## CORPORATE POWER AND THE POLITICS OF CHANGE

In *Corporate Power and the Politics of Change*, Matteo Gatti examines how corporations have taken on roles traditionally reserved for governments – advocating on social issues, setting internal norms, and stepping in where public institutions fall short. This phenomenon, called corporate governing, takes two forms: socioeconomic advocacy, when companies take public stances, and government substitution, when they deliver services or protections the state does not provide. Drawing on legal doctrine and insights from the social sciences, Gatti shows how this shift reflects broader pressures within firms and deep dysfunction outside them. The rise of corporate governing has also triggered political, legal, and cultural backlash that challenges its legitimacy and reach. Clear-eyed and timely, this book offers a framework for understanding how corporate power reshapes policymaking and what that means for business and democracy.

Matteo Gatti is Professor of Law at Rutgers Law School and Research Member of the European Corporate Governance Institute. His research on corporate law and political economy has appeared in leading journals and is cited in legal and policy literature.

# Corporate Power and the Politics of Change

**MATTEO GATTI**
Rutgers Law School

CAMBRIDGE
UNIVERSITY PRESS

CAMBRIDGE
UNIVERSITY PRESS

Shaftesbury Road, Cambridge CB2 8EA, United Kingdom

One Liberty Plaza, 20th Floor, New York, NY 10006, USA

477 Williamstown Road, Port Melbourne, VIC 3207, Australia

314–321, 3rd Floor, Plot 3, Splendor Forum, Jasola District Centre, New Delhi – 110025, India

103 Penang Road, #05–06/07, Visioncrest Commercial, Singapore 238467

Cambridge University Press is part of Cambridge University Press & Assessment, a department of the University of Cambridge.

We share the University's mission to contribute to society through the pursuit of education, learning and research at the highest international levels of excellence.

www.cambridge.org
Information on this title: www.cambridge.org/9781009704441

DOI: 10.1017/9781009704465



When citing this work, please include a reference to the DOI 10.1017/9781009704465

First published 2026

*A catalogue record for this publication is available from the British Library*

*Library of Congress Cataloging-in-Publication Data*
NAMES: Gatti, Matteo, 1995– author.
TITLE: Corporate power and the politics of change / Matteo Gatti, Rutgers Law School.
DESCRIPTION: Cambridge, United Kingdom ; New York, NY : Cambridge University Press, 2026. | Includes bibliographical references and index.
IDENTIFIERS: LCCN 2025024995 (print) | LCCN 2025024996 (ebook) | ISBN 9781009704441 (hardback) | ISBN 9781009704465 (ebook)
SUBJECTS: LCSH: Corporation law. | Corporation law – Political aspects.
CLASSIFICATION: LCC K1315 .G38 2026 (print) | LCC K1315 (ebook) | DDC 346/.066–dc23/eng/20250522
LC record available at https://lccn.loc.gov/2025024995
LC ebook record available at https://lccn.loc.gov/2025024996

ISBN 978-1-009-70444-1 Hardback
ISBN 978-1-009-70449-6 Paperback

*This one goes out to the ones I love –*

*Catherine, Valentina, and Leandro –*

*for your support, your patience, and the joy of being around you.*

The interest of the dealers … in any particular branch of trade or manufactures, is always in some respects different from, and even opposite to, that of the public.

ADAM SMITH, THE WEALTH OF NATIONS 372 (Collier ed., 1902) (1776)

# Summary of Contents

# Contents

# Figures

# Tables

# Acknowledgments

This book, in a way, was born over after-work pints of Guinness with my colleague, Professor Chrystin Ondersma, at a bar in Newark in the fall of 2018. We were watching a Europa League match – RB Leipzig vs. Celtic, if memory serves – when a news segment on a nearby television flashed to Chrys' mentor, Senator Elizabeth Warren, discussing her newly introduced Accountable Capitalism Act. The bill aimed to federalize corporate law for large corporations and expand director fiduciary duties beyond shareholders to a broader set of constituencies.

Chrys, a bankruptcy and human rights scholar, turned to me.

"What do you think?"

"Won't happen. Wouldn't work for stakeholders anyway," I said.

That sparked a back-and-forth. "Let's write something together!" she went. I hesitated – Milanese pragmatism, I suppose – but she won the argument, and write we did. That conversation led to three articles over four years, projects I'm immensely proud of. I first explored these ideas in the 1990s while studying law in Italy, but it took that moment to bring them to life. I owe you, Professor Ondersma.

Eventually, we each pursued our own book projects. Mine became this book – a natural progression of my earlier work on stakeholder capitalism. I first conceived the book's core ideas one fall evening in 2021 while coming back from Newark to Brooklyn. I still remember making a left onto Chambers from West Broadway when – bang! – it all clicked. I had to jot down the first outline the moment I got home. Feels like yesterday.

I was fortunate to have chosen this project. Researching and writing it was rewarding, and I know that I'll miss it. But all things must pass.

I owe a deep debt of professional gratitude to many. I am particularly thankful to Anne van Aaken, Emilie Aguirre, Carlos Ball, Lucian Bebchuk, Matt Bodie, Johanna Bond, Bill Bratton, Laura Castelli, Emiliano Catan, John Coates, Sarah Dadush, Jens Dammann, Paul Davies, Marco Dell'Erba, Jon Dubin, Doug Eakeley, Luca Enriques, Lisa Fairfax, Jill Fisch, Edoardo Gambaro, Martin Gelter, Rachel

Godsil, Suren Gomtsyan, Carlos Gonzales, Jeff Gordon, Zohar Goshen, Alperen Gözlügöl, Sergio Gramitto Ricci, Stuart Greene, Caleb Griffin, Sean Griffith, Yuliya Guseva, Adil Haque, Rainer Haselmann, Chris Havasy, Stacy Hawkins, Jennifer Hill, Christina Ho, Klaus Hopt, Alan Hyde, Alan Kluegel, Aneil Kovvali, Arthur Laby, John Leubsdorf, Zhao Li, Tom Lin, Ann Lipton, Dorothy Lund, Joan MacLeod Heminway, Franco Maccabruni, Carlo Marchetti, Amelia Miazad, Alexander Morell, Casimiro Antonio Nigro, David Noll, Elizabeth Pollman, Jim Pope, Wolf-Georg Ringe, Adriana Robertson, Ed Rock, Mark Roe, Sandro Romano, Roberto Sacchi, Sabrina Safrin, Carlo Scaglioni, Simone Sepe, Fadi Shaheen, Roy Shapira, Reilly Steel, Giovanni Strampelli, Leo Strine, Roberto Tallarita, Eric Talley, Matteo Tonello, Tobias Tröger, David Troutt, Stefan Voigt, and Luigi Zingales.

I am grateful for the thoughtful feedback received at the SJD Seminar at Bocconi University School of Law (May 2023), the National Business Law Scholars Conference (June 2023), the Center for Advanced Studies – Foundations of Law and Finance at Goethe University Frankfurt (October 2023), the Law & Society Association Annual Meeting (June 2024), the Hamburg Lecture Series in Law and Economics at the University of Hamburg (November 2024), the Brooklyn Law School Seminar (November 2024), the Rutgers Law School Faculty Colloquium (February 2025), and Columbia Law School's conference, "Bylaws, Bills, and Ballots: Understanding the Nexus Between Business, Law, and Politics in the 21st Century."

To my dedicated research assistants – in the order they joined my team – Tom Daly, Walter Wynkoop, Matt Chiota, Tinghe Yao, Youngchae Cho, Priten Patel, and Nikita Kulkarni: your contributions were invaluable. Thank you for your hard work and commitment.

I am grateful to Rutgers Law School, the Pratt Fund, the Schuchman Fund, Goethe University in Frankfurt, and all other institutions that supported me and provided forums to present early versions of this book.

The initial ideas in this book were explored in my article *Corporate Governing: Understanding Corporations as Agents of Socioeconomic Change*, 50 J. Corp. L. 149 (2024). I am grateful to the *Journal of Corporation Law* for giving these ideas their first home.

I am very grateful to Matt Gallaway for believing in and championing this book, and to everyone at Cambridge University Press for their responsiveness, professionalism, and collegial spirit. It has been both an honor and a pleasure to work with you all.

To the reader – whether you've stuck around for the whole thing or dipped in and out – I hope I met your expectations. Thank you for engaging with my ideas.

To my friends, near and far, across oceans and time zones: I love you. You know who you are. Fate, serendipity, or just life brought us together, and I am grateful for every moment.

To Catherine, you're why I landed in New York City more than twenty years ago (we were young!). What a ride it's been. You're an amazing partner and a brilliant person. Thanks for this fantastic voyage. I love you a lot.

To Valentina, my wonderful daughter – you changed my life, and I would do anything for you. You make me a proud dad every single day, and our hangs are the best. I can't wait for our next trip together. And, of course, to the legendary Leandro Nilo Gatti, my beautiful boy – the sweetest soul I know. You bring me a lot of joy and teach me so many things. Maybe one day, some of you little Gattis will read this book, or – more realistically – just these final notes. I loved having you by my side while I worked on it – yes, I was impatient and cranky at times, and yes, you were gracious. I love you.

Shoutouts to all the other Gattis and extended family – our aunts, uncles, cousins, pets, and others – there are so many of us!

Thanks to my beloved brother, Marco, for always tirelessly holding down the fort in Milan while I am here; to my trailblazing sister-in-law, Nicole; and to my phenomenal nephews, Pietro and Tito.

Finally, I honor the memory of my father, Stefano Gatti (1935–2023), and my mother, Ucci Dell'Orto Gatti (1939–2025), both of whom passed while this project was underway. I was the luckiest son. I love you immensely, and I've felt you with me throughout the writing. Now that the book must come to an end, I intend to carry you forward – but I will miss you so very much.

# Introduction

A Corporate Power and the Politics of Change: Understanding "Corporate Governing"
B Two Types of Corporate Governing: Corporate Socioeconomic Advocacy and Government Substitution
C Key Questions Driving the Book
D Existing Literature; Contributions and Structure of the Book

In 2018, Nike featured former NFL quarterback Colin Kaepernick – known for kneeling during the national anthem to protest racial injustice and police brutality – in its thirtieth anniversary "Just Do It" campaign.[1] The tagline – "Believe in something. Even if it means sacrificing everything" – was crafted to align with Kaepernick's positioning as an athlete-turned activist.[2] The move was controversial, sparking widespread debate. Critics destroyed Nike products, and the hashtag #BoycottNike trended on social media.[3] However, Nike's market research had already indicated that its young, urban, and socially engaged core consumers would respond positively.[4]

Behind the scenes, the campaign was no walk in the park. For starters, Nike nearly dropped Kaepernick a year earlier.[5] After he opted out of his contract with the San Francisco 49ers in 2017 and remained unsigned by any NFL team, Nike executives were uncertain about how to position him in their marketing.[6] Without a team affiliation, he no longer fit their typical sponsorship model, and the sports marketing group initially decided to remove him from their roster of sponsored athletes.[7] However, Nigel Powell, Nike's longtime head of communications,

1 Alex Abad-Santos, *Nike's Colin Kaepernick Ad Sparked a Boycott – and Earned $6 Billion for Nike*, Vox (Sept. 24, 2018), www.vox.com/2018/9/24/17895704/nike-colin-kaepernick-boycott-6-billion.
2 *Id.*
3 *Id.*
4 *Id.*
5 Julie Creswell, Kevin Draper & Sapna Maheshwari, *Nike Nearly Dropped Colin Kaepernick before Embracing Him*, N.Y. Times (Sept. 26, 2018), www.nytimes.com/2018/09/26/sports/nike-colin-kaepernick.html.
6 *Id.*
7 *Id.*

strongly opposed the move, fearing backlash from consumers and the media.[8] Powell argued that severing ties with Kaepernick would make Nike appear aligned with the NFL against him, potentially alienating the younger, urban demographic that admired Kaepernick's activism – an audience more crucial to Nike's business than the older, more conservative NFL fan base.[9]

Yet, despite being kept on the Nike roster, discussions about making Kaepernick the face of the "Just Do It" campaign began much later and only after outside pressure.[10] His lawyers argued that the company was contractually obligated to feature him rather than keep him inactive.[11] At the same time, Nike's longtime ad agency pushed for Kaepernick to take a central role in a campaign.[12] The expected fallout was considered manageable as Nike's partnership with the NFL was essentially folding after 2020 – it would no longer produce league merchandise for consumers.[13] Most importantly, Nike recognized that Kaepernick's controversy was a strategic advantage – his supporters closely mirrored the brand's target demographic.[14] After all, the company had long embraced athletes challenging societal norms, from Serena Williams advocating for gender equity to its support for LGBTQ+ representation in sports.[15]

The ad was a big success. Nike's online sales surged by 31 percent immediately after its release.[16] Despite an initial dip, the company's stock rebounded to record highs, adding an estimated $6 billion to its market value.[17] The data reinforced Nike's longstanding approach: Controversy could be lucrative when appropriately managed.[18]

Nike's activist branding extended beyond marketing. In 2020, following the George Floyd protests, it released an ad titled "For once, Don't Do It," an inversion of its famous slogan, calling on viewers to recognize and address racism. More substantively, in June 2020, Nike committed $40 million over four years to support organizations that address racial injustice.[19]

Research shows that consumers support corporations they perceive as genuinely "values-driven," rewarding those that align with their beliefs.[20] Nike's consistent

8 *Id.*

9 *Id.*

10 *Id.*

11 *Id.*

12 *Id.*

13 *Id.*

14 *Id.*

15 Ann Lipton, *The Revolution Will Be Marketed*, BUS. LAW PROF. BLOG (Sept. 8, 2018), https://lawprofessors.typepad.com/business_law/2018/09/the-revolution-will-be-marketed.html.

16 Abad-Santos, *supra* note 1.

17 *Id. See also* Aneil Kovvali, *Stark Choices for Corporate Reform*, 123 COLUM. L. REV. 693, 742 (2023).

18 Lipton, *supra* note 15.

19 Nike News, *NIKE, Inc. Statement on Commitment to the Black Community*, June 5, 2020, https://about.nike.com/en/impact-resources/nike-inc-statement-on-commitment-to-the-black-community [https://perma.cc/BKY4-6RV9].

20 Daniel Korschun, Hoori Rafieian, Anubhav Aggarwal & Scott D. Swain, *Taking a Stand: Consumer Responses When Companies Get (or Don't Get) Political* 34, Working Paper (2019), https://papers.ssrn.com/sol3/papers.cfm?abstract_id=2806476. *See infra* Chapter 4, Sections 2 and 3.

integration of social advocacy into its brand gave it a competitive edge over companies whose forays into activism seem opportunistic. This credibility helped Nike translate controversy into brand loyalty and financial success, while others have faced backlash or market instability.[21]

* * *

Not all corporate political moves yield the same results. In early 2022, Florida lawmakers presented the "Parental Rights in Education" bill,[22] better known as "Don't Say Gay," which restricts discussions on sexual orientation and gender identity in classrooms.[23] The bill ignited a public fight between the Sunshine State and one of the largest businesses operating there, The Walt Disney Company.

Disney's entanglement in the controversy began not with a bold public statement but with a revelation from the *Orlando Sentinel* – the company had been quietly funneling political donations to the bill's sponsor and cosponsors.[24] The news caught Disney off guard. On the surface, there was nothing unusual about it as the company routinely donated to politicians from both parties, leveraging its influence in Florida, where its parks and resorts make it an economic heavyweight. But this was different. The bill's chief sponsor, Dennis Baxley, had long supported anti-LGBTQ+ legislation, making Disney's financial backing look less like routine corporate lobbying and more like an endorsement of his agenda.[25]

At first, Disney tried to manage the fallout with a carefully worded, generically pro-LGBTQ+ statement from CEO Bob Chapek, avoiding outright condemning the bill.[26] But the strategy backfired. Critics saw it as a glaring contradiction – how could a company that draped itself in rainbow flags every June and built an empire on family-friendly storytelling stay silent on an issue that directly impacted the communities it claimed to champion? The backlash was swift. Activists, Florida Democrats, and the public turned their attention to Disney, demanding a stronger response.[27]

[21] *See* Susan Fournier, Shuba Srinivasan & Patrick Marrinan, *Turning Socio-political Risk to Your Brand's Advantage*, 13.2 NIM Marketing Intel. Rev. 18, 22–24 (2021) (mentioning Nike's extensive history in advocating for social change, especially on racial matters in America). Kovvali, *supra* note 17.

[22] H.B. 1557, 2022 Leg. (Fla. 2022) (codified at Fla. Stat. Ann. § 1001.42(8)(c)(3) (West 2024).

[23] Dana Goldstein, *Opponents Call It the "Don't Say Gay" Bill. Here's What It Says*, N.Y. Times (Mar. 18, 2022), www.nytimes.com/2022/03/18/us/dont-say-gay-bill-florida.html.

[24] Scott Maxwell, *Florida's Anti-Gay Crusade Is Funded by Disneys of the World*, Orlando Sentinel (Feb. 25, 2022), www.orlandosentinel.com/opinion/scott-maxwell-commentary/os-prem-op-florida-business-disney-dont-say-gay-scott-maxwell-20220225-b7pxbrc4pfdmxbm2yp05bpw23e-story.html.

[25] Ramishah Maruf, *Disney CEO Refuses to Publicly Condemn "Don't Say Gay" Bill but Commits to Inclusivity*, CNN (Mar. 7, 2022), https://amp.cnn.com/cnn/2022/03/07/media/disney-chapek-dont-say-gay-bill/index.html.

[26] Simeone v. Walt Disney Co., 302 A.3d 956, 960 (Del. Ch. 2023).

[27] Maruf, *supra* note 25.

Then came internal pushback. Creatives from Disney's animation division took to social media to highlight what they saw as contradictions in the company's stance.[28] *Owl House* creator Dana Terrace and *Ghost and Molly McGee* director Sam King called out Disney's pattern of celebrating LGBTQ+ representation in public while stifling it behind the scenes.[29] Their frustrations struck a nerve. As #BoycottDisney trended on Twitter, audiences who had once praised the company's moves toward inclusivity began to question just how deep that commitment ran.[30] Disney, a company that had spent decades perfecting the art of controlling its image, suddenly struggled to manage a narrative slipping out of its hands.

To ease tensions with its stakeholders, Disney sidestepped one crisis only to walk straight into another – arguably an even larger one – as it ultimately took on the politicians.

In complete damage control, the day after an emergency meeting on the company's political strategy, with Chapek and Corporate Affairs Chief Geoff Morrell trying to contain the fallout, Disney held its annual stockholder meeting on March 9, 2022.[31] There, Chapek admitted the company's low-profile approach had "not quite gotten the job done"[32] and that Disney was joining a petition against similar legislation and would support efforts to protect the LGBTQ+ community.[33] He also noted he had called Governor Ron DeSantis that morning to express Disney's "disappointment."[34] DeSantis reacted by criticizing "woke corporations" like Disney and calling out their hypocrisy for being silent with governments like China.[35]

Meanwhile, Chapek was still scrambling to reassure employees. "We need to be a better ally," he wrote in a memo on March 11, 2022, trying to placate staff.[36] But by March 28, DeSantis signed the bill into law,[37] and Disney – boxed in and outmaneuvered – finally chose to go public with its opposition:

> Florida's HB 1557, also known as the "Don't Say Gay" bill, should never have passed and should never have been signed into law. Our goal as a company is for this law to be repealed by the legislature or struck down in the courts, and we remain committed to supporting the national and state organizations working to achieve that.[38]

[28] Caroline Atwood, *Burning Cabins and Rainbow Mickeys: Disney's Florida "Don't Say Gay" Controversy and Definitions of America in U.S. Disney Parks*, TÉOROS, 43-1 | 2024, https://journals.openedition.org/teoros/12443.

[29] *Id.*

[30] *Id.*

[31] *Simeone*, 302 A.3d 956, at 960.

[32] *Id.*

[33] *Id.* at 960–61.

[34] *Id.* at 961.

[35] *Id.*

[36] *Id.* at 961.

[37] *Id.*

[38] *Id.*

The battle was on. Florida retaliated by revoking the self-governance rights Disney had in some districts, and DeSantis stated that Disney was accountable for some prior taxes and debts.[39] After Disney's stock price declined,[40] a shareholder unsuccessfully sought access to its books and records.[41] Litigation between Disney and Florida concerning Disney's self-governance rights ensued but settled.[42]

Bob Chapek was ultimately replaced as CEO by his predecessor, Bob Iger, who returned to the role he had successfully held for fifteen years.[43] Since his return, Iger has stood by the substance of Disney's stance on HB 1557, signaling continuity in the company's position:

> Frankly, the company was within its right – even though I'm not sure it was handled very well – … to speak up on an issue, constitutionally protected right of free speech [sic][.] … To retaliate against the company in a way that would be harmful to the business was not something we could sit back and tolerate.[44]

* * *

Tech firms have long waded into socioeconomic issues, but as political backlash heats up, their paths split.

Take Apple, one of the world's largest companies. In the summer of 2020, as protests spilled into the streets and corporations scrambled to find their moral footing, Apple announced a $100 million Racial Equity and Justice Initiative.[45] The goal: to chip away at systemic inequities in education, economic opportunity, and

[39] *Simeone*, 302 A.3d at 961–62

[40] *Id.* at 962–63 (mentioning that "stock price fell during the summer [of 2022] from $145.70 per share on March 1 to $91.84 on July 14. On November 9 – the day after Governor DeSantis was reelected – Disney's stock fell to $86.75 per share").

[41] *Id.* at 956–57. For a discussion on the *Simeone* case, see *infra* Chapter 3, Section C.3.

[42] The Florida legislature ultimately chose not to dissolve Disney's governance rights, but Governor Ron DeSantis moved to strip Disney of its self-governing authority by appointing a state-controlled board to oversee the district. Yet, before DeSantis' takeover, the outgoing Disney-backed board enacted restrictive covenants and a development agreement securing Disney's rights. In response, DeSantis signed legislation empowering the new board to invalidate those agreements, triggering lawsuits between Disney and the state. *Id.* at 965–66. The legal battle culminated in a March 2024 settlement under which the prior board's development agreement was nullified, and Disney agreed to negotiate new terms aligned with the district's 2020 comprehensive plan. Dawn Chmielewski & Lisa Richwine, *Disney, Florida Settle Bitter Legal Feud over Disney World District*, REUTERS (Mar. 27, 2024), www.reuters.com/legal/florida-governor-disney-reach-settlement-ap-reports-2024-03-27/.

[43] Meg James, *Behind the Stunning Exit of Disney CEO Bob Chapek*, L.A. TIMES (Nov. 21, 2022), www.latimes.com/entertainment-arts/business/story/2022-11-21/bob-chapek-disney-ouster-bob-iger.

[44] Andrew Zhang, *Disney CEO Responds to DeSantis: "Preposterous" That Company Is Sexualizing Kids*, POLITICO (July 13, 2023), www.politico.com/news/2023/07/13/disney-ceo-bob-iger-desantis-00106214.

[45] Apple Newsroom, *Apple Launches Major New Racial Equity and Justice Initiative Projects*, Jan. 13, 2021, www.apple.com/newsroom/2021/01/apple-launches-major-new-racial-equity-and-justice-initiative-projects-to-challenge-systemic-racism-advance-racial-equity-nationwide/.

criminal justice.[46] There was the Propel Center, an ambitious innovation hub for Historically Black Colleges and Universities (HBCUs). A Developer Academy in Detroit, offering free coding classes to underrepresented students.[47] And by 2023, the company doubled down, pledging over $200 million toward education, minority entrepreneurship, and legal advocacy for marginalized groups.[48]

Apple's engagement with social issues precedes these initiatives. In 2016, the company opposed North Carolina's "bathroom bill," which restricted LGBTQ+ rights. Alongside other major corporations, Apple signed statements condemning the law and supported legal efforts to overturn it.[49]

Apple did not hesitate to criticize the highest officials. In response to President Trump's remarks equating white supremacists and counter-protesters following the August 2017 "Unite the Right" rally in Charlottesville, Virginia, Apple CEO Tim Cook sent an email to employees expressing his disagreement with the President and announcing that Apple will be making contributions of $1 million each to the Southern Poverty Law Center and the Anti-Defamation League.[50]

The company also played a role in the immigration debate, again pushing back against Trump's policies. In response to the Trump administration's attempt to rescind Deferred Action for Childhood Arrivals (DACA), Apple publicly defended its employees who were Dreamers and joined legal efforts supporting the program:[51] in 2019, it filed an amicus brief at the Supreme Court advocating for DACA's preservation.[52] There was also the matter of Trump's exit from the Paris Agreement. Apple, along with a parade of other big names, bought full-page ads in the country's leading newspapers to publicly condemn the move.[53]

46 *Id.*

47 *Id.*

48 Apple Newsroom, *Apple's Racial Equity and Justice Initiative Surpasses $200 Million*, June 13, 2023, www.apple.com/newsroom/2023/06/apples-racial-equity-and-justice-initiative-surpasses-200m-usd-in-investments/.

49 Jon Swartz, *Google, Apple, Facebook, Others Oppose N.C. Law*, USA TODAY (Mar. 25, 2016), www.usatoday.com/story/tech/2016/03/25/tech-leaders-join-ranks-opposing-nc-law/82263478/.

50 David Choi, *Apple CEO Tim Cook's message to His Employees after the Charlottesville Violence*, WORLD ECON. F., (Aug. 17, 2017), www.weforum.org/stories/2017/08/apple-ceo-tim-cooks-message-to-his-employees-after-the-charlottesville-violence/ (reporting that Cook stated: "I disagree with the president and others who believe that there is a moral equivalence between white supremacists and Nazis, and those who oppose them by standing up for human rights. Equating the two runs counter to our ideals as Americans.").

51 Tom C.W. Lin, *Incorporating Social Activism*, 98 B.U. L. REV. 1535, 1553–54 (2018).

52 Camilo Montoya-Galvez, *Apple's Tim Cook Urges Supreme Court to Save DACA in Amicus Brief*, CBS NEWS (Oct. 3, 2019), www.cbsnews.com/news/apples-tim-cook-urges-supreme-court-to-save-daca-in-amicus-brief/. *See infra* Chapter 1, Section B.1.

53 Daniel Victor, *"Climate Change Is Real": Many U.S. Companies Lament Paris Accord Exit*, N.Y. TIMES (June 11 2017), www.nytimes.com/2017/06/01/business/climate-change-tesla-corporations-paris-accord.html.

In 2025, Apple faced a shareholder proposal to eliminate its diversity, equity, and inclusion (DEI) programs,[54] reflecting the growing hostility toward DEI.[55] The board opposed the proposal, stating that the company does not engage in discriminatory practices and accusing the proponent of overstepping – seeking to micromanage routine business decisions under the guise of shareholder oversight.[56] Apple shareholders ultimately rejected it by a wide margin.[57] More broadly, Apple reaffirmed its commitment to DEI as other companies retreated from it.[58]

* * *

Unlike Apple, other "activists" in Big Tech faltered. Meta – formerly Facebook – was once a leading force in corporate activism, much like Apple. Then, things changed.

For years, Meta positioned itself as one of corporate America's most politically engaged companies. It took a stand on major social issues, often facing both internal and external pressures to do so. When Donald Trump posted "when the looting starts, the shooting starts" amid the George Floyd protests, Facebook employees staged virtual walkouts, openly rebuking CEO Mark Zuckerberg's decision to leave the post up.[59] The backlash wasn't just internal – activists and advertisers launched the "Stop Hate for Profit" campaign, pressuring Facebook to strengthen its policies on hate speech and misinformation.[60] While Zuckerberg stood by his original decision, the combination of employee dissent, advertiser revolt, and civil society mobilization pushed Facebook into making incremental policy shifts.[61]

This was not the first time Facebook opposed Trump's policies, as, just like Apple, the company joined corporate opposition to Trump's withdrawal from the Paris Agreement[62] and Trump's termination of DACA.[63] The company also vocally

[54] Conor Murray, *Apple Urges Shareholders to Reject Anti-DEI Policy*, FORBES (Jan. 13, 2025), www.forbes.com/sites/conormurray/2025/01/13/apple-urges-shareholders-to-reject-anti-dei-policy/. *See infra* Chapter 1, Section C.

[55] *See infra* Chapter 1, Section C. *See* Murray, *supra* note 54.

[56] *Id.*

[57] Mark Gurman, *Apple to Keep DEI Efforts, though Some Adjustments Possible*, BLOOMBERG (Feb. 25, 2025), www.bloomberg.com/news/articles/2025-02-25/apple-to-keep-dei-efforts-though-some-adjustments-possible.

[58] David Hood, *Apple, Microsoft Defend DEI as Big Tech Rivals Back Down*, BLOOMBERG LAW (Jan. 20, 2025), https://news.bloomberglaw.com/daily-labor-report/apple-microsoft-defend-dei-as-big-tech-rivals-back-down. *See infra* Chapter 1, Section C.4.

[59] *See* Anat Alon-Beck, *Times They Are A-Changin': When Tech Employees Revolt*, 80 MD. L. REV. 120, 133–35 (2020).

[60] *Id.* at 135.

[61] *Id.*

[62] *See* Victor, *supra* note 53 (mentioning that Facebook was one of several companies publishing full-page advertisements in prominent newspapers in order to publicly demonstrate their resentment).

[63] *See* Lin, *supra* note 51, at 1553–54.

opposed anti-LGBTQ+ policies such as North Carolina's HB2, which targeted transgender individuals.[64]

Facebook's political engagement reached its peak following the January 6 attack on the US Capitol. In its aftermath, the company barred Trump from its platform, citing the risk of inciting violence and spreading misinformation.[65] However, the ban was not permanent. As political and legal pressures intensified, Meta lifted the restriction and later, in a further turn, agreed to a $25 million settlement with Trump – underscoring the evolving, and increasingly fraught, relationship between social media platforms and political figures.[66]

Ultimately, as the political landscape shifted, so did Meta's approach. The company began retreating from its most visible commitments when Trump's second administration took shape. Once a vocal advocate, the company began scaling back its diversity programs – adjusting hiring practices, supplier policies, and internal training efforts.[67] After Mark Zuckerberg's video announcing the abandonment of DEI initiatives and a push for more "masculine energy" in corporate culture[68] – emphasizing aggression and less censorship – Meta's VP of HR, Janelle Gale, framed these changes as necessary responses to an evolving legal landscape, citing shifts in US DEI policies.[69] A company that once saw sociopolitical engagement as an asset was now treating it as a liability.[70]

* * *

64 *Id.* at 1547–50 (mentioning that Facebook, alongside more than 200 corporations, signed a letter with the Human Rights Campaign advocating for the law's repeal).

65 *See* Grace Dean, *From Cutting All Ties with Trump to Pulling Political Donations, Here's How Corporate America Has Responded to the Capitol Insurrection*, BUS. INSIDER (Jan 17, 2021, 7:55 AM), www.businessinsider.com/capitol-siege-trump-company-responses-riots-political-donations-2021-1.

66 Annie Linskey & Rebecca Ballhaus, *Meta to Pay $25 Million to Settle 2021 Trump Lawsuit: President Had Sued Social-Media Company after His Accounts Were Suspended Following Jan. 6 Riot*, WALL ST. J. (Jan. 29, 2025), www.wsj.com/us-news/law/trump-signs-agreement-calling-for-meta-to-pay-25-million-to-settle-suit-6f734c8c.

67 Kurt Wagner & Jeff Green, *Meta Retreats from Diversity and Inclusion, Appeasing Trump*, BLOOMBERG (Jan. 10, 2025, 3:45 PM), www.bloomberg.com/news/articles/2025-01-10/meta-rolls-back-diveristy-and-inclusion-efforts-appeasing-trump.

68 Johana Bhuiyan & Dara Kerr, *Zuckerberg's Swerve: How Diversity Went from Being a Meta Priority to Getting Cancelled*, GUARDIAN (Feb. 11, 2025), www.theguardian.com/technology/ng-interactive/2025/feb/11/dei-meta-facebook. Zuckerberg was heavily criticized for what was seen as an opportunistic move to appease Donald Trump. For an account from a former employee noting that Facebook had previously profited from positioning itself as a DEI champion, see Bärí A. Williams, *Zuckerberg Has Shown Us Who He Really Is. Believe Him*, FAST CO. (Jan. 30, 2025), www.fastcompany.com/91269069/users-should-boycott-meta-over-ending-dei.

69 Kate Gibson & Emmet Lyons, *Meta Ends Diversity Programs, Joining McDonald's, Walmart and Other Major Companies to Back Off DEI*, CBS NEWS (Jan. 16, 2025), www.cbsnews.com/news/meta-dei-programs-mcdonalds-walmart-ford-diversity/.

70 Natalie Sherman, *Meta and Amazon Scale Back Diversity Initiatives*, BBC (Jan. 10, 2025), www.bbc.com/news/articles/cgmy7xpw3pyo.

What played out at Meta played out elsewhere too – from McDonald's to Amazon, Walmart to Ford.[71] Different logos, same pattern. The corporate world perceived a tidal change. Its embrace of environmental, social, and governance (ESG) and DEI initiatives was once a boardroom mantra. Yet it has since turned into a political lightning rod, and with it, a growing risk for business. Conservative politicians, business leaders, and plaintiffs launched a battle against such initiatives, with figures like Donald Trump and Elon Musk emerging as their most influential critics.[72] Trump's second administration moved swiftly to dismantle DEI efforts, while social media-fueled campaigns, litigation, and shareholder activism pressured companies to reconsider their commitments.[73] Many – like Meta – reversed course.[74] The Supreme Court's decision in *Students for Fair Admissions v. President and Fellows of Harvard College*,[75] which struck down affirmative action in college admissions, added significant momentum, setting off a wave of legal challenges that sought to apply the same reasoning to corporate diversity programs.

Litigation has since become a primary battleground. Conservative legal groups, seizing on the post-*Students for Fair Admissions* legal landscape, argued that race-conscious corporate policies violate civil rights laws. *American Alliance for Equal Rights v. Fearless Fund* captured the new direction: The Eleventh Circuit blocked a grant program aimed at supporting Black women entrepreneurs – a signal that judicial skepticism toward corporate DEI efforts is no longer theoretical, but operational.[76]

Meanwhile, Republican-led states launched their offensives on the legislative front, passing laws restricting ESG-based investment strategies. Texas blocked financial firms that refused to back fossil fuels, while Florida divested billions from institutions that factored social and environmental goals into investment decisions.[77] Similar efforts occurred on the DEI front.

The sharpest turn came at the federal level. The second Trump administration moved quickly – dismantling diversity programs in government, rescinding affirmative action rules for federal contractors, and instructing agencies to take a closer look at corporate DEI initiatives.[78]

The message is clear: Corporations must rethink what had long been viewed as a strategic imperative, but is now seen as a potential risk. Facing mounting legal and

[71] *Id.*
[72] *See infra* Chapter 1, Sections C.1 and C.2.
[73] *See infra* Chapter 1, Sections C.1–C.3.
[74] *See infra* Chapter 1, Section C.4.
[75] Students for Fair Admissions, Inc. v. President and Fellows of Harvard College, 600 U.S. 181 (2023) (ruling by a vote of 6 to 3 that the admissions programs used by Harvard College and the University of North Carolina violated Title VI and the Constitution's equal protection clause).
[76] American Alliance for Equal Rights v. Fearless Fund Management, LLC, No. 23-13138 (11th Cir. June 3, 2024). *See infra* Chapter 1, Section C.2.
[77] *See infra* Chapter 1, Section C.3.
[78] *See infra* Chapter 1, Section C.3.

political pressures, companies are reassessing their approach to social responsibility, weighing their commitments against an increasingly hostile environment.

## A CORPORATE POWER AND THE POLITICS OF CHANGE: UNDERSTANDING "CORPORATE GOVERNING"

The corporate stories above are not isolated, but form what I call "corporate governing." Over the past decade, businesses have increasingly found themselves at the center of political and social debates, with expectations to take positions on issues ranging from racial justice and climate policy to LGBTQ+ rights and voting access. Whether through public statements, lobbying, or operational decisions, corporations have assumed a role seemingly beyond their traditional business domain. This development has been celebrated and contested, as corporate involvement in these territories has transformed from internal business strategy into political battleground.

Supporters argue that the strategy is sound. It reflects evolving stakeholder expectations and can serve as a force for positive change, particularly in areas where government action is slow or absent.[79] They point to corporate-led climate initiatives, diversity programs, and advocacy for underrepresented communities as evidence that business can advance broader societal goals.

Critics, by contrast, argue that such engagement is not only bad for business but also distorts the political process – granting unelected executives disproportionate influence over matters of public concern.[80] The backlash has intensified, driven by advocacy campaigns, legal challenges, political pressure, and policy interventions that have placed corporations under growing scrutiny.[81]

As previously noted, the Supreme Court's decision in *Students for Fair Admissions* emboldened legal attacks on corporate diversity initiatives. Republican-led administrations have also moved to curtail ESG investment strategies and scale back DEI programs, reinforcing the sense that corporate governing is entering a period of heightened legal and political risk.[82]

*Corporate Power and the Politics of Change* examines this shifting landscape, tracing how corporations play a prominent role in policymaking and governance. It interrogates this phenomenon's legal and normative implications, exploring its promises and risks. The central question is not simply whether corporations may or should engage in public affairs but how their involvement reshapes markets, institutions, and democracy. To begin the inquiry, I must be clear on what I mean by corporate governing.

79 *See infra* Chapter 5, Section B.1.
80 *See infra* Chapter 5, Section B.2.
81 *See infra* Chapter 1, Section C.
82 *See infra* Chapter 1, Section C.3.

## B TWO TYPES OF CORPORATE GOVERNING: CORPORATE SOCIOECONOMIC ADVOCACY AND GOVERNMENT SUBSTITUTION

Corporate governing is the exercise of corporate power to drive change. Companies exert influence in two primary ways.

The first is what I call *corporate socioeconomic advocacy*[83] – when businesses take stands on political and social issues, shaping debates that arguably extend far beyond their balance sheets. This isn't just traditional lobbying. It's Apple and Facebook throwing their weight to protest exiting the Paris Agreement or terminating DACA. It's Disney pushing back against Florida's "Don't Say Gay" law. Whether to protect their brand, appeal to stakeholders, or hedge against future risks, corporations have increasingly positioned themselves as political actors, capable of shaping public sentiment as effectively as any politician. While some applaud this phenomenon, others are outraged.[84] Recent polling shows that Americans are experiencing some fatigue when hearing corporations speak on socioeconomic issues.[85]

The second way corporations exert power through corporate governing is what I call *government substitution*: Corporations step in to provide resources, services, or protections, in other words, perform quasi-governmental roles when the actual government cannot (because of its dysfunction) or does not want to (because of

83 In the communications discipline, this phenomenon has been defined as "corporate social advocacy." *See, for example*, Melissa D. Dodd & Dustin W. Supa, *Conceptualizing and Measuring 'Corporate Social Advocacy' Communication: Examining the Impact on Corporate Financial Performance*, 8 PUB. RELS. J., no. 3, 2014, at 1, 1 (describing how corporate social advocacy refers to an "organization making a public statement or taking a public stance on social-political issues"). For an attempt to differentiate this type of activity from traditional corporate social responsibility (CSR) and corporate political donations and lobbying, see Anna Toniolo, *Corporate Participation in Social Debates*, 3 U. CHI. BUS. L. REV. 368 (2024) (noting that CSR is generally non-partisan and consensus-driven, whereas corporate activism, unlike the discreet nature of corporate lobbying, is intentionally public and often polarizing, reflecting stakeholders' sociopolitical values.).

84 Marketing scholars highlight that the partisan nature of sociopolitical issues is a key element for brand activism. *See* Christine Moorman, *Commentary: Brand Activism in a Political World*, 39 J. PUB. POL'Y & MKTG. 388, 389 (2020). Moorman adds:

> [A]n essential feature of political activism is the partisan nature of the issue on which the activities are focused. This means there will be firm stakeholders – consumers, partners, employees, policy makers, and so on – who want to maintain the status quo on these issues and those who seek a changed world. As a result, when brands engage on these topics, they need to pick a side and either challenge or defend the status quo.

*Id. See also* Yashoda Bhagwat, Nooshin L. Warren, Joshua T. Beck & George F. Watson, IV, *Corporate Sociopolitical Activism and Firm Value*, 84 J. MKTG., no. 5, 2020, at 1 ("Although [corporate social activism or] CSA may strengthen relationships with some stakeholders who agree with the firm, it will likely damage relationships with those who disagree.").

85 According to a Bentley University and Gallup survey of May 2024 states, "Americans' support for businesses taking a public stance on current events continues to wane in 2024: 38% of Americans say businesses should take a public stance on current events, down from 41% in 2023 and 48% in 2022." Bentley Univ. & Gallup, *Business in Society 2024 Report* (2024), at 6, www.gallup.com/file/analytics/649841/bentley-university-gallup-business-society-2024-report.pdf.

its political credo) perform such functions.[86] Corporations undertake actions that are traditionally carried out by governments in lieu of, or in addition to, governments. This isn't new – employers have long provided healthcare in the US because the government didn't. But in recent years, companies have expanded their role in areas where the state is absent or unwilling to act. When Dick's Sporting Goods stopped selling assault rifles to customers under twenty-one, it was setting a policy stricter than federal law.[87] When Lotus Development extended corporate benefits to employees' domestic partners in the early 1990s, it wasn't just about internal policy – it was extending rights unavailable under then-applicable law.[88] When JPMorgan Chase made a $30 billion pledge aimed at closing the racial wealth gap through race-based lending and investments in Black, Hispanic, and Latino communities, it was effectively engaging in economic policy.[89]

These two forces – corporate socioeconomic advocacy and government substitution – are intertwined: together, they form *corporate governing*. Methodologically, I consider corporate socioeconomic advocacy a type of corporate governing activity, as opposed to mere advocacy, because of the political power corporations have in the policymaking process. With corporate messaging, corporations send signals to markets and stakeholders about what to expect from their future internal and external actions. As Martin Petrin said, "corporations have structural power by being able to set the agenda and by their ability to shape the economic environment."[90] The two activities are tied together because "talk" (corporate socioeconomic advocacy) is often a complement of action (government substitution). In other words, corporate political messaging and advocacy complements measures, initiatives, and activities corporations have been doing for decades. To get a sense of the phenomenon, corporate actions, as opposed to mere statements, represented 40 percent of the sample in a study analyzing 293 events of corporate sociopolitical activism initiated by 149 firms across thirty-nine industries between 2011 and October 2016.[91]

86 *See, for example*, Dirk Matten & Andrew Crane, *Corporate Citizenship: Toward an Extended Theoretical Conceptualization*, 30 ACAD. MGMT. REV. 166, 172 (2005) (describing that corporations intervene due to the result of globalization, when states can no longer guarantee the provision of traditional public goods).

87 Joseph Pisani, *US Companies Take a Stand, Raise Age to Purchase Guns*, AP NEWS (Mar. 1, 2018), https://apnews.com/article/north-america-us-news-ap-top-news-ar-state-wire-shootingsa70d3d6e213d4b3a8af92ffd1849b725.

88 CARLOS A. BALL, THE QUEERING OF CORPORATE AMERICA: HOW BIG BUSINESS WENT FROM LGBTQ ADVERSARY TO ALLY 105–12 (2019).

89 Megan Armstrong, Eathyn Edwards & Duwain Pinder, *Corporate Commitments to Racial Justice: An Update*, MCKINSEY (Feb. 21, 2023), www.mckinsey.com/bem/our-insights/corporate-commitments-to-racial-justice-an-update.

90 *See* Martin Petrin, *Beyond Shareholder Value: Exploring Justifications for a Broader Corporate Purpose*, *in* RESEARCH HANDBOOK ON CORPORATE PURPOSE AND PERSONHOOD 345 (Elizabeth Pollman & Robert B. Thompson, eds., 2020).

91 Bhagwat, Warren, Beck & Watson, *supra* note 84, at 16.

## C KEY QUESTIONS DRIVING THE BOOK

As the backlash against corporate governing grows, firms are now confronting a fundamental question: Should they be in this space at all? Or are they overstepping, wielding power never meant to be theirs?

Much of the debate around corporate governing is tied to its use in connection with specific political projects. Some celebrate businesses that take a stand for reproductive rights or push for stronger climate policies. Others champion efforts to penalize corporations that "discriminate" against the gun industry or refuse to do business with fossil fuel producers. But these conversations often focus on the moment's politics, missing the larger structural shift underway.

*Corporate Power and the Politics of Change* pauses judgment on those immediate battles to examine corporate governing as an institutional phenomenon – one that is reshaping the relationship between business and the state. Rather than asking whether any given political stance is right or wrong, this book interrogates the broader question: What happens when corporations assume roles traditionally reserved for governments?

Corporate governing has been framed in many ways – sometimes as a market-driven correction to political dysfunction, sometimes as a dangerous overreach by unelected executives. *Corporate Power and the Politics of Change* seeks to move beyond those binaries, systematically analyzing how corporate governing operates, what legal and policy frameworks exist to regulate it, and whether those frameworks are equipped to handle its growing influence. The book examines the promises and risks of corporate governing, first from a corporate perspective, considering market incentives, strategic positioning, and legal exposure, and then from a societal one, exploring its impact on social activists, society at large, and democratic institutions. It also looks at possible corporate and policy guardrails, asking whether new governance structures or regulatory interventions could help mitigate potential harms. Finally, it surveys how firms respond to the backlash, whether by doubling on advocacy, quietly retreating, or finding new ways to navigate an increasingly complex political landscape.

These questions animate the book throughout the various chapters. How did corporate governing evolve, and why has it become more contentious? Does it align with traditional corporate law and fiduciary duties, or does it stretch legal boundaries? What are its business, strategic, societal, and political implications? What unintended consequences might arise from businesses assuming quasi-governmental roles? And how should corporate govern*ance* adapt to this new reality?

The goal is not to take sides but to provide a deeper, more comprehensive understanding of corporate governing – how it works, why it matters, and what it means for the future of business and society.

## D EXISTING LITERATURE; CONTRIBUTIONS AND STRUCTURE OF THE BOOK

Corporations increasingly engage in political and social issues to protect their business interests, particularly in recruiting and retaining talent and attracting consumers.[92] A 2019 Accenture survey found that 62% of consumers expect companies to take a stand on social issues, 53% would voice complaints if dissatisfied with a brand's stance, 47% would switch to a competitor, and 17% may never return.[93] Beyond self-interest, corporations are often seen as political actors of last resort, especially in the US, where congressional paralysis has left businesses to fill governance gaps.[94] This expectation pressures corporations to take stances on hot-button political issues, even at the risk of backlash. The push for corporate action often comes from employees[95] and institutional investors who embrace ESG principles.[96]

Scholarly perspectives on corporate activism vary. Some cautiously support this evolving role,[97] arguing that corporate purpose extends beyond shareholder value[98] and that political engagement should be analyzed under a risk management perspective.[99] Others express skepticism or outright opposition.[100] Critics warn that corporate activism can distract from core business responsibilities[101] or even distort

[92] *See infra* Chapter 4, Section A.3.

[93] Abas Mirzaei, Dean C. Wilkie & Helen Siuki, *Woke Brand Activism Authenticity or the Lack of It*, 139 J. BUS. RES. 1, 1 (2022).

[94] *See infra* Chapter 2, Section B.3.

[95] Jennifer S. Fan, *Employees as Regulators: The New Private Ordering in High Technology Companies*, 2019 UTAH L. REV. 973 (2020); Alon-Beck, *supra* note 59. *See infra* Chapter 2, Section A.1.a.

[96] *See generally* Michal Barzuza, Quinn Curtis & David H. Webber, *Shareholder Value(s): Index Fund ESG Activism and the New Millennial Corporate Governance*, 93 S. CAL. L. REV. 1243, 1250 (2020); Dorothy S. Lund, *Asset Managers as Regulators*, 171 U. PA. L. REV. 77 (2023). *See infra* Chapter 2, Section A.1.b.

[97] *See generally* Lin, *supra* note 51 (describing the phenomenon in favorable terms); TOM C.W. LIN, THE CAPITALIST AND THE ACTIVIST: CORPORATE SOCIAL ACTIVISM AND THE NEW BUSINESS OF CHANGE (2022) (same); Jennifer S. Fan, *Woke Capital: The Role of Corporations in Social Movements*, 9 HARV. BUS. L. REV. 441 (2019) (same); Daniel Korschun & N. Craig Smith, *Companies Can't Avoid Politics – and Shouldn't Try To*, HARV. BUS. REV., Mar. 7, 2018 (same).

[98] *Cf.* Oliver Hart & Luigi Zingales, *Companies Should Maximize Shareholder Welfare Not Market Value*, 2 J.L. FIN. & ACCT. 247 (2017) (arguing that shareholders favor long-term welfare over strict value maximization); Kovvali, *supra* note 17 (endorsing stakeholder governance).

[99] Omari Scott Simmons, *Political Risk Management*, 64 WM. & MARY L. REV. 707, 713–14 (2023); Lisa M. Fairfax, *Reframing the Corporate Political Speech Debate*, Working Paper (2025) (unpublished manuscript, on file with author), at 6–9 (arguing for enterprise-wide, risk-based approaches to managing corporate political speech).

[100] STEPHEN M. BAINBRIDGE, THE PROFIT MOTIVE: DEFENDING SHAREHOLDER VALUE MAXIMIZATION (2023) (arguing that activism is bad for business); Jill E. Fisch & Jeff Schwartz, *How Did Corporations Get Stuck in Politics and Can They Escape?*, 3 U. CHI. BUS. L. REV. 325 (2024) (criticizing the phenomenon and arguing that corporations should collectively opt for silence on political issues).

[101] BAINBRIDGE, *supra* note 100, at 96.

democratic processes.[102] Popular discourse reflects these concerns, with some politicians building their careers in opposition to "woke" corporations.[103] In the middle are some voices suggesting that when engaging in activism, corporations inevitably face political legitimacy challenges that need to be addressed via policy fixes like enhanced transparency and stakeholder engagement.[104]

This book builds on existing literature on corporate activism, which has traditionally framed the phenomenon within the context of social activism and movements,[105] as well as on scholarship that critiques or challenges it.[106] While some authors view corporate involvement positively,[107] others argue that its political implications remain problematic even when social activism aligns with business interests.[108] They contend that corporate leaders act as unelected policymakers,[109] risking the alienation of stakeholders over divisive topics.[110] Stephen Bainbridge's recent work echoes these concerns, questioning not only the democratic legitimacy of corporate activism[111] but also its profitability.[112]

* * *

[102] Saura Masconale & Simone M. Sepe, *Citizen Corp. – Corporate Activism and Democracy*, 100 WASH. U.L. REV. 257, 260, 278–81 (2022).

[103] VIVEK RAMASWAMY, WOKE INC.: INSIDE CORPORATE AMERICA'S SOCIAL JUSTICE SCAM (2021). *See* Josh Kraushaar, *"Woke, Inc." Author Launches GOP Presidential Campaign*, AXIOS (Feb. 21, 2023), www.axios.com/2023/02/22/vivek-ramaswamy-2024-presidential-election [https://perma.cc/P9EW-MZ25]; Jessica Guynn, *"Woke Mind Virus"? Why Red America Has Declared War on Corporate America*, USA TODAY (Jan. 4, 2023), www.usatoday.com/story/money/2023/01/04/desantis-republicans-woke-big-business-war/10947073002 [https://perma.cc/5YW8-ZTYZ].

[104] Stavros Gadinis & Chris Havasy, *The Quest for Legitimacy: A Public Law Blueprint for Corporate Law*, 57 U.C. DAVIS L. REV. 1581 (2024).

[105] *See* Lin, *supra* note 51, at 1535 (framing the new reality of business and social activism in America); LIN, *supra* note 97, at 89; Fan, *supra* note 97 (arguing that corporate activism holds the promise of being a force for social change).

[106] *See supra* notes 100–104.

[107] *See* LIN, *supra* note 105, at 163 ("Contemporary corporate social activism offers not only a new path to social progress, but also a new perspective for our roles in making this progress real. It offers us a way to see ourselves in a broader, more diverse, and more complete fashion – beyond narrow definitions of activist and capitalist – as a complete person."); Fan, *supra* note 105, at 445 ("[D]espite the perils associated with the involvement of corporate law within social movements, there is the promise of meaningful change.").

[108] *See* Masconale & Sepe, *supra* note 102, at 305–11; Leo E. Strine, Jr., *Good Corporate Citizenship We Can All Get Behind? Toward a Principled, Non-Ideological Approach to Making Money the Right Way*, 78 BUS. LAW. 329, 357–58 (2023).

[109] *See for example*, Milton Friedman, *The Social Responsibility of Business Is to Increase Its Profits*, NY TIMES MAG. 32, Sept. 13, 1970; Masconale & Sepe, *supra* note 102, at 305–11.

[110] Strine, *supra* note 108, at 357.

[111] BAINBRIDGE, *supra* note 100, at 149–51 (noting that "exercise of political power by undemocratically selected technocrats skilled predominately in business and finance amounts to authoritarianism by the wrong authorities").

[112] *Id.* at 105–24.

*Corporate Power and the Politics of Change* advances the existing literature through five main contributions.

*First*, I map and categorize various areas of corporate governing. Chapter 1 examines the evolving role of corporations as agents of change, distinguishing between the two forms of corporate governing: government substitution, where firms step in to address societal needs in the absence of effective government action, and corporate socioeconomic advocacy, where businesses publicly engage in political and social issues. These dual functions – providing direct support to stakeholders while shaping public discourse – reflect a historical trajectory dating back to corporations' origins as instruments of public goods and extending through critical junctures like the Progressive Era, the 1960s, and beyond.[113]

In Section B, Chapter 1 maps contemporary corporate initiatives across key policy areas, including racial equity, gender and reproductive rights, LGBTQ+ rights, climate action, voting rights, and gun control. This section highlights direct corporate interventions – such as funding racial justice initiatives, offering reproductive healthcare benefits, and enforcing workplace diversity programs – and public advocacy efforts, such as corporate opposition to restrictive voting laws and environmental deregulation. Section B closes by introducing the emergence of conservative corporate governing, where firms take conservative positions or roll back earlier prosocial initiatives.

To be sure, corporate governing has faced intensifying pushback from conservative forces. In Section C, Chapter 1 explores the "anti-woke" movement, detailing political advocacy, litigation, and legislative efforts designed to curb corporate engagement in ESG and DEI. The second Trump administration accelerated this trend, deploying executive orders and regulatory actions to dismantle DEI programs. As a result, many companies have recalibrated their strategies, with some retreating from high-profile initiatives while others maintain their commitments despite heightened scrutiny.

Chapter 1 argues that while corporate governing is under significant pressure, it remains a defining feature of the modern corporate landscape. Whether corporations continue to act as substitutes for government action or as politically engaged entities will depend on ongoing legal, political, and market developments.

* * *

*Second*, in Chapter 2, I explore the key drivers behind corporate governing, examining both internal corporate dynamics and broader societal forces that shape corporate engagement in public policy.

Within firms, bottom-up pressure from employees – particularly Millennials and Gen Z – has been a critical force, compelling corporations to address social issues through workplace policies and public advocacy.[114] Investors – especially large asset

[113] *See infra* Chapter 1, Section A.

[114] *See infra* Chapter 2, Section A.1.a.

managers and ESG-focused funds – have also tried to steer corporate behavior, using shareholder engagement and capital allocation to push environmental and social priorities.[115] At the same time, top-down shifts in corporate purpose, including the revival of stakeholderism, have nudged companies to look beyond short-term profit maximization.[116]

And yet, corporate lobbying and political speech remain a parallel, often contradictory force. Businesses continue to spend heavily to shape public policy – frequently in ways that undercut the very values they promote in press releases and ESG reports.[117]

Beyond these corporate-level drivers, Chapter 2 situates corporate governing within broader social and political trends. It examines how movements such as #MeToo, Black Lives Matter, the Climate Movement, and March for Our Lives have pressured companies to take actions and stands on social justice issues, particularly in an era of digital activism.[118]

The first Trump presidency marked a turning point too, as corporations actively opposed policies such as the Muslim Ban, the withdrawal from the Paris Climate Agreement and the termination of DACA.[119]

This era also highlighted the growing expectation that corporations act when traditional political channels fail, a reality exacerbated by congressional gridlock, polarization, and structural barriers to reform. Chapter 2 details how systemic dysfunction – driven by perpetual campaigning, gerrymandering, the filibuster, and the disproportionate influence of small states in the US Senate – has made corporate intervention more prominent in policymaking.[120]

* * *

*Third*, I develop doctrinal and normative frameworks for analyzing both forms of corporate governing.

Chapter 3 maps the relevant legal terrain, asking whether these practices expose companies to meaningful legal risk. Critics often object that corporations are reaching beyond their proper sphere when they weigh in on social and political issues. This book provides a counterpoint: Corporate governing is, in many cases, part of doing business.

Most such actions fall within the broad discretion afforded to directors and officers, and are generally protected by the business judgment rule. Chapter 3 offers a framework for evaluating corporate governing, distinguishing between *government substitution* – where firms fill regulatory or functional voids – and *corporate socio-economic advocacy* – where firms take public stands on contested issues. Case law,

115 *See infra* Chapter 2, Section A.1.b.
116 *See infra* Chapter 2, Section A.2.
117 *See infra* Chapter 2, Section A.3.
118 *See infra* Chapter 2, Section B.1.
119 *See infra* Chapter 2, Section B.2.
120 *See infra* Chapter 2, Section B.3.

including the 2023 Delaware Chancery Court decision in *Simeone v. Walt Disney Company*,[121] suggests that both forms remain well within the bounds of corporate law.[122] Nor do oversight duties, as currently understood, impose significant additional obligations.[123]

While fiduciary duties impose minimal constraints, compliance risks are beginning to surface. Though not binding on private companies, the long arc of the Supreme Court's decision in *Students for Fair Admissions*[124] has already chilled some corporate DEI efforts and may lead federal courts to further narrow the legal space for such initiatives. Chapter 3 also briefly flags emerging risks from securities fraud litigation and the growing wave of anti-ESG and anti-DEI legislation.[125]

* * *

After analyzing legal risk, the book in Chapter 4 addresses the multifaceted merits of corporate governing. The debate has been contentious and inconclusive partly because it lumps separate normative dimensions. Chapter 4 separates *four distinct normative questions*. The first two focus on corporate considerations: Is there a business case for corporate governing – does it enhance firm value? Even so, is it strategically sensible for a corporation to engage in it? The latter two questions address broader societal and political implications: Does corporate governing advance the goals of social activists and benefit society at large? Does corporate governing, in turn, pose a risk to democratic institutions?

The answers to the first two questions are cautiously affirmative: For some firms, corporate governing may enhance value and be strategically sound, depending on factors like the specific policy issue, firm characteristics, perceived authenticity of the initiative, alignment with the firm's core mission and prior messaging, and the expectations of its stakeholders and the various markets in which the firm operates, such as product, labor, and stock markets.[126] Like any initiative, corporate governing is risky but potentially profitable, and most companies plan for these risks. Importantly, corporate governing initiatives are voluntary, shaped by a firm's strategic choices rather than legal mandates. Companies embrace them when they perceive value or advantage – some have thrived as a result, while others have not. Without clear evidence of widespread harm, limiting these initiatives on business grounds becomes a challenging case to make.[127]

The other two questions are more problematic. Not so much for social activists who know the risk of corporate co-opting and can always part ways with corporate

[121] *See supra* note 26.
[122] *See* Chapter 3, Sections B and C.
[123] *See* Chapter 3, Section D.
[124] *See supra* note 75 and accompanying text.
[125] *See* Chapter 3, Section E.
[126] *See infra* Chapter 4, Sections A and B.
[127] *See infra* Chapter 4, Sections A.3.c.iii.

partners if the results are unsatisfactory.[128] However, whether corporate governing benefits society is more challenging and often politically divisive.[129] Another risk is that delegating socioeconomic issues to corporations might lead citizens to disengage from traditional politics and government.[130] The book further digs into these issues in Chapter 5.

* * *

*Fourth*, based on the proposed normative framework, in Chapter 5, this book investigates the promises and risks of corporate governing from both corporate and societal perspectives. Under the former, corporate governing – when strategically planned and executed – can enhance recruitment, improve employee morale, strengthen branding, and even boost long-term profitability.[131] However, it also carries risks, including alienating stakeholders with opposing views, unsettling shareholders, and creating tensions within the existing corporate governance framework when broader agendas conflict with shareholder and stakeholder expectations.[132] While these challenges are not insurmountable, they may require policy or private ordering refinements to ensure corporate governing aligns with business objectives and governance structures.

From a societal perspective, the implications of corporate governing are more challenging. On the one hand, it can achieve political and social goals that traditional politics struggles to secure, as demonstrated by the corporate sector's critical role in advancing LGBTQ+ rights.[133] Yet, on the other hand, corporate governing also raises several societal risks: It is undemocratic as it lacks accountability and representativeness; it is divisive and anti-pluralistic; its reach is partial; corporations might lose interest or, worse, be opportunistic, absent, or antagonistic to society's quests; and prioritizing the corporate channel over traditional politics is risky, as it may ultimately discourage citizens from engaging in the latter.[134]

These risks include not doing enough for societal issues and weakening democratic institutions. First, corporate governing is *insufficient*: Corporations will not foster true social progress in areas where their interests conflict with society, like tax, antitrust, labor, privacy, and financial reform, among many others.[135] The limitations of corporate governing go beyond concerns about the conflicts of big business; they stem from the fundamental structural incapacity of private actors and markets to tackle large-scale societal challenges effectively. Addressing such issues

[128] *See infra* Chapter 4, Section C.1.
[129] *See infra* Chapter 4, Section C.2.
[130] *See infra* Chapter 4, Section D.
[131] *See infra* Chapter 5, Section A.1.
[132] *See infra* Chapter 5, Section A.2.
[133] *See infra* Chapter 5, Section B.1.
[134] *See infra* Chapter 5, Section B.2.a.
[135] *See infra* Chapter 5, Section B.2.b.i.

requires durable, systemic, coordinated, and enforceable solutions – capabilities that only states can reliably provide.[136] Corporations, by their very nature, lack these mechanisms, a fact made strikingly clear by their swift retreat from prior commitments under the pressure of the second Trump administration.[137] This is an important cautionary tale to remember before embarking on potentially perilous policy changes that would entrust executives with more extensive mandates and roles than they currently have.

Under a separate line of criticism, corporate governing is *dangerous*. Two main reasons for that: First, it can be undemocratic, sacrificing dissenter rights over policies that bypass the democratic process;[138] second, it risks weakening politics and democratic institutions if corporations dominate the reform space.[139] Chapter 5 argues that while the undemocratic nature of corporate governing may be less severe than some claim, the real concern lies in its potential to undermine politics. This shift – where corporations take on policymaking roles – could normalize corporate influence in areas traditionally reserved for the state, reducing transparency and accountability while consolidating power in unelected private actors. Over time, corporate governing may not just supplement politics but replace it, exacerbating the imbalance between public and private power in ways that threaten democratic stability. Needless to say, the aftermath of the 2024 election - and Elon Musk's short tenure in formal political power through the Department of Government Efficiency (DOGE) - has exponentially heightened this type of risk.

* * *

*Fifth*, and finally, in Chapter 6, the book explores potential corporate governance safeguards to manage corporate governing risks, particularly in corporate socioeconomic advocacy. After describing the constraints imposed by *Citizens United*[140] and the business judgment rule, this chapter examines regulatory and market-based solutions to mitigate risks while preserving corporate speech and discretion.

Chapter 6 first considers disclosure as a soft intervention, questioning whether and how corporations should provide more precise insights into their policy agendas, lobbying, and advocacy efforts through periodic reports.[141] Chapter 6 then evaluates board empowerment and oversight mechanisms, including disinterested

136 Daron Acemoglu & James A. Robinson, Why Nations Fail: The Origins of Power, Prosperity, and Poverty 75–76 (2012).

137 *See supra* Chapter 1, Section C.4.

138 *See infra* Chapter 5, Sections B.2.b.ii.x and B.2.b.ii.y.

139 *See infra* Chapter 5, Section B.2.b.ii.z.

140 Citizens United v. Fed. Election Comm'n, 558 U.S. 310, 336–66 (2010) (prohibiting the government from restricting independent expenditures for political communications by corporations, including nonprofit corporations, labor unions, and other associations, so long as such spending is independent of a party or a candidate).

141 *See infra* Chapter 6, Section B.2.

director involvement, dedicated committees, enhanced board accountability, and shareholder approval for corporate governing initiatives.[142]

However, Chapter 6 questions the viability of legislative interventions to advance corporate governing reform, given the political polarization surrounding the issue. It then explores how, in the absence of legal reform, market forces – such as investor pressure, litigation risks, and internal corporate policies – may shape corporate governing.[143]

Indeed, many firms have adopted internal policies to navigate political and social engagement, particularly in response to mounting litigation risks and evolving investor expectations. Analyzing disclosures from two samples of S&P 500 companies – the S&P 100 and the smallest 100 in the index – Chapter 6 identifies patterns in how corporations structure their internal guidelines and ensure transparency around corporate governing activities.[144] The findings reveal variation across industries and firm sizes, with larger companies being more explicit about their advocacy strategies. The survey also finds that many frame their initiatives as aligned with business and industry interests rather than broader societal concerns.

Notably, Chapter 6 underscores that clarity and transparency in corporate governing are not just external expectations but serve the best interests of corporations themselves. By articulating clear policies, defining decision-making processes, and ensuring consistency in their advocacy efforts, companies may limit reputational backlash, reduce litigation risks, and preempt regulatory scrutiny. In an environment where corporate governing increasingly attracts legal and political challenges, proactive disclosure and structured internal governance can function as legitimacy and risk management tools.

While corporate governance mechanisms can help manage risk at the firm level, they are insufficient to address the broader societal implications of corporate governing. Reliance on corporations to fill policy gaps raises concerns about democratic accountability and long-term governance stability – issues that extend beyond the corporate sphere and require broader political reform. Market forces, including shareholder activism, consumer pressure, and reputational risks, continue to shape corporate governing decisions, but whether they provide sufficient discipline at the societal level remains an open question.

As no easy policy fixes exist, addressing this risk requires ambitious efforts from multiple actors to prevent the erosion of reform through traditional democratic institutions. This demands changes in norms, political goodwill, and possibly political reform – all areas where corporate governance can assist but not be the driving force.

* * *

142 *See infra* Chapter 6, Section B.3.
143 *See infra* Chapter 6, Section C.
144 *See infra* Chapter 6, Section D.

*A note to the reader.*

Chapters 1 and 2, which introduce the phenomenon of corporate governing and explore its key drivers, are written with a general audience in mind. Chapters 3–6 are more technical. Chapters 3 and 6 contain the book's most concentrated legal analysis. They are aimed primarily at lawyers and social scientists, though remain accessible to non-specialists. Chapters 4 and 5 address the normative dimensions of corporate governing with a broader lens, drawing on insights from law, economics, finance, management, marketing, political theory, and political science. While intended for a wide readership, they are denser than Chapters 1 and 2.

# PART I

# The Landscape

# 1

# Corporations as Agents of Socioeconomic Change

## *Where Are We Now?*

This chapter examines corporate governing efforts by major corporations, distinguishing between two primary dimensions: *government substitution* and *corporate socioeconomic advocacy*. Government substitution occurs when corporations step in to address societal needs that governments fail to meet – whether due to political inaction or constitutional paralysis – by implementing internal policies that directly protect stakeholders. Corporate socioeconomic advocacy, on the other hand, involves businesses taking public stances on policy issues, using executive messaging, lobbying, and other forms of political engagement to influence broader societal outcomes.

Section A briefly traces corporations' origins as instruments of public goods and the circumstances under which they have engaged in social and political matters. While corporations are profit-driven enterprises, over time, including during the Progressive and Civil Rights Eras, external pressures have pushed them into a quasi-public role.

Section B analyzes contemporary corporate governing, illustrating how businesses engage in various socioeconomic issues, often in ways that provoke controversy or resistance. The discussion covers numerous corporate initiatives in racial equity, women's and reproductive rights, LGBTQ+ rights, climate, voting rights, and gun control. I examine how major corporations – such as JPMorgan Chase's $30 billion pledge to close the racial wealth gap, Apple's racial justice fund, and Disney's high-profile clash with Florida lawmakers – have taken action and how some have scaled back under political pressure. This section highlights both the breadth and complexity of corporate governing today, where actions can range from funding social justice programs to lobbying against restrictive voting laws or even limiting firearm sales in response to mass shootings. I also explore the rise of *conservative corporate governing*, where some firms actively align with conservative values or reverse their prosocial initiatives in response to legal and political pressures.

Section C examines whether corporate governing has slowed in the face of the growing conservative backlash, which accelerated after the Supreme Court's affirmative action ruling and has intensified under Trump's second administration.

With conservative forces back in power, corporations now face heightened scrutiny, litigation, and political pressure to retreat – particularly on ESG and DEI fronts. Still, it remains too soon to tell whether this marks a full-scale reversal or merely a recalibration.



This chapter examines the role of corporations in driving socioeconomic change, focusing on two distinct but interconnected forms of action. The first, which I call *government substitution*, occurs when corporations address societal needs that governments fail to meet – whether by choice or because of political gridlock. These internal corporate actions are designed to protect one or more constituencies directly. The second, *corporate socioeconomic advocacy*, involves external efforts: corporations taking public stands on policy issues. Using tools like the "CEO megaphone" and corporate messaging, they seek to promote, oppose, or adjust public policies at various levels – international, national, state, or local.

These two activities often complement each other. Not only do corporations implement initiatives to safeguard specific internal and societal interests, but they also advocate for broader policy outcomes – whether reinforcing or challenging governmental efforts. Together, these interconnected actions represent two facets of the same coin: The broader phenomenon of corporate governing, where businesses actively engage with societal and political challenges.

To be sure, neither phenomenon is new. Corporations were initially used as unique governmental arms to achieve public goods – not just in the US but everywhere since the Romans.[1] This is not surprising because corporations are creatures of the state, and in their early days, they operated in a reciprocal arrangement:

[1] On the origins of business corporations as entities used by nation-states to provide (outsourced) public services since Ancient Rome, see Sergio Alberto Gramitto Ricci, *Archeology, Language, and Nature of Business Corporations*, 89 Miss. L.J. 43 (2019) (tracing the use of the corporate form as a legal

The state granted charters to enable private investment in enterprises that aligned with its geopolitical or political interests.[2] This was especially true for the colonies: While British and Dutch merchants, investors, and speculators used this legal instrument as an eminently private way to foster their wealth,[3] the place where their outbound investment was taking place had a primary public interest in its success.[4]

In the early years of the United States, by 1800, judges and jurists regarded business enterprises such as banks, insurance companies, and transportation facilities as arms of the state: "The archetypal American corporation of the eighteenth century is the municipality, a public body charged with carrying out public functions."[5] When the Constitution was adopted, few business corporations were chartered, all with an overarching public vocation: "two banks, two insurance companies, six canal companies, and two toll bridge operators."[6] While corporations slowly but surely succeeded in becoming eminently private enterprises, during the Progressive Era, they were pressured to implement the first employee benefit plans and pension systems.[7] It was after the 1960s that some corporations started to exemplify the type of social activism that has become more commonplace today[8]. Over the last ten years, corporate involvement in the public sphere reached an all-time high: To get a sense, the share of US corporations who engage in socioeconomic advocacy has increased from roughly 10 percent to 38 percent between 2011 and 2019.[9] A testament to its significance is the wide backlash it generated from conservatives.[10]

technology that combined public and private interests and allowed Rome to provide services on a vast territory).

[2] *See* Thomas Hobbes, Leviathan 172 (Oxford, 1909) (1651) (conceiving business corporations as "bodies politic" of a smaller nature than the actual state).

[3] *Id.* at 178 ("The end … of these Bodies of Merchants, being not a Common benefit to the whole Body, … but the particular gaine of every adventurer.").

[4] Carlos A. Ball, The Queering of Corporate America: How Big Business Went from LGBTQ Adversary to Ally 10 (2019) ("The colonists and early Americans largely viewed corporations as entities whose function was to help society achieve public ends.").

[5] Morton J. Horwitz, The Transformation of American Law, 1780–1860 110–112 (1977). *See also* John Coates IV, *Corporate Speech and the First Amendment: History, Data, and Implications*, 30 Const. Comment. 223, 226 (2015) (noting that "corporations from their inception in English (and hence, American) history were extensions of government").

[6] Adam Winkler, We the Corporations: How American Businesses Won Their Civil Rights 4 (2018).

[7] Ball, *supra* note 4, at 13 (mentioning corporate disability benefits and retirement programs at Procter & Gamble as early as 1915).

[8] Tom C.W. Lin, *Incorporating Social Activism*, 98 B.U. L. Rev. 1535, 1541 (2018). While others remained uninvolved, some companies openly supported civil rights leaders and organizations. *Id.* at 1541–42 (noting that businesses also directly assisted in the enactment of the Civil Rights Acts of 1964 and 1968).

[9] Swarnodeep Homroy & Shubhashis Gangopadhyay, *Strategic CEO Activism in Polarized Markets*, J. Fin. & Quantitative Analysis 1, 2 (2023), doi:10.1017/S0022109023001382.

[10] *See infra* Section C.

In this chapter, after a brief historical excursus to contextualize the phenomenon (Section A), I map selected instances of recent corporate governing initiatives, which I organize by subject matter of intervention and distinguish between government substitution and corporate socioeconomic advocacy (Section B). This chapter closes with an account of the political and legal backlash against corporate governing and assesses whether less involvement is going to become the new standard (Section C).

## A CORPORATE GOVERNING IN HISTORICAL CONTEXT

The role of corporations in achieving social objectives has developed and adapted over the centuries. As anticipated, in their early days, corporations were precisely conceived to absolve a public function. During Ancient Rome, corporations were often organized for social purposes, such as running homes for the poor and elderly, hospitals, orphanages, and asylums.[11] This pattern was replicated in medieval England, where the Crown chartered corporations not to seek profits but to run municipalities, churches, and universities.[12] The earliest entities resembling a modern-day corporation, the English East India Company and the Dutch *Vereenigde Oostindische Compagnie*, were chartered in the colonial era to develop the newly conquered lands and facilitate trading, both foreign policy goals of their home nations.[13]

In America, during the colonial period, corporations were first established under the authority of the British Crown; after the Revolutionary War, state legislatures took over the chartering process.[14] At the time, corporations were relatively rare and still primarily created via special charter for public or social purposes, like building infrastructure or supporting charitable organizations.[15]

When the era of special charters ended, giving way to general corporation statutes adopted by states across the US,[16] the social mission of corporations progressively faded, and profit-making became more central.[17] In the nineteenth century, especially after the Civil War, American society viewed corporations as profit-first and profit-only private entities.[18]

11 Eric C. Chaffee, *The Origins of Corporate Social Responsibility*, 85 U. Cin. L. Rev. 347, 351 (2017).

12 Leo E. Strine Jr. & Nicholas Walter, *Originalist or Original: The Difficulties of Reconciling Citizens United with Corporate Law History*, 91 Notre Dame L. Rev. 877, 891 (2016).

13 Elizabeth Pollman, *Reconceiving Corporate Personhood*, 2011 Utah L. Rev. 1629, 1632 (2011).

14 Chaffee, *supra* note 11, at 353.

15 *Id*; Winkler, *supra* note 6, at 43.

16 Henry Hansmann & Mariana Pargendler, *The Evolution of Shareholder Voting Rights Separation of Ownership and Consumption*, 123 Yale L.J. 948, 993–94 (2014).

17 Chaffee, *supra* note 11, at 354–55.

18 Ball, *supra* note 4, at 11.

As corporations expanded and monopolized industries in the early 1900s, public unease grew during the Progressive Era, leading to calls for reforms and for large corporations to act more responsibly.[19] Under mounting pressure, some of the nation's wealthiest families established charitable foundations to redistribute their wealth.[20] This period saw the introduction of the first employee benefit plans, pension systems, disability benefits, retirement programs, and the eight-hour workday policy.[21]

However, during the Great Depression, these corporate welfare policies proved vastly inadequate. In response, New Deal policies replaced them with large government-led social programs, diminishing the relevance of the corporate sector in addressing social issues.[22]

Then came World War II. During wartime, businesses fulfilled a vital social role by supporting the war efforts, contributing to national production, and supplying essential goods and services.[23] Corporations retooled their operations to produce military equipment, vehicles, and supplies at an unprecedented scale, which was critical to the war's success.[24] This support for the wartime economy highlighted the ability of businesses to serve broader societal needs beyond just generating profit.

World War II also brought a massive overhaul in workforce composition. The war significantly expanded the participation of women and racial minorities in the labor force because of a labor shortage due to the mass enlistment of men. As women were encouraged to take up jobs in manufacturing – particularly in industries critical to the war effort such as munitions, shipbuilding, and aircraft production – their entry into the workforce helped ease labor shortages and, in turn, opened new employment opportunities for minorities within the wartime economy.[25] The contributions of women and minorities during the war helped to lay the groundwork for future civil rights advancements, as their participation challenged traditional gender roles and racial barriers in the labor market.[26] In the 1940s, corporations like General Electric and The Radio Corporation of America were the first to embrace equal opportunity policies.[27]

19 *Id.* at 13.

20 *Id.*

21 *Id.*

22 *Id.* at 14.

23 President Franklin Delano Roosevelt established the War Production Board, which brought together industry leaders to oversee the nation's transition from civilian to military manufacturing. Ralph E. Gomory & Richard Sylla, *The American Corporation*, 142(2) DAEDALUS 102, 105 (2013) (noting that "[c]orporations recovered much of the prestige they lost during the Depression through their contributions to the successful outcome of World War II.").

24 *Id.*

25 Executive Order 8802, 3 C.F.R. (1941); NEIL A. WYNN, THE AFRICAN AMERICAN EXPERIENCE DURING WORLD WAR II (2010).

26 SUSAN M. HARTMANN, THE HOME FRONT AND BEYOND: AMERICAN WOMEN IN THE 1940S (1982); Karen Tucker Anderson, *Last Hired, First Fired: Black Women Workers during World War II*, 69 J. AM. HIST. 82 (1982).

27 BALL, *supra* note 4, at 22.

While after World War II, corporations did little more than engage in philanthropy on the social front,[28] Howard Bowen's *Social Responsibilities of the Businessman*,[29] published in 1953, is seen as the starting point for modern corporate social responsibility (CSR). His book argued that businesses should think beyond profit and consider their broader impact on society, setting the stage for the evolution of CSR in the following years.

Bowen's idea wasn't new – Chapter 3 highlights a similar argument by Henry Ford, who, in the late 1910s, defended against a lawsuit by the Dodge brothers, accusing him of prioritizing social goals, like lowering car prices and creating jobs, over maximizing shareholder profits.[30] Famously, though, that argument did not serve Ford well, as he lost the case in what was considered the corporate law trial of the century.[31] In the aftermath of the *Dodge v. Ford* case, two leading corporate law scholars, Adolf Berle of Columbia and Merrick Dodd of Harvard, sparked a debate – one that continues to this day – over the proper beneficiaries of directors' fiduciary duties: Should they serve only shareholders (as Berle argued), or broader constituencies (as Dodd contended)?[32] Thus, when CSR was first advocated, it was not a novel concept but rather a reformulation of preexisting tensions over the role and responsibilities of corporations in society.

In the meantime, postwar conservatism, intensified by anxieties over the rise of international communism, led many to look to business, rather than government, for prominent social leadership.[33] This is one reason the CSR discourse resonated strongly in academic and business circles. The other important factor was the significant societal upheaval experienced in the 1960s, driven by the Civil Rights Movement. In 1970, protesters stormed Honeywell's annual shareholder meeting, forcing to adjourn it after just 14 minutes.[34]

The scholarly debate intensified. Keith Davis argued that mounting social, economic, and political pressures demanded businesses reassess their social

[28] Archie B. Carroll, A *History of Corporate Social Responsibility: Concepts and Practices, in* THE OXFORD HANDBOOK OF CORPORATE SOCIAL RESPONSIBILITY 19 (Andrew Crane et al. eds., 2008) [hereinafter, Carroll, A *History of Corporate Social Responsibility*]. During the 1960s, corporate philanthropy evolved from personalized giving by industrial magnates to more formalized company-wide programs, with firms like Dayton Hudson (now Target) and Cummins Engine Co. leading through their "Five Percent Clubs." Archie B. Carroll, *Corporate Social Responsibility: The Centerpiece of Competing and Complementary Frameworks*, 44 ORG. DYNAMICS 87 (2015) [hereinafter, Carroll, *Corporate Social Responsibility*].

[29] HOWARD R. BOWEN, SOCIAL RESPONSIBILITIES OF THE BUSINESSMAN (Iowa, 2013) (1953).

[30] Dodge v. Ford Motor Co., 170 N.W. 668, 684 (Mich. 1919).

[31] *Id.* For a legal analysis, see *infra* Chapter 3, Section B.3.

[32] For a discussion on stakeholderism, see *infra* Chapter 2, Section A.2.

[33] *See* MORRELL HEALD, THE SOCIAL RESPONSIBILITIES OF BUSINESS: COMPANY AND COMMUNITY 1900–1960 83 (1988)

[34] Benjamin C. Waterhouse, *The Personal, the Political and the Profitable: Business and Protest Culture, 1960s–1980s*, FIN. HIST., Spring 2017, at 14, 15.

responsibilities, linking CSR to both social power and economic benefits.[35] In contrast, future Nobel laureate Milton Friedman challenged CSR, contending that business and politics be kept separate and the former should focus solely on profit-making – a debate that would influence discussions on CSR for decades.[36]

On top of the broader debate on corporate responsibility, the emergence of civil rights organizations, feminist groups, and environmental organizations pressured corporations to take on more significant social obligations, catalyzing the mainstreaming of CSR by the late 1960s and early 1970s, when social activists and organizations targeted corporations directly.[37] For instance, activists purchased shares in the Greyhound Bus Company to use shareholder meetings as a forum for highlighting racial discrimination in the private sector.[38] A similar strategy disrupted Eastman Kodak's annual shareholder meetings, pressuring the company over its lack of racial diversity in hiring and promotions.[39] Eventually, Kodak conceded, agreeing to create a job training program and later helping establish the Rochester Business Opportunities Corporation to support minority-owned businesses.[40]

Notably, these bottom-up pressures were, in a sense, encouraged by big business itself. Before civil rights legislation was enacted, the National Association of Manufacturers (NAM) argued that voluntary corporate action was preferable to government-mandated reforms, citing fears of backlash, increased racial division, and expanded government bureaucracy.[41]

Companies like International Harvester, General Electric, and RCA took early steps by implementing nondiscrimination policies as early as the 1940s; by the 1960s, they were testifying before Congress in favor of equal opportunity laws.[42] In Atlanta, Coca-Cola rallied white businesses to celebrate Dr. Martin Luther King

[35] Keith Davis, *Can Business Afford to Ignore Social Responsibilities?* 2 Cal. Mgmt. Rev. 70 (1960).

[36] Milton Friedman, Capitalism and Freedom (1962); Milton Friedman, *The Social Responsibility of Business is to Increase Its Profits*, N.Y. Times Mag., Sept. 13, 1970. *See infra* Chapter 2, Section A.2.

[37] *See* Sarah A. Soule, Contention and Corporate Social Responsibility 54–58 & 62–63 (2009) (chronicling some of the most prominent protests in the United States targeting corporations in the 1970s on issues such as Vietnam, South Africa, and environmental disasters).

[38] Ball, *supra* note 4, at 19.

[39] *Id.*

[40] Soule, *supra* note 37, at 60.

[41] Ball, *supra* note 4, at 20. Somewhere in the middle, the Johnson Administration sought to bridge the divide between corporations and activists when it promoted public–private partnerships on social issues. In 1968, President Lyndon Johnson created the National Alliance of Businessmen (NAB) to encourage large employers to hire economically disadvantaged individuals. Led by the president of Ford Motor Company and including executives from companies like Alcoa and Coca-Cola, the NAB sought to address racial inequality in the workforce. Although these programs eventually declined due to economic pressures and political opposition, they underscored the role of corporate leaders in addressing social issues. *Id.* at 25.

[42] *Id.* at 22.

Jr.'s Nobel Prize in 1964,[43] while the likes of Avon, Xerox, and McDonald's began incorporating African Americans into their recruitment, marketing, and investment strategies.[44]

Between the 1970s and 1990s, corporations faced increasing public scrutiny that forced them to adjust in response to sustained protests. These demonstrations often targeted harmful or unethical business practices, drawing inspiration from the anti-war activism of the 1960s and 1970s.[45] In the late 1970s, Nabisco faced criticism because its Aurora subsidiary marketed toys perceived as too violent and sexist.[46] A few years later, Burger King was pressured by animal rights activists to remove its veal sandwich due to concerns over the inhumane treatment of calves.[47]

At the same time, businesses began proactively integrating social responsibility into their core operations rather than merely reacting to backlash. Companies like The Body Shop in the UK and Ben & Jerry's in the US built their brands around ethical sourcing, environmental sustainability, and social activism, marking a shift from traditional corporate philanthropy to CSR as a defining business strategy.[48]

As corporate engagement with social issues deepened, companies also started paying closer attention to *shareholder* demands on these matters. Corporations began voluntarily incorporating public interest resolutions into their proxy statements and negotiating with politically active investors to manage public relations risks and mitigate the reputational damage that shareholder activism could inflict – especially when confronted by high-profile groups such as churches and socially conscious investors.[49] Executives recognized that addressing specific demands could preempt negative media coverage and prevent shareholder meetings from becoming forums for criticism of their social performance.[50]

The Reagan administration's rollback of federal protections for vulnerable groups in the 1980s fueled corporate activism, as businesses stepped in to fill the gaps left by government inaction – a pattern that would resurface cyclically in the following decades, particularly during the first Trump presidency.[51] Some argue that this was Reagan's precise goal, as he urged companies and private initiatives to address social problems, calling for volunteerism and advocating for the private sector to

43 Tom C.W. Lin, The Corporation and the Activist: Corporate Social Activism and the New Business of Change 24 (2022).

44 *Id.* at 24–25 (noting that many other corporations opposed integration).

45 Soule, *supra* note 37, at 56–58 (documenting the protests that targeted Dow Chemical and Honeywell).

46 *Id.* at 55–56.

47 *Id.* at 55.

48 Carroll, *A History of Corporate Social Responsibility*, *supra* note 28.

49 David Vogel, Kindred Strangers: The Uneasy Relationship between Politics and Business in America 167–68 (1996).

50 *Id.*

51 *See infra* Chapter 2, Section B.2.

fill the gap left by federal and state social service funding cuts.[52] Thus, despite the Reagan administration's opposition to affirmative action, some corporations continued addressing inequality.[53] In 1981, corporate executives opposed federal rollbacks by filing amicus briefs and testifying before Congress.[54]

During this time, activists intensified targeting large corporations, recognizing their sensitivity to brand reputation and negative publicity. With many LGBTQ+ employees and limited legal protections, activists exposed discriminatory practices at prominent companies like phone providers, Coors, and TV networks.[55]

Corporate responses followed. Most notably, in the early 1990s, Lotus Development extended benefits to employees' domestic partners, a move Carlos Ball identifies as a landmark in the relationship between corporate America and LGBTQ+ rights.[56] Lotus's decision signaled a broader shift as companies began integrating social issues into their core business strategies – not just as a reaction to regulation but as a proactive way to attract and retain talent while managing reputational risks.[57]

Collaboration between corporations and activists, advocacy groups, employee resource groups, and trade associations on socioeconomic issues became the norm in the new millennium.[58] Businesses became expected to act responsibly and lead social change.[59] As the rest of this chapter illustrates, they have played an active role – though not without facing intense criticism and heavy countermeasures from conservative forces.

## B MAPPING CORPORATE GOVERNING

In this section, I review selected instances of corporate governing initiatives at some major corporations and cover some of their most impactful – and often controversial – actions in response to momentous societal events. Notably, I distinguish between government substitution and corporate socioeconomic advocacy and present the categories in this order to show that corporations often engage in political messaging as a complement to their pro-stakeholder measures, initiatives, and activities. Below, I survey initiatives in six areas: race and immigration, women's and reproductive rights, LGBTQ+ rights, climate, reactions to January 6 and voting

52 *See* Carroll, *Corporate Social Responsibility*, *supra* note 28, at 88.

53 BALL, *supra* note 4, at 26–27.

54 *Id.* (noting that this period saw corporate America distance itself from the term "affirmative action," shifting toward "diversity" initiatives instead).

55 *Id.* at 31–58 (noting that TV networks were accused of negatively portraying non-heterosexual individuals).

56 *Id.* at 105–12

57 *See infra* Chapter 4, Section A.3.b.

58 *See* LIN, *supra* note 43, at 21.

59 *Id.* at 22.

restriction laws, and gun control. Additionally, I examine the rise of "conservative corporate governing," consisting of corporations that either adhere to conservative values from the outset or, under political pressure, roll back prior prosocial commitments – such as those on DEI or climate – shifting toward conservative positions.

### 1 *Race and Immigration*

The aftermath of the murders of George Floyd and Breonna Taylor sparked nationwide protests and a racial reckoning of a scale unseen in decades. Corporate America felt the impact. In response, many companies adopted policies and programs aimed at advancing racial justice.[60] Several major firms moved to support underrepresented and underserved communities, often positioning these efforts as long due and aligned with long-term business interests.[61]

*Government Substitution*. Between May 2020 and October 2022, companies pledged approximately $340 billion to achieve racial equality, most coming from the financial industry.[62] A study by McKinsey indicates that 93 percent of the total pledges were from financial sector companies, focusing on areas such as affordable housing and small business development.[63] This period saw significant commitments: JPMorgan Chase pledged $30 billion to close the racial wealth gap through race-based lending and investments in Black, Hispanic, and Latino communities.[64] PepsiCo committed $400 million over five years to support Black communities and increase Black representation within the company, which included expanding recruitment at Historically Black Colleges and Universities (HBCUs) and investing in Black-owned businesses.[65]

In the tech sector, Apple created a coding camp for Black coders and computer engineers and set aside $100 million to fund its Racial Equity and Justice Initiative

60 *See generally* Megan Armstrong, Eathyn Edwards & Duwain Pinder, *Corporate Commitments to Racial Justice: An Update*, McKinsey (Feb. 21, 2023), www.mckinsey.com/bem/our-insights/corporate-commitments-to-racial-justice-an-update.

61 Lin, *supra* note 43, at 89.

62 Armstrong, Edwards & Pinder, *supra* note 60.

63 *Id.* (noting that "[f]rom May 2021 through October 2022, 16 Fortune 1000 finance companies made up 93.0 percent of the value of commitments, followed by 4.5 percent from 11 businesses worth $588 billion in the retail sector, 1.3 percent from eight companies in the food and restaurant industry, and less than 1.0 percent for any other sector.").

64 *Id.* To be fair, concerns have emerged regarding the actual disbursement and impact of these funds, with some estimates indicating that only a small fraction of the pledged amounts has been effectively utilized. Creative Investment Research, *Corporate Donations to Black Lives Matter Total $67 Billion*, PRLog (2021), www.prlog.org/12874879-corporate-donations-to-black-lives-matter-total-67-billion.html ("As of Thursday, June 24, 2021, 261 corporations have pledged $67.186 billion to BLM. We estimate that cash disbursed so far totals $652 million.").

65 Lisa M. Fairfax, *Racial Rhetoric or Reality? Cautious Optimism on the Link between Corporate #BLM Speech and Behavior*, 2022 Colum. Bus. L. Rev. 118, 140 (highlighting these actions as examples of corporate efforts to align public statements with tangible initiatives addressing racial inequality.)

"to help dismantle systemic barriers to opportunity and combat injustices faced by communities of color."[66] Apple's initiative focuses on education, economic equality, and criminal justice reform.[67] Among various measures, Apple launched an innovation and learning hub for HBCUs, a developer academy to support coding and tech education for students in Detroit, and venture capital funding for Black and Brown entrepreneurs.[68] In launching the initiatives, its CEO Tim Cook stated, "We are all accountable to the urgent work of building a more just, more equitable world."[69]

Google, now Alphabet, committed $175 million to support African American entrepreneurs, job seekers, students, and developers as part of its racial equity initiatives.[70] This package included $100 million for Black-led capital firms and startups, $50 million for small businesses serving the Black community, and $15 million for job training programs.[71] In 2020, the company aimed to increase Black representation at senior levels by 30 percent by 2025, with efforts focused on mentoring and advocating for underrepresented staff and a pledge to open senior positions to external candidates and invest in cities with significant Black populations, such as Atlanta, Chicago, and London.[72] Additionally, Google invested in education and AI representation to close gaps in computer science and STEM fields.[73]

Retail and media companies were also active. Sephora and other national retailers like Macy's and Gap pledged to source 15 percent of their product offerings from Black-owned businesses.[74] Target committed to spending more than $2 billion with Black-owned businesses by the end of 2025.[75]

[66] Apple Inc., *Apple Launches Major New Racial Equity and Justice Initiative Projects to Challenge Systemic Racism, Advance Racial Equity Nationwide*, Apple Newsroom (Jan. 13, 2021), www.apple.com/newsroom/2021/01/apple-launches-major-new-racial-equity-and-justice-initiative-projects-to-challenge-systemic-racism-advance-racial-equity-nationwide/.

[67] *See* Kif Leswing, *Tim Cook Commits $100 Million to Apple Program for Racial Justice after Killing of George Floyd*, CNBC (June 11, 2020, 12:55 PM), www.cnbc.com/2020/06/11/apple-racial-equity-and-justice-initiative-100m.html.

[68] *See* Apple, *supra* note 66.

[69] *Id.*

[70] *See* Jacob Kastrenakes, *Google Commits $175 Million to Racial Equity with Focus on Black-Owned Businesses*, The Verge (June 17, 2020, 5:22 PM), www.theverge.com/2020/6/17/21294692/google-175-million-racial-equity-black-businesses-entrepreneurs-commitment.

[71] *Id.*

[72] *See* Sundar Pichai, *Commitments to Racial Equity*, Google Blog (June 17, 2020), https://blog.google/inside-google/company-announcements/commitments-racial-equity/ (mentioning that Google would set up a talent liaison to mentor and advocate for underrepresented staff and convened a task force to develop accountability measures in hiring, performance management, and retention).

[73] *Id.*

[74] Lin, *supra* note 43, at 89; *see also* Melissa Repko & Lauren Thomas, *After George Floyd Was Killed, Retailers Pledged to Put Black-Owned Brands on Shelves. Here's How It's Going*, CNBC (May 25, 2021, 2:34 PM), www.cnbc.com/2021/05/25/retailers-diversity-pledges-put-more-black-owned-brands-on-shelves.html (describing other initiatives by companies like Lowe's, Ulta Beauty, Walmart, and Nordstrom's).

[75] This included adding products from over 500 Black-owned companies across various categories and introducing programs to help Black-owned businesses grow and scale their operations, thanks to

Viacom and WarnerMedia launched initiatives to fund and air more social justice content.[76] Netflix pledged to invest $100 million, or 2 percent of its cash equivalents, into banks that primarily work with Black communities.[77]

Corporations like Nike, Twitter, Target, General Motors, and Lyft decided to recognize Juneteenth as a paid holiday for their employees.[78] JPMorgan Chase and Capital One chose to close their banks early.[79] Many of the over 460 companies observing Juneteenth provided holiday pay to their workers.[80] Given the broad support, Congress subsequently established Juneteenth as a federal holiday.[81]

Following the George Floyd protests in May 2020, companies like Twitter and Facebook faced intense pressure from employees, activists, and advertisers to respond to President Trump's post – "when the looting starts, the shooting starts" – a historically charged phrase calling for violent action against protesters.[82] Facebook employees, through public statements and a virtual walkout, opposed CEO Mark Zuckerberg's decision to leave the post up, leading to reputational damage and financial fallout.[83] The "Stop Hate for Profit" campaign pressured major advertisers like Unilever and Verizon to withdraw their ads.[84] Twitter labeled Trump's tweet as a violation of its rules against glorifying violence,[85] and Facebook, under mounting pressure, eventually introduced policies to address hate speech.[86]

*Corporate Socioeconomic Advocacy*. As mentioned earlier, the outcry for the murders of George Floyd and Breonna Taylor was a significant turning point for racial relations in the US, and corporations took part to demonstrate their commitment to social justice. Almost nine out of ten Fortune 100 companies

grants and media funds to enhance visibility. Target Corporation, *Target Commits to Spending More than $2 Billion with Black-Owned Businesses by 2025*, TARGET NEWSROOM (Apr. 7, 2021), https://corporate.target.com/press/release/2021/04/target-commits-to-spending-more-than-2-billion-wit. The initiative was dismissed a few years later when Target succumbed to conservative pressure. *See infra* Section C.4.

76 LIN, *supra* note 43, at 89.

77 *Id.*

78 Gillian Friedman, *Here's What Companies Are Promising to Do to Fight Racism*, N.Y. TIMES (Aug. 23, 2020), www.nytimes.com/article/companies-racism-george-floyd-protests.html.

79 *Id.*

80 *See* Keira Wingate, *BestBuy, Target and Starbucks Are among the Companies Celebrating Juneteenth as PTO or Holiday Pay*, USA TODAY (June 20, 2021, 7:58 PM), www.usatoday.com/story/money/2021/06/18/companies-federal-holiday-juneteenth-off-employees/7740121002/.

81 *See* Lexi Lonas, *Biden Signs Bill Establishing Juneteenth as Federal Holiday*, THE HILL (June 17, 2021), https://thehill.com/changing-america/respect/equality/559079-biden-signs-bill-establishing-juneteenth-as-federal-holiday/.

82 *See* Anat Alon-Beck, *Times They Are A-Changin': When Tech Employees Revolt*, 80 MD. L. REV. 120, 133–35 (2020).

83 *Id.* at 133.

84 *Id.* at 134.

85 *Id.*

86 *Id.* at 135. These policies have been reserved since. *See infra* Section C.4.

and 66 percent of Fortune 500 companies issued public statements condemning racism, supporting the Black Lives Matter movement, and "pledging to help eradicate racist policies and practices both within their own institutions and the broader society."[87]

On the immigration front, corporations were not shy in publicizing their reactions to other events that defined Trump's first term in office.[88] The Trump Muslim Ban, an executive order that went into effect in January 2017, was met with severe opposition from US corporations and their leaders,[89] and at least 153 large and mid-size companies spoke out against it.[90] Close to a 100 tech companies went further, filing an amicus brief protesting the order.[91] A Nike executive condemned President Trump's order in an email to employees.[92] The CEO of Netflix expressed his distaste for the policy on social media and indicated it would hurt their employees worldwide.[93] When the Supreme Court upheld a third version of the ban in 2018, the president of Microsoft and the CEO of Airbnb released public statements condemning the decision.[94]

Corporate CEOs expressed their discontent with President Trump's handling and equivocation of the August 2017 "Unite the Right" rally in Charlottesville, Virginia.[95] The rally was led by white nationalists, and the resulting riots culminated in the death of activist Heather Heyer.[96] Trump faced criticism for blaming both the rally participants and the demonstrators opposing them and also adding that there were "very fine people on both sides."[97] While some CEOs, such as Apple's Tim Cook, Goldman Sachs's Lloyd Blankfein, and Walmart's Doug

87 Fairfax, *supra* note 65, at 120.

88 Lin, *supra* note 8, at 1550–52.

89 *Id.*

90 Vanessa Fuhrmans, *A Watershed Moment in CEO Activism*, WALL STREET J. (Apr. 4, 2017, 9:00 AM), www.wsj.com/articles/a-watershed-moment-in-ceo-activism-1491310803 (indicating that, "In 84% of instances, it was the CEO directly who took the stand.").

91 Jennifer S. Fan, *Woke Capital: The Role of Corporations in Social Movements*, 9 HARV. BUS. L. REV. 441, 459 (2019) (mentioning that Google, Lyft, and Twitter pledged or donated millions of dollars to the American Civil Liberties Union (ACLU) and other groups supporting immigrants and refugees).

92 Tony Connelly, *Nike's Mark Parker Condemns Trump's Muslim Travel Ban in Staff Email Rallying Support for Sir Mo Farah*, THE DRUM (Jan. 30, 2017, 9:31 AM), www.thedrum.com/news/2017/01/30/nikes-mark-parker-condemns-trumps-muslim-travel-ban-staff-email-rallying-support-sir (mentioning that the executive encouraged employees to stand up for the company's commitment to diversity).

93 *See* T.C. Sottek, *Netflix CEO: "Trump's Actions Are So Un-American It Pains Us All,"* VERGE (Jan. 28, 2017, 5:14 PM), www.theverge.com/2017/1/28/14426536/netflix-reed-hastings-trump-immigration-executive-order.

94 Fan, *supra* note 91, at 466.

95 Lin, *supra* note 8, at 1552–53.

96 Maev Kennedy, *Heather Heyer, Victim of Charlottesville Car Attack, Was Civil Rights Activist*, THE GUARDIAN (Aug. 13, 2017), www.theguardian.com/us-news/2017/aug/13/woman-killed-at-white-supremacist-rally-in-charlottesville-named.

97 *Full Text: Trump's Comments on White Supremacists, "Alt-Left" in Charlottesville*, POLITICO (Aug. 15, 2017), www.politico.com/story/2017/08/15/full-text-trump-comments-white-supremacists-alt-left-transcript-241662.

McMillon, issued strong public statements condemning white supremacy, racism, and violence,[98] others – including the leaders of Merck, Intel, and Under Armour – resigned from presidential advisory councils,[99] which Trump preemptively disbanded via Twitter.[100]

President Trump's decision to terminate the DACA program[101] in 2017 prompted numerous corporate executives to publicly oppose the move, emphasizing the program's importance to their workforce and the broader economy.[102] Facebook's Mark Zuckerberg and Apple's Tim Cook were two of the most prominent CEOs who made public statements opposing Trump's decision.[103] Microsoft, Google, Goldman Sachs, Disney, and eBay executives also encouraged Congress to defend DACA.[104]

Data from a 2018 survey run by researchers at the Rock Center for Corporate Governance at Stanford (the "2018 Stanford Survey") show that the public generally supports corporate involvement in racial issues, though a sizeable fraction of the population is against it.[105] More recent data from a Bentley University and Gallup survey of May 2024 (the "2024 Bentley/Gallup Survey") reveal a regression in support of corporate advocacy in general[106] and on racial issues in particular: only 43 percent of Americans are in favor, compared to 54 percent in the 2018 Stanford Survey.[107]

[98] Nour Kteily & Francesca Gino, *Why CEOs Can't Stay Silent in the Wake of Events Like Charlottesville*, HARV. BUS. REV. (Aug. 14, 2017), https://hbr.org/2017/08/why-ceos-cant-stay-silent-in-the-wake-of-events-like-charlottesville.

[99] Michael Herman, *Three CEOs Resign from Trump Council over Charlottesville*, Reuters (Aug. 14, 2017), www.reuters.com/article/business/three-ceos-resign-from-trump-council-over-charlottesville-idUSKCN1AU1FM/. *See also* Weber Shandwick, *The Business Response to the Charlottesville Protests* (Sept. 2017), https://cms.webershandwick.com/wp-content/uploads/2017/09/Business_Response_to_the_Charlottesville_Protests.pdf.

[100] Lin, *supra* note 8, at 1553

[101] *Deferred Action for Childhood Arrivals*, 77 Fed. Reg. 53,757 (Aug. 15, 2012). The program is a US immigration policy that provides temporary protection from deportation and work authorization to certain undocumented individuals who were brought to the US as children.

[102] Lin, *supra* note 8, at 1553–54.

[103] *Id.*

[104] *See* Zach Wichter, *C.E.O.s See a "Sad Day" after Trump's DACA Decision*, N.Y. TIMES (Sept. 5, 2017), www.nytimes.com/2017/09/05/business/chief-executives-see-a-sad-day-after-trumps-daca-decision.html#:~:text=%E2%80%9CThis%20is%20a%20sad%20day,then%20punish%20them%20for%20it.%E2%80%9D.

[105] David F. Larcker, Stephen A. Miles, Brian Tayan & Kim Wright-Violich, *The Double-Edged Sword of CEO Activism* 4, Rock Center for Corporate Governance at Stanford University Closer Look Series: Topics, Issues and Controversies in Corporate Governance (2018), www.ssrn.com/abstract=3283297 (finding that 54 percent of Americans support CEO activism about racial issues, while 29 percent do not).

[106] Bentley Univ. & Gallup, *Business in Society 2024 Report* (2024), at 6, www.gallup.com/file/analytics/649841/bentley-university-gallup-business-society-2024-report.pdf (reporting that only "38% of Americans say businesses should take a public stance on current events, down from 41% in 2023 and 48% in 2022.").

[107] *Id.* at 14.

### 2 *Women's Rights, Gender Equity, and Reproductive Rights*

Most companies run internal programs aimed at advancing women in the workplace – mentorship tracks, leadership pipelines, and affinity groups. While women remain underrepresented in corporate boardrooms,[108] the trend is improving, slowly.[109] According to The Conference Board and ESGAUGE, women held 32 percent of S&P 500 board seats in 2023, up from just 23 percent in 2018.[110] Much of that progress didn't come from within – it came from pressure. Major index funds, including State Street and BlackRock, began demanding gender diversity on boards,[111] and backed it up with votes. In 2017, State Street voted against directors at 400 companies that had no women on their boards. A year later, BlackRock announced it would oppose nominating committees that failed to show meaningful progress.[112]

*Government Substitution*. Once a leaked Supreme Court memo warned that *Roe v. Wade* was likely to be overturned, as it ultimately was with the *Dobbs* decision,[113] some companies announced that they would cover travel expenses for any employees seeking to terminate pregnancies.[114] Starbucks, Tesla, Yelp, Airbnb, Netflix, Patagonia, DoorDash, JPMorgan Chase, Levi Strauss, PayPal, Amazon, and Reddit each indicated they would reimburse – directly or via health insurance coverage – their employees and families for travel expenses associated with transportation to an abortion-friendly state.[115] Shortly after, many more adopted similar policies, including Johnson & Johnson, Meta, and Disney.[116] Researchers at Yale's School of Management conducted a study summarizing the policies adopted by 118 of the first companies to

[108] Yun Li, *More Women in the Boardroom Could Drive Higher Credit Ratings and Stock Returns for Firms – They Still Hold Just 29% of Seats*, CNBC (Mar. 11, 2022, 10:13 AM), www.cnbc.com/2022/03/11/women-gain-ground-in-the-boardroom-holding-29percent-of-director-seats-in-2022.html.

[109] *See* Katelyn Fossett, A *"Watershed Year" for Women on Corporate Boards*, POLITICO (Apr. 15, 2022, 12:01 PM), www.politico.com/newsletters/women-rule/2022/04/15/a-watershed-year-for-women-on-corporate-boards-00025478 ("A recent report from the Women Business Collaborative (WBC) and 50-50 Women on Boards found that 2021 was a 'watershed year' for women on corporate boards, with the largest ever year-over-year increase in board seats held by women among companies in the Russell 3000.").

[110] *US Corporate Board Diversity: Boards Are More Diverse than Ever, but the Pace of Growth Is Slowing*, THE CONF. BD. (Nov. 9, 2023), www.conference-board.org/press/press-release-board-diversity-2023.

[111] *See* Michal Barzuza, Quinn Curtis & David H. Webber, *Shareholder Value(s): Index Fund ESG Activism and the New Millennial Corporate Governance*, 93 S. CAL. L. REV. 1243, 1265–69 (2020).

[112] *Id.* at 1268–69. For an overview of investor pressure on socioeconomic issues, see *infra* Chapter 2, Section A.1.b. *See also infra* Section C, for a description of the backlash and retreat.

[113] Dobbs v. Jackson Women's Health Org., 142 S. Ct. 2228 (2022) (holding that since the Constitution makes no reference to abortion and no such right is therefore protected by any of its provisions, the authority to regulate abortion must be returned to the states and their elected representatives).

[114] Emma Goldberg, *These Companies Will Cover Travel Expenses for Employee Abortions*, N.Y. TIMES (Aug. 19, 2022), www.nytimes.com/article/abortion-companies-travel-expenses.html.

[115] *Id.*

[116] *Id. See also generally* Anna Toniolo, *Corporate Participation in Social Debates*, 3 U. CHI. BUS. L. REV. 361 (2024) (describing corporate reactions in connection with the overturning of *Roe*).

respond to the *Dobbs* decision.[117] However, these announcements came with serious risks as state legislatures vowed to punish employers who facilitate abortions.[118]

Corporations adopted initiatives to protect women's rights on other fronts. The #MeToo movement made corporations reconsider certain practices, like forced arbitration of sexual harassment claims and change reporting and investigation processes. A flurry of firms, including Microsoft,[119] Uber,[120] and Google,[121] changed their internal policies and abandoned arbitration. Ultimately, in 2022, Congress passed legislation to bar the practice.[122] Netflix commissioned a diversity study that revealed that 52 percent of the company's films in 2018 and 2019 featured girls or women in starring roles.[123] The study prompted a $100 million investment to improve diversity in movies and shows – in front and behind the camera.[124]

High-profile issues like board representation and the gender pay gap became focal points for corporate DEI initiatives. While California's attempt to mandate board diversity was struck down on constitutional grounds,[125] companies have continued to expand representation voluntarily – women now hold 32 percent of S&P 500 board seats, up from 23 percent in 2018.[126] Cisco, for example, reports

[117] *See* Jeffrey Sonnenfeld, Steven Tian & Georgia Hirsty, *A List of Companies Supporting Abortion Rights After the Roe v. Wade Ruling Shows Which Firms Are Stepping Up, and Why*, FORTUNE (June 30, 2022), https://fortune.com/2022/06/30/companies-supporting-abortion-rights-roe-v-wade-first-movers/.

[118] Lawmakers in Texas were quick to threaten Citigroup and Lyft for establishing reimbursement policies. Daniel Wiessner, *Legal Clashes Await U.S. Companies Covering Workers' Abortion Costs*, REUTERS (June 27, 2022, 4:08 PM), www.reuters.com/world/us/legal-clashes-await-us-companies-covering-workers-abortion-costs-2022-06-26/. Like Texas, Oklahoma law allowed citizens to sue anyone aiding or abetting an abortion as early as six weeks into a pregnancy. Chris Marr & Robert Iafolla, *Can States Ban Employer Abortion Aid? Post-Roe Limits Explained*, BLOOMBERG L. (June 28, 2022, 10:17 AM), https://news.bloomberglaw.com/daily-labor-report/can-states-ban-employer-abortion-aid-post-roe-limits-explained.; Marshall Mort, Jane Piehler, Shawn E. Lampron, Daniel J. McCoy & Marie C. Bafuset, *Considerations for Employers Reimbursing Out-of-State Travel for Abortion Procedures*, 35 BENEFITS L.J., no. 3, Autumn 2022, at 6, 12 (discussing Texas state representatives' attempt to introduce legislation that bans employer-sponsored abortion).

[119] Brad Smith, *Microsoft Endorses Senate Bill to Address Sexual Harassment*, MICROSOFT.COM (Dec. 19, 2017), https://blogs.microsoft.com/on-the-issues/2017/12/19/microsoft-endorses-senate-bill-address-sexual-harassment/

[120] Daisuke Wakabayashi, *Uber Eliminates Forced Arbitration for Sexual Misconduct Claims*, N.Y. TIMES (May 15, 2018), www.nytimes.com/2018/05/15/technology/uber-sex-misconduct.html

[121] Kate Conger & Daisuke Wakabayashi, *Google Overhauls Sexual Misconduct Policy after Employee Walkout*, N.Y. TIMES (Nov. 8, 2018), www.nytimes.com/2018/11/08/technology/google-arbitration-sexual-harassment.html

[122] Deborah A. Widiss, *New Law Limits Mandatory Arbitration in Cases Involving Sexual Assault or Sexual Harassment*, 50 A.B.A. LAB. & EMP'T L. NEWS, no. 13, Fall 2022, at 13, 13.

[123] Nicole Sperling, *Netflix Productions Are More Diverse than Studio Films, Study Shows*, N.Y. TIMES (Feb. 26, 2021), www.nytimes.com/2021/02/26/business/media/netflix-diversity-movies-original-series.html.

[124] LIN, *supra* note 60, at 94.; *Women in the Workplace* 2023, MCKINSEY & CO. (Oct. 5, 2023), www.mckinsey.com/featured-insights/diversity-and-inclusion/women-in-the-workplace (as shown in exhibit 7)

[125] Crest v. Padilla, No. 19STCV27561, at 3–4 (Cal. Super. Ct. May 13, 2022) (holding that California's SB 826, which mandated female representation on corporate boards, violated the Equal Protection Clause of the California Constitution).

[126] *See supra* note 110.

that 42 percent of its board and executive team are women,[127] whereas Johnson & Johnson pledged to reach 50 percent global gender parity in management by 2025.[128] On pay, firms like Mastercard and Salesforce have responded with audits, public disclosures, and salary adjustments[129] – Salesforce committed $3 million after a 2015 audit revealed disparities.[130] These moves suggest that some companies are willing to act preemptively, even without legal mandates – but how widespread or durable the commitment is remains an open question.

*Corporate Socioeconomic Advocacy*. Although the *Dobbs* case overturning *Roe v. Wade* dominated the headlines, survey data from The Conference Board showed that only around 10 percent of US companies made public statements about the Supreme Court decision.[131] A study by Anna Toniolo found that only 117 US public corporations issued statements, most of which were directed at employees and carefully avoided taking a stance on abortion.[132] Among the few that did respond to *Dobbs*, many limited their statements to employee benefits – such as covering travel expenses for abortions but steered clear of the broader political controversy.[133]

Before the *Dobbs* upheaval, another history-defining moment – like the #MeToo movement – pushed corporations to take a stand. For example, Microsoft issued a statement supporting a Senate bipartisan bill to address sexual harassment and end forced arbitration,[134] in which it admitted that "[t]he easiest mistake any employer can make is to assume that 'this could never happen here.'"[135]

According to the 2018 Stanford Survey, public support for corporations taking a stand on gender issues and abortion is mixed. Gender issues scored a net-favorable position (40 percent in favor versus 37 percent against), but addressing abortion did

[127] *Creating a World of Potential, Annual Report* (2023), CISCO.COM, at 11 www.cisco.com/c/dam/en_us/about/annual-report/cisco-annual-report-2023.pdf (Last visited July 21, 2024).

[128] 9 *Companies around the World That Are Embracing Diversity in a BIG Way*, SOCIAL TALENT, www.socialtalent.com/blog/diversity-and-inclusion/9-companies-around-the-world-that-are-embracing-diversity (last visited July 21, 2024)

[129] Ann Cairns, *Mastercard's Commitment to Gender Balance*, MASTERCARD NEWSROOM (Feb. 27, 2020), www.mastercard.com/news/perspectives/2020/for-women-for-everyone-mastercard-s-commitment-to-gender-balance/; Chris Brummer & Leo E. Strine. Jr., *Duty and Diversity*, 75 VAND. L. REV. 1 (2022).

[130] Jena McGregor, *Why Salesforce Is Investing Another $3 Million to Close Its Pay Gap*, WASH. POST (Apr. 4, 2017), www.washingtonpost.com/news/on-leadership/wp/2017/04/04/why-salesforce-is-investing-another-3-million-to-close-its-pay-gap/.

[131] *See* Paul Washington, *The US Corporate Response to Recent Supreme Court Decisions*, THE CONF. BD. (July 19, 2022), www.conference-board.org/topics/civil-just-society/US-corporate-response-to-Supreme-Court-decisions.

[132] Toniolo, *supra* note 116, at 363, 367, and 377 (noting the stark contrast to other recent social and political events, such as the Black Lives Matter movement, where corporate statements were much more common).

[133] *Id.* at 387. For Toniolo, companies chose silence over the risk of backlash on contentious issues, so-called corporate hushing. *Id.* at 396–97.

[134] Ending Forced Arbitration of Sexual Harassment Act of 2017, S. 2203, 115th Cong. (2017), which was eventually approved by Congress in 2022. *See* Ending Forced Arbitration of Sexual Assault and Sexual Harassment Act of 2021, Pub. L. No. 117-90, 136 Stat. 26 (2022).

[135] Smith, *supra* note 119.

not (37 percent versus 39 percent).[136] The 2024 Bentley/Gallup Survey does not list women's rights as a standalone category, but DEI scored relatively high, with 53 percent of Americans in favor.[137] By contrast, corporate speech on abortion drew support from only 20 percent.[138]

### 3 *LGBTQ+ Rights*

The support of LGBTQ+ rights has been one of the main staples of corporate governing in the US since the early 1990s when Lotus Development extended corporate benefits to its employees' domestic partners, which was shortly followed by other employers in Silicon Valley and elsewhere.[139] This shift did not occur overnight but came after decades of pressure from activist campaigns. In the 1970s, activists organized boycotts and other actions targeting phone companies for discriminatory hiring practices, TV networks for negative depictions of queer individuals, and Coors for both its discriminatory policies and anti-union stance.[140]

*Government Substitution.* Since Lotus Development's change in policy, corporations have played a significant role in supporting LGBTQ+ rights: "[C]ompanies have helped to spur a rapid evolution in public opinion in the United States, with a majority of Americans now supporting not only marriage equality but also laws to prevent discrimination against gay people."[141]

For instance, in response to North Carolina's 2016 House Bill 2 ("North Carolina HB2"), which required transgender individuals to use the public restrooms that corresponded with their biological sex,[142] Target introduced a bathroom policy allowing transgender employees and customers to use the bathroom that corresponds with their gender identity.[143] The company later announced that it would spend $20 million to add a private bathroom to each store.[144]

[136] Larcker, Miles, Tayan & Wright-Violich, supra note 105, at 4.

[137] Bentley Univ. & Gallup, *supra* note 106, at 14.

[138] *Id.*

[139] Ball, *supra* note 4, at 105–12.

[140] *Id.* at 31–58.

[141] Richard Socarides, *Corporate America's Evolution on L.G.B.T. Rights*, New Yorker (Apr. 27, 2015), www.newyorker.com/business/currency/corporate-americas-evolutionon-l-g-b-t-rights, cited by Fan, *supra* note 91, at 477). A 2022 study from The Conference Board indicated that LGBTQ+ rights is the second most frequently addressed topic by corporations, trailing only racial equality. *See* Washington, *supra* note 131.

[142] *See* Lin, *supra* note 8, at 1547–50.

[143] Nathan Layne, *Retailer Target Says Transgender People Can Use Bathroom of Their Choice*, Reuters (Apr. 19, 2016, 6:05 PM), www.reuters.com/article/us-target-lgbt/retailer-target-says-transgender-people-can-use-bathroom-of-their-choice-idUSKCN0XG2VU. Because North Carolina's law did not affect private businesses, Target was free to set its own policy contradicting the state's bill.

[144] Khadeeja Safdar, *Target Adds Private Bathrooms to Quell Transgender Debate*, Wall St. J. (Aug. 18, 2016, 5:53 PM), www.wsj.com/articles/target-to-spend-20-million-to-roll-out-private-bathrooms-to-all-stores-1471453630.

In 2016, Airbnb adopted an "Open Doors" policy requiring all hosts and guests to agree to a nondiscrimination code mandating that they "treat all fellow members of [the Airbnb] community, regardless of race, religion, national origin, disability, sex, gender identity, sexual orientation or age, with respect, and without judgment or bias."[145]

However, some measures – arguably not government substitution in the strict sense, since they didn't address gaps left by state inaction but instead reflected market-facing, symbolic gestures – sparked controversy and, in some cases, litigation. During Pride Month, many American corporations launch themed ad campaigns or sell special product collections.[146] Yet, in 2023, Target's LGBTQ+ merchandise faced backlash from conservative groups and individuals, who argued that the campaign was inappropriately aimed at children.[147] According to news stories, Target's stock declined at least 14 percent during the boycotts over the Pride Month collections in a single month.[148] Target attempted to minimize the backlash by removing some of the products from its shelves,[149] but doing so subjected the company to criticism from the LGBTQ+ community, which was upset that Target gave in to conservative pressure.[150]

Bud Light and its parent company, Anheuser-Busch, faced a swift backlash after launching an LGBTQ+ support campaign featuring Dylan Mulvaney, a transgender social media influencer.[151] The partnership triggered boycotts and public outcry among conservative consumers.[152] Boycotts led sales of Bud Light to fall by 20 percent, resulting in a reported $25 billion loss in market value,[153] and the marketing executives who led the campaign were put on leave of absence.[154]

145 Shannon McMahon, *Airbnb Launches "Open Doors" Policy to Combat Discrimination*, SMARTER TRAVEL (Sept. 9, 2016), www.smartertravel.com/airbnb-launches-policy-to-combat-discrimination/; *see also* Katie Benner, *Airbnb Adopts Rules to Fight Discrimination by Its Hosts*, N.Y. TIMES (Sept. 8, 2016), www.nytimes.com/2016/09/09/technology/airbnb-anti-discrimination-rules.html.

146 *See* Emily Stewart, *Target Giving in to Conservative Pressure on Pride Is Not a Great Sign*, VOX (May 25, 2023), www.vox.com/politics/2023/5/25/23737338/target-abprallen-pride-boycott-bud-light-trans-controversy-stock-price.

147 *Id.*

148 *See* Nick Halter, *Target, In the Crosshairs, Is Taking a Beating on Wall Street*, AXIOS (June 2, 2023), www.axios.com/local/twin-cities/2023/06/02/target-stock-prices-tumble-pride-boycotts.

149 *See* Stewart, *supra* note 146.

150 *See* Anne D'Innocenzio & Dee-ann Durbin, *Target on the Defensive after Removing LGBTQ+-Themed Products*, L.A. TIMES (May 24, 2023, 4:38 PM), www.latimes.com/business/story/2023-05-24/target-on-the-defensive-after-removing-lgbtq-themed-products (mentioning that the president of the Human Rights Campaign criticized Target for pushing Pride Month displays "into the proverbial closet.")

151 *See* Matthew Impelli, *Anheuser-Busch Stock Drops 20% as Bud Light Sales Struggle*, NEWSWEEK (May 31, 2023, 1:36 PM), www.newsweek.com/anheuser-busch-stock-drops-20-percent-bud-light-sales-struggle-1803680.

152 *Id.*

153 Derek Saul, *Anheuser-Busch Faces "Permanent" 15% Decline In Bud Light Sales – But Now May Be "Attractive" Time to Buy Stock*, FORBES (June 6, 2023, 1:12 PM), www.forbes.com/sites/dereksaul/2023/06/06/anheuser-busch-faces-permanent-15-decline-in-bud-light-sales-but-now-may-be-attractive-time-to-buy-stock/?sh=4cf85895197c.

154 Elizabeth Napolitano, *Bud Light Executives Put on Leave after Dylan Mulvaney Uproar, Report Says*, CBS NEWS (Apr. 25, 2023), www.cbsnews.com/news/bud-light-dylan-mulvaney-transgender-anheuser-busch/.

Not only did the outcry impact stock prices and result in downgraded ratings for both Target and Anheuser-Busch,[155] but Target also became subject to securities litigation that survived a motion to dismiss.[156]

*Corporate Socioeconomic Advocacy*. This is an area in which corporations have shown to be willing to challenge government actions. The response to North Carolina HB2, which mandated bathroom use based on birth sex, displayed the efficacy of corporate intervention.[157] Companies like Apple, Bank of America, Facebook, General Electric, and Google disapproved of the North Carolina legislature's action.[158] More than 200 corporations signed a letter with the Human Rights Campaign advocating repealing the law.[159] When companies like PayPal and Deutsche Bank canceled business expansion in the state, North Carolina's losses grew to over $3 billion.[160] Eventually, the law was partially repealed after a new governor took over in 2017.[161]

The feud between Disney and Florida Governor Ron DeSantis described in the Introduction is possibly the most high-profile fight between a large corporation and an elected politician. After DeSantis signed an Act commonly called "Don't Say Gay," Disney and its then-CEO publicly criticized the law and vowed to aid in its repeal.[162] As tensions escalated, DeSantis signed legislation removing some of Disney's special privileges, and litigation ensued, with each side suing the other.[163] Meanwhile, the Delaware Chancery Court denied a shareholder request under

[155] *See* Nick Halter, *Target, In the Crosshairs, Is Taking a Beating on Wall Street*, AXIOS (June 2, 2023), www.axios.com/local/twin-cities/2023/06/02/target-stock-prices-tumble-pride-boycotts; Kristopher J. Brooks, *Bud Light Gets Stock Downgrade Just Weeks after Dylan Mulvaney Fallout*, CBS NEWS (May 12, 2023), www.cbsnews.com/news/bud-light-dylan-mulvaney-stock-downgrade-anheuser-busch-sales [https://perma.cc/X9NH-K6B7].

[156] Brian Craig v. Target Corp., No. 2:23-cv-599-JLB-KCD (M.D. Fla. Dec. 4, 2024) (denying defendants' motion to dismiss securities fraud claims, holding that plaintiffs adequately plead material misrepresentations, scienter, and loss causation regarding Target's alleged failure to disclose risks associated with ESG/DEI initiatives and a 2023 Pride Month campaign). For an analysis, see *infra* Chapter 3, Sections B.4 and E.1.

[157] *See* Lin, *supra* note 8, at 1547–50.

[158] *Id.* at 1548–49.

[159] *Id.* at 1549.

[160] *Id.*

[161] *Id.*

[162] *See supra* Introduction. *See also* Saura Masconale & Simone M. Sepe, *Citizen Corp. – Corporate Activism and Democracy*, 100 WASH. U. L. REV. 257, 271 (2022); Elizabeth Blair, *After Protests, Disney CEO Speaks out against Florida's "Don't Say Gay" Bill*, NPR (Mar. 10, 2022, 9:10 AM), www.npr.org/2022/03/08/1085130633/disney-response-florida-bill-dont-say-gay (detailing then-CEO Bob Chapek's announcement that "Disney has signed the Human Rights Campaign's statement opposing similar legislative efforts. He also said the company will pledge five million dollars to organizations "working to protect" LGBTQ+ rights, including the Human Rights Campaign (HRC).").

[163] *Id.* The case was ultimately settled. *See supra* Introduction.

Section 220 of the Delaware General Corporation Law ("DGCL")[164] to obtain books and records, which was seeking access to emails amongst Disney directors in connection with the dispute with the Governor.[165]

The issue is hardly uncontroversial: according to the 2018 Stanford Survey, 43 percent support corporate activism about LGBTQ+ rights, while 32 percent do not.[166] While the 2024 Bentley/Gallup Survey shows 53 percent of Americans in favor of corporations speaking on DEI issues,[167] only 33 percent are in favor of addressing LGBTQ+ (down from 37 percent in 2023).[168]

## 4 *Climate*

Over the last few decades, increasing temperatures and various natural climate-related disasters have raised society's concerns about climate risk. Climate is *the* defining policy issue of our times: it is urgent, of enormous magnitude, and extremely difficult to solve. Given the role corporations play in the global economy, it is no surprise that climate risk has become one of the thorniest issues C-suites have been grappling with. While Chapter 2 offers a deeper dive into climate's role in shaping corporate governing, it bears noting here that major institutional investors and proxy advisors have pushed companies toward more climate-conscious practices – demanding transparency on climate risk, emissions targets, and sustainability efforts.[169]

Compared to other areas, climate initiatives are less controversial, and environmental concerns appear more widely held. Some polls show that nearly seven in ten Americans (69 percent) favor the US becoming carbon neutral by 2050 and that although Republicans over sixty-five oppose this initiative, 67 percent under thirty are in support.[170] Overall, 54 percent of Americans see climate change as a major threat,[171] yet it is still difficult for many corporations to revise their current business models to adapt to the changing landscape.

[164] DEL. CODE ANN. tit. 8, § 220(b) (2023).

[165] For an analysis, see *infra* Chapter 3, Section C.3.

[166] Larcker, Miles, Tayan & Wright-Violich, *supra* note 105, at 4.

[167] Bentley Univ. & Gallup, *supra* note 106, at 14.

[168] *Id.*

[169] *See* Madison Condon, *Externalities and the Common Owner*, 95 WASH. L. REV. 1, 5–7 (2020); *see generally*, Peter Eavis & Clifford Krauss, *What's Really behind Corporate Promises on Climate Change?*, N.Y. TIMES (May 12, 2021), www.nytimes.com/2021/02/22/business/energy-environment/corporations-climate-change.html ("Just over a third of the 500 companies in the S&P 500 stock index have set ambitious targets, it found, while 215 had no target at all. The rest had weak targets.").

[170] *See* Alec Tyson, Cary Funk & Brian Kennedy, *What the Data Says about Americans' Views of Climate Change*, PEW RSCH. CTR. (Apr. 18, 2023) www.pewresearch.org/short-reads/2023/04/18/for-earth-day-key-facts-about-americans-views-of-climate-change-and-renewable-energy/.

[171] *Id.*

Meanwhile, the Biden SEC's proposed climate disclosure rules[172] – already scaled back after multiple challenges and currently stayed[173] – are bound to be dropped by the Trump SEC, as confirmed by its Acting Chair.[174]

*Government Substitution*. Walmart set some of its first sustainability goals when it partnered with the Environmental Defense Fund back in 2005.[175] The company committed to removing one billion tons of greenhouse gas emissions from its global supply chain by 2030.[176] One of its initiatives, "Project Gigaton," encourages its suppliers to decrease their carbon footprints.[177] Seventy percent of Walmart's suppliers participate in the program and commit to reducing emissions.[178]

Amazon made similar efforts, committing to become net-zero carbon by 2040.[179] The company also allocated $2 billion toward developing decarbonization technologies and deploying renewable energy.[180]

In 2023, United Airlines launched a fund for sustainable aviation fuel.[181] The fund was established to invest in startups producing sustainable fuel for commercial airplanes.[182] Companies like Air Canada, Boeing, JPMorgan Chase, Honeywell International, and General Electric have all contributed to the fund, giving it a total of $100 million as initial investments.[183]

*Corporate Socioeconomic Advocacy*. When President Trump announced his decision to withdraw the United States from the Paris Agreement in 2017, corporate leaders

172 *SEC Proposes Rules to Enhance and Standardize Climate-Related Disclosures for Investors*, U.S. Securities and Exchange Commission, www.sec.gov/newsroom/press-releases/2022-46 (last updated July 14, 2022).

173 *U.S. SEC Climate Disclosure Rules Spark Flurry of Litigation*, Jones Day (June 2024), www.jonesday.com/en/insights/2024/06/us-sec-climate-disclosure-rules-spark-flurry-of-litigation.

174 Mark T. Uyeda, *Statement by Acting Chair Uyeda on Climate Related Disclosure Rules*, Harv. L. Sch. F. on Corp. Governance (Mar. 8, 2025), https://corpgov.law.harvard.edu/2025/03/08/statement-by-acting-chair-uyeda-on-climate-related-disclosure-rules/ (stating, in his capacity as Acting Chair of the SEC, that the agency lacks statutory authority to impose climate disclosure rules and directing staff to notify the court of changed circumstances in pending litigation).

175 *See Our Partnership with Walmart Brings Big Change*, Env't Def. Fund (July 27, 2019), www.edf.org/partnerships/walmart.

176 *Id.*

177 Dieter Holger, *Walmart Makes Progress on Emissions Target By Winning over Suppliers, CSO Says*, Wall St. J. (Apr. 12, 2022, 12:55 PM), www.wsj.com/articles/walmart-makes-progress-on-emissions-target-by-winning-over-suppliers-cso-says-11649782501.

178 *Id.*

179 *See Amazon Announces $2 Billion Climate Pledge Fund to Invest in Companies Building Products, Services, and Technologies to Decarbonize the Economy and Protect the Planet*, Amazon (June 23, 2020), https://press.aboutamazon.com/2020/6/amazon-announces-2-billion-climate-pledge-fund-to-invest-in-companies-building-products-services-and-technologies-to-decarbonize-the-economy-and-protect-the-planet.

180 *Id.*

181 Amrith Ramkumar, *United Airlines Creates Fund for Sustainable Aviation Fuel*, Wall St. J. (Feb. 21, 2023, 8:00 AM), www.wsj.com/articles/united-airlines-creates-fund-for-sustainable-aviation-fuel-1f24de23.

182 *Id.*

183 *Id.*

expressed disappointment and promised to continue their efforts to tackle the effects of climate change.[184] Elon Musk and Bob Iger chose to leave Trump's economic advisory council based on their disagreement with the choice.[185] Companies like Apple, Facebook, Google, and Microsoft took out full-page ads in major newspapers to publicly oppose the policy.[186] Many CEOs from these and other corporations also expressed their dissatisfaction on social media.[187]

Immediately following Donald Trump's reelection, while maintaining a non-confrontational tone, ExxonMobil's CEO urged the US not to exit the Paris Agreement for a second time.[188] Yet, after January 20, 2025, when President Donald Trump signed the Executive Order to withdraw the United States from the Paris Agreement,[189] virtually all companies that publicly criticized him back in 2017 remained silent.[190]

Climate is one of the least divisive socioeconomic issues on which corporations intervene: according to the 2018 Stanford Survey, the public generally supports CEO activism on environmental issues; polling shows significant public support on issues such as clean air or water (78 percent), renewable energy (68 percent), sustainability (65 percent), and climate change (65 percent).[191] The 2024 Bentley/Gallup Survey indicates a decline in approval percentages, yet a majority of Americans still support corporations taking a stance on climate change (53 percent, down one percentage point from 2023).[192]

## 5 *January 6, Voting Rights*

Democratic institutions in the US continue to experience significant stress tests. As Donald Trump, his political allies, journalists, and other media personalities embraced the narrative that the results of the 2020 presidential election were

184 *See* Daniel Victor, *"Climate Change Is Real": Many U.S. Companies Lament Paris Accord Exit*, N.Y. Times (June 11, 2017), www.nytimes.com/2017/06/01/business/climate-change-tesla-corporations-paris-accord.html.

185 *Id.*

186 *Id.*

187 *Id.*

188 Rebecca F. Elliott, *Exxon Chief to Trump: Don't Withdraw from Paris Climate Deal*, N.Y. Times (Nov. 12, 2024), www.nytimes.com/2024/11/12/business/energy-environment/exxon-mobil-baku-climate-cop29.html (mentioning that, according to the CEO, frequent policy changes create uncertainty and inefficiencies, and the US should maintain its commitment to the global climate accord).

189 Seth Kerschner, Taylor Pullins & Suzanne Knijnenburg, *US Withdrawal from the Paris Agreement: Impact and Next Steps*, White & Case (Jan. 21, 2025), www.whitecase.com/insight-alert/us-withdrawal-paris-agreement-impact-and-next-steps.

190 Corbin Hiar & Sara Schonhardt, *"Everyone's Afraid to Offend the President": How the Tech Giants Went Silent on Paris*, Politico (Jan. 26, 2025), www.politico.com/news/2025/01/26/trump-tech-giants-paris-climate-agreement-withdrawal-00200328.

191 *See* Larcker, Miles, Tayan & Wright-Violich, *supra* note 105, at 4.

192 Bentley Univ. & Gallup, *supra* note 106, at 14.

"stolen," many citizens began questioning the validity of the US democratic system.[193] A University of Amherst poll revealed that over a third of Americans believed President Biden's victory was illegitimate.[194] That sentiment culminated in the January 6, 2021 insurrection, when a pro-Trump mob stormed the US Capitol in an attempt to halt the certification of the election results. The episode marked a violent rupture in American political life – and yet, election denial remained a cornerstone of Trump's 2024 campaign.[195]

Meanwhile, Georgia led a wave of states enacting laws that made it harder for voters to exercise their rights,[196] with disproportionately adverse effects on racial minorities: The provisions include limited drop boxes for mail ballots, more rigid voter identification requirements for absentee balloting, and prohibitions on providing food or water to people waiting in line to vote.[197] Over the past years, state legislatures have been highly active in reshaping election laws. Between January 1, 2021, and September 16, 2024, at least thirty states enacted seventy-eight restrictive voting laws, with sixty-three taking effect in twenty-nine states during the 2024 election.[198]

*Government Substitution*. After January 6, Facebook blocked President Trump's account, and Twitter suspended his account.[199] Because Trump declined to condemn the rioters, social media companies restricted his access to their platforms based on his potential to incite violence and spread misinformation.[200] Furthermore, Twitter removed 70,000 accounts associated with the far-right conspiracy theory

[193] *See* Lisa Hagen, *Poll: A Third of Americans Question Legitimacy of Biden Victory Nearly a Year since Jan. 6*, USNews & World Rep. (Dec. 28, 2021, 2:40 PM), www.usnews.com/news/politics/articles/2021-12-28/poll-a-third-of-americans-question-legitimacy-of-biden-victory-nearly-a-year-since-jan-6.

[194] *Id.*

[195] Robert Yoon, *Trump's Drumbeat of Lies about the 2020 Election Keeps Getting Louder. Here Are the Facts*, AP News (Aug. 27, 2023), https://apnews.com/article/trump-2020-election-lies-debunked-4fc26546b07962fdbf9d66e739fbb50d

[196] Jane C. Timm, *19 States Enacted Voting Restrictions in 2021. What's Next?*, NBC News (Dec. 21, 2021, 7:02 AM), www.nbcnews.com/politics/elections/19-states-enacted-voting-restrictions-2021-rcna8342.

[197] *See* Richard Fausset, Nick Corasaniti & Mark Leibovich, *Why the Georgia G.O.P.'s Voting Rollbacks Will Hit Black People Hard*, N.Y. Times (Mar. 25, 2021), www.nytimes.com/2021/03/25/us/politics/georgia-black-voters.html.

[198] Common provisions include stricter voter identification requirements, reductions in early voting periods, limitations on mail-in voting, and more stringent voter registration procedures. Such measures have raised concerns among voting rights advocates about potential disenfranchisement, particularly among marginalized communities The seventy-eight restrictive laws since January 1, 2021, make up over two-thirds of all restrictive laws passed since the Supreme Court's 2013 *Shelby County v. Holder* decision (570 U.S. 529 (2013)), which weakened the Voting Rights Act. As of September 2024, at least 31 states passed 114 restrictive voting laws in the 11 years since that ruling. *Voting Laws Roundup: September 2024*, Brennan Ctr. for Just. (Sept. 2024), www.brennancenter.org/our-work/research-reports/voting-laws-roundup-september-2024.

[199] *See* Grace Dean, *From Cutting All Ties with Trump to Pulling Political Donations, Here's How Corporate America Has Responded to the Capitol Insurrection*, Bus. Insider (Jan 17, 2021, 7:55 AM), www.businessinsider.com/capitol-siege-trump-company-responses-riots-political-donations-2021–1.

[200] *See id.*

known as QAnon.[201] Many Trump acolytes were blocked as well.[202] Ultimately, these restrictions were relaxed and fell away for various reasons – Meta (formerly known as Facebook) even had to settle with Trump for $25 million.[203] Yet, at the time, private corporations quickly responded to the January 6 events when political actors couldn't or wouldn't.[204]

Companies also adopted initiatives to boost voting rights: Apple and Twitter gave their employees paid time off to vote in November elections or volunteer at a polling location.[205] Thousands joined the Time to Vote movement, which was created by Levi's, Patagonia, and PayPal, to formally encourage workers to vote by offering paid time off on Election Day.[206]

*Corporate Socioeconomic Advocacy*. January 6 prompted a long list of companies to no longer donate to politicians or groups that refused to acknowledge the legitimacy of the election:[207] corporations like Amazon, AT&T, American Express, Coca-Cola, Deloitte, Facebook, Intel, Microsoft, Nike, and a host of other companies indicated that they would pause political action committee (PAC) contributions and other donations to lawmakers who voted against election certification.[208]

Further, the discriminatory provisions of Georgia's 2021 SB 202 voting law sparked outrage among large Georgia-headquartered corporations and their executives.[209] Merck's CEO Ken Frazier called for companies to stand against government efforts to restrict voting rights.[210] Alongside Frazier were Coca-Cola and Delta,

201 *Id.*

202 *Id.*

203 Annie Linskey & Rebecca Ballhaus, *Meta to Pay $25 Million to Settle 2021 Trump Lawsuit: President Had Sued Social-Media Company after His Accounts Were Suspended Following Jan. 6 Riot*, WALL ST. J. (Jan. 29, 2025), www.wsj.com/us-news/law/trump-signs-agreement-calling-for-meta-to-pay-25-million-to-settle-suit-6f734c8c.

204 The political response cannot be as swift and effective as the response by private enterprises, given that the latter are not constrained by First Amendment concerns. *See generally* ELIZABETH ANDERSON, PRIVATE GOVERNMENT: HOW EMPLOYERS RULE OUR LIVES (AND WHY WE DON'T TALK ABOUT IT) (2017). On the tension between regulating online hate speech and the First Amendment, see Claudia E. Haupt, *Democratic Self-Defense*, 93 FORDHAM L. REV. 1377 (2025) (describing divergent approaches between red and blue states).

205 Lauren Frias, *Apple Joins Twitter in Policy Giving Employees Paid Time Off to Vote in the November Election*, BUS. INSIDER (July 24, 2020, 8:02 PM), www.businessinsider.com/apple-giving-employees-paid-time-off-vote-volunteer-election-day-2020-7.

206 Kate Gibson, *Election Day 2024: Time Off to Vote – State Laws and Employer Policies*, CBS NEWS, (Nov. 5, 2024), www.cbsnews.com/news/election-day-2024-time-off-to-vote-state-law-employers/.

207 *See* Dean, *supra* note 199.

208 Melinda Fakuade, *A Running List of Corporate Responses to the Capitol Riot*, VOX (Jan. 14, 2021, 11:45 AM), www.vox.com/the-goods/22227717/brands-corporate-response-capitol-dc-riot-insurrection-mob-pac-donations.

209 Masconale & Sepe, *supra* note 162, at 271.

210 Kevin Stankiewicz, *"There Is No Middle Ground" – Black CEOs Urge Companies to Oppose Restrictive Voting Laws*, CNBC (Mar. 31, 2021, 4:28 PM), www.cnbc.com/2021/03/31/ken-frazier-black-ceos-urge-firms-to-oppose-restrictive-voting-laws.html.

who criticized their home state's new voting law.[211] Hundreds of other companies followed Frazier's lead and signed a statement opposing any legislation making it harder for people to vote.[212] The MLB even removed its All-Star game from Atlanta, indicating its support for voting rights.[213] In July of 2021, major corporations formed a coalition when they signed a letter urging Congress to pass new legislation expanding the 1965 Voting Rights Act.[214] They asked Congress to enact an updated law restoring some of the provisions of the original Voting Rights Act and reversing the *Shelby County v. Holder*[215] decision that eliminated portions of the law.[216]

## 6 *Guns*

In the United States, mass shootings sadly remain common occurrences, averaging more than 600 annually – nearly two per day – according to the Gun Violence Archive, which defines such events as those involving four or more injuries or deaths.[217] While corporations remained silent after the 2012 Sandy Hook shooting, the 2018 mass shooting at Marjory Stoneman Douglas High School in Parkland, Florida, spurred corporate engagement in gun control initiatives.[218]

*Government Substitution*. After the Parkland tragedy, where seventeen people were killed with a semiautomatic AR-15 rifle, large retailers and financial institutions instituted new policies.[219]

Dick's Sporting Goods, Kroger, and L.L. Bean implemented stricter policies than those required by federal law.[220] Following the Parkland shooting,

211 David Shepardson & Uday Sampath Kumar, *Delta, Coca-Cola Blast Home State Georgia's Voting Restrictions As "Unacceptable,"* Reuters (Mar. 31, 2021, 7:25 AM), www.reuters.com/article/us-usa-georgia-voting-companies/delta-coca-cola-blast-home-state-georgias-voting-restrictions-as-unacceptable-idUSKBN2BN1M9.

212 David Gelles & Andrew Ross Sorkin, *Hundreds of Companies Unite to Oppose Voting Limits, but Others Abstain*, N.Y. Times (May 27, 2021), www.nytimes.com/2021/04/14/business/ceos-corporate-america-voting-rights.html.

213 Kevin Draper, James Wagner, Reid J. Epstein & Nick Corasaniti, *M.L.B. Pulls All-Star Game from Georgia in Response to Voting Law*, N.Y. Times (Apr. 6, 2021), www.nytimes.com/2021/04/02/us/politics/mlb-all-star-game-moved-atlanta-georgia.html.

214 Tucker Higgins, *More than 150 Companies Call on Congress to Strengthen Voting Rights Act*, CNBC (July 14, 2021, 12:46 PM), www.cnbc.com/2021/07/14/companies-call-on-congress-to-strengthen-voting-rights-act.html.

215 Shelby Cnty., Ala. v. Holder, 570 U.S. 529 (2013) (holding that the Voting Rights Act's original coverage formula used to determine which states were subject to preclearance when amending voting regulations or passing voting laws was outdated, therefore rendering the provision unconstitutional).

216 Higgins, *supra* note 214.

217 *How Many US Mass Shootings Have There Been in 2024?* BBC News, www.bbc.com/news/world-us-canada-41488081.

218 *See* Lin, *supra* note 8, at 1554–57; Masconale & Sepe, *supra* note 162, at 270.

219 *See* Lin, *supra* note 8, at 1554–57.

220 Joseph Pisani, *US Companies Take a Stand, Raise Age to Purchase Guns*, AP News (Mar. 1, 2018), https://apnews.com/article/north-america-us-news-ap-top-news-ar-state-wire-shootingsa70d3d6e213d4

Dick's immediately halted sales of all assault-style rifles, removed high-capacity magazines from its inventory, and pledged never to sell them again.[221] Not only did the store halt sales, but it also destroyed $5 million worth of rifles that it had in stock at the time.[222]

On its end, back in 2015, Walmart stopped selling handguns and military-style rifles, such as the AR-15.[223] The company discontinued sales of handgun and short-barrel rifle ammunition that can be used in large-capacity clips on military-style weapons,[224] and raised the age limit to purchase firearms or ammunition to 21.[225] Additionally, Walmart required a "green light" on a background check, whereas federal law only requires the absence of a "red light."[226] Walmart also adopted a policy of videotaping the point of sale for firearms, allowing only trained associates to sell firearms.[227]

Financial institutions introduced new policies in response to mounting pressures.[228] Following advocacy from employees whose children endured the Parkland school tragedy, Citigroup implemented a policy targeting its client gun retailers.[229] The bank imposed restrictions, barring clients from selling bump stocks, high-capacity magazines, firearms without background checks, or guns to individuals under twenty-one – a threshold supported by data showing that eighteen- to twenty-one-year-olds commit firearm-related homicides at a rate roughly four times that of those aged twenty-one and older.[230] Despite this initiative, Citigroup stood alone; few other banks adopted similar measures to pressure retailers.[231] Instead, some institutions, such as Bank of America and JPMorgan Chase, focused on manufacturers,

b3a8af92ffd1849b725 (mentioning that Kroger commented that gun retail outlets must go beyond what current US laws require).

221 Lin, *supra* note 8, at 1554–57.

222 Laura M. Holson, *Dick's Sporting Goods Destroyed $5 Million Worth of Guns* N.Y. Times (Oct. 8, 2019), www.nytimes.com/2019/10/08/business/dicks-sporting-goods-destroying-guns-rifles.html.

223 Nandita Bose & Melissa Fares, *Walmart Faces Pressure to Stop Gun Sales after Latest U.S. Mass Shootings*, Reuters (Aug. 5, 2019, 3:39 PM), www.reuters.com/article/us-walmart-guns-pressure/walmart-faces-pressure-to-stop-gun-sales-after-latest-u-s-mass-shootings-idUSKCN1UV22X.

224 Russell Redman, *Walmart, Kroger Take Action after Shootings: Retailers Crack Down on "Open Carry" of Guns*, Supermarket News (Sept. 5, 2019), www.supermarketnews.com/retail-financial/walmart-kroger-take-action-after-shootings.

225 Bose & Fares, *supra* note 223.

226 Redman, *supra* note 224.

227 *Id.*

228 Lin, *supra* note 43, at 1556.

229 David Benoit, *Inside Citigroup's Attempt to Rally Wall Street to Pressure Gun Sellers: The Bank Adopted New Gun Policies after the 2018 Parkland Shooting, but Rivals Didn't Follow. "We Were Kind of Lonely," the Former CEO Recalled*, Wall St. J. (June 25, 2022), www.wsj.com/articles/citigroup-tried-and-failed-to-rally-banks-to-pressure-gun-sellers-11656124086.

230 *Id.*

231 *Id.*

refusing loans to companies producing military-style firearms for civilian markets, while others, like Wells Fargo, opted to remain neutral.[232]

*Corporate Socioeconomic Advocacy*. After the 2022 mass shooting that killed 19 children and 2 adults at an elementary school in Uvalde, Texas, more than 200 CEOs sent a letter to Congress to urge passing gun control legislation.[233] Pointing to a study finding that incidents involving guns have become the number one cause of child deaths, business leaders from companies like Condé Nast and Levi Strauss expressed their desire for stronger firearm regulations.[234] Two separate shootings at Walmart stores in 2019 sparked a similar outcry from corporate executives.[235] The CEOs of Uber, Gap, Lyft, and Twitter were some of the influential figures who signed a letter urging the Senate to pass a law requiring background checks on all gun sales.[236]

Corporate involvement in gun control issues is supported by the public but not by a wide margin: According to the 2018 Stanford Survey, 45 percent of Americans are in favor of corporations taking a stand, while 35 percent are unfavorable.[237] The 2024 Bentley/Gallup Survey indicates a decline of those in favor, which is now down to 32 percent (it was 39 percent in 2023), but does not mention how many are against.[238]

## 7 *Conservative Corporate Governing*

Given the corporate actions and initiatives discussed so far, one might assume that corporate governing uniquely advances progressive causes. This impression would be misleading. While much of corporate governing promotes prosocial policies, many corporations have embraced conservative-aligned initiatives or rolled back prior commitments under political pressure. These actions, some dating back decades, others reflecting a repositioning after the 2024 election – what some have referred to as CEOs "bending the knee" to Trump[239] – illustrate that corporate governing is not a monolith but reflects the diverse and often conflicting ideological forces shaping the business landscape.

232 *Id.*

233 Colin Lodewick, *Over 200 CEOs Demand Action on Gun Control Not Just Because It's the Right Thing to Do: They Say It Costs $280 Billion a Year for Taxpayers*, FORTUNE (June 9, 2022, 2:52 PM), https://fortune.com/2022/06/09/ceos-demand-action-gun-control-senate-uvalde-shooting/.

234 *Id.*

235 *See* Amelia Lucas, *Chief Executives of 145 Companies Urge Senate to Pass Gun Control Laws*, CNBC (Sep. 12, 2019, 2:25 PM), www.cnbc.com/2019/09/12/chief-executives-of-145-companies-urge-senate-to-pass-gun-control-laws.html.

236 *Id.*

237 Larcker, Miles, Tayan & Wright-Violich, *supra* note 105, at 4.

238 Bentley Univ. & Gallup, *supra* note 106, at 14.

239 Brian Schwartz, Dana Mattioli & Rebecca Ballhaus, *The Week CEOs Bent the Knee to Trump*, WALL ST. J. (Dec. 13, 2024, 9:00 PM ET), www.wsj.com/politics/policy/donald-trump-ceos-corporate-influence-second-term-df1455f7.

Prominent examples of the former group include companies like Chick-fil-A,[240] Hobby Lobby,[241] MyPillow,[242] and – of course – Trump's Truth Social,[243] all aligning policies and platforms with conservative values. Chick-fil-A's public stance on issues such as same-sex marriage, combined with donations to organizations opposing LGBTQ+ rights,[244] cemented its reputation as a bastion of conservative corporate values.[245] Similarly, Hobby Lobby's refusal to provide certain types of contraception through employee health plans – a position upheld by the US Supreme Court in its decision *Burwell v. Hobby Lobby Stores, Inc.*[246] – underscores how some corporations embed religious and conservative principles into their governing frameworks.[247]

In the media sphere, News Corp and X (formerly known as Twitter) represent examples of corporate governing aligned with conservative interests. These companies actively shape public opinion on political and cultural issues through their platforms, championing positions that resonate with conservative audiences and policymakers.[248] Musk's acquisition of Twitter marked a turning point for

[240] Emma Green, *Chick-fil-A: Selling Chicken with a Side of God*, The Atlantic (Sept. 8, 2014), www.theatlantic.com/business/archive/2014/09/chick-fil-a-selling-chicken-with-a-side-of-god/379776/.

[241] Jerry Bowyer, *What Makes Hobby Lobby a Christian Company? Hint: It's Not a Greed or a Misogyny Thing*, Forbes (Apr. 25, 2017, 9:00 AM), www.forbes.com/sites/jerrybowyer/2017/04/25/what-makes-hobby-lobby-a-christian-company-hint-its-not-a-greed-or-a-misogyny-thing/.

[242] Alexandra Berzon, Charles Homans & Ken Bensinger, *How Mike Lindell's Pillow Business Propels the Election Denial Movement*, N.Y. Times (Oct. 27, 2022), www.nytimes.com/2022/10/27/us/politics/lindell-mypillow-trump-election-deniers.html.

[243] *What We Know about Truth Social, Donald Trump's Social Media Platform*, AP (Mar. 27, 2024), https://apnews.com/article/truth-social-donald-trump-djt-ipo-digital-world-7437d5dcc491a1459a078195ae547987 Naomi Forman-Katz & Galen Stocking, *Key Facts about Truth Social as Donald Trump Runs for U.S. President Again*, Pew Rsch. Ctr. (Nov. 18, 2022), www.pewresearch.org/short-reads/2022/11/18/key-facts-about-truth-social-as-donald-trump-runs-for-u-s-president-again/.

[244] Hugo Greenhalgh, *Fast-Food Chain Chick-fil-A Changes Donations after Facing LGBT Protests*, Reuters (Nov. 18, 2019), www.reuters.com/article/usa-lgbt-business/update-3-fast-food-chain-chick-fil-a-changes-donations-after-facing-lgbt-protests-idINL8N27Y51S (discussing how Chick-Fil-A once donated to organizations opposing LGBTQ+ rights but then stopped amid backlash).

[245] Jordan Valinsky, *Chick-fil-A Faces Backlash over Fake Controversy*, CNN (June 2, 2023), www.cnn.com/2023/06/02/business/chick-fil-a-fake-controversy/index.html (explaining how Chick-Fil-A has long been in support of conservative values, including directly referencing God on their DEI page, and are now targets of activists).

[246] Burwell v. Hobby Lobby Stores, Inc., 573 U.S. 682 (2014) (allowing exemptions for close corporations from a regulation that its owners religiously object to if there is a less restrictive means of furthering the law's interest).

[247] Mary Agnes Carey, *Hobby Lobby Ruling Cuts into Contraceptive Mandate*, NPR (June 30, 2014, 5:03 PM), www.npr.org/sections/health-shots/2014/06/30/327065968/hobby-lobby-ruling-cuts-into-contraceptive-mandate.

[248] Reuters, *Divisive Ailes Gave Conservatives a TV Home at Fox News*, Reuters (July 21, 2016, 10:16 PM), www.reuters.com/article/lifestyle/divisive-ailes-gave-conservatives-a-tv-home-at-fox-news-idUSKCN1012RL/; Pew Research Center, *After Musk's Takeover, Big Shifts in How Republican and Democratic Twitter Users View the Platform*, Pew Rsch. Ctr. (May 1, 2023), www.pewresearch.org/short-reads/2023/05/01/after-musks-takeover-big-shifts-in-how-republican-and-democratic-twitter-users-view-the-platform/.

the platform, as he rebranded it as X and significantly reshaped its policies with changes that included abandoning content moderation, reinstating previously banned accounts, and amplifying content aligned with conservative, libertarian, and hard-right viewpoints.[249] News Corp's flagship network, Fox News, with its online and TV properties, has been dubbed as "America's leading propaganda outlet."[250] Together, News Corp and X demonstrate how media platforms can affect broader societal attitudes and contributing to the polarization of public discourse. Both platforms were crucial contributors to secure Trump a second term[251] and got rewarded with cabinet and other high-profile political appointments.[252]

Other corporations have adjusted their initiatives and advocacy efforts to appease political actors and avoid conservative backlash.

Meta provides a notable example. Initially robust in fact-checking and engaged in DEI initiatives, the company performed a public pivot right before the start of the Trump second administration, relaxing its policies to avoid political scrutiny and compliance costs,[253] especially in the aftermath of the Supreme Court's decision invalidating affirmative action.[254] Similarly, companies like Walmart, McDonald's, and several others have scaled back their DEI programs in response to legal and political challenges.[255]

These shifts reveal that some corporations previously engaged in liberal or progressive corporate governing have now recalibrated – or, in some cases, reversed course entirely – in response to conservative pressures. While some of these

[249] *Id.*

[250] Yochai Benkler, Robert Faris & Hal Roberts, Network Propaganda: Manipulation, Disinformation, and Radicalization in American Politics 147 (2018).

[251] A computational analysis suggests that algorithmic adjustments on X (formerly Twitter) in mid-July 2024 coincided with Elon Musk's endorsement of Donald Trump and resulted in a significant engagement boost for Musk's account, as well as an asymmetric increase in visibility for Republican-leaning content. Timothy Graham & Mark Andrejevic, *A Computational Analysis of Potential Algorithmic Bias on Platform X during the 2024 US Election* (2024) (working paper), https://eprints.qut.edu.au/253211.

[252] Elon Musk was appointed as head of the Department of Governmental Efficiency (DOGE). Fox personalities were appointed to around twenty cabinet and other positions. Justin Baragona, *Trump Gets the Fox News Band Back together for His Second Administration*, The Independent (Jan. 14, 2025, 17:35 GMT), www.independent.co.uk/news/world/americas/us-politics/donald-trump-fox-news-second-administration-b2678911.html.

[253] Amy Thomson & Hannah Miller, *Meta Cuts Fact-Checkers after Content Moderation Went "Too Far,"* Bloomberg (Jan. 7, 2025, 5:00 PM), www.bloomberg.com/news/articles/2025-01-07/meta-cuts-fact-checkers-after-content-moderation-went-too-far; Kurt Wagner & Jeff Green, *Meta Retreats from Diversity and Inclusion, Appeasing Trump*, Bloomberg (Jan. 10, 2025, 3:45 PM), www.bloomberg.com/news/articles/2025-01-10/meta-rolls-back-diveristy-and-inclusion-efforts-appeasing-trump.

[254] *See infra* notes 277–280 and accompanying text.

[255] Richa Naidu & Simon Jessop, *Before Trump's Return, Some Top U.S. Firms Had Already Gone Cold on Diversity Pledges*, Reuters (Jan. 27, 2025, 7:15 AM), www.reuters.com/world/us/before-trumps-return-some-top-us-firms-had-already-gone-cold-diversity-pledges-2025-01-27/. *See infra* Section C.4.

changes may reflect risk aversion or performative balancing rather than a full ideological shift, the material consequences remain: Those who once benefited from corporate policies now face their withdrawal. Whether corporations are actively embracing conservative corporate governing or simply yielding to pressure, the outcome is the same – a net gain for conservative causes – which is why these actions must be understood as part of conservative corporate governing.

Ultimately, conservative-aligned corporate governing highlights that this phenomenon is not exclusive to progressive or liberal causes but is complex and shaped by the broader sociopolitical landscape in which corporations operate.

## C "COUNTER REFORM": CONSERVATIVE BACKLASH AGAINST CORPORATE GOVERNING

Following rapid expansion – particularly in its progressive type – corporate governing now faces significant headwinds. Its trajectory has been undermined by shifts in the political landscape, an intensifying conservative backlash, and overt efforts to obstruct initiatives tied to climate action and DEI.

Conservative politicians and influential public figures like Elon Musk have spearheaded some of the most visible opposition, framing corporate governing efforts as overreach or a misalignment with corporate and public values. These dynamics are further intensified by Trump's re-election, which has escalated cultural tensions and set the stage for heightened regulatory pushback.

I examine this phenomenon through four key lenses: advocacy by key political players (Section C.1); litigation by conservative stakeholders (Section C.2); legislative and regulatory efforts to curtail ESG and DEI initiatives at both state and federal levels (Section C.3); finally, the corporate sector's strategic recalibrations in the new political landscape under the second Trump administration (Section C.4).

### 1 *Advocacy*

The last few years have witnessed the rise of a movement that overtly opposes corporate efforts in the social sphere. This "anti-woke" movement has gained significant momentum, challenging corporate initiatives such as ESG and DEI programs. As this section illustrates, corporate governing critics argue that efforts in such spheres constitute overreach, undermine shareholder interests, and impose cultural agendas misaligned with traditional values. This countermovement has been propelled by influential political and business figures who view it as a necessary response to the perceived excesses of modern Corporate America.

One of the opening salvos was a *Wall Street Journal* op-ed by former Vice President Mike Pence, who described ESG as a "pernicious," "devastating," and "hypocritical" political bias.[256] His opinion also denounced ESG scores for being "inherently political" and ignoring business and employees' interests. Another impactful *Wall Street Journal* op-ed, co-authored by former Attorney General Bill Barr – another member of the first Trump administration – criticized ESG policies, this time targeting Delaware, the state of incorporation for most major US public companies, for allowing its corporate law to become increasingly politicized.[257]

Without a doubt, Donald Trump is one of the central figures in the anti-ESG/DEI movement. He has repeatedly criticized DEI initiatives as fostering anti-white discrimination and compromising merit-based systems.[258] He has argued that DEI programs lead to hiring less qualified individuals, claiming they undermine efficiency and effectiveness in various sectors.[259] Unsurprisingly, his second administration acted aggressively to target DEI initiatives with a flurry of executive orders, which I address in Section C.3.[260]

Elon Musk also emerged as one of the most prominent critics of "woke" culture. He has described "wokeness" as "divisive, exclusionary, and hateful," asserting that DEI initiatives represent "discrimination based on race."[261] Amid various controversies, Musk mocked gender identity norms, declaring "pronouns suck,"[262] and dismissed DEI as "racism by another name."[263] After acquiring Twitter, he fired the trust and safety team, reinstated previously banned accounts,[264] and recast the platform as

[256] Mike Pence, *Republicans Can Stop ESG Political Bias*, WALL ST. J. (May 26, 2022, 1:50 PM), www.wsj.com/articles/only-republicans-can-stop-the-esg-madness-woke-musk-consumer-demand-free-speech-corporate-america-11653574189. To be sure, Republican unease with the phenomenon predates Pence's op-ed. *See* Stavros Gadinis & Chris Havasy, *The Quest for Legitimacy: A Public Law Blueprint for Corporate Law*, 57 U.C. DAVIS L. REV. 1581, 1613–14 & n.124–25 (2024) (mentioning Senators Rubio and McConnell fiercely opposing corporate political involvement as early as 2021) (citing Burgess Everett, *McConnell: Big Business Acting Like "Woke Parallel Government,"* POLITICO (Apr. 5, 2021, 11:13 AM EDT), www.politico.com/news/2021/04/05/mcconnell-corporate-america-woke-parallel-government-479042 [https://perma.cc/9A5F-FSZ8].).

[257] William P. Barr & Jonathan Berry, *Delaware Is Trying Hard to Drive Away Corporations*, WALL ST. J. (Nov. 24, 2023), www.wsj.com/articles/delaware-is-trying-hard-to-drive-away-corporations-business-environmental-socialgovernance-investing-780f812a.

[258] Keeanga-Yamahtta Taylor, *The War on Diversity, Equity, and Inclusion*, NEW YORKER (Feb. 8, 2025), www.newyorker.com/news/the-lede/the-war-on-diversity-equity-and-inclusion?_sp=59d8c1bf-9743-4b8d-b494-98aba6d5f5c8.1739241185574.

[259] Lindsay Ellis & Alex Leary, *Fight against DEI Dominates Start of Trump's Second Term*, WALL ST. J. (Jan. 31, 2025), www.wsj.com/politics/policy/fight-against-dei-dominates-start-of-trumps-second-term-fea62a30.

[260] *See infra* Section C.3.

[261] Tim Higgins, *Why Elon Musk Won't Stop Talking about a "Woke Mind Virus,"* WALL ST. J. (Dec. 13, 2023), www.wsj.com/tech/elon-musk-woke-mind-virus-41576aa6.

[262] Elon Musk (@elonmusk), *Pronouns suck*, X (July 25, 2020, 1:44 PM), https://x.com/elonmusk/status/1286869404874088448.

[263] Kwan Wei Kevin Tan, *Elon Musk is Allying with Bill Ackman and Raging against DEI*, BUSINESS INSIDER (Jan. 4, 2024), www.businessinsider.com/elon-musk-says-dei-is-just-another-word-for-racism-2024-1.

[264] Matt O'Brien & Barbara Ortutay, *Musk's Twitter Disbands Its Trust and Safety Advisory Group*, ASSOCIATED PRESS (Dec. 12, 2022), https://apnews.com/article/elon-musk-twitter-inc-technology-business-a9b795e8050de12319b82b5dd7118cd7.

a bulwark against "woke mind virus" culture[265] – terms he regularly deploys to frame progressive causes as threats to free speech and merit. Finally, on the corporate front, Musk relocated the headquarters of X and SpaceX to Texas, citing disagreements with California's policies, including those related to LGBTQ+ rights.[266]

Vivek Ramaswamy, biotech entrepreneur, former Republican presidential contender, and author of *Woke, Inc.*, was among the first to spotlight the influence of "woke" corporations, arguing in his book that ESG practices erode shareholder primacy and economic efficiency.[267] Through his investment firm, Strive Asset Management, he pressures corporations to abandon ESG initiatives in favor of a shareholder-first approach.[268] Some business and financial leaders amplified the anti-woke movement, with billionaire figures like Peter Thiel and Bill Ackman positioning it as a defense of economic freedom and cultural neutrality.[269] For example, Ackman launched a full-blown attack on DEI policies and programs at schools and in the corporate world with a 4,000-word manifesto on X.[270] Ackman called DEI "inherently a racist and illegal movement in its implementation even if it purports to work on behalf of the so-called oppressed."[271]

Conservative think tanks play a relevant part as well. Some, like the Heritage Foundation, which authored Project 2025, are well-known and primarily active in lobbying,[272] while others have targeted corporations with anti-ESG/DEI shareholder proposals[273] or litigation.[274]

[265] Liam Reilly, *Musk Links Trans People to Tesla Attacks the Same Day His Estranged Daughter Criticizes Him in Teen Vogue Interview*, CNN (Mar. 20, 2025), www.cnn.com/2025/03/20/media/vivian-wilson-teen-vogue-criticism-musk-tesla-trans/index.html.

[266] *Musk Says SpaceX Will Move Headquarters to Texas from California*, REUTERS (July 16, 2024, 4:00 PM), www.reuters.com/technology/musk-says-spacex-will-move-headquarters-texas-california-2024-07-16/.

[267] VIVEK RAMASWAMY, WOKE INC.: INSIDE CORPORATE AMERICA'S SOCIAL JUSTICE SCAM (2021). *See* Josh Kraushaar, *"Woke, Inc." Author Launches GOP Presidential Campaign*, AXIOS (Feb. 21, 2023), www.axios.com/2023/02/22/vivek-ramaswamy-2024-presidential-election [https://perma.cc/P9EW-MZ25].

[268] Liz Hoffman & Charley Grant, *Upstart Money Manager Gets Billionaires to Back the Anti-BlackRock*, WALL ST. J. (May 10, 2022), www.wsj.com/articles/upstart-money-manager-gets-billionaires-to-back-the-anti-blackrock-11652134919.

[269] *Id.*

[270] Paige McGlauflin & Azure Gilman, *Bill Ackman's Manifesto Is the Latest High-Profile Attack on DEI but Workplace Experts Say Companies Are Resetting – Not Backtracking*, FORTUNE (Jan. 5, 2024), https://fortune.com/2024/01/05/bill-ackman-twitter-manifesto-attack-dei-diversity-programs/ (on file with the *Journal of Corporation Law*).

[271] *Id.*

[272] Lila MacLellan, *Major Players in the Anti-DEI Movement: Here's Who's Pressuring Goldman Sachs, Pfizer, IBM, and Other Fortune 500 Companies to Drop Their Policies*, FORTUNE (Feb. 1, 2025, 4:00 AM EST), https://fortune.com/2025/02/01/anti-dei-guide-groups-people-attackin-goldman-ibm-pfizer-jpmorgan-salesforce/.

[273] On the shareholder proposals front, the National Center for Public Policy Research targeted, among others, Costco, Apple, Levi's, Goldman Sachs, and others, while recipients of proposals by the National Legal and Policy Center included McDonald's, JPMorgan Chase, and Goldman Sachs. *Id.*

[274] *See infra* Section C.2.

And it's not just high-profile names: conservative grassroots activists also have an impactful role. For instance, Nashville-based video director Robby Starbuck has been running successful social media campaigns to pressure corporations into abandoning their DEI initiatives.[275] With viral videos, he singled out firms like Tractor Supply, John Deere, Lowe's, and Harley-Davidson, prompting them to scale back their DEI commitments.[276]

### 2 *Litigation*

The attacks extended beyond public condemnation and reached the courts, with efforts that intensified after the US Supreme Court struck down affirmative action in college admissions.[277] The ruling curtailed race-conscious admissions policies,[278] raising immediate questions about its implications for corporations. While the decision did not directly apply to private employers,[279] companies have been reassessing their diversity programs to mitigate legal and practical risks,[280] often scaling back or restructuring their DEI efforts, as Section C.4 further illustrates.

Amid this legal uncertainty, conservative figures like Edward Blum and organizations like the American Alliance for Equal Rights (AAER) have seized the moment to escalate their challenges.[281] Having played a key role in dismantling affirmative action,[282]

[275] *See* MacLellan, *supra* note 272.

[276] *Inside Robby Starbuck's Campaign to End DEI, One Company at a Time*, WALL ST. J. (Feb. 19, 2025), www.wsj.com/video/inside-robby-starbucks-campaign-to-end-dei-one-company-at-a-time/B6EFA738-AD30-4462-9E88-720274FF027B.

[277] Students for Fair Admissions, Inc. v. President and Fellows of Harvard College, 600 U.S. 181 (2023) (ruling by a vote of 6 to 3 that the admissions programs used by Harvard College and the University of North Carolina violated Title VI and the Constitution's equal protection clause). *See* Emily Birnbaum, *Trump Allies Attack Corporate "Bigotry" against White men*, BLOOMBERG (Dec. 11, 2023, 7:00 AM), www.bloomberg.com/news/articles/2023-12-11/trump-allies-blame-companies-of-discriminating-against-white-men-in-dei-push.

[278] Nina Totenberg, *Supreme Court Guts Affirmative Action, Effectively Ending Race-Conscious Admissions*, NPR (June 29, 2023), www.npr.org/2023/06/29/1181138066/affirmative-action-supreme-court-decision; Adewale A. Maye, *The Supreme Court's Ban on Affirmative Action Means Colleges Will Struggle to Meet Goals of Diversity and Equal Opportunity*, ECONOMIC POLICY INSTITUTE (June 29, 2023), www.epi.org/blog/the-supreme-courts-ban-on-affirmative-action-means-colleges-will-struggle-to-meet-goals-of-diversity-and-equal-opportunity/.

[279] Kenji Yoshino & David Glasgow, *What SCOTUS's Affirmative Action Decision Means for Corporate DEI*, HARVARD BUSINESS REVIEW (July 12, 2023), https://hbr.org/2023/07/what-scotuss-affirmative-action-decision-means-for-corporate-dei.

[280] Andrea R. Lucas, *With Supreme Court Affirmative Action Ruling, It's Time for Companies to Take a Hard Look at Their Corporate Diversity Programs*, REUTERS (June 29, 2023), www.reuters.com/legal/legalindustry/with-supreme-court-affirmative-action-ruling-its-time-companies-take-hard-look-2023-06-29/.

[281] Tali Arbel, *The Case against Bill Ackman and Elon Musk's Anti-DEI Stance*, WALL ST. J. (Feb. 7, 2024, 1:42 PM), www.wsj.com/business/dei-diversity-initiatives-advocacy-elon-musk-bill-ackman-b64caeea.

[282] Max Abelson, Simone Foxman & Ava Benny-Morrison, *Wall Street's DEI Retreat Has Begun*, BLOOMBERG (Mar. 3, 2024, 9:34 PM), www.bloomberg.com/news/articles/2024-03-04/goldman-jpmorgan-cut-dei-efforts-over-lawsuit-threats.

Blum and AAER swiftly turned their attention to corporate diversity programs, filing lawsuits that argue these initiatives violate federal civil rights laws.[283] Their litigation targets included two law firms accused of unlawfully discriminating against white candidates through diversity fellowships[284] and the venture capital firm Fearless Fund, which faced allegations that its startup grants for African American women imposed racially exclusive eligibility criteria.[285] In the case against Fearless Fund, AAER argued that its Strivers Grant Contest – which awarded $20,000 to businesses owned by Black women[286] – was discriminatory.[287] While Fearless Fund launched the program to address poor representation of women of color among venture capital recipients and evidence of hardships in obtaining investments,[288] Blum claimed that "race-exclusive programs like the one the Fearless Fund promoted are divisive and illegal."[289] In June 2024, the Eleventh Circuit ruled in favor of AAER, issuing a preliminary injunction; a few months later, Fearless Fund settled the lawsuit and closed the grant contest.[290]

The uptick in litigation against DEI initiatives is also fueled by President Trump's longtime aide and ally Stephen Miller, whose conservative organization, America First Legal (AFL), aims to eradicate diversity initiatives in business.[291] AFL efforts include litigating against CBS and Paramount Global for allegedly discriminating against a white, straight writer,[292] and challenging the NFL's Rooney Rule, which mandates interviewing minority candidates for specific positions.[293] During the 2022–23 period, AFL filed 25 complaints with the US Equal Employment Opportunity Commission against companies such as Meta, Macy's, BlackRock, and

283 *Id.*

284 Nate Raymond, *Activist behind US Affirmative Action Cases Sue Major Law Firms*, Reuters (Aug. 22, 2023, 10:23 PM), www.reuters.com/legal/activist-behind-us-affirmative-action-cases-sues-major-law-firms-2023-08-22/.

285 Arbel, *supra* note 281.

286 Alexandra Olson, *Fearless Fund Drops Grant Program for Black Women Business Owners in Lawsuit settlement*, The Associated Press (Sept. 11, 2024), https://apnews.com/article/fearless-fund-dei-lawsuit-ed-blum-227a457ded5460061b4300a7ad16d18a.

287 Kiara Alfonseca, *Fearless Fund Ends Program for Black. Women, Settling Discrimination Lawsuit*, ABC News (Sept. 11, 2024), https://abcnews.go.com/US/fearless-fund-ends-program-black-women-settling-discrimination/story?id=113597707.

288 *Id.*

289 Alexandra Olson, *Fearless Fund Drops Grant Program for Black Women Business Owners In Lawsuit Settlement*, The Associated Press (Sept. 11, 2024), https://apnews.com/article/fearless-fund-dei-lawsuit-ed-blum-227a457ded5460061b4300a7ad16d18a.

290 American Alliance for Equal Rights v. Fearless Fund Management, LLC, No. 23-13138 (11th Cir. June 3, 2024). *See* Olson, *supra* note 289.

291 Alex Thompson, *Exclusive: Trump Allies Plot Anti-racism Protections – for White People*, Axios (Apr. 1, 2024), www.axios.com/2024/04/01/trump-reverse-racism-civil-rights.

292 *Historic lawsuit – America First Legal Sues CBS for Alleged Anti-white Discrimination*, America Legal First (Feb. 29, 2024), https://aflegal.org/historic-lawsuit-america-first-legal-sues-cbs-for-alleged-illegal-anti-white-discrimination/.

293 Arbel, *supra* note 281.

NASCAR.[294] AFL also challenged BlackRock for a scholarship program that supposedly favors Black, Hispanic, LGBTQ+, and disabled students.[295]

Anti-climate litigation is prominent too. Recently, a federal district court found that American Airlines and its Employee Benefits Committee violated their ERISA duty of loyalty by subordinating the financial interests of plan participants to corporate ESG objectives in managing the company's 401(k) plans.[296]

The climate fight extends beyond private suits, as state attorneys general entered the ring, steering policy through litigation. In 2022, nineteen of them sent a letter to BlackRock, accusing the asset manager of breaching its fiduciary duties when encouraging portfolio companies to combat climate change.[297] Tensions escalated further. In November 2024, Texas Attorney General Ken Paxton, joined by ten other Republican-led states, sued BlackRock, State Street, and Vanguard, accusing them of colluding to starve coal producers of capital and conspiring to tilt the market in favor of net-zero goals.[298] The lawsuit doesn't just challenge ESG; it repositions it – as an antitrust violation, a threat to fair competition, an overreach that must be checked. The case signals a shift, where climate-conscious investing is no longer just a market choice but a legal battleground.

### 3 *Legislative and Regulatory Efforts*

Conservatives complemented advocacy and litigation with a wave of legislative and regulatory efforts aimed at curbing ESG and DEI initiatives. Republican lawmakers have introduced numerous anti-ESG bills,[299] with 88 laws in effect across 26 states by mid-2024.[300] Texas led the charge with a 2021 law barring government contracts with financial firms boycotting fossil fuels, targeting companies like Goldman Sachs and Citigroup.[301] The Texas Comptroller criticized

294 Birnbaum, *supra* note 277.

295 BlackRock eliminated the online references to those cohorts for the program. *Id.*

296 *Spence v. American Airlines, Inc.*, No. 4:23-cv-00552 (N.D. Tex. Jan. 10, 2025). The court held that American Airlines improperly delegated substantial authority to BlackRock despite, according to the judge, its well-documented ESG activism, which led to conflicts of interest and fiduciary mismanagement ultimately prioritizing corporate and third-party interests over those of plan beneficiaries.

297 BlackRock denied the characterization. Brooke Masters, *BlackRock Denies Republican Claims of Climate "Activism,"* Fin. Times (Sept. 7, 2022), www.ft.com/content/a4af6919-b1cc-4c15-b17c-46186fddbd4c.

298 Justin Jacobs, *Texas Leads Republican States in Antitrust Case against ESG Investment Firms*, Fin. Times (Nov. 29, 2024), www.ft.com/content/dc34dffe-c92f-4743-8991-f0ec173d083b.

299 David H. Webber, *It's Time for ESG to Fight Back*, Barron's (Nov. 11, 2022, 11:59 am), www.barrons.com/articles/esg-investing-blackrock-profits-51668185876.

300 *Navigating State Regulation of* ESG, Ropes & Gray, www.ropesgray.com/en/sites/navigating-state-regulation-of-esg (last updated July 11, 2024).

301 Michelle Celarier, *The Backlash against* ESG *Faces Its Own Backlash*, Institutional Investor (Mar. 7, 2023), www.institutionalinvestor.com/article/2bstpooh7569w263f3w1s/culture/the-backlash-against-esg-faces-its-own-backlash.

ESG as an "opaque and perverse system,"[302] mandating divestment from non-compliant firms and prohibiting contracts with companies discriminating against firearm manufacturers.[303] Florida has also aggressively opposed ESG since 2022, with Governor DeSantis labeling it "financial fraud."[304] The state enacted laws barring financial institutions from discrimination based on beliefs,[305] required investment decisions to focus solely on pecuniary factors,[306] and divested $2 billion from BlackRock for its pro-ESG stance.[307] In 2023, Florida led a coalition of eighteen states to counter the ESG agenda, citing its destabilizing economic effects.[308]

DEI has become another express target of legislative efforts by conservatives. At the state level, since Florida and Texas moved to ban DEI offices at their public universities in 2023 in the aftermath of *Students for Fair Admissions*, a flurry of red states joined the anti-DEI movement.[309] By June 2024, one could count over 100 anti-DEI bills introduced or passed nationwide.[310]

It has not been quiet at the federal level, either. In November 2024, Representative Michael Cloud introduced the Dismantle DEI Act, also sponsored by JD Vance, then-Senator and now the Vice President of the United States, which intends to suspend all DEI-related activities within federal agencies.[311] To no one's surprise, Trump immediately moved aggressively against DEI initiatives from the outset of his second term.

[302] Mitchell Ferman, *Texas Bans Local, State Government Entities from Doing Business with Firms that "Boycott" Fossil Fuels*, Texas Tribune (Aug. 24, 2022), www.texastribune.org/2022/08/24/texas-boycott-companies-fossil-fuels/.

[303] Danielle Moran, *Why Texas Is Banning Banks over Their ESG Policies*, Bloomberg (Mar. 20, 2024, 12:40 pm), www.bloomberg.com/news/articles/2024-03-20/why-texas-is-banning-blackrock-citi-other-banks-over-esg-investing?embedded-checkout=true.

[304] *Governor Ron DeSantis Signs Legislation to Protect Floridians' Financial Future & Economic Liberty*, Florida Governor Ron DeSantis (May 2, 2023), www.flgov.com/2023/05/02/governor-ron-desantis-signs-legislation-to-protect-floridians-financial-future-economic-liberty/.

[305] *Id.*

[306] *Id.*

[307] *Chief Financial Officer Directive* 2023-01, Florida Department of Financial Services, www.myfloridacfo.com/docs-sf/cfo-news-libraries/news-documents/2023/cfo-directive--2023-1.pdf?sfvrsn=3868d4f_2 (last visited July 21, 2024).

[308] *Governor Ron DeSantis Leads Alliance of 18 States to Fight against Biden's ESG Financial Fraud*, Florida Governor Ron DeSantis (Mar. 16, 2023), www.flgov.com/2023/03/16/governor-ron-desantis-leads-alliance-of-18-states-to-fight-against-bidens-esg-financial-fraud/.

[309] Johanna Alonso, *DEI Bans Flourished in 2024, Politicians Aren's Finished.*, Inside Higher Ed (Dec. 16, 2024), www.insidehighered.com/news/faculty-issues/diversity-equity/2024/12/16/how-battle-over-dei-shook-out-2024-and-whats-come.

[310] Julie Kratz, *Anti-DEI Legislation: How We Got Here with Tips to Combat It*, Forbes (June 18, 2024), www.forbes.com/sites/juliekratz/2024/06/09/anti-dei-legislation-how-we-got-here-with-tips-to-combat-it/.

[311] Dismantle DEI Act of 2024, S. 4516, 118th Cong. (2024). Christopher Wilkinson & Jeremy Wright, *The Dismantle DEI Act: One Potential Blueprint for Forthcoming Attacks on DEI*, Perkins Coie (Jan. 17, 2025), https://perkinscoie.com/insights/update/dismantle-dei-act-one-potential-blueprint-forthcoming-attacks-dei.

First, he issued an executive order suspending DEI programs and eliminating so-called discriminatory policies within the government.[312] Among the immediate administrative measures was the termination of chief diversity officer positions established under the Biden administration.[313] Second, he signed another executive order rolling back equity policies and mandating that government forms and documents recognize only two genders, effectively erasing legal recognition of gender identity.[314]

While these orders targeted the public sector, a third executive order, issued the same day,[315] extended Trump's anti-DEI agenda into the private sector.[316] This order revoked a Biden-era mandate requiring federal contractors and subcontractors to implement race- and gender-conscious affirmative action programs.[317] Importantly, it also directed federal agencies to pursue enforcement actions against DEI policies in the private sector.[318] The Attorney General and the Office of Management and Budget were tasked with delivering a report within 120 days on ways to "encourage" the private sector to eliminate DEI programs.[319] Agencies were further instructed to prioritize up to nine civil compliance investigations into major corporations, large nonprofits, professional associations, and universities with billion-dollar endowments.[320] With this order, the administration dramatically expands federal scrutiny over DEI initiatives, signaling that private employers and institutions would need to ensure their policies could withstand legal challenges.[321]

Unsurprisingly, the new Trump administration also inverted direction on sustainability matters. Among other things, the SEC made it clear that it will not back

[312] Erica L. Green & Zach Montague, *Trump Signs Two Orders to Dismantle Equity Policies*, N.Y. TIMES (Jan. 20, 2025), www.nytimes.com/2025/01/20/us/politics/trump-transgender-race-education .html?smid=url-share.

[313] *Id.*

[314] *Id.*

[315] *Ending Illegal Discrimination and Restoring Merit-Based Opportunity*, THE WHITE HOUSE (Jan. 21, 2025), www.whitehouse.gov/presidential-actions/2025/01/ending-illegal-discrimination-and-restoring-merit-based-opportunity/.

[316] Sweeping Executive Order Targets DEI initiatives in the Private and Public Sectors, O'MELVENY (Jan. 23, 2025), www.omm.com/insights/alerts-publications/sweeping-executive-order-targets-dei-initiatives-in-the-private-and-public-sectors/.

[317] Alexis Cherry & Denise Giraudo, *Analyzing President Trump's Latest Executive Order Titled "Ending Illegal Discrimination and Restoring Merit-Based Opportunity,"* SHEPPARD MULLIN (Jan. 28, 2025), www.laboremploymentlawblog.com/2025/01/articles/discrimination/analyzing-president-trumps-latest-executive-order-titled-ending-illegal-discrimination-and-restoring-merit-based-opportunity/.

[318] *Ending Illegal Discrimination and Restoring Merit-Based Opportunity*, *supra* note 315.

[319] *Id.* Section 4(b).

[320] *Id.* (requiring the report to outline key sectors of concern, identify major breaches, propose measures to deter unlawful practices, and include up to nine civil compliance investigations targeting large corporations, nonprofits, and institutions, along with strategies for private sector compliance, potential litigation, and regulatory actions).

[321] *Trump Targets OFCCP, DEI in Executive Order*, CROWELL (Jan. 22, 2025), www.crowell.com/en/insights/client-alerts/trump-targets-ofccp-dei-in-executive-order.

the Biden-era proposed climate disclosures[322] and released new interpretative guidelines that make it harder for institutional investors to exert pressure on corporations, thus chilling engagement on the ESG front.[323] The US exited the Paris Climate Agreement for the second time.[324]

## 4 *Are Corporations Retreating?*

The backlash had already reached the C-suite long before the flurry of presidential executive orders. Though the Supreme Court's affirmative action decision did not apply to corporations, its language inevitably sparked speculation about its wide-ranging implications.[325] Companies have been quietly adjusting – if not abandoning – their diversity programs[326] and terminology[327] to mitigate legal risks amid uncertainty and the new political landscape in Washington.[328]

In response to lawsuits, some firms broadened their diversity programs to include more applicants.[329] For example, Pfizer removed race-based eligibility from its Breakthrough Fellowship Program in 2023 following a lawsuit, and several law firms

[322] *See supra* note 174 and accompanying text.

[323] The SEC's new guidance expands the definition of "influencing control" to include certain ESG engagements, clarifying that investors pressing companies on governance or sustainability – such as conditioning director support on policy changes – may be required to file a Schedule 13D instead of the less burdensome Schedule 13G, creating a chilling effect on institutional investor advocacy due to heightened compliance costs and regulatory scrutiny. *See* SEC, *Compliance & Disclosure Interpretations: Exchange Act Sections 13(d) and 13(g) and Regulation 13D-G Beneficial Ownership Reporting*, U.S. Sec. & Exch. Comm'n (Feb. 11, 2025), www.sec.gov/rules-regulations/staff-guidance/compliance-disclosure-interpretations/exchange-act-sections-13d-13g-regulation-13d-g-beneficial-ownership-reporting; Marc Rotter, *SEC Staff Publishes New Guidance on When Shareholder Engagement on ESG and Other Matters Requires Schedule 13D Filings*, Ropes & Gray (Feb. 11, 2025), www.ropesgray.com/en/insights/viewpoints/102jzvp/sec-staff-publishes-new-guidance-on-when-shareholder-engagement-on-esg-and-other.

[324] *See supra* Section B.4.

[325] Francesca L. Odell, Jennifer Kennedy Park & Charity E. Lee, *How Boards Should Be Thinking about the Supreme Court's SFFA Affirmative Action Decision*, Harv. L. Sch. F. on Corp. Governance (Feb. 14, 2024), https://corpgov.law.harvard.edu/2024/02/14/how-boards-should-be-thinking-about-the-supreme-courts-sffa-affirmative-action-decision/#more-162363.

[326] Alexander Olson, Haleluya Hadero & Anne D'Innocenzio, *As Diversity, Equity, and Inclusion Come Under Legal Attack, Companies Quietly Alter Their Programs*, AP News (Jan. 14, 2024), https://apnews.com/article/dei-diversity-corporations-affirmative-action-309864f08e6ec63a45d18ca5f25d7540.

[327] Jeff Green & Simone Foxman, *Uber and Citi Cut "Anti-Racist" from Corporate Vocabulary Following DEI Backlash*, Bloomberg (Mar. 1, 2024, 6:30 AM), www.bloomberg.com/news/articles/2024-03-01/uber-citi-among-us-companies-dropping-anti-racist-tag-with-dei-backlash?sref=5pcoIoxz.

[328] During the 2024 election, tech elites and venture capitalists were vocal in supporting Donald Trump, reflecting a broader rightward shift. Nicole Narea, *Why Tech Titans Are Turning toward Trump*, Vox (July 17, 2024, 6:30 AM), www.vox.com/politics/361087/trump-silicon-valley-fundraising-musk-andreessen-horowitz.

[329] Olson, Hadero & D'Innocenzio, *supra* note 326.

expanded diversity fellowships to include all students.[330] Although the lawsuit was dismissed, Pfizer removed the race-based eligibility requirement in 2023.[331]

Corporations are also more cautious with their diversity language.[332] Uber removed the term "anti-racist" from its corporate filings,[333] and about 20 percent of the eighty-two regulatory filings reviewed by Bloomberg News in early 2024 modified or removed diversity-related language.[334]

As noted earlier, Meta vocally scaled back its diversity programs, citing legal and political risks.[335] It adjusted programs for hiring, training, and picking suppliers.[336] The company described the retreat from DEI as necessary because the "legal and policy landscape surrounding diversity, equity and inclusion efforts in the United States is changing."[337] Other companies such as Amazon, Walmart, McDonald's, and Ford also reshaped their DEI efforts.[338] In its internal memo circulated on December 2024, Amazon said the company is "winding down outdated programs and materials."[339] It also changed the "Our Positions" webpage by slimming down sections once dedicated to DEI policies.[340] Walmart reduced its emphasis on DEI in hiring practices,[341] while McDonald's quietly eliminated some of its public-facing DEI commitment,[342] and transformed its diversity team into the Global Inclusion Team.[343]

A retreat is taking place also on Wall Street, with large institutional investors like Vanguard announcing they would stop pushing for gender, racial, or ethnic

[330] Nate Raymond, *Group Suing over Pfizer Diversity Fellowship Program Loses US Appeal*, Reuters (Mar. 6, 2024, 7:42 PM), www.reuters.com/legal/group-suing-over-pfizer-diversity-fellowship-program-loses-us-appeal-2024-03-06/.

[331] Olson, Hadero & D'Innocenzio, *supra* note 326.

[332] *See* Green & Foxman, *supra* note 327.

[333] *Id.*

[334] *Id.*

[335] Natalie Sherman, *Meta and Amazon Scale Back Diversity Initiatives*, BBC (Jan. 10, 2025), www.bbc.com/news/articles/cgmy7xpw3pyo.

[336] Katie Paul & Judy Babu, *Meta, Amazon Scale Back Diversity Programs Ahead of Trump Inauguration*, Reuters (Jan. 10, 2025), www.reuters.com/sustainability/society-equity/meta-end-diversity-programs-ahead-trump-inauguration-2025-01-10/.

[337] Kate Gibson & Emmet Lyons, *Meta Ends Diversity Programs, Joining McDonald's, Walmart and Other Major Companies to Back Off DEI*, CBS NEWS (Jan. 16, 2025), www.cbsnews.com/news/meta-dei-programs-mcdonalds-walmart-ford-diversity/.

[338] Natalie Sherman, *Meta and Amazon Scale Back Diversity Initiatives*, BBC (Jan. 10, 2025), www.bbc.com/news/articles/cgmy7xpw3pyo.

[339] Annie Palmer, *Amazon to Halt Some of Its DEI Programs: Internal Memo*, CNBC (Jan. 10, 2025), www.cnbc.com/2025/01/10/amazon-halt-dei-programs-.html.

[340] *Id.*

[341] Heather Haddon, *McDonald's Drops Diversity Targets for Employees, Suppliers*, Wall St. J. (Jan. 6, 2025, 2:30 PM), www.wsj.com/livecoverage/stock-market-today-dow-sp500-nasdaq-live-01-06-2025/card/mcdonald-s-drops-diversity-targets-for-employees-suppliers-8HY6qot7iprVPxODSQuc.

[342] Sarah Nassauer, *Walmart Rolls Back DEI Programs*, Wall St. J. (Nov. 15, 2024, 10:00 AM), www.wsj.com/business/retail/walmart-rolls-back-dei-programs-66a5201a.

[343] David Goldman, *McDonald's Is Ending Some of Its DEI Practices*, CNN Business (Jan 6, 2025), www.cnn.com/2025/01/06/business/mcdonalds-dei/index.html.

diversity in corporate governance and the Nasdaq swiftly rescinding its board diversity disclosure rule.[344] Even proxy advisors like Institutional Shareholder Services (ISS) and Glass Lewis took notice of the changed environment. While ISS went as far as stating it will no longer consider board diversity in its voting recommendations to its institutional investor clients (citing Trump's executive orders),[345] Glass Lewis reaffirmed its diversity-related voting policies, but noted it will flag its diversity-related recommendations and provide alternative rationales to clients.[346]

Data indicate a general retreat from DEI initiatives in the private sector, beyond corporate America. Leopard Solution group found a decline in diverse entry-level hires in the top 200 American law firms, dropping from 2,371 in 2022 to 2,049 in 2023, with a significant decrease in ethnically diverse lateral hires.[347] Venture capital funding for businesses owned by Black and Latina women fell to less than 1 percent, compared to a peak of 1.05 percent in 2021.[348] All the while, the number of anti-DEI shareholder proposals has more than tripled since 2020.[349]

Despite all of this, while many companies are curtailing DEI initiatives, some remain committed.[350] Microsoft, for instance, reaffirmed its stance in December 2024, with its Chief Diversity Officer publicly stating that "Microsoft's diversity and inclusion work is more important than ever."[351] Similarly, Apple defended its commitment to fostering "a culture of belonging where everyone can do their best work."[352] At its 2025 annual meeting, Apple convinced shareholders to reject a proposal to dismantle its DEI programs.[353] Costco's shareholders also followed their management's lead and defeated a similar proposal.[354] In the consulting industry,

344 Rob Copeland, *Fearing Trump, Wall Street Sounds a Retreat on Diversity Efforts*, N.Y. TIMES (Feb. 11, 2025), www.nytimes.com/2025/02/11/business/trump-dei-wall-street.html.

345 Ross Kerber, *ISS Ends Diversity Considerations for US Boardrooms, Citing Trump Orders*, REUTERS (Feb. 11, 2025), www.reuters.com/business/finance/iss-ends-diversity-considerations-us-boardrooms-citing-trump-orders-2025-02-11/.

346 Ross Kerber, *Proxy Adviser Glass Lewis Sticks with Diversity Guidance, Will Flag Risks*, REUTERS (Mar. 4, 2025), www.reuters.com/sustainability/boards-policy-regulation/proxy-adviser-glass-lewis-sticks-with-diversity-guidance-will-flag-risks-2025-03-04/.

347 Joe Miller, *Biggest US Law Firms Hired Fewer Diverse Candidates Amid DEI Backlash*, FIN. TIMES (Mar. 7, 2024), www.ft.com/content/df5f4d76-3a37-40f6-8bee-6161f56b6af7

348 Olson, Hadero & D'Innocenzio, *supra* note 326.

349 Emily Peck, *Anti-DEI Shareholder Proposals Tripled since 2020*, AXIOS (Jan. 8, 2025), www.axios.com/2025/01/08/dei-diversity-backlash-starbucks-apple-trump.

350 Gibson, *supra* note 15.

351 David Hood, *Apple, Microsoft Defend DEI as Big Tech Rivals Back Down*, BLOOMBERG LAW (Jan. 20, 2025), https://news.bloomberglaw.com/daily-labor-report/apple-microsoft-defend-dei-as-big-tech-rivals-back-down.

352 *Id.*

353 Mark Gurman, *Apple to Keep DEI Efforts, though Some Adjustments Possible*, BLOOMBERG (Feb. 25, 2025), www.bloomberg.com/news/articles/2025-02-25/apple-to-keep-dei-efforts-though-some-adjustments-possible (reporting that Apple will maintain its diversity, equity, and inclusion initiatives despite external pressures, though it may implement adjustments in response to evolving legal requirements).

354 Reuters, *Costco Shareholders Just Destroyed an Anti-DEI Push*, CNN (Jan. 24, 2025), www.cnn.com/2025/01/24/business/costco-dei/index.html (reporting that Costco shareholders overwhelmingly

McKinsey & Co. took a notably defiant stance, with Global Managing Partner Bob Sternfels stating in a memo that the firm would "boldly pursue" both diversity and meritocracy despite government pressure.[355]

The back-and-forth from Goldman Sachs and JPMorgan Chase – first doubling down on DEI,[356] then hedging with careful caveats – lays bare the business and legal uncertainty firms are trying to navigate. Through a spokesperson, Goldman Sachs reaffirmed that it "strongly believe[s] that organizations benefit from diverse perspectives" and remains committed to operating DEI programs in compliance with the law.[357] Similarly, Jamie Dimon, CEO of JPMorgan Chase, defended the bank's efforts, stating that it "will continue to reach out to the Black community, the Hispanic community, the veterans community, [and] LGBTQ …."[358] However, in early 2025, Goldman Sachs dropped its IPO policy requiring companies to have at least two diverse board members before assisting them in going public, citing "legal developments."[359] Meanwhile, Dimon acknowledged that some of JPMorgan's DEI-related spending had become excessive and inefficient, announcing plans to cut certain programs – a move he insisted was driven by cost concerns rather than political pressure.[360]

As of December 2024, just before Trump's wave of anti-DEI executive orders, I conducted a survey and found that nearly every S&P 100 company was still publicly committed to diversity: 95 out of 100 had gender equity goals, 96 out of 100 had racial equity goals, and 83 out of 100 had commitments tied to sexual orientation and gender identity.[361] Following Trump's executive orders, a survey of 350 C-suite executives run by employment law firm Littler found most companies plan to maintain their DEI commitments, with some expanding initiatives in 2024, but a significant subset scaling back (24 percent in 2025 jumping from 6 percent in 2024).[362]

rejected a proposal to curb the company's diversity, equity, and inclusion initiatives, demonstrating strong investor support for existing DEI policies). *See also* Sarah Nassauer, *Why Costco Isn't Joining the Backlash against DEI*, WALL ST. J. (Jan. 2025), www.wsj.com/business/costco-dei-policies-0e7a3f11.

355 Ambereen Choudhury & Amy Bainbridge, *McKinsey Champions Diversity while Rivals Abandon Targets*, BLOOMBERG (Feb. 12, 2025, 9:35 AM EST), www.bloomberg.com/news/articles/2025-02-12/mckinsey-strikes-defiant-tone-on-diversity-while-rivals-balk (noting that rival Accenture dropped DEI initiatives citing political pressures).

356 Emily Fitter, Jeff Green & Simone Foxman, *JPMorgan, Goldman CEOs Resist Calls to Roll Back DEI Programs*, BLOOMBERG (Jan. 22, 2025, 8:00 AM), www.bloomberg.com/news/articles/2025-01-22/jpmorgan-goldman-ceos-resist-calls-to-roll-back-dei-programs.

357 Kiara Alfonseca, *These Companies Are Standing By Their DEI Policies amid Backlash*, ABC NEWS (Jan. 23, 2025), https://abcnews.go.com/Business/companies-sticking-dei-amid-backlash/story?id=118037109.

358 *Id.*

359 Copeland, *supra note* 344.

360 *Id.*

361 *See infra* Chapter 6, Section D.

362 *See* Littler Mendelson P.C., *Littler's Inclusion, Equity and Diversity C-Suite Survey Report 2025* (Feb. 26, 2025), www.littler.com/publication-press/publication/littler-csuite-survey-report-2025.

Taken together, all these developments highlight a growing divide in the corporate world. While some companies retreat to avoid legal scrutiny, others attempt to reframe DEI initiatives to weather the shifting political and regulatory landscape. I come back to assessing DEI-related legal risk in Chapter 3.[363]

* * *

Though ESG and DEI efforts have been under sustained attack, it remains too early to determine whether this will lead to a definitive retreat from corporate governing activities. Anti-ESG/DEI initiatives are expected to intensify, and the second Trump administration appears more politically coordinated and institutionally assertive than during its first term, particularly in its confrontational stance toward corporations seen as oppositional. However, assuming corporations will entirely abandon these initiatives or disengage from broader social and environmental commitments is unrealistic, given stakeholder expectations and global market pressures. All in all, the landscape remains fluid.

[363] *See infra* Chapter 3, Section E.2.

# 2

# Corporations as Agents of Socioeconomic Change

## *Why Now?*

This chapter examines the various forces driving corporate governing, from internal dynamics to broader societal pressures. Within firms, a notable catalyst for change has been the rise of Millennial and Gen Z employees. Their collective push for prosocial commitments – often amplified through social media – has placed new demands on executives, prompting a reexamination of corporate priorities and a sharper focus on ESG concerns. At the same time, investors began to treat ESG as financially material, reshaping how companies align long-term strategy with stakeholder expectations. This dual pressure has challenged the shareholder-centric model and encouraged directors to broaden their understanding of corporate purpose. To round out the analysis, this chapter also explores corporate political spending and lobbying, offering a concise account of how these activities influence corporate direction and public positioning.

In Section B, this chapter expands its focus to the broader societal landscape, situating corporate governing within the cultural and political upheavals of the mid-to-late 2010s – many of them amplified by social media. Movements such as Black Lives Matter, #MeToo, the Climate Movement, and March for Our Lives reshaped public expectations and placed new pressures on companies to take a stand. During the first Trump administration, corporate activism surged in response to policies like the Muslim Ban, the withdrawal from the Paris Agreement, and the termination of DACA. Companies filed amicus briefs, executives resigned from advisory councils, and major platforms limited Trump's reach following the January 6 insurrection. By the start of his second term, however, corporate voices have largely fallen silent. Another key driver of corporate involvement in the public sphere is the state of traditional politics. Polarization and gridlock have made meaningful reform difficult. Gerrymandering and compressed election cycles pull representatives toward the extremes, while procedural tools like the filibuster in the US Senate reinforce stasis. In this vacuum, corporations increasingly position themselves as agents of change, stepping in where political institutions fail to act.

- A Firm-Level Drivers for Corporate Governing
  - 1 Workforce and Investor Bottom-Up Demands
    - a Workforce Pressure
    - b Investor Pressure: ESG Investing and Engagement
  - 2 Top-Down Recalibration of Corporate Purpose: Stakeholderism
  - 3 Rent Protection: Corporate Political Spending, Lobbying, and Politics at Work
- B Societal Drivers for Corporate Involvement
  - 1 Shocks, Reckonings, Citizens Demand, and the Role of Social Media
  - 2 The Trump Presidency: Then (and Now?)
  - 3 Failure of Traditional Politics

Corporations' business has been intertwined with public affairs for a long time.[1] In the 1980s and 1990s, the consensus was that corporations could work in parallel tracks with the public sector and take over several functions of the former and run them as eminently private enterprises.[2] However, the contraction of the public sector and political dysfunction have created a void that has pulled corporations into addressing broader societal challenges – at times as direct beneficiaries of privatized public functions like prisons and military services,[3] some other times because corporations engage in government substitution.[4] Two prominent corporate law scholars, Marcel Kahan and Ed Rock, have observed a welfarist era of corporate governance.[5] Meanwhile, social activists paid attention. Tom Lin noted, "As the spheres of government and business converge, social activists will understandably seek change not only through the traditional avenues of government and public policy but also through the private boulevards of business and corporate policy."[6]

[1] *See* Chapter 1, Section A.

[2] John B. Goodman & Gary W. Loveman, *Does Privatization Serve the Public Interest?*, HARV. BUS. REV. (Nov.–Dec. 1991), https://hbr.org/1991/11/does-privatization-serve-the-public-interest.

[3] Tom C.W. Lin, *Incorporating Social Activism*, 98 B.U. L. REV. 1535, 1558–61 (2018) (noting at 1559 that "[c]ontemporary corporations and businesses exert their influence on traditional, public government functions like never before. Privately owned for-profit schools, prisons, utilities, and military forces – once hard to imagine – are now common. The US government regularly uses private contractors affiliated with major corporations for combat missions, intelligence affairs, and diplomatic efforts.").

[4] *See supra* Chapter 1, Section B. A body of literature examines regulatory models in which governments formally or informally delegate rule-making and enforcement responsibilities to private actors. Management-based regulation, for example, refers to a structured regulatory approach in which the state requires firms to develop internal compliance systems to achieve public objectives, often through statutes, formal rules, or agency-issued guidance. See Cary Coglianese & David Lazer, *Management-Based Regulation: Prescribing Private Management to Achieve Public Goals*, 37 LAW & SOC'Y REV. 691, 691–730 (2003). However, the phenomenon discussed in this book differs in a crucial respect: rather than a public directive – whether binding or suggestive – corporate governing today often arises *in the absence* of any state initiative, and instead emerges as a reaction to political dysfunction, societal pressure, or stakeholder expectations. It is not a planned instrument of governance, but a patchwork response to policy failure.

[5] Marcel Kahan & Edward Rock, *The Emergence of Welfarist Corporate Governance*, Eur. Corp. Governance Inst. Law Working Paper, No. 683/2023, Draft December 22, 2022 (on file with author).

[6] Lin, *supra* note 3, at 1561.

In this chapter, I briefly sketch the main drivers of corporate engagement in public policy issues. Section A addresses firm-level drivers, while Section B deals with broader societal phenomena.

## A FIRM-LEVEL DRIVERS FOR CORPORATE GOVERNING

Some drivers for corporate involvement derive from internal dynamics: These include bottom-up pressures from the workforce or investors (especially those who care about ESG matters) and top-down interventions from directors, especially by boards embracing stakeholderism. In the background, corporate political spending and lobbying, less visibly, blur the line between business and politics. The ensuing subsections illustrate these dynamics.

### 1 *Workforce and Investor Bottom-Up Demands*

#### a Workforce Pressure

Employees have played a crucial role in driving change within organizations, particularly in the tech industry.[7] Big Tech companies made concessions after employees challenged existing social norms.[8] In response to the mishandling of sexual misconduct cases, over 20,000 Google employees walked out in November 2018. Shortly afterward, the company conceded, abandoning mandatory arbitration for harassment and discrimination claims and committing to greater transparency.[9] Many other companies, including Facebook and Airbnb, followed suit.[10]

[7] Recent empirical research indicates that senior management in certain industries, notably technology, tends to support progressive causes more than those in other sectors, like energy. Reilly Steel, *The Political Transformation of Corporate America, 2001–2022*, at 3, forthcoming AM. POL. SCI. REV. (working draft Mar. 29, 2025), https://static1.squarespace.com/static/6019c4d665a1bd185288d428/t/67e7648118c6d849a51480da/1743217798724/Steel_Political_Transformation_of_Corporate_America_3-28-25.pdf.

[8] *See* Jennifer S. Fan, *Employees as Regulators: The New Private Ordering in High Technology Companies*, 2019 UTAH L. REV. 973, 1008–14 (2020) (discussing mandatory arbitration provisions and the elimination of the provisions by certain companies in the wake of the #MeToo Movement); Anat Alon-Beck, *Times They Are A-Changin': When Tech Employees Revolt*, 80 MD. L. REV. 120 (2020) (discussing the role of tech workers in pushing for corporate policy changes). *See also* Daisuke Wakabayashi & Jessica Silver-Greenberg, *Facebook to Drop Forced Arbitration in Harassment Cases*, N.Y. TIMES (Nov. 9, 2018), www.nytimes.com/2018/11/09/technology/facebook-arbitration-harassment.html; Jena McGregor, *Google and Facebook Ended Forced Arbitration for Sexual Harassment Claims. Why More Companies Could Follow.*, WASH. POST (Nov. 12, 2018), www.washingtonpost.com/business/2018/11/12/google-facebook-ended-forced-arbitration-sex-harassment-claims-why-more-companies-could-follow/.

[9] Fan, *supra* note 8, at 974–75.

[10] Kate Clark, *Airbnb Ends Forced Arbitration Days after Google, Facebook Did the Same*, TECHCRUNCH (Nov. 12, 2018, 2:49 PM), https://techcrunch.com/2018/11/12/airbnbends-forced-arbitration-days-after-google-facebook-did-the-same/.

This exemplifies what Jennifer Fan labeled as "employee-initiated private ordering," whereby employees influence corporate practices on moral and ethical issues, which extend beyond employee matters and sexual harassment to other areas like providing military drone technology, doing business with anti-democratic countries, and helping with anti-immigration efforts.[11] While these actions can lead to significant legal changes within companies, they can be impactful even when ultimately unsuccessful, because they force companies to take a position publicly.[12]

Tech employees are more vocal for a series of reasons: They are highly educated, trained, and well-paid, making them valuable assets to firms where turnover is costly.[13] The competitive "war for talent" compels companies to prioritize attracting, engaging, and retaining top employees, thereby granting these individuals a degree of influence over corporate practices.[14]

The phenomenon is by no means a prerogative of tech firms. For example, several corporations spoke out after the *Dobbs* decision because of employee pressure, especially women.[15] Following a series of mass shootings, Walmart employees organized protests and walkouts, prompting the company to change its gun and ammunition sales policies.[16] Similarly, advocacy from employees whose children were affected by the Parkland school tragedy led Citigroup to implement restrictions on its gun retailer clients, barring sales of certain firearms and accessories.[17] Wayfair employees staged a walkout to protest the company's furniture sale to migrant detention centers, demanding ethical business practices.[18] The famous feud between Disney and DeSantis occurred after employees and showrunners protested against the CEO's initially passive reaction to the proposed "Don't Say Gay Bill."[19]

It was movements like #MeToo and BLM that sparked conversations about workplace culture and compelled employers to reevaluate their practices and create new roles within their organizations to lead or improve efforts in DEI.[20] Employees became

11 *See generally* Fan, *supra* note 8, at 998–1017.

12 *Id.* at 976.

13 Alon-Beck, *supra* note 8, at 136.

14 *Id.*

15 Anna Toniolo, *Corporate Participation in Social Debates*, 3 U. Chi. Bus. L. Rev. 361, 365 (2024) at 365.

16 Stephen Miles, David F. Lacker & Brian Tayan, *Protests from Within: Engaging with Employee Activists* at 1 (March 8, 2021). Stanford Closer Look Series, https://ssrn.com/abstract=3801120.

17 David Benoit, *Inside Citigroup's Attempt to Rally Wall Street to Pressure Gun Sellers: The Bank Adopted New Gun Policies after the 2018 Parkland Shooting, but Rivals Didn't Follow. "We Were Kind of Lonely," the Former CEO Recalled*, Wall St. J. (June 25, 2022), www.wsj.com/articles/citigroup-tried-and-failed-to-rally-banks-to-pressure-gun-sellers-11656124086.

18 Kari Paul, *Wayfair Workers to Walk Off Job over Partnership with Detention Centers*, The Guardian (June 25, 2019, 8:14 PM), www.theguardian.com/us-news/2019/jun/25/wayfair-walkout-border-facility-furniture.

19 Elizabeth Blair, *After Protests, Disney CEO Speaks out Against Florida's "Don't Say Gay" Bill*, NPR (Mar. 10, 2022, 9:10 AM), www.npr.org/2022/03/08/1085130633/disney-response-florida-bill-dont-say-gay.

20 Megan Reitz & John Higgins, *Leading in an Age of Employee Activism*, 63 MIT Sloan Mgmt. Rev., no. 3 (2022), available at https://sloanreview.mit.edu/article/leading-in-an-age-of-employee-activism/; Geri Strengel, *Black Lives Matter Protests Moves Corporate D&I Initiatives Center Stage*,

more eager and empowered to speak up, shedding light on misconduct and holding employers accountable. A 2019 Weber Shandwick survey shows that nearly four in ten employees (38 percent) speak up to support or criticize their employers' actions over a controversial issue that affects society.[21] The same survey shows that 75 percent of employees in the United States agreed with the statement that "employees are right to speak up against their employers."[22] The uptick around the decade's turn is apparent: Marketing Scenario Analytica data show a 50 percent increase in employee activism events between 2018 and 2020 during the two-month measurement period of May and June, with events nearly tripling from 2019 to 2020.[23] Additionally, the scope of issues driving employee activism expanded beyond the treatment of women in the workplace to encompass a broader range of social, political, and environmental concerns.[24]

A study by Reilly Steel reveals that a small but very influential component of the workforce in corporate America, senior management, has shifted ideologically leftward, with senior managers – but not CEOs – now more liberal.[25] His work suggests that the phenomenon is partly due to increased diversity, with more women and people of color in leadership.[26]

At a minimum, more progressive senior management is likely more receptive to employee-driven activism,[27] reshaping expectations for employers and reinforcing the idea that workers can be agents of change within and beyond their organizations.

### b Investor Pressure: ESG Investing and Engagement

Investor pressure mirrored workforce activism, with institutional investors – especially large asset managers – driving ESG's rise.[28] Over the past decade, ESG became so influential in corporate governance that it provoked an equally forceful backlash.[29]

FORBES (June 17, 2020), www.forbes.com/sites/geristengel/2020/06/17/black-lives-matter-protests-moves-corporate-di-initiatives-into-the-spotlight/?sh=7429f6327a0d.

21 Among these activists, Millennials are the most likely generation to engage (48%), significantly more than Gen Xers (33%) and Boomers (27 percent), often targeting other employees (46%) and top leaders (43%) more than financial investors (12%) or the news media (11%). *See Employee Activism in the Age of Purpose: Employees (Up)rising*, WEBER SHANDWICK (May 29, 2019), https://webershandwick.com/news/employee-activism-in-the-age-of-purpose-employees-uprising.

22 *Id.* at 7.

23 *Id.* (cited by Miles, Larcker & Tayan, *supra* note 16, at 1).

24 *See Employee Activism in the Age of Purpose: Employees (Up)rising*, *supra* note 21, at 13.

25 *See generally* Steel, *supra* note 7, at 3 (noting that CEOs remain more conservative).

26 *Id.* at 24–25 (suggesting that another important factor is that a growing number of corporate leaders come from liberal areas). The proposition that increased diversity spurs broader perspectives in the corporate world traces back decades in scholarship. *See* DAVID VOGEL, KINDRED STRANGERS: THE UNEASY RELATIONSHIP BETWEEN POLITICS AND BUSINESS IN AMERICA 169–70 (1996).

27 This is confirmed by Steel's study, which shows that firms with more progressive directors and executives are much more likely to take public stances to support progressive causes. *Id.* at 4–5.

28 For a history of the term "ESG," see Elizabeth Pollman, *The Making and Meaning of ESG*, 14 HARV. BUS. L. REV. 403 (2024).

29 *See supra* Chapter 1, Section C.

Elizabeth Pollman traces the origins of ESG back to the late 1990s when the United Nations promoted initiatives for more collaboration with the business sector.[30] This change was marked by the launch of the UN Global Compact in 2000 by then-Secretary General Kofi Annan, who called on businesses to align their operations with universal principles covering human rights, labor, environment, and anti-corruption.[31] A turning point came in 2004 with the "Who Cares Wins" report,[32] which first coined ESG and emphasized integrating social and environmental factors into financial analysis and investment decisions.[33] By the 2010s, ESG investing surged as institutional investors embraced these metrics. By 2021, ESG was mentioned in nearly 20% of corporate earnings calls, and 72% of institutional investors incorporated ESG factors into their strategies.[34]

Institutional investor ownership expanded, driven by passive investing. By 2017, institutions controlled 78% of US corporate equity and 80% of the S&P 500.[35] This shift reflected the exponential growth of passive funds, which surged from managing $2.3 trillion at the beginning of 2010[36] to $15.1 trillion by the end of 2023.[37] In this setting, three asset managers such as Vanguard, State Street, and BlackRock, often referred to as the "Big Three,"[38] remarkably expanded over the past two decades, attracting considerable attention due to their size – they collectively manage over $22 trillion in investor assets – and to their significant passive investment business (ETFs and index mutual funds).[39]

Sustainable funds also grew, reaching $3.4 trillion by 2023 or 7.2 percent of total assets under management.[40] Investments in the US in funds using ESG data

30 *See* Pollman, *supra* note 28 at 411.

31 *Id.* at 411–12.

32 *Id.* at 413.

33 *Id.* at 413.

34 *Id.* at 417–18.

35 Anna Christie, *The Agency Costs of Sustainable Capitalism*, 55 UC DAVIS L. REV. 875, 888–89 (2021).

36 *Id.* at 888.

37 Patturaja Murugaboopathy, *Global Passive Equity Funds' Assets Eclipsed Active in 2023 for First Time*, REUTERS (Feb. 1, 2024), www.reuters.com/markets/us/global-markets-funds-passive-2024-02-01/ (noting that passive investments' net funds surpassed those of active funds for the first time in 2023).

38 The unqualified use of this shorthand has been criticized by Dorothy S. Lund & Adriana Robertson, *Giant Asset Managers, the Big Three, and Index Investing*, *in* BOARD-SHAREHOLDER DIALOGUE: POLICY DEBATE, LEGAL CONSTRAINTS AND BEST PRACTICES 158 (Luca Enriques & Giovanni Strampelli eds. 2023) (showing that the index fund industry comprises other asset manager players and that the business of Vanguard, State Street, and BlackRock is not limited to index funds).

39 Alon Brav, Dorothy S. Lund & Lin Zhao, *Financing Decisions, and Institutional Ownership of the U.S. Equity Market*, Eur. Corp. Governance Inst.L. Working Paper (Jan. 13, 2024), No. 749/2024, at 8, https://papers.ssrn.com/sol3/papers.cfm?abstract_id=4693837. *See also* JOHN C. COATES, THE PROBLEM OF TWELVE: WHEN A FEW FINANCIAL INSTITUTIONS CONTROL EVERYTHING 27–50 (2023).

40 *Sustainable Funds Outperformed Peers in 2023*, MORGAN STANLEY (Feb. 29, 2024), www.morganstanley.com/ideas/sustainable-funds-performance-2023-full-year.

nearly doubled between 2016 and 2020, surpassing $40 trillion.[41] In response, companies faced mounting pressure from investors, particularly in the younger generations, Millenials and Gen Z, who push businesses to prioritize social and environmental themes.[42] BlackRock's Larry Fink's 2019 letter underscored this shift, citing the "largest transfer of wealth in history" as $24 trillion moved from baby boomers to millennials.[43]

Corporate prosociality resurfaced.[44] Investor activism translated into shareholder proposals, with support for environmental and social initiatives peaking in 2022. By then, such proposals comprised most of those submitted to Russell 3000 companies,[45] achieving record levels of support around the turn of the decade, with the percentage receiving over 30% approval climbing from zero in 2000 to 36% in 2018.[46] While recent support has declined,[47] overall shareholder proposal

41 Quinn Curtis, Jill Fisch & Adriana Z. Robertson, *Do ESG Funds Deliver on Their Promises?*, 120 MICH. L. REV. 393, 404 (2021).

42 *See generally* Michal Barzuza, Quinn Curtis & David H. Webber, *Shareholder Value(s): Index Fund ESG Activism and the New Millennial Corporate Governance*, 93 S. CAL. L. REV. 1243 (2020) (arguing that the efforts of the Big Three index funds (BlackRockVanguard, and State Street) were motivated by a desire to appeal to the social values of millennial investors). *See also* Ruby Brownen-Trinh & Ajan Orujov, *Corporate Socio-political Activism and Retail Investors: Evidence from the Black Lives Matter campaign*, 80 J. CORP. FIN. 102417 (2023).

43 *See* Bernard S. Sharfman, *Opportunism in the Shareholder Voting and Engagement of the "Big Three" Investment Advisers to Index Funds*, 48 J. CORP. L. 463, 481 (2023).

44 For accounts on the historical impact of the corporate accountability movement on the political system and on corporations, see VOGEL, *supra* note 26, at 166–90; SARAH A. SOULE, CONTENTION AND CORPORATE SOCIAL RESPONSIBILITY 54–58 & 62–63 (2009). *See also supra* Chapter 1, Section A.

45 Daniel Litowitz & Lara Aryani, *Trends in E&S Proposals in the 2022 Proxy Season*, HARV. L. SCH.: F. ON CORP. GOVERNANCE (Nov. 28, 2022), https://corpgov.law.harvard.edu/2022/11/28/trends-in-es-proposals-in-the-2022-proxy-season/..The number of environmental and social proposals increased from 133 in 2021 to 142 in 2022. *2023 Proxy Season Preview and 2022 Proxy Season Highlights*, BROADRIDGE www.broadridge.com/_assets/pdf/broadridge-2023-proxypulse-report.pdf (last visited July 7, 2023).

46 Kahan & Rock, *supra* note 5, at 19. Voting outcomes alone don't tell the full story. Many shareholder proposals are deemed successful not because they win votes, but because they prompt companies to act – often quietly, before a vote even takes place. That's not captured in raw outcome data. Consider proposals on corporate political disclosures: Jill Fisch and Adriana Robertson show that many of these have led to meaningful improvements in transparency, even when withdrawn or voted down. *See* Jill E. Fisch & Adriana Z. Robertson, *Corporate Political Disclosure and Shareholder Voting* (2025) (on file with author).

47 *Compare* Kenneth Khoo & Roberto Tallarita, *Expanding Shareholder Voice: The Impact of SEC Guidance on Environmental and Social Proposals*, European Corporate Governance Institute – Law Working Paper No. 764/2024 (2024), at 2, https://ssrn.com/abstract=4913660 (finding that environmental proposal backing dropped from 40.24% in 2021 to 19.01% in 2023, while support for social proposals fell from 35.27% to 16.96% over the same period) *with* Merel Spierings, *2024 Proxy Season Review: Corporate Resilience in a Polarized Landscape*, HARV. L. SCH. F. ON CORP. GOVERNANCE (Oct. 12, 2024), https://corpgov.law.harvard.edu/2024/10/12/2024-proxy-season-review-corporate-resilience-in-a-polarized-landscape/ (noting that in 2024 shareholder proposals surged, but a smaller percentage reached a vote as companies became more assertive and effective in countering the rise of prescriptive and repetitive submissions).

activity has not. On the contrary, the 2024 proxy season saw a record number of submissions, unfolding in a highly politicized climate where corporations remain on edge[48] and conservative investors intensify their scrutiny of DEI and human capital policies.[49]

BlackRock played a central role in ESG's ascent. In 2018, its CEO Larry Fink wrote a letter urging companies to create long-term value for all stakeholders,[50] reinforcing BlackRock's commitment through engagement and voting.[51] Holding shares of some 14,000 companies worldwide, in 2019, the asset manager divested from coal stocks,[52] and by 2022, Fink encouraged CEOs to set emissions reduction targets.[53] State Street and Vanguard followed,[54] emphasizing climate risks and gender diversity. In 2017, State Street's Fearless Girl campaign – featuring a bronze statue of a girl facing Wall Street's charging bull – publicly underscored its commitment to gender diversity.[55] The initiative promoted a State Street investment fund focused on companies with gender-diverse boards, which prompted competitors like BlackRock and Vanguard to pressure firms to improve board diversity[56] and vote against boards with poor performance in this area.[57] Institutional investor impetus also pushed retail investors toward sustainable capitalism.[58]

ESG's rise was so phenomenal it sparked a fierce backlash in response.[59] Accused of ambiguity, political bias, and greenwashing, Fink dropped the label[60] for "energy pragmatism."[61] Critics saw ESG as vague, enabling corporate greenwashing.[62]

48 *See generally* Geeyoung Min, *Shareholder Direct Democracy*, 74 Emory L. J. 381 (2024) (chronicling the tensions between shareholders and management about shareholder proposals).

49 2025 *Proxy Season Preview*, The Conf. Bd. (Feb. 2025), www.conference-board.org/press/2025-proxy-season-preview.

50 Larry Fink, 2018 *Letter to CEOs: A Sense of Purpose*, BlackRock (2018), www.blackrock.com/corporate/investor-relations/2018-larry-fink-ceo-letter [https://perma.cc/3YYU-MAEL]. *See* Barzuza, Curtis & Webber, *supra* note 42, at 1273.

51 Sean Griffith & Dorothy Lund, *Conflicted Mutual Fund Voting in Corporate Law*, 99 B.U.L. Rev. 1151, 1186 (2019).

52 Barzuza, Curtis & Webber, *supra* note 42, at 1274.

53 Kahan & Rock, *supra* note 5, at 18.

54 *See* Barzuza, Curtis & Webber, *supra* note 42, at 1275.

55 *Id.* at 1266.

56 Bethany McLean, *The Backstory behind That "Fearless Girl" Statue on Wall Street*, The Atlantic (Mar. 13, 2017), www.theatlantic.com/business/archive/2017/03/fearless-girl-wall-street/519393.

57 Barzuza, Curtis & Webber, *supra* note 42, at 1266.

58 Sergio Alberto Gramitto Ricci & Christina M. Sautter, *Corporate Governance Gaming: The Collective Power of Retail Investors*, 22 Nev. L.J. 51, 92–96 (2021) (describing how prosocial attitudes of retail investors shift corporate voting preferences impacting corporations and society).

59 *See supra* Chapter 1, Section C.

60 Pollman, *supra* note 29, at 406 (mentioning that Fink considers the term weaponized by both the left and the right). *See also id.* 430–33.

61 Jon McGowan, *BlackRock's Fink Calls for Energy Pragmatism, Omits ESG from Annual Letter*, Forbes (Mar. 27, 2024), www.forbes.com/sites/jonmcgowan/2024/03/27/blackrocks-fink-calls-for-energy-pragmatism-omits-esg-from-annual-letter/.

62 Pollman, *supra* note 29, at 436.

Conservatives seized the moment[63] – Texas and other states passed anti-ESG laws,[64] while in mid-2024, Rep. Jim Jordan's House Judiciary Committee probed asset managers for alleged anticompetitive collusion.[65] That November, Texas and ten Republican-led states sued BlackRock, Vanguard, and State Street for purported antitrust violations.[66] The Trump SEC reinforced this shift, shelving Biden-era climate disclosure proposals and tightening shareholder engagement rules, making it more difficult for asset managers to exert pressure.[67]

Despite the backlash, shareholder pressure remains a powerful tool. Investors will likely adapt to the shifting regulatory and political landscape. At the same time, corporations depend on institutional investor support and cannot afford to ignore their concerns.[68]

### 2 *Top-Down Recalibration of Corporate Purpose: Stakeholderism*

Given the bottom-up pressure from workers and investors, it is no coincidence that, in recent years, the long-standing debate on corporate purpose – whether corporations must maximize wealth for shareholders or serve all stakeholders, including employees, creditors, consumers, suppliers, and the general interest – revamped virtually everywhere around the world.[69]

In the United States, scholarly debate over the proper purpose of the corporation can be traced to the early 1930s exchange between Adolph Berle and Merrick Dodd.[70] The exchange was likely ignited by the famous *Dodge v. Ford* case of 1919, which ruled against Henry Ford and held that the purpose of a corporation is to produce profits for shareholders.[71] While Berle argued that "corporate powers were held in trust for shareholders," Dodd maintained that "these powers were held in trust for the entire community."[72]

63 *See supra* Chapter 1, Section C.
64 *See supra* Chapter 1, Section C.3.
65 Isla Binnie, *Exclusive: US House Panel Finds Wall St. "Colluded" to Curb Emissions*, REUTERS (June 11, 2024), www.reuters.com/sustainability/us-house-committee-report-finds-wall-street-colluded-curb-emissions-2024-06-11/.
66 *See supra* Chapter 1, Section C.2.
67 The SEC new guidance broadens the definition of "influencing control," increasing the risk that ESG-focused investors must file a burdensome Schedule 13D, discouraging active corporate engagement. *See supra* Chapter 1, Section C.3.
68 *See generally* Dorothy S. Lund, *Asset Managers as Regulators*, 171 U. PA. L. REV. 77 (2023) (arguing that asset managers wield regulatory-like influence over corporations through their investment and voting power, shaping corporate policies and practices without formal regulatory authority).
69 For an account of the debates in other parts of the world, see Martin Gelter & Geneviève Helleringer, *Lift Not the Painted Veil! To Whom Are Directors' Duties Really Owed?*, 2015 U. ILL. L. REV. 1069, 1089–92 (2015) (describing corporate purpose debates in Germany, France, Italy, and the UK).
70 Adolph A. Berle, Jr., *Corporate Powers as Powers in Trust*, 44 HARV. L. REV. 1049 (1931); E. Merrick Dodd, Jr., *For Whom Are Corporate Managers Trustees?*, 45 HARV. L. REV. 1145 (1932).
71 Dodge v. Ford Motor Co., 170 N.W. 668, 684 (Mich. 1919). *See infra* Chapter 3, Section B.3.
72 ADOLPH A. BERLE, THE 20TH CENTURY CAPITALIST REVOLUTION 169 (1954).

The debate reached national prominence in 1970 when future Nobel Prize winner Milton Friedman published a famous article in the *New York Times Magazine*.[73] In the article, Friedman dismissed CSR theories, arguing that corporate executives would be spending "someone else's money" and that their primary responsibility should be to maximize shareholder wealth.[74] Over the next several decades, mainstream financial economists and legal scholars endorsed shareholder wealth maximization,[75] and in 2001, Reinier Kraakman and Henry Hansmann declared the triumph of shareholder value.[76]

Nonetheless, other voices kept advocating for a stakeholder approach. Prominent champions include Martin Lipton, who rebuked hostile takeovers in the 1980s by, among other things, empowering directors in the name of stakeholder interests,[77] and Margaret Blair and Lynn Stout, who set forth a view of the corporation as a joint project comprised of various team members working together for mutual gain.[78]

While participants in the academic debate continued to dispute what directors were required to do under the law,[79] financial, business, and political leaders chipped in. In his 2018 letter, BlackRock's CEO Larry Fink warned:

> To prosper over time, every company must not only deliver financial performance, but also show how it makes a positive contribution to society. Companies must

[73] Milton Friedman, *The Social Responsibility of Business is to Increase Its Profits*, NY TIMES MAG. 32, Sept. 13, 1970.

[74] *Id.*

[75] *See* Michael C. Jensen & William H. Meckling, *Theory of the Firm: Managerial Behavior, Agency Costs and Ownership Structure*, 3 J. FIN. ECON. 305 (1976) (arguing that managers of corporations should act as agents of shareholders and focus exclusively on their wealth); ROBERT C. CLARK, CORPORATE LAW 682 (1986) (noting that courts stand behind the idea that the purpose of the business corporation is to make profits for its shareholders); Stephen M. Bainbridge, *Director Primacy: The Means and Ends of Corporate Governance*, 97 NW. U. L. REV. 547, 563 (2003) (noting that "most corporate law scholars embrace some variant of shareholder primacy"); D. Gordon Smith, *The Shareholder Primacy Norm*, 23 J. CORP. L. 277, 280 (1998) ("The shareholder primacy norm is considered fundamental to corporate law."); Henry Hansmann & Reinier Kraakman, *The End of History for Corporate Law*, 89 GEO. L.J. 439, 439 (2001).

[76] *Id.* at 440–41 (noting consensus amongst scholars, business officials, and policymakers that "managers of the corporation should be charged with the obligation to manage the corporation in the interests of the shareholders.").

[77] *See* Martin Lipton, *Takeover Bids in the Target's Boardroom*, 35 BUS. LAW. 101 (1979).

[78] *See* Margaret M. Blair & Lynn A. Stout, *A Team Production Theory of Corporate Law*, 85 VA. L. REV. 247, 250–51 (1999).

[79] *Compare* Leo E. Strine, Jr., *The Dangers of Denial: The Need for A Clear-Eyed Understanding of the Power and Accountability Structure Established by the Delaware General Corporation Law*, 50 WAKE FOREST L. REV. 761, 768 (2015) (concluding that "directors must make stockholder welfare their sole end, and that other interests may be taken into consideration only as a means of promoting stockholder welfare.") *with* LYNN STOUT, THE SHAREHOLDER VALUE MYTH: HOW PUTTING SHAREHOLDERS FIRST HARMS INVESTORS, CORPORATIONS, AND THE PUBLIC 31 (2012) (arguing that the business judgment rule and other judicial doctrines in Delaware allow boards broad latitude to make decisions for businesses).

> benefit all of their stakeholders, including shareholders, employees, customers, and the communities in which they operate.[80]

Not long later, in August 2019, the Business Roundtable, the lobbying organization of CEOs of America's largest corporations, embraced the stakeholder approach in an impactful one-pager signed by its CEO members titled "Statement on the Purpose of a Corporation" (the BRT Statement).[81] The statement emphasized the importance of all stakeholders – customers, employees, suppliers, communities, and shareholders – [82] and pledged to deliver value to customers, ensure fair compensation and development opportunities for employees, engage ethically with suppliers, support sustainability and community well-being, and generate long-term value for shareholders through transparency and engagement.[83]

The works of British Economist Colin Mayer and prominent American legal practitioner Martin Lipton heavily influenced the BRT Statement. Mayer proposed a new agenda for establishing the corporation as a force for societal prosperity in two books.[84] Lipton long advocated for corporations and institutional investors to collaborate on long-term, sustainable strategies, aiming to both preempt regulatory intervention and mitigate short-termism through private sector solutions.[85]

Fink and especially the BRT Statement reignited the scholarly debate. While most accounts were critical of the BRT Statement, which was found opportunistic[86] and incapable of redressing societal ails,[87] others were supportive.[88]

80 Larry Fink, *2018 Letter to CEOs: A Sense of Purpose*, BlackRock (2018), www.blackrock.com/corporate/investor-relations/2018-larry-fink-ceo-letter [https://perma.cc/3YYU-MAEL].

81 *Statement on the Purpose of a Corporation*, Bus. Roundtable (Aug. 19, 2019), www.businessroundtable.org/business-roundtable-redefines-the-purpose-of-a-corporation-to-promote-an-economy-that-serves-all-americans.

82 *Id.*

83 *Id.*

84 *See generally* Colin Mayer, Prosperity: Better Business Makes Greater Good (2018) *and* Colin Mayer, Firm Commitment: Why the Corporation is Failing Us and How to Restore Trust in It (2013).

85 In August 2016, Martin Lipton issued a memorandum for the International Business Council of the World Economic Forum, calling for a paradigm shift in corporate governance. *See* Martin Lipton, *Corporate Governance: The New Paradigm*, Harv. L. Sch. F. on Corp. Governance (Jan. 11, 2017), https://corpgov.law.harvard.edu/2017/01/11/corporate-governance-the-new-paradigm/#1.

86 *See for example*, Lucian A. Bebchuk & Roberto Tallarita, *The Illusory Promise of Stakeholder Governance*, 106 Cornell L. Rev. 91, 91 (2020).

87 Matteo Gatti & Chrystin Ondersma, *Can A Broader Corporate Purpose Redress Inequality? The Stakeholder Approach Chimera*, 46 J. Corp. L. 1 (2020).

88 *See for example*, Leo E. Strine, Jr., *Restoration: The Role Stakeholder Governance Must Play in Recreating a Fair and Sustainable American Economy: A Reply to Professor Rock*, 76 Bus. Lawyer 397 (2021); Aneil Kovvali, *Stark Choices for Corporate Reform*, 123 Colum. L. Rev. 693 (2023). For a study finding that corporations whose CEOs had signed the BRT Statement experienced statistically significant positive abnormal stock market returns relative to other corporations, see Jens Dammann & Daniel Lawrence, CEOs' *Endorsements of Stakeholder Values: Cheap Talk or Meaningful Signal? An Empirical Analysis*, 49 J. Corp. L. 577 (2024).

Importantly, politicians took notice: Senators Elizabeth Warren and Bernie Sanders embraced the stakeholder approach in bills to reform corporate law they proposed while vying for the Democratic nomination in the 2020 presidential election.[89]

Intuitively, as Chapter 3 further illustrates, when corporate law formally endorses a stakeholder approach, directors could virtually justify all corporate governing initiatives. Regardless, Chapter 3 also makes it clear that directors enjoy sufficient discretion even under a shareholder approach. In any event, no matter where the law stands on the issue, stakeholderism is once again on the table, likely emboldening executives who pursue a corporate governing agenda.

### 3 *Rent Protection: Corporate Political Spending, Lobbying, and Politics at Work*

Corporations are well-equipped and motivated to engage politically due to their extensive lobbying expertise. Each year, they make considerable expenditures to protect and advance their interests.[90] Corporate money in US politics accelerated in the wake of the controversial Supreme Court decision in *Citizens United*, which prohibited the government to restrict independent expenditures for political communications by corporations so long as such spending is independent of a party or a candidate.[91] Not only has political spending increased since then,[92] but the 2024 election was one of the most expensive ever.[93] All the while,

[89] *See* Accountable Capitalism Act, S. 3348, 115th Cong. § 5 (2018); *Corporate Accountability and Democracy Plan*, BernieSanders.com, https://berniesanders.com/issues/corporate-accountability-and-democracy/ [https://perma.cc/EF45-BPGV].

[90] For instance, in the US, Fortune 100 companies spent $2 billion on lobbying efforts between 2014 and 2017, the US Chamber of Commerce spent nearly $82 million in the first nine months of 2020 (and over $77 million in 2019), and the Business Roundtable spent around $17 million in the first nine months of 2020 (and almost $20 million in 2019). Matteo Gatti & Chrystin Ondersma, *Stakeholder Syndrome: Does Stakeholderism Derail Effective Protections for Weaker Constituencies?*, 100 N.C. L. Rev. 167, 210 (2021).

[91] *See* Citizens United v. Fed. Election Comm'n, 558 U.S. 310, 336–66 (2010).

[92] In the five years after *Citizens United*, super PACs, corporations, labor unions, and other outside groups spent almost $2 billion on federal elections – two and a half times more than in the years preceding *Citizens United*. *See* Daniel I. Weiner, Citizens United Five Years Later, Brennan Ctr. for Just. 4 (2015), www.brennancenter.org/sites/default/files/2019-08/Report_Citizens_United_%205_%20Years_%20Later.pdf [https://perma.cc/3LXQ-MLKX].

[93] During the 2024 election cycle, high-net-worth donors from diverse industries – ranging from tech entrepreneurs like Dustin Moskovitz and Reid Hoffman, co-founders of Facebook and LinkedIn, to legacy business magnates such as Timothy Mellon of the Mellon banking family and Miriam Adelson of Las Vegas Sands – contributing from tens to hundreds of million dollars to political campaigns. Alan Kronenberg, *The Biggest Political Donors of the 2024 Election*, U.S. News & World Rep. (Nov. 5, 2024), www.usnews.com/news/elections/articles/2024-11-05/the-biggest-political-donors-of-the-2024-election. Notably, Elon Musk donated nearly a quarter of a billion dollars to PACs supporting Donald Trump's campaign. Sarah E. Needleman & Anthony DeBarros, *Elon Musk Donated*

corporations lobby heavily to prevent any rule requiring them to disclose how much they spend on political campaigns.[94]

Low visibility is, in fact, a strategy.[95] The lobbying effort typically occurs without the public noticing, thanks to indirect lobbying via intermediaries such as the US Chamber of Commerce and the Business Roundtable.[96] The Chamber of Commerce does not disclose the identities of its donors[97] and overwhelmingly directs its lobbying expenditures to conservative candidates and committees.[98] Smaller organizations – such as the American Legislative Exchange Council (ALEC) – raise money from corporations and conservative foundations and then draft and lobby pro-business legislation on such issues as minimum wage, "right to work" bills, tort reform, and tax cuts.[99] Hence, in many cases, several corporations professing to support progressive causes donate substantial sums to legislation that goes in the opposite direction.[100] This is part of a broader phenomenon: Many super-wealthy donors

*Over $250 Million to Pro-Trump Super PACs*, WALL ST. J. (Dec. 6, 2024), www.wsj.com/politics/elections/elon-musk-trump-republican-super-pac-investment-78a725cb.

94 *See* Luigi Zingales, *Corporations Fight Push for Donation Disclosure*, GULF TIMES (June 3, 2013, 11:24 PM), www.gulf-times.com/story/355016/Corporations-fight-push-for-donation-disclosure [https://perma.cc/G24M-3USK]; Lucian A. Bebchuk, Robert J. Jackson Jr., James D. Nelson & Roberto Tallarita, *The Untenable Case for Keeping Investors in the Dark*, 10 HARV. BUS. L. REV. 1, 3–4 (2020).

95 BENJAMIN I. PAGE & MARTIN GILENS, DEMOCRACY IN AMERICA? WHAT HAS GONE WRONG AND WHAT WE CAN DO ABOUT IT 140 (2017) ("One of the keys to understanding lobbying is that most of it proceeds out of the public eye, in *low-visibility* settings where no public awareness or opposition is likely to arise." Emphasis in original.).

96 John M. de Figueiredo & Brian Kelleher Richter, *Advancing the Empirical Research on Lobbying*, 17 ANN. REV. POL. SCI. 163, 165 (2014) (noting that large corporations are far more represented in these lobbying efforts than small business interests, with the latter typically using trade associations). *See* Lucian A. Bebchuk & Robert Jackson, *Shining Light on Corporate Political Spending*, 101 GEO. L.J. 923, 931 (2013). In 2012, interest groups spent $3.5 billion to lobby the federal government, several times more than the roughly $750 million interest groups and that PACs (including super-PACs) were spending annually on campaign contributions at the time.

97 DAN DUDIS, THE CHAMBER OF SECRETS: AN INVESTIGATION INTO WHO FUNDS THE NOTORIOUSLY OPAQUE U.S. CHAMBER OF COMMERCE, PUB. CITIZEN 3 (Sept. 13, 2017), https://chamberofcommercewatch.org/wp-content/uploads/2017/09/Chamber_of_Secrets_members_report.pdf.

98 The lobbying activity of the US Chamber of Commerce includes opposing minimum wage increases, labor and employment provisions of bills designed to enhance family and medical leave, bills designed to protect pregnant women from discrimination, occupational safety and health rights, and so forth. *See* the full list at *Downloadable Lobbying Databases*, U.S. SENATE, www.senate.gov/legislative/Public_Disclosure/database_download.htm [https://perma.cc/7YBS-YF6U].

99 *See* Mike McIntire, *Conservative Nonprofit Acts as a Stealth Business Lobbyist*, N.Y. TIMES (Apr. 21, 2012), www.nytimes.com/2012/04/22/us/alec-a-tax-exempt-group-mixes-legislators-and-lobbyists.html?pagewanted=all (noting that corporate representatives sit at ALEC conferences with legislators on various task forces that address topics like telecom, health care, and product liability).

100 Corporate funds were used to "seat candidates who have gerrymandered legislative districts and put in place ballot restrictions harming black people; opposed action to address climate change; opposed LGBTQ+ rights; attacked the Affordable Care Act, including during the pandemic; and sought to restrain women's reproductive rights." Strine, *supra* note 88, at 422, n.84.

in the US are not necessarily conservative on social issues yet donate to conservative politicians because they support their economic policies.[101]

Similarly, corporations sometimes advance their self-interest by creating or funneling money to faux grassroots organizations that purport to act in pursuit of social causes. This lobbying, known as "astroturf activism,"[102] shapes public perception by creating fake citizen groups or scientific bodies to publish articles or ostensible "research" that undermines climate change or health science evidence.[103] It is not just the money spent – disinformation campaigns by lobbying groups have significantly confused public opinion on many critical issues, climate first and foremost.[104]

In addition, employers mobilize their own workers – sometimes in coercive ways – to lobby for business-friendly causes: Workers' support to their employers notably includes helping to persuade public opinion.[105] Political scientists show how employer mobilization shapes congressional work, as legislative staffers find it helpful "especially when it involves having employees express their support for or opposition to particular policy proposals."[106]

## B SOCIETAL DRIVERS FOR CORPORATE INVOLVEMENT

Corporations engage in corporate governing also for macro reasons. Below, I illustrate three significant drivers: broad societal shifts, reactions to the first Trump presidency, and political paralysis.

[101] Benjamin I. Page, Jason Seawright & Matthew J. Lacombe, Billionaires and Stealth Politics 86–87 (2019) (mentioning that both Robert Koch and Sheldon Alston went on record as pro-choice but nevertheless supported Republicans for their policies on the budget and their anti-union stance).

[102] *See* John Braithwaite & Peter Drahos, Global Business Regulation 489 (2000) (providing examples of astroturf NGOs, including Consumers for World Trade, a pro-GATT industry coalition, Citizens for Sensible Control of Acid Rain, a coal and electricity industry coalition, and the National Wetlands Coalition, a coalition of US oil companies and real estate developers); *see also generally* Melissa J. Durkee, *Astroturf Activism*, 69 Stan. L. Rev. 201 (2017) (discussing the ways in which businesses imitate grassroot organizations).

[103] *See* George Monbiot, *The Denial Industry*, Guardian (Sept. 19, 2006, 10:45 AM), www.theguardian.com/environment/2006/sep/19/ethicalliving.g2?INTCMP=SRCH. Businesses also hire teams of individuals who pose as disinterested members of the public (often creating multiple profiles), but in fact promote corporate causes. George Monbiot, *The Need to Protect the Internet from 'Astroturfing' Grows Ever More Urgent*, Guardian (Feb. 23, 2011, 7:01 AM), www.theguardian.com/environment/georgemonbiot/2011/feb/23/need-to-protect-internet-from-astroturfing.

[104] Zohar Goshen, Assaf Hamdani & Alex Raskolnikov, *Poor ESG: Regressive Effects of Climate Stewardship, forthcoming* BYU L. Rev., Eur. Corp. Governance Inst. – Law Working Paper No. 764/2024 (2024), at 12, https://ssrn.com/abstract=4771137 (chronicling the efforts by the likes of the Global Climate Coalition in combating environmental laws and regulations).

[105] *See* Alexander Hertel-Fernandez, Politics at Work: How Companies Turn Their Workers into Lobbyists 118 (2018).

[106] *Id.* at 164 (describing survey work showing that 49 percent of congressional staffers find it "extremely or very useful" when employees "offer assistance with legislation"); *see also id.* at 163–72 (examining how employer mobilization can impact congressional decision-making).

### 1 *Shocks, Reckonings, Citizens Demand, and the Role of Social Media*

With the Great Recession still unfolding, the 2010s saw the rise of grassroots movements challenging the socioeconomic status quo in ways unseen since the Sixties. A wave of transformative activism mobilized younger generations.[107] Occupy Wall Street erupted in 2011, sparking a national debate on economic inequality. Protesters chanting, "We are the 99%," thrust wealth disparity into public discourse and put economic justice on the agenda.[108] The Fight for $15 followed in 2012, expanding from NYC fast-food workers to a broader movement that reshaped minimum wage debates.[109] While no federal change occurred, public pressure and legislative changes in blue states prompted many private employers to raise wages.[110]

Social activism gained momentum. Black Lives Matter emerged in 2013 after Trayvon Martin's killing and intensified in 2020 following the deaths of George Floyd and Breonna Taylor, prompting several corporate policy shifts.[111] The #MeToo movement surged in 2017 as survivors of harassment shared their stories online,[112] leading corporations like Microsoft and Uber to end forced arbitration for harassment claims, as mentioned above.[113] March for Our Lives, founded by Parkland school shooting survivors in 2018, mobilized millions for gun reform.[114] Though political action was stuck, corporations like Dick's Sporting Goods and Walmart changed firearm sales policies and supported gun control legislation, aligning with the movement's goals.[115]

Climate activism intensified, led by figures like Greta Thunberg and groups such as the Youth Climate Strike and Extinction Rebellion.[116] Investor and public pressure pushed corporations to commit to sustainability goals – Walmart and Amazon pledged emission reductions, while corporate leaders reaffirmed support for the Paris Agreement.[117]

[107] *See* Lin, *supra* note 3, at 1547; Barzuza, Curtis & Webber, *supra* note 42, at 1283–1303.

[108] James A. Anderson, *Some Say Occupy Wall Street Did Nothing. It Changed Us More than We Think*, Time (Nov. 15, 2021), https://time.com/6117696/occupy-wall-street-10-years-later/.

[109] Kate Andrias, *The New Labor Law*, 126 Yale L.J. 2, 47–53 (2016).

[110] *Id.*

[111] *See supra* Chapter 1, Section B.1.

[112] Holly Corbett, *#MeToo Five Years Later: How the Movement Started and What Needs to Change*, Forbes (Oct. 27, 2022), www.forbes.com/sites/hollycorbett/2022/10/27/metoo-five-years-later-how-the-movement-started-and-what-needs-to-change/.

[113] *See supra* Chapter 1, Section B.2.

[114] Ashraf Khalil & Darlene Superville, *"Enough Is Enough": Thousands Demand New Gun Safety Laws*, AP (June 11, 2022), https://apnews.com/article/enough-is-enough-thousands-demand-new-gun-safety-laws.

[115] *See supra* Chapter 1, Section B.6.

[116] Megan Carnegie, *Gen Z: How Young People Are Changing Activism*, BBC Worklife (Aug. 8, 2022), www.bbc.com/worklife/article/20220803-gen-z-how-young-people-are-changing-activism.

[117] *See supra* Chapter 1, Section B.4.

These movements reshaped how corporations engage with social and political issues, propelled by grassroots activism and amplified through social media. Millennials and Gen Z played a central role, both inside firms and in the broader public sphere, pressing for change through workplace advocacy, consumer action, and digital campaigns.[118] With 56 percent of millennials expecting CEOs to take public stands,[119] companies faced growing pressure to align with evolving social expectations.[120] Outside corporate walls, younger generations mobilized to hold institutions accountable,[121] using social media to expand their reach and sharpen their demands.[122]

Indeed, social media platforms revolutionized social activism, empowering individuals to form movements much faster and on a larger scale.[123] Social media significantly impacted markets and businesses[124] by facilitating the rapid spread of awareness and engagement through viral videos and hashtag campaigns.[125] Platforms like Diet Prada and brand watchdogs emerged as influential forces in exposing wrongdoing and holding companies accountable for their actions.[126] Executives fear damaging viral videos or negative trending hashtags more than a

118 To be sure, societal pressures to corporations, especially via consumer markets, are not new. *See supra* Chapter 1, Section A. *See also* See David Vogel, *The Private Regulation of Global Corporate Conduct: Achievements and Limitations*, 49 Bus. & Soc'y 68, 76–77 (2010) (explaining that many self-regulation codes corporations have adopted over the years stem from citizen campaigns targeting corporate practices, using boycotts, public pressure, and naming-and-shaming as regulatory strategies).

119 *See* Jennifer S. Fan, *Woke Capital: The Role of Corporations in Social Movements*, 9 Harv. Bus. L. Rev. 441, 454 (2019) (citing Weber Shandwick & KCR Research, CEO Activism in 2017: High Noon in the C-Suite 5 (July 24, 2017), www.webershandwick.com/news/article/ceo-activism-in-2017-high-noon-in-the-c-suite).

120 *See* Barzuza, Curtis & Webber, *supra* note 42, at 1296–97 (mentioning the Wayfair debacle, whereby its employees walked out because the company entered into and honored a contract to supply furniture to a migrant detention center during the Trump era).

121 Fan, *supra* note 119, at 474 (discussing how in the aftermath of the Parkland shooting, "the students moved the corporations to action; they are also the ones sustaining the gun control movement").

122 Since the dawn of radio, media has played a crucial role in shaping the relationship between business and society. *See* Morrell Heald, The Social Responsibilities of Business: Company and Community 1900–1960 83 (1988) (noting how in the 1920s, "the expansion of advertising and public relations fields and especially the new medium of radio strengthened the channels of communication between business and society.").

123 Zeynep Tufekci, Twitter and Tear Gas: The Power and Fragility of Networked Protest (2017) (describing the potential and the limits of online social movements); Marcia Mundt, Karen Ross & Charla M. Burnett, *Scaling Social Movements through Social Media: The Case of Black Lives Matter*, 4:4 Social Media + Soc'y (2018), https://journals.sagepub.com/doi/epub/10.1177/2056305118807911.

124 *See for example*, Lund, *supra* note 68, at 139 (mentioning that the Big Three have changed their traditionally passive stance on political contributions after bad press: BlackRock's shift occurred after pressure from academics and unfavorable press).

125 Lin, *supra* note 3, at 1544.

126 Jonah Engel Bromwich, *We're All Drinking Diet Prada Now*, N.Y. Times (Mar. 14, 2019), www.nytimes.com/2019/03/14/fashion/diet-prada.html.

newspaper story for the potentially far more profound negative impact of these forms of communications on their brand reputation and stock prices.[127]

All this increased exposure encouraged corporations to take a more active role in addressing and solving social issues. Most public companies decided not to remain silent on topics debated nationally because silence could raise negative implications.[128] For example, Disney initially attempted to remain neutral on the "Don't Say Gay" bill, but stakeholders reacted strongly and, facing mounting pressure, Disney was ultimately compelled to take a public stand against the legislation.[129] Corporations also feel peer pressure to speak when other corporations are expressly denouncing silence, like when Netflix, in the aftermath of George Floyd's killing, issued a statement that said: "To be silent is to be complicit."[130]

To be sure, in recent years, social media has also become a powerful vehicle for right-wing populism. Donald Trump's political rise was largely fueled by his social media presence – a dynamic that intensified after he and several allies were banned from major platforms following January 6.[131] The crackdown led to a migration to alternative platforms like Truth Social (founded by Trump), Gab, and Parler.[132] Meanwhile, X, under Elon Musk, has amplified right-wing narratives and conspiracies,[133] and Meta distanced itself from political content, curbing progressive engagement.[134] Conservatives have also mobilized grassroots campaigns against corporate governing.[135] Robby Starbuck, with 780,000 followers on

[127] Lin, *supra* note 3, at 1545; Chris Brummer & Leo E. Strine, Jr., *Duty and Diversity*, 75 VAND. L. REV. 1, 45 (2022) (describing how social media amplified the damaging consequences for Papa John's after its founder used a racial epithet and criticized Colin Kaepernick, and how competitors used their own social media to take advantage of the debacle); Dammann & Lawrence, *supra* note 88, at 16 (noting that "'naming and shaming' matters since there is broad evidence to suggest that, by and large, CEOs care deeply about their public reputations." (Citing Matthew S. Johnson, *Regulation by Shaming: Deterrence Effects of Publicizing Violations of Workplace Safety and Health Laws*, 110 AM. ECON. REV. 1866, 1866 (2020))).

[128] Saura Masconale & Simone M. Sepe, *Citizen Corp.–Corporate Activism and Democracy*, 100 WASH. U.L. REV. 257, 269 (2022).

[129] *See supra* Introduction.

[130] Lisa M. Fairfax, *Racial Rhetoric or Reality? Cautious Optimism on the Link between Corporate #BLM Speech and Behavior*, 2022 COLUM. BUS. L. REV. 118, 121 (2022).

[131] *See supra* Chapter 1, Section B.5.

[132] Sheera Frenkel, *Liberals Are Left Out in the Cold as Social Media Veers Right*, N.Y. TIMES (Nov. 17, 2024), www.nytimes.com/2024/11/17/technology/election-right-wing-social-media.html.

[133] Ann. Lipton, *The Legitimation of Shareholder Primacy*, forthcoming J. CORP. L., Eur. Corp. Governance Inst. Law Working Paper, No. 826/2025, https://papers.ssrn.com/sol3/papers.cfm?abstract_id=5120765, at 13 ("Musk ... bought a social network with global influence and turned it into a hotbed of misinformation, harassment, and conspiracy theorizing").

[134] Frenkel, *supra* note 132.

[135] Chip Cutter & Joseph Pisani, *The Activist Pushing Companies to Ditch Their Diversity Policies*, WALL ST. J. (Aug. 3, 2024), www.wsj.com/business/the-activist-pushing-companies-to-ditch-their-diversity-policies-aeb82873.

X and regular amplification from Musk himself, led successful pressure campaigns against Tractor Supply, John Deere, Lowe's, and Harley-Davidson – pushing them to scale back DEI commitments.[136]

Once an amplifier of prosocial activism, now social media is a battleground, where populist movements push back against it. As polarization deepens, the question is how it will evolve during the second Trump presidency.

## 2 *The Trump Presidency: Then (and Now?)*

Speaking of which: Trump. In the words of Saura Masconale and Simone Sepe, "the expansive phase of corporate activism began in reaction to the politics of the … [first] Trump administration."[137] As mentioned in Chapter 1, various instances of corporate governing emerged in response to controversial policies and positions advanced during Trump's first presidency.

Numerous corporations and their executives openly opposed several of President Trump's decisions. Consider the Muslim Ban, where 153 companies spoke out against it, and about 100 tech companies filed an amicus brief protesting the order.[138] Another example is the withdrawal from the Paris Climate Agreement when thirty CEOs took out a full-page ad in the *Wall Street Journal* urging not to withdraw, several executives resigned from the President's business advisory council, and Larry Fink discussed how BlackRock would pressure portfolio companies to comply with the Paris Climate Agreement.[139] The handling of the Charlottesville Unite the Right march resulted in stern criticism and several resignations by executives sitting on the American Manufacturing Council.[140] The termination of DACA was opposed by the likes of Mark Zuckerberg and Tim Cook, as well as executives at Microsoft, Google, Goldman Sachs, Disney, and eBay.[141] The decision to roll back National Monuments prompted the Patagonia website to display the message "The President Stole Your Land."[142] Trump's handling of the January 6 insurrection led Facebook, Twitter, and other social media companies to restrict his access to their platforms.[143]

[136] Jennifer Williams, *Companies Walk a Tightrope on Diversity; "No Industry Should Feel Safe,"* WALL ST. J. (Nov. 14, 2024), www.wsj.com/articles/companies-walk-a-tightrope-on-diversity-no-industry-should-feel-safe-39a1d82d.

[137] Masconale & Sepe, *supra* note 128, at 312.

[138] *See supra* Chapter 1, Section B.1.

[139] *See supra* Chapter 1, Section B.4.

[140] *See supra* Chapter 1, Section B.1.

[141] *See supra* Chapter 1, Section B.1.

[142] David Gelles, *Patagonia v. Trump*, N.Y. TIMES (May 5, 2018), www.nytimes.com/2018/05/05/business/patagonia-trump-bears-ears.html.

[143] *See* Grace Dean, *From Cutting All Ties with Trump to Pulling Political Donations, Here's How Corporate America Has Responded to the Capitol Insurrection*, BUS. INSIDER (Jan 17, 2021, 7:55 AM), www.businessinsider.com/capitol-siege-trump-company-responses-riots-political-donations-2021–1.

These tweets by the CEOs of Google and TripAdvisor are emblematic of CEOs public opposition to Trump's policies during his first term:

> The stories and images of families being separated at the border are gut-wrenching. Urging our government to work together to find a better, more humane way that is reflective of our value as a nation. #keepfamilestogether – Sundar Pinchai, CEO Google[.]
>
> Retweet on refugee policy: Another new low from the Trump administration. Unconscionable. Remember this cruelty when you vote. Not just in the next election but in every election. Not a single republican official has condemned this. The "moderates" and "centrists" are just as cruel – Stephen Kaufer, CEO TripAdvisor.[144]

Yet, during the initial months of Trump's second administration, Corporate America was notably silent. In fact, many companies, especially in Big Tech, displayed an ostensible pivot in support of Trump 2.0.[145] The reasons range from strategic calculus to fear of retribution. If compared to the corporate outcry experienced in the 2017–2020 period, the contrast is striking.[146]

True, this silence has not been entirely uniform. A handful of executives have voiced concerns, though in a markedly more restrained manner than before. Ford CEO Jim Farley criticized Trump's tariffs for introducing "cost and chaos" to American manufacturing,[147] while ExxonMobil's Darren Woods warned against another US withdrawal from the Paris Climate Agreement, arguing that such instability creates uncertainty for long-term investment.[148] JPMorgan Chase's Jamie Dimon reaffirmed his company's commitment to diversity programs despite the administration's anti-DEI stance, stating bluntly, "bring them on" when asked

[144] Quoted in David F. Larcker, Stephen A. Miles, Brian Tayan & Kim Wright-Violich, *The Double-Edged Sword of CEO Activism* 3, Rock Center for Corporate Governance at Stanford University Closer Look Series: Topics, Issues and Controversies in Corporate Governance (2018), www.ssrn .com/abstract=3283297.

[145] Kyle Chayka, *Techno-Fascism Comes to America*, New Yorker (Feb. 26, 2025), www.newyorker.com/ culture/infinite-scroll/techno-fascism-comes-to-america-elon-musk (mentioning Silicon Valley's alliance with Trump).

[146] Jeffrey A. Sonnenfeld & Stephen Henriques, *Memo to the Business Elite: It's Time to Stand Up*, N.Y. Times (Mar. 4, 2025), www.nytimes.com/2025/03/04/opinion/business-ceo-trump-tariffs.html (arguing that corporate leaders must take a public stand against Trump's tariff policies and their broader economic and democratic risks).

[147] Nora Eckert, Allison Lampert & Ernest Scheyder, *Executives Plot Strategy to Deal with "Cost and Chaos" of Trump Tariffs*, Reuters (Feb. 11, 2025), www.reuters.com/business/autos-transportation/ ford-ceo-decries-cost-chaos-trump-tariffs-2025-02-11/ (reporting that business executives are strategizing to mitigate the economic impact of Trump's tariffs on global trade and supply chains).

[148] Lamar Johnson, *ExxonMobil Urges Trump Not to Withdraw from Paris Agreement Again*, Utility Dive (Nov. 14, 2024), www.utilitydive.com/news/exxonmobil-ceo-darren-woods-urges-trump-not-to-withdraw-us-from-paris-agreement-2024/732929 (reporting that ExxonMobil warned of significant consequences if the US withdraws from the Paris Climate Agreement for a second time).

about legal threats.[149] Meta's chief AI scientist Yann LeCun condemned Trump's crackdown on academic research, likening it to a modern-day witch hunt and warning that it could drive top talent away from the US.[150]

Still, such critiques remain exceptions, and unlike in Trump's first term, they have not coalesced into a broader corporate resistance. Instead, many companies have opted for quiet compliance, with some even rebranding their DEI and ESG initiatives to avoid scrutiny.[151] Whether this calculated restraint will hold as Trump's policies take shape – or whether pressure from employees, investors, or the international business community will force more vocal opposition – remains an open question.

## 3 *Failure of Traditional Politics*

Another critical driver of corporate governing is politics itself – slow, captured, and in perennial gridlock. As a result, corporations are seen as more reliable agents of change than traditional politics.[152]

Marcel Kahan and Ed Rock explain that as political gridlock impedes the effective regulation of activities that generate externalities (for example, through the imposition of a carbon tax), it is rational for investors to expect corporations to act.[153] Zohar Goshen, Assaf Hamdani, and Alex Raskolnikov present the rise of the ESG movement as a market-driven response aimed at filling the policy void left by government inaction on climate change.[154] They detail a series of legislative and regulatory failures to address climate change, from the US Senate's failure to

[149] Caroline Colvin, *While Trump's Anti-DEI Executive Orders Pile Up, JPMorgan Chase CEO Doesn't Flinch*, ESG Dive (Jan. 27, 2025), www.esgdive.com/news/jpmorgan-chase-ceo-jamie-dimon-doesnt-flinch-on-dei/738358/ (reporting that JPMorgan Chase CEO Jamie Dimon dismissed activist pressure against the company's DEI initiatives, challenging critics to "bring them on"). *See also supra* Chapter 1, Section C.4.

[150] Effie Webb, *Meta's Chief AI Scientist Says the Trump Administration Has Started a "Witch Hunt" in Academia*, Business Insider (Mar. 11, 2025), www.businessinsider.com/yann-lecun-meta-trump-academia-witch-hunt-musk-ai-2025#:~:text=Meta%27s%20chief%20AI%20scientist%20has,US%27s%20position%20in%20AI%20research (reporting that Meta's AI chief, Yann LeCun, criticized the Trump administration's policies as driving scientists away from US institutions).

[151] *See supra* Chapter 1, Section C.4.

[152] *See for example*, Fan, *supra* note 10, at 452, 471 (noting that "[the] institutional failure has created a vacuum which corporations are now filling." *Id.*); Lund, *supra* note 68, at 90–92; Kahan & Rock, *supra* note 5, at 47–48; Strine, *supra* note 88; Kovvali, *supra* note 88; Goshen, Hamdani & Raskolnikov, *supra* note 104, at 16–17 ("In the face of Congress's poor record in addressing the grave risk of climate change, the climate stewardship component of ESG has emerged as a promising solution to the government inaction").

[153] Kahan & Rock, *supra* note 5, at 17. *See also id.* at 47: "the political system has proven unable to deal with the problems facing society in an effective way."

[154] Goshen, Hamdani & Raskolnikov, *supra* note 104, at 11–16.

ratify the Kyoto Protocol in 1997 to the repeated inability to pass cap-and-trade proposals, carbon taxes, and comprehensive energy efficiency standards.[155] They also highlight the protracted struggle over the Paris Agreement as emblematic of these shortcomings.[156]

But what makes American politics so dysfunctional? This question has long preoccupied political theorists, scientists, and constitutional law scholars, who identify a range of contributing factors.[157]

Citizens' political divide is fostered by cable news and social media echo chambers,[158] which thrive on division, outrage, and anger to boost ratings and engagement.[159] As politicians campaign, they amplify extreme voter sentiments and court donors who benefit from partisan rifts.[160] House elections, held every two years, exacerbate polarization due to their frequency. The quick election cycle pressures representatives to continuously campaign, making them more likely to adopt extreme positions that appeal to their party's base.[161] Consequently, this results in increased partisan rhetoric and reduced willingness to compromise, as representatives focus on short-term electoral gains rather than long-term legislative collaboration.[162] Additionally, while not the main driver of polarization, the current primary system weakens party control and favors inexperienced, often fringe, candidates who cater to their base,[163] further shrinking the pool of moderates.[164]

155 *Id.*

156 *Id.* at 14–15.

157 *See generally* Richard H. Pildes, *The Age of Fragmented Politics*, 32 J. DEMOCRACY 146 (2021) (describing how social media and other novel ways of communication exacerbated polarization and fragmentation in politics, making it extremely hard to govern and pass reforms).

158 *Id.*

159 *Id. See also* Paul Barrett, Justin Hendrix & Grant Sims, *How Tech Platforms Fuel U.S. Political Polarization and What Government Can Do about It*, BROOKINGS (SEPT. 27, 2021), www.brookings.edu/blog/techtank/2021/09/27/how-tech-platforms-fuel-u-s-political-polarization-and-what-government-can-do-about-it/; Hailey Reissman, *Cable News Networks Have Grown More Polarized, Study Finds*, ANNENBERG SCHOOL FOR COMMUNICATION, UNIVERSITY OF PENNSYLVANIA (Aug. 1, 2022), www.asc.upenn.edu/news-events/news/cable-news-networks-have-grown-more-polarized-study-finds.

160 Xiaoyan Lu, Jianxi Gao & Boleslaw K. Szymanski, *The Evolution of Polarization in the Legislative Branch of Government*, THE ROYAL SOCIETY (July 17, 2019), https://doi.org/10.1098/rsif.2019.0010.

161 *Why Is the Electoral Cycle of America's Congress So Short?*, THE ECONOMIST (Sept. 20, 2022), www.economist.com/the-economist-explains/2022/09/20/why-is-the-electoral-cycle-of-americas-congress-so-short.

162 *Cf.* KEVIN M. KRAUSE & JULIAN E. ZELINER, FAULT LINES: A HISTORY OF THE UNITED STATES SINCE 1974, 296–98 (2019) (chronicling the political calculous behind the choice of Republicans in Congress to not cooperate with the Obama administration in connection with the economic stimulus bill to combat the Great Recession).

163 Seth Masket & Hans Noel, *How Did We Get Here: Primaries, Polarization, and Party Control*, PROTECT DEMOCRACY (Oct. 12, 2023), https://protectdemocracy.org/work/how-did-we-get-here-primaries-polarization-and-party-control/; PAGE & GILENS, *supra* note 95, at 58.

164 ANDREW B. HALL, WHO WANTS TO RUN? HOW THE DEVALUING OF POLITICAL OFFICE DRIVES POLARIZATION (2019).

Gerrymandered districts also fuel polarization by creating safe districts that reinforce partisan divides.[165] Moreover, state legislatures have become incubators of polarization and extreme candidates, some of whom eventually ascend to Congress.[166]

More generally, US constitutional design makes it hard to pass reforms at the federal level. To advance an agenda, one political party must control the Presidency and both legislative chambers of Congress, a condition known as a trifecta, which is infrequent in federal politics: A government trifecta at the federal level has been achieved, before the 2024 elections, only in twelve of the preceding forty-two years.[167] The absence of a trifecta leads to gridlock and partisan stalemates, further intensifying polarization and impeding effective governance.

The Senate's structure and rules play a pivotal role. To be fair, in the minds of the framers, the Senate was supposed to act as a check on legislative impetus: "George Washington is said to have told Jefferson that the framers had created the Senate to 'cool' House legislation just as a saucer was used to cool hot tea."[168] Yet, the Senate's structure, where each state is represented by two senators regardless of population,[169] gives disproportionate power to smaller, less populous, and primarily white states,[170] which results in the Senate being unrepresentative of the broader population.[171] To get a sense, in the first two years of the Biden presidency,

[165] Fred Dews, *A Primer on Gerrymandering and Political Polarization*, BROOKINGS (July 6, 2017), www.brookings.edu/articles/a-primer-on-gerrymandering-and-political-polarization/.

[166] Cassandra Handan-Nader, Andrew C. W. Myers & Andrew B. Hall, *Polarization and State Legislative Elections*, 2022 STAN. INST. FOR ECON. POL'Y RSCH.

[167] After the 2024 elections, it will be fourteen years out of forty-four. Wikipedia, *Control of the U.S. Senate and House of Representatives: 1855–2025*, (last visited, July 27, 2023), https://upload.wikimedia.org/wikipedia/commons/7/72/Combined--Control_of_the_U.S._House_of_Representatives_-_Control_of_the_U.S._Senate.png.

[168] UNITED STATES SENATE, www.senate.gov/artandhistory/history/minute/Senate_Created.htm (last visited Aug. 20, 2024). *See also* ROBERT A. CARO, MASTER OF THE SENATE 9 (2002) (disclaiming that the story may be apocryphal).

[169] U.S. CONST. art. 1, § 3, cl. 1. (amended 1912).

[170] David B. Froomkin & A. Michael Froomkin, *Saving Democracy from the Senate*, 2024 UTAH L. REV. 397; Dan Balz, Clara Ence Morse & Nick Mourtoupalas, *The Hidden Biases at Play in the U.S. Senate*, THE WASHINGTON POST (Nov. 17, 2023, 6:00 AM), www.washingtonpost.com/politics/interactive/2023/us-senate-bias-white-rural-voters/. Smaller states like Connecticut, Delaware, and New Jersey fiercely opposed proportional representation in the Senate, rejecting proposals from figures like Hamilton and Madison in favor of equal representation to protect their influence. *See* STEVEN LEVITSKY & DANIEL ZIBLATT, THE TYRANNY OF THE MINORITY: WHY AMERICAN DEMOCRACY REACHED THE BREAKING POINT 155 (2023) (mentioning that the constitutional convention nearly collapsed when the Delaware delegate Bedford threatened to exit the Union if states were not given equal representation).

[171] To be sure, the rules for electing the President through the Electoral College also reflect underrepresentation dynamics, granting smaller states a disproportionately higher share of electoral votes relative to their population sizes. *See* ERWIN CHEMERINSKY, NO DEMOCRACY LASTS FOREVER: HOW THE CONSTITUTION THREATENS THE *United* STATES 38–45 (2024).

the fifty Democratic senators represented 42 million more people than did the fifty Republican senators.[172]

To make things even worse, the filibuster rule in the Senate enables a minority to obstruct legislation by requiring a sixty-vote supermajority to proceed. While initially intended to protect minority rights and foster compromise, the filibuster has long been used as an effective tool for partisan obstructionism.[173] As Erwin Chemerinsky notes, "senators representing less than 25 percent of the population can block any legislation."[174] With money's influence in politics enabling lobbying groups to capture key politicians,[175] this practice prevents reformist policies. It entrenches gridlock, creating a system filled with counter-majoritarian barriers[176] that hinder policies favored by a majority of citizens.[177]

The Senate has blocked numerous significant bills, including early twentieth-century anti-lynching legislation, multiple anti-poll tax measures in the 1940s, the 1946 Fair Employment Practices Bill, and a 1970 amendment to abolish the Electoral College.[178] In November 2021, the John R. Lewis Voting Rights Advancement Act was added to the list.[179] In all such cases, the filibuster was a powerful tool to prevent their passage.[180]

Today, several issues systematically fail to be reformed despite consensus among voters of the necessity of change:[181] labor reform, minimum wage, and gun control are measures that, when polled, garner strong approval from voters. For example, according to a 2020 Gallup poll, 65 percent of Americans approve of unions (83 percent of registered Democrats, 45 percent of registered Republicans, and 64 percent of independents),[182] six out of ten Americans support a federal $15 minimum wage,[183] while

[172] *Id.* at 11.

[173] Catherine Fisk & Erwin Chemerinsky, *The Filibuster*, 49 Stan. L. Rev. 181 (1997).

[174] Chemerinsky, *supra* note 171, at 12.

[175] *See supra* Section A.3.

[176] For an analysis of the risks of supermajority rules, see generally Melissa Schwartzberg, Counting the Many: The Origins and Limits of Supermajority Rule (2013), (noting that while supermajorities protect the rights of minorities in theory, in practice they foster interests of powerful and well-organized minorities).

[177] Tim Wu, *The Oppression of the Supermajority*, N.Y. Times (Mar. 5, 2019), www.nytimes.com/2019/03/05/opinion/oppression-majority.html; Levitsky & Ziblatt, *supra* note 170, at 164.

[178] *The Case against the Filibuster*, Brennan Center for Justice (Oct. 30, 2020), www.brennancenter.org/our-work/research-reports/case-against-filibuster.

[179] Levitsky & Ziblatt, *supra* note 170, at 136.

[180] *Id.* at 163.

[181] Page, & Gilens, *supra* note 95, at 53 ("gridlock in Washington … prevents the adoption of new policies that large majorities of Americans want.").

[182] Megan Brenan, *At 65%, Approval of Labor Unions in U.S. Remains High*, Gallup (Sept. 3, 2020), https://news.gallup.com/poll/318980/approval-labor-unions-remains-high.aspx.

[183] Amina Dunn, *Most Americans Support a $15 Federal Minimum Wage*, Pew Research Center (Apr. 22, 2021), www.pewresearch.org/fact-tank/2021/04/22/most-americans-support-a-15-federal-minimum-wage/.

seven out of ten support gun control legislation.[184] Other areas whereby citizens' consensus is thwarted by political inertia include climate change, immigration reform, and tax reform, among many others.[185] A study by Gilens and Page confirms the bias toward inaction: They found that even when large majorities, such as 70 or 80 percent, favor a change, they succeed less than half the time.[186] As one of them said, "Under most circumstances, the preferences of the vast majority of Americans appear to have essentially no impact on which policies the government does or doesn't adopt."[187]

Finally, judicial review also complicates reform, and this has long been an issue. For example, several Supreme Court decisions struck down key New Deal legislation, frustrating President Roosevelt to the point where he considered expanding the Court with justices supporting his agenda.[188] Federal courts, especially the Supreme Court, have played a crucial role in maintaining the status quo on social and economic issues: Consider, for example, its long-standing anti-labor jurisprudence[189] and general pro-business stance.[190] Conversely, the Supreme Court has not hesitated to change the status quo when contrary to its political views, overturning *Roe v. Wade* and *Chevron* in just two years, each along partisan lines.[191] The presence of judges with ideological leanings can shape court decisions and

[184] Sara Burnett, *AP-NORC Poll: Most in US Say They Want Stricter Gun Laws*, AP NEWS (Aug. 23, 2022), https://apnews.com/article/gun-violence-covid-health-chicago-c912ecc5619e925c5ea7447d36808715.

[185] PAGE & GILENS, *supra* note 95, at 53–54, 73–88 (listing (i) many factors leading to inertia, including the power of wealthy individuals, the clout of corporations and interest groups, polarization, limited voter choice, unrepresentativeness, misinformation, and constitutional design and (ii) many policies that did note get passed despite large citizen support).

[186] They also note that when a 55% majority favors a policy change, it is no more likely to happen than when only a 25% minority supports it, with changes occurring about a quarter of the time in both cases. *Id.* at 71 (citing Martin Gilens & Benjamin I. Page, *Testing Theories of American Politics: Elites, Interest Groups, and Average Citizens*, 12 PERSP. ON POL. 564 (2014)).

[187] MARTIN GILENS, AFFLUENCE AND INFLUENCE: ECONOMIC INEQUALITY AND POLITICAL POWER IN AMERICA 1 (2012).

[188] *See for example*, Joshua Braver, *Court-Packing: An American Tradition?*, 61 B.C. L. REV. 2747, 2752–53 (2020).

[189] *See for example*, Andrias, *supra* note 109, at 17 (noting that "the [Supreme] Court, among other things, undercut the [National Labor Relation] Act's protection of the right to strike, made it easier for employers to oppose union campaigns, and generally shored up managerial rights of control over the workplace.").

[190] *See for example*, Elizabeth Pollman, *The Supreme Court and the Pro-Business Paradox*, 135 HARV. L. REV. 220 (2021) (noting that the US Supreme Court has developed a "pro-business" reputation, often expanding corporate rights while narrowing corporate liability and accountability).

[191] *See* Dobbs v. Jackson Women's Health Org., 142 S. Ct. 2228 (2022) (holding that since the Constitution makes no reference to abortion and no such right is therefore protected by any of its provisions, the authority to regulate abortion must be returned to the states and their elected representatives) *and* Loper Bright Enters. v. Raimondo, 144 S. Ct. 2244 (2024) (holding that courts need not, and under the Administrative Procedure Act (APA) may not, defer to an agency's interpretation of the law simply because a statute is ambiguous; overruling Chevron, U.S.A., Inc. v. Natural Resources Defense Council, Inc., 467 U.S. 837, 104 S.Ct. 2778, 81 L.Ed.2d 694.).

influence the direction of public policy.[192] This politicization of the judiciary further deepens partisan divisions, contributes to the dysfunction of the political system, and, at times, imperils the rule of law itself.[193]

* * *

With American politics mired in gridlock, polarization, procedural choke points, and the churn of perpetual campaigning, meaningful change through traditional channels feels increasingly out of reach. That's why the corporate route isn't just seen as an alternative but as the only realistic path left – not because it's ideal, but because, at times, it feels like the only game in town.

192 Lund, *supra* note 68, at 91: "Even after rules are promulgated, they are often challenged and given a 'hard look' by courts that may lead to invalidation."

193 *See* Ryan D. Doerfler & Samuel Moyn, *Democratizing the Supreme Court*, 109 CAL. L. REV. 1703 (2021) (noting how the Supreme Court, with its conservative majority, is likely to obstruct progressive efforts by striking down or undermining legislation aimed at social, economic, and environmental changes).

# PART II

# The Law and the Merits

# 3

# Corporate Governing and the Law

This chapter contains a legal analysis of corporate governing. Contrary to concerns, established case law and legal scholarship suggest that corporate governing does not pose significant challenges from a corporate law perspective. After introducing a framework for evaluating corporate governing actions, I begin with government substitution, where corporations take on quasi-governmental roles in the absence of state action. Legal precedents support treating these actions as business decisions, shielding directors under the business judgment rule. I then examine corporate socioeconomic advocacy, which has sparked greater controversy. While critics challenge its legitimacy, case law – especially the 2023 Delaware Chancery Court decision in *Simeone v. The Walt Disney Company* – reinforces board discretion in addressing societal issues. In *Simeone*, the court rejected a shareholder's demand to inspect Disney's records related to its opposition to Florida's "Don't Say Gay" legislation, ruling that the plaintiff failed to demonstrate a credible basis for wrongdoing. The decision underscores Delaware courts' reluctance to scrutinize corporate speech on social issues absent clear evidence of fiduciary breaches. Director liability for oversight failures also remains unlikely. Although Delaware courts have expanded *Caremark* duties to mission-critical risks, they have shown little inclination to extend this to political risks absent clear legal violations or egregious circumstances. Yet, while corporate law offers broad discretion, legal risks persist in other areas such as securities fraud and ESG/DEI compliance. The scrutiny of ESG initiatives and corporate DEI policies underscores the ongoing legal and political pressures in these areas.

In this chapter, I examine the legal dimensions of corporate governing: Do corporate governing actions and initiatives pose significant legal risks for corporations and their directors and officers? From a corporate law standpoint, both case law and legal scholarship suggest the answer is no: Despite criticism, corporate governing does not present major fiduciary duty concerns.

To begin with, corporate governing is a nonissue from an authority standpoint. Since ultra vires doctrines have long been discarded, directors and officers are fully authorized to adopt any measure.[1] Issues relating to corporate purpose are litigated under fiduciary duties doctrines.[2] When it comes to such doctrines, it is helpful to run separate analyses for the two types of corporate governing activities: I address government substitution in Section B and then turn my attention to corporate socioeconomic advocacy in Section C. Section D investigates if the recent extension of director oversight duties may have any impact on the analysis. Section E closes this chapter by looking into areas where legal risk is less trivial: securities fraud and legal compliance, especially concerning DEI.

## A FRAMEWORK FOR EVALUATING CORPORATE GOVERNING ACTIONS AND INITIATIVES

Preliminarily, Section A offers a framework for evaluating the corporate governing actions and initiatives surveyed throughout this book. This framework underpins the legal analysis that follows in this chapter and sets the stage for the normative assessments developed in Chapters 4 and 5.

[1] *See e.g.* STEPHEN M. BAINBRIDGE, THE PROFIT MOTIVE: DEFENDING SHAREHOLDER VALUE MAXIMIZATION 13 (2023) ("at one time issues of corporate social responsibility were litigated under the *ultra vires* doctrine. Today, however, with the erosion of the ultra vires doctrine, questions of corporate purpose doctrine are litigated not under that doctrine but under that of fiduciary obligation."). *See also* Leo E. Strine, Jr., *Good Corporate Citizenship We Can All Get Behind? Toward a Principled, Non-Ideological Approach to Making Money the Right Way*, 78 BUS. LAW. 329, 340 (2023) (noting that "as a matter of statutory corporate law, corporations are typically empowered to conduct their affairs toward any lawful end by any lawful means.").

[2] *See* Dalia T. Mitchell, *From* Dodge *to* eBay: *The Elusive Corporate Purpose*, 13 VA. L. & BUS. REV. 155, 175 (2019).

As discussed in Chapter 1, corporations have increasingly engaged with socioeconomic issues that, at first impression, may appear tangential to their core business activities. Some scholars have characterized these engagements – what this book terms corporate socioeconomic advocacy – as involving positions on matters "not directly related to their company's core business."[3] Others echo this view, suggesting, for instance, that "policy changes in areas such as LGBTQ+ rights, while likely relevant for many firms' employees, would hardly drive a business's financial performance."[4]

This book advances a different, perhaps counterintuitive, argument: Corporate governing is part of running a business. Contrary to conventional framing, an issue need not have a direct or narrow connection to a company's core operations (however defined), nor must it promise immediate financial returns, to warrant managerial attention. As the Delaware Court of Chancery recognized in *Simeone v. Disney*,[5] contentious policies can significantly influence corporate culture and employee morale and – one might add – consumer sentiment.[6] These factors, in turn, bear directly on a firm's performance and strategic positioning, a point well understood by corporate leadership.

Some issues affect the corporation in a *direct* and immediate sense. For example, when Lotus Development extended employee benefits to domestic partners,[7] it was not merely making a symbolic gesture – it was advancing a policy of equal pay for equal work. In doing so, it deepened its relationship with both existing and prospective members of its workforce. Similarly, policies designed to reimburse travel for abortion-related healthcare[8] are not solely expressive acts; they are efforts to retain female employees who might otherwise leave or relocate. Such measures often serve to protect stakeholders despite public policy, especially when government action is perceived as antagonistic. Other initiatives focus on strengthening relationships with external constituencies, such as consumers or communities affected by the corporation's activities.[9] These efforts – while not always yielding quantifiable results in the short term – aim to foster goodwill, reinforce reputational capital, and cultivate long-term stakeholder loyalty.

Other matters may implicate the corporation more *indirectly*. Climate-related initiatives offer an illustration. In some cases, firms adopt climate policies to mitigate

3 Aaron K. Chatterji & Michael W. Toffel, *Assessing the Impact of CEO Activism*, 32 Org. & Env't. 159 (2019).

4 Anna Toniolo, *Corporate Participation in Social Debates*, 3 U. Chi. Bus. L. Rev. 361, 368 (2024) (citing Chatterji & Toffeland conceding, this is essentially a matter of framing.

5 *See* Simeone v. Walt Disney Co., 302 A.3d 956, 972 (Del. Ch. 2023).

6 *Id.*

7 *See supra* Chapter 1, Section B.3.

8 *See supra* Chapter 1, Section B.2.

9 For example, Viacom and WarnerMedia aimed at increasing social justice content or at Sephora, which pledged to source 15 percent of its product offerings from Black-owned businesses. *See supra* Chapter 1, Section B.1.

risks directly associated with physical vulnerability – such as exposure to wildfires, floods, or extreme weather events. In others, the initiatives are more collective in nature: Actions that may not yield immediate firm-specific benefits but that seek to address systemic environmental risks in the long run.[10] In either case, the rationale is consistent with sound risk management and long-term value preservation.[11]

Corporate governing takes two broad forms: internal and external. Internal initiatives involve formal changes within the firm – improving compensation and benefits, expanding healthcare access, ending mandatory arbitration, advancing workplace equity, or modifying product lines. Some extend further, adopting stricter environmental standards or revising supply chain practices. External initiatives, by contrast, involve public messaging by CEOs or corporate leadership aimed at shaping public opinion or influencing policymakers, including legislators, regulators, and courts.

A study of 293 sociopolitical activism events across 149 firms and 39 industries found that roughly 40 percent involved internal policy changes rather than public statements.[12] These initiatives reflect a form of government substitution: firms stepping in where the state does not. By contrast, external messaging aligns with what this book calls corporate socioeconomic advocacy.[13] The sections that follow examine both forms through the lens of corporate law, assessing their legal foundations, limits, and implications.

## B GOVERNMENT SUBSTITUTION AND FIDUCIARY DUTIES

This type of conduct occurs when a corporation takes on a quasi-governmental role when the actual government is incapable or for political reasons unwilling to perform. The corporate purpose literature and case law have long analyzed the adoption of corporate measures for the benefit of some corporate constituencies or society.[14]

10 *Cf.* Madison Condon, *Externalities and the Common Owner*, 95 WASH. L. REV. 1, 5 (2020) (arguing that climate activism by some in the institutional investor industry is explainable as a way to tame systemic risk); John C. Coffee, Jr., *ESG, Common Ownership, and Systematic Risk: How They Intersect*, Eur. Corp. Governance Inst. Law Working Paper, No. 541/2020 (2021), https://papers.ssrn.com/sol3/papers.cfm?abstract_id=3678197 (arguing that large index funds have been pushing for mandating ESG disclosures to help reduce systemic risk); Jeffrey N. Gordon, *Systematic Stewardship*, 47 J. CORP. L. 627 (2022).

11 *See infra* Chapter 5, Section A.

12 Yashoda Bhagwat, Nooshin L. Warren, Joshua T. Beck & George F. Watson, IV, *Corporate Sociopolitical Activism and Firm Value*, 84:5 J. MARKETING 1, 21 (2020).

13 Of course, external initiatives also include outright political contributions from corporations to candidates, PACs, and other intermediaries such as ALEC and the Chamber of Commerce, which is a theme that I briefly touch upon *supra* in Chapter 2, Section A.3, but is outside the core of my inquiry and well-covered in the literature: *see e.g.* Lucian A. Bebchuk & Robert Jackson, *Shining Light on Corporate Political Spending*, 101 GEO. L.J. 923, 931 (2013).

14 *See e.g.* AP Smith Mfg. Co. v. Barlow, 98 A.2d 581, 13 N.J. 145, 13 N.J. Eq. 145 (1953) (validating charitable contributions). For an analysis, see *infra* notes 26–27 and accompanying text.

The fundamental question is whether this type of conduct is consistent with profit maximization. Of course, whether profit maximization is *the* goal corporations must pursue is debated, given the revamping of stakeholder theories, as mentioned in Chapter 2.[15] Thus, to address the legality of government substitution, it is best to perform separate analyses depending on the perspective taken with respect to corporate purpose – stakeholderism or shareholderism.

### 1 *Stakeholderist Lens*

Under a stakeholderist view of the firm, there should be few questions on the legality of government substitution. Stakeholderism recognizes that corporations have broader responsibilities beyond maximizing shareholder value, and performing quasi-governmental functions can be seen as fulfilling those responsibilities.[16] At a minimum, the legal recognition of government substitution is less problematic in jurisdictions that have adopted a constituency statute, which expressly permits consideration of goals beyond shareholder value. In the words of former Chief Justice Leo Strine,

> In a majority of American states … specific statutes empower boards to take action benefiting certain corporate constituencies, and thus enhance board discretion even further.[17]

### 2 *Shareholderist Lens and the Business Judgment Rule*

Even under Delaware's shareholderist framework, where "the directors' fiduciary duties run to the corporation and its stockholders[,]"[18] as long as a corporate action can be tied to long-term value, the business judgment rule stands as a shield.[19] This

[15] *See supra* Chapter 2, Section A.2.

[16] *See supra* Chapter 2, Section A.2.

[17] *See* Strine, *supra* note 1, at 340 (citing Lucian Bebchuk, Kobi Kastiel & Roberto Tallarita, *For Whom Corporate Leaders Bargain*, 94 S. Cal. L. Rev. 1467, 1489 (2021) (finding thirty-three states with constituency statutes in force during the period from 2000 to 2019)). *See e.g.* Pennsylvania Statutes Title 15 Pa.C.S.A. Corporations and Unincorporated Associations § 1715 (allowing, but not requiring, directors to look after interests of non-shareholder constituencies).

[18] *See* McRitchie v. Zuckerberg, 315 A.3d 518, 536–37 (Del. Ch. 2024) (citing at n.24 several cases, including N. Am. Catholic Educ. Programming Found., Inc. v. Gheewalla, 930 A.2d 92, 99 (Del. 2007); Quickturn Design Sys., Inc. v. Shapiro, 721 A.2d 1281, 1292 (Del. 1998); Mills Acquisition Co. v. Macmillan, Inc., 559 A.2d 1261, 1280 (Del. 1989); Polk v. Good, 507 A.2d 531, 536 (Del. 1986); Cede & Co. v. Technicolor, Inc., 634 A.2d 345, 367 (Del. 1993); Unocal Corp. v. Mesa Petroleum Co., 493 A.2d 946, 955 (Del. 1985)).

[19] *See* Holger Spamann & Jacob Fisher, *Corporate Purpose: Theoretical and Empirical Foundations/Confusions*, Eur. Corp. Governance Inst. Law Working Paper, No. 664/2022 (2022), at 10, http://ssrn.com/abstract_id=4269517 (arguing that "fiduciary duties are not enforceable with … precision, i.e., the shareholder/stakeholder distinction makes no practical legal difference").

is because, as Ann Lipton put it, while shareholder wealth maximization remains the doctrinal standard, "courts *in practical effect* softened the harsh consequences of a shareholder primacist rule by mitigating its application."[20] The business judgment rule shields directors and officers from personal liability for their decisions so long as they demonstrate that they had no interest in the subject matter and that their actions were reasonably informed and rational.[21] While the justification for the rule is to incentivize responsible risk-taking for the benefit of the business and its investors,[22] "the vast majority of corporate law scholars have come to appreciate that fiduciary duty law grants boards wide discretion to advance the interests of non-shareholders."[23] Indeed, establishing the prerequisites of the business judgment rule – disinterest,[24] reasonable information, and rationality – is not particularly hard, as case law can attest.[25] In practical terms, if the long-term benefits of corporate actions are articulated and proper decision-making processes are followed, the business judgment rule will protect directors and managers from liability.

20 Ann M. Lipton, *Book Review, Will the Real Shareholder Primacy Please Stand Up? The Profit Motive: Defending Shareholder Value Maximization*, by Stephen M. Bainbridge, Cambridge: Cambridge University Press, 2023. Pp. 223. $34.99., 137 Harv. L. Rev. 1584, 1596 (2024) (describing the account of the view that "the business judgment rule – and courts' general reluctance to interfere with managerial decisionmaking – amounts to a de facto retreat from shareholder wealth maximization.") (emphasis in original).

21 *See* American Law Institute, Principles of Corporate Governance (1994), Section 4.01(C).

22 *See* Stephen M. Bainbridge, *The Business Judgment Rule as Abstention Doctrine*, 57 Vand. L. Rev. 83, 107 (2004); Stavros Gadinis & Chris Havasy, *The Quest for Legitimacy: A Public Law Blueprint for Corporate Law*, 57 U.C. Davis L. Rev. 1581, 1600 (2024).

23 *See* Lisa Fairfax, *Stakeholderism, Corporate Purpose, and Credible Commitment*, 108 Va. L. Rev. 1163, 1206 n.225 (citing Jill E. Fisch & Steven Davidoff Solomon, *Should Corporations Have a Purpose?*, 99 Tex. L. Rev. 1309, 1323 (2021) (noting that "the proposition that existing law prohibits corporate decision makers from considering and incorporating the interests of stakeholders and society" is overstated)). *See also* Matteo Gatti & Chrystin Ondersma, *Can A Broader Corporate Purpose Redress Inequality? The Stakeholder Approach Chimera*, 46 J. Corp. L. 1, 10 (2020); Bebchuk, Kastiel & Tallarita, *supra* note 17, at 751; Strine, *supra* note 1, at 340.

24 As elaborated in Chapter 6, the mere allegation that a director holds political views should not, on its own, displace the business judgment rule. If interestedness were read too broadly, no director would qualify as disinterested – everyone holds views on contested issues. Excluding liberal directors from voting on prosocial initiatives due to alleged conflicts would ignore the parallel reality that conservative directors bring their own preferences – just in the opposite direction. To set aside the business judgment rule on such grounds would be an overreach, unsupported by doctrine and unworkable in practice. *See infra* Chapter 6, Section B.3.

25 *See e.g.* Shlensky v. Wrigley, 237 N.E.2d 776, 779 (Ill. App. Ct. 1968) (not second-guessing a decision to not install lights at Chicago Cubs' baseball stadium Wrigley Field, which according to the plaintiff resulted in the loss of potentially significant revenue and establishing that "the authority of the directors in the conduct of the business of the corporation must be regarded as absolute when they act within the law, and the court is without authority to substitute its judgment for that of the directors."); Kamin v. Am. Express Co., 383 N.Y.S.2d 807, 810–11 (Sup. Ct. 1976) (not second-guessing a decision to forego a significant tax advantage to avoid a capital loss in the income statement and establishing that "[t]he directors' room rather than the courtroom is the appropriate forum for thrashing out purely business questions ....").

### 3 *Case Law*

Legal precedents support the idea that actions of government substitution in which some corporate stakeholders are awarded better treatment than the bare minimum under applicable law can be treated as business decisions and thus qualify for the protection of the business judgment rule. For instance, courts have long validated corporate philanthropy. The *AP Smith Manufacturing*[26] case established that decisions regarding philanthropy are no different from any other decisions entrusted to the board of directors and, therefore, their decisions should be subject to the same degree of judicial deference.[27]

If dedicating some resources to charity does not constitute a breach of fiduciary duties, then neither does choosing a course of action that does not explicitly prioritize short-term profits. Decision-makers who forego potential profits out of concern for some long-term implications of the underlying project enjoy the protection of the business judgment rule: In *Shlensky v. Wrigley*, a case present in several corporate law casebooks, the court was satisfied with finding that directors resolved not to install lights in the Chicago Cubs baseball stadium – which meant no nighttime games and less profits – because directors did not want to alienate residents in the surrounding neighborhood.[28]

Notably, even cases that seem to limit directors' freedom to depart from profit maximization, such as the famous *Dodge v. Ford*[29] case and its more modern iteration, *eBay v. Newmark*,[30] can be reconciled with the judicial deference described above. Several commentators of *Dodge* and *eBay* maintain that such cases had an adverse outcome for the directors due to their "confessional" nature because, during deposition, the defendants explicitly admitted their goal was not to benefit shareholders.[31] But the consensus among courts and scholars is that, absent

[26] *AP Smith Mfg.*, 98 A.2d 581, at 160–61.

[27] *See* BAINBRIDGE, *supra* note 1, at 45 (quoting Nancy J. Knauer, *The Paradox of Corporate Giving*, 44 DEPAUL L. REV. 1, 19–20 (1994): "corporate managers and fundraisers agree that corporate transfers to charity represent a calculated purchase of advertising services or goodwill"). *See also* David Rosenberg, *Delaware's "Expanding Duty of Loyalty" and Illegal Conduct: A Step towards Corporate Social Responsibility*, 52 SANTA CLARA L. REV. 81, 103 n.16 (2012) ("Corporate philanthropy or altruism is certainly protected from review in most cases by the business judgment rule."); Geoffrey Miller, *Narrative and Truth in Judicial Opinions: Corporate Charitable Giving Cases*, 2009 MICH. ST. L. REV. 831, 839 (2009).

[28] *Shlensky*, 237 N.E.2d 776, at 180–81.

[29] 170 N.W. 668, 684 (Mich. 1919) (holding that the purpose of a corporation is to produce profits for shareholders but adding that a judge will not second-guess decisions stemming from the business judgment of directors).

[30] eBay Domestic Holdings, Inc. v. Newmark, 16 A.3d 1, 11 (Del. Ch. 2010) (holding that "directors of a corporation cannot implement a corporate policy that reduces the corporation's value or profitability without a compelling justification that such a policy advances the corporation's long-term interests.").

[31] *See* BAINBRIDGE, *supra* note 1, at 46; Leo E. Strine, Jr., *The Dangers of Denial: The Need for A Clear-Eyed Understanding of the Power and Accountability Structure Established by the Delaware General Corporation Law*, 50 WAKE FOREST L. REV. 761, 777 (2015) (labeling *Dodge* and *eBay* as

such an explicit admission, directors benefit from the deference of the business judgment rule if the record supports a reasonable belief that the action – say, expanding employee benefits – is *rationally related* to the long-term interests of shareholders.[32] The logic is that a more satisfied workforce can enhance productivity, improve retention, and drive innovation, all of which contribute to shareholder value.[33]

## 4 *Summary (and Disclaimer)*

In sum, even if a jurisdiction does not adhere to stakeholderism, the broad protection warranted by the business judgment rule makes government substitution-type activity hard to challenge on corporate law grounds.

This conclusion should be understood within its specific context – fiduciary duties of directors and officers. It does not imply that all government substitution initiatives inherently comply with applicable law. As anticipated, compliance with DEI initiatives has become a flashpoint, situated between the Supreme Court's rejection of affirmative action in college admissions[34] and a wave of anti-DEI measures targeting the corporate sector and beyond.[35] I analyze this issue in Section E.

"confession cases"). *See also* Spamann & Fischer, *supra* note 19, at 12 (noting that a close read of *eBay* stands only for not allowing to deploy a pill to defend a business strategy that overtly does not embrace profit maximization, and adding that "the defendant directors and controlling shareholders … won another count and thus the war because [the Court] allowed them to keep eBay off of the company's … board.").

32 Bainbridge, *supra* note 1, at 60 (quoting Revlon Inc. v. MacAndrews & Forbes Hldgs., Inc., 506 A.2d 173, 182). *See also* Edward B. Rock, *For Whom Is the Corporation Managed in 2020?: The Debate over Corporate Purpose*, 76 Bus. Law. 363, 379 (2021) ("[I]n managing the business, the board of directors may consider the interests of other stakeholders, so long as there is some 'rational relation' to shareholder value." Cited by *Simeone*, 302 A.3d 956, at 971 n.138); Spamann & Fischer, *supra* note 19, at 11 (noting that the shareholder/stakeholder distinction is not enforceable because of the business judgment rule and arguing there is not a single case of managers or directors being held personally liable for furthering stakeholder interests over shareholder interests); Strine, *supra* note 1, at 338. *See infra* note 65 and accompanying text.

33 *See* Alex Edmans, *Does the Stock Market Fully Value Intangibles? Employee Satisfaction and Equity Prices*, 101 J. Fin. Econ. 621 (2011) (finding that firms with high employee satisfaction outperform in long-run stock returns); Hamid Boustanifar & Young Dae Kang, *Employee Satisfaction and Long-Run Stock Returns, 1984–2020*, 78 Fin. Analysts J. 129 (2022) (analyzing data from 1984–2020 and concluding that employee satisfaction is positively associated with long-term stock performance). *See also* Zoe Adams & Simon Deakin, *Corporate Governance and Employment Relations*, *in* The Oxford Handbook of Corporate Law and Governance 1037, 1038, 1057, 1060–61 (Jeffrey N. Gordon & Wolf-Georg Ringe eds., 2018) (surveying a body of empirical work suggesting that worker protections are positively correlated with productivity and innovation at the firm level). *See infra* Chapter 4, Section A.3.b.

34 *Students for Fair Admissions v. President & Fellows of Harvard.*, 600 U.S. 181 (2023) (holding that race-based affirmative action programs in college admissions processes violate Title VI of the Civil Rights Act of 1964 as well as the Equal Protection Clause of the Fourteenth Amendment).

35 *See supra* Chapter 1, Section C.

## C CORPORATE SOCIOECONOMIC ADVOCACY AND FIDUCIARY DUTIES

Corporate socioeconomic advocacy raises similar issues but has generated more uproar from its detractors. The refrain usually is that corporations should worry more about the results of their operations and less about politics.[36] Despite this, even critics of the phenomenon concede that the conduct is not problematic from a positive law angle.[37] Recent case law confirms this. The Delaware Chancery Court in *Simeone v. The Walt Disney Company* denied a plaintiff's books and records request under Section 220 DGCL.[38] The request challenged Disney's board over its opposition to Florida's "Don't Say Gay" law and sought access to internal board communications. As discussed in Section C.3, the effort failed.

### 1 A *Different Type of Corporate Speech*

Corporate socioeconomic advocacy represents a unique form of corporate speech where corporations advocate for prosocial causes that may seemingly not align with their immediate business interests. Unlike traditional lobbying, which typically pursues interests related to the corporation and its bottom line,[39] this type seeks to advance broader goals.

Given the significant expansion of corporate political speech stemming from cases like *Citizens United*[40] and *Hobby Lobby*,[41] few would question the legality of corporate advocacy in the abstract. In *Citizens United*, the Supreme Court ruled in 2010 that the First Amendment prohibits the government from restricting independent expenditures for political communications by corporations when not related to

[36] Stephen Bainbridge, *Investors Want Returns, Not Political Fights*, BARRON'S (July 6, 2023), www.barrons.com/articles/investors-wants-returns-not-political-fights-codc18b; Phil Gramm & Mike Solon, *Keep Politics out of the Boardroom*, WALL ST. J. (July 19, 2018), www.wsj.com/articles/keep-politics-out-of-the-boardroom-1531952912.

[37] Jill E. Fisch & Jeff Schwartz, *How Did Corporations Get Stuck in Politics and Can They Escape?*, 3 U. CHI. BUS. L. REV 342 (2024) (arguing that "the scope of the business judgment rule largely insulates corporate political posturing from legal attack unless a corporation's expenditures are so egregious that they constitute waste.").

[38] *Simeone*, 302 A.3d 956, at 960.

[39] The goal is to typically reduce costs (less taxes and regulations, cheaper labor) or increase revenue (winning subsidies or procurement contracts). *See* BENJAMIN I. PAGE & MARTIN GILENS, DEMOCRACY IN AMERICA? WHAT HAS GONE WRONG AND WHAT WE CAN DO ABOUT IT 139 (2020). *See also supra* Chapter 2, Section A.3.

[40] Citizens United v. Fed. Election Comm'n, 558 U.S. 310, 336–66 (2010) (prohibiting the government from restricting independent expenditures for political communications by corporations, including nonprofit corporations, labor unions, and other associations, so long as such spending is independent of a party or a candidate). *See supra* Chapter 2, Section A.3.

[41] Burwell v. Hobby Lobby Stores, Inc., 573 U.S. 682 (2014) (allowing exemptions for close corporations from a regulation that its owners religiously object to if there is a less restrictive means of furthering the law's interest).

a party or a candidate.[42] This landmark decision effectively allowed corporations to spend unlimited amounts on political advocacy, broadening corporate speech rights' scope. Similarly, a few years later, in *Hobby Lobby*, the Supreme Court held that closely held for-profit corporations could be exempt from regulations that violate their religious beliefs under the Religious Freedom Restoration Act.[43] Although this case focused on religious beliefs and concerns a private corporation, it reinforced the idea that corporations possess certain speech rights that allow expression and to act on their convictions.

Therefore, at first glance, such expansion of corporate speech rights suggests that a corporation may use its clout (and funds) to push a socioeconomic agenda because the government cannot limit corporate speech. Social advocates have capitalized on this expansion of corporate powers, urging corporations to engage in socioeconomic advocacy that aligns with their goals.[44] While corporate interests backing these Supreme Court decisions never intended this outcome, the irony is unmistakable: Having championed expanded corporate political speech, they now criticize companies for using it to support progressive causes.[45]

### 2 *Fiduciary Duties, Waivers, and (Again) the Business Judgment Rule*

Regardless of its viability under a First Amendment perspective, some speech could theoretically generate director or officer liability if it breaches the director's fiduciary duties. One could hypothesize a scenario in which a CEO's reckless social media rant is so incendiary and offensive that it alienates a substantial portion of the corporation's customer base, leading to significant revenue losses.[46] The question then arises under which circumstances advocating for socioeconomic goals could trigger breaches of fiduciary duties. The answer is rarely.

For companies not subject to the duty of care under Section 102(b)(7) of the DGCL (around 90 percent of Delaware corporations),[47] only bad faith could trigger liability. Even though corporations may adopt charter provisions that eliminate directors' personal liability for breaching the duty of care, they cannot eliminate liability for "breach of the director's duty of loyalty … or … for acts or omissions not

42 *See supra* note 40.

43 *See supra* note 41.

44 *See* Tom C.W. Lin, *Incorporating Social Activism*, 98 B.U. L. Rev. 1535, 1573 (2018).

45 *See* Strine, *supra* note 1, at 350.

46 The hypothetical is not far-fetched, as there are already examples of businesses collapsing due to social media controversies and related public meltdowns. See Mary Roeloffs, *Shopify Shuts Down Kanye West's Yeezy Site after Days of Selling Only One Thing – A Swastika T-Shirt*, Forbes (Feb. 11, 2025), www.forbes.com/sites/maryroeloffs/2025/02/11/shopify-shuts-down-kanye-wests-yeezy-site-after-days-of-selling-only-one-thing-a-swastika-t-shirt/.

47 Roberta Romano, *Corporate Governance in the Aftermath of the Insurance Crisis*, 39 Emory L.J. 1155, 1160–61 (1990) (mentioning that, by 1990, more than 90 percent of 180 randomly sampled Delaware corporations had amended the charter to adopt the exculpatory provision).

in good faith[.]"[48] For corporations with a Section 102(b)(7) waiver, the main issue is determining whether directors failed to act in good faith. Courts equate bad faith with "utter dereliction of duty:" Bad faith is triggered whenever a "fiduciary intentionally fails to act in the face of a known duty to act, demonstrating a conscious disregard for his duties."[49]

If bad faith is the liability standard, it sets a high bar for plaintiffs who must establish a conscious disregard for one's duties.[50] It is unclear how expressing views on policy matters that, at least on their face, affect various stakeholders of the corporation can ever amount to that. Again, even under a strict shareholderist approach, defendants could point out that the socioeconomic matters the corporation is advocating for would benefit the long-term welfare of the corporation and its stockholders.[51] Under a stakeholderist approach, even the faintest doubts would dissipate.

That said, even if the corporation has not waived the duty of care in its charter, the analysis remains essentially the same due to the broad discretion granted to directors and officers under the business judgment rule, as I mentioned in Section B.3. As long as directors can demonstrate that their actions are disinterested, informed, and rational[52] – which is not difficult to do[53] – they will be shielded from liability. This is something that even academics who, on the merits, oppose enhanced corporate speech concede as a matter of law:

> [fiduciary] duties do not compel directors to use corporate funds to speak, or avoid speaking, in political controversies as they believe shareholders would prefer because the most basic of corporate law doctrines – the "business judgment rule" – precludes judicial review of board decisions, absent evidence of a conflict of interest or a complete failure to exercise any care.[54]

48 *See* DEL. CODE ANN. tit. 8, § 102(b)(7) (2023), a provision that was passed in 1986 in the aftermath of *Smith v. Van Gorkom*, 488 A.2d 858, which shattered the calm waters of the business judgment rule to impose monetary liability for failure to comply with the duty of care in the sale of the company. Under Section 102(b)(7) of the DGCL, the certificate of incorporation of a Delaware corporation may contain a "provision eliminating … the personal liability of a director … for monetary damages for breach of fiduciary duty …, [except]: (i) [f]or any breach of the director's duty of loyalty …; (ii) for acts or omissions not in good faith or which involve intentional misconduct or a knowing violation of law …." Corporations routinely include charter provisions of this kind. Holger Spamann, *Monetary Liability for Breach of the Duty of Care?*, 8 J. LEG. ANALYSIS 337, 338 (2016).

49 *See* Lyondell Chem. Co. v. Ryan, 970 A.2d 235, 243 (Del. 2009) (citing Brehm v. Eisner (In re Walt Disney Co. Derivative Litig.), 906 A.2d 27, 67 (Del. 2006)).

50 *See Lyondell*, 970 A.2d, at 243.

51 For more detail, see *infra* Section IV.A.3.c.

52 *See* AMERICAN LAW INSTITUTE, PRINCIPLES OF CORPORATE GOVERNANCE (1994), Section 4.01(C).

53 *See supra* note 25.

54 John C. Coates et al., Brief of Corporate Law Professors as Amici Curie in Support of Respondents, *Friedrichs v. California Teachers Ass'n* No. 14-915 (U.S. Nov. 2015), at 8 https://scholarship.law.duke.edu/faculty_scholarship/3546 (discussing how the Supreme Court's assumptions about shareholder control over corporate political spending are flawed, noting that individual shareholders often lack information and the ability to prevent their investments from being used for political speech they

### 3 *Simeone v. Disney*

This analysis is confirmed by the Chancery Court *Simeone* decision, which in June 2023 denied a Section 220 claim to inspect Disney's books and records concerning the corporation's decision to criticize Florida's "Don't Say Gay" Bill.[55] One of the reasons for such denial was that the shareholder did "not provide[] a credible basis from which to infer possible wrongdoing."[56]

In *Simeone*, the plaintiff claimed that Disney's public opposition to HB 1557 breached fiduciary duties, arguing that the company's stance triggered retaliation from Florida officials, cost Disney key self-governance rights, and led to shareholder losses.[57] However, the court rejected this assertion because the plaintiff merely disagreed with a board decision,[58] something that, absent decision-making pathologies, warrant judicial deference even if "the decision turned out poorly in hindsight."[59]

On the one hand, Vice Chancellor Lori Will recognized the challenges a corporation faces when addressing divisive topics, especially given that shareholders have diverse preferences beyond the "shared goal of corporate profitability [, which] may not align with the company's position on political, religious, or social matters."[60] On the other hand, the Vice Chancellor noted that (i) shareholders understand that "the board is empowered to direct the corporation's affairs"[61] and (ii) the board "held the sort of deliberations that a board should undertake when the corporation's voice is used on matters of social significance."[62] Disney's public stand wasn't aprioristic. The company initially opted for silence, and only after discussing with the board "the communications plan, philosophy and

disagree with). *See also* Victor Brudney, *Business Corporations and Stockholders' Rights under the First Amendment*, 91 YALE L.J. 235, 257–58 (1981).

55 *Simeone*, 302 A.3d 956, at 966 (establishing that "plaintiff does not meet the standard for a Section 220 inspection for three independent reasons[:] [f]irst, the purposes described in the demand are not the plaintiff's own purposes [but rater of his counsel doing work for the Thomas More Society][;] [s]econd, the plaintiff has not provided a credible basis from which to infer possible wrongdoing[;] [t]hird, the defendant has provided the plaintiff with all necessary and essential documents").

56 *Id.*

57 *Id.* at 969.

58 *Id.* at 972.

59 *Id.* at 969.

60 *Id.* at 969–70.

61 *Id.* (citing 8 *Del. C.* § 141(a) and noting that the Disney shareholders were on notice because of a publicly available internal policy on political engagement). *Cf.* The Walt Disney Company, *Political Giving and Participation in the Formulation of Public Policy in the United States* at 1 (July 2020), https://thewaltdisneycompany.com/app/uploads/2020/07/Political-Giving-and-Participation-in-the-Formulation-of-Public-Policy-2020.pdf. *But see*, for a response to this line of arguing, Lucian A. Bebchuk & Robert J. Jackson, Jr., *Corporate Political Speech: Who Decides?*, 124 HARV. L. REV. 83, 113 (2010) (referring to "generic objections that may be raised in response to the many existing mandatory corporate law rules that protect minority shareholders from diversions of value by the majority").

62 *Simeone*, 302 A.3d 956, at 970.

approach regarding Florida legislation and employee response"[63] did the CEO announce opposition to the bill.[64]

The Chancery Court confirmed long-standing Delaware case law allowing boards to exercise business judgment to pursue the interests of corporate stakeholders as "rationally related" to building long-term value.[65] Quoting *eBay*, Vice Chancellor Will abstained from questioning "rational judgments about how promoting non-stockholder interests ... ultimately promote stockholder value."[66] Further, the Chancery Court also denied that Disney "'ignored a known risk' of negative consequences from opposing the legislation[,]"[67] by noting that while the board "could have avoided political blowback by remaining silent on HB 1557[,] ... doing so could have damaged the company's corporate culture and employee morale."[68] For the court, "the weighing of these key risks by disinterested [directors did] not evidence a potential lack of due care, let alone bad faith."[69]

## D OVERSIGHT DUTIES?

Thus far, the analysis has focused on corporate decisions that directly shape business outcomes. But what if the alleged loss stems from a failure to oversee risks associated with certain initiatives taken by management? The Target controversy provides a useful hypothetical: the company faced conservative backlash and boycotts over its Pride merchandise display, allegedly aimed at children, leading to financial losses.[70] One could argue the directors failed to oversee the political risk embedded in the managerial decision to sell the merchandise. While Target is not a Delaware corporation, and the ensuing analysis cannot be squarely applied to its specific case, the hypothetical can arise in similar circumstances. Can directors be liable for ignoring or not sufficiently monitoring the underlying political risks of corporate governing initiatives?

Under Delaware law, the *Caremark* doctrine requires directors to implement monitoring systems for legal compliance and respond to red flags.[71] Liability arises

[63] *Id.*

[64] *Id.* at 970–71.

[65] *Id.* at 971 (citing, among other things, Revlon, 506 A.2d 173, at 182: "A board may have regard for various constituencies in discharging its responsibilities, provided there are rationally related benefits accruing to the stockholders."). *See also supra* note 32.

[66] *Id.* at 971. *Cf. eBay*, 16 A.3d 1, at 34.

[67] *Simeone*, 302 A.3d 956, at 972.

[68] *Id.*

[69] *Id.*

[70] *See supra* Chapter 1, Section B.3. Shareholders sued Target, but pursued claims under Rule 10b-5 for securities fraud not under corporate law. Brian Craig v. Target Corp., No. 2:23-cv-599-JLB-KCD (M.D. Fla. Dec. 4, 2024). Note that Target is incorporated in Minnesota, not Delaware, so the entire section displays a pure hypothetical. *See infra* Section E.1.

[71] In re Caremark International Inc. Derivative Litigation, 698 A.2d 959 (Del. Ch. 1996).

when directors either fail to establish such systems or knowingly ignore misconduct warnings.[72] Proving a *Caremark* claim is difficult, as it requires showing bad faith – an intentional dereliction of duty or conscious disregard of responsibilities[73] – typically evidenced by a major corporate failure that went unaddressed. Early understandings of the doctrine identified *Caremark* breaches with liability stemming from failures in legal and regulatory compliance. Yet, it is an open question whether the scope of *Caremark* evolved with *Marchand v. Barnhill*, which highlighted a duty of oversight of mission-critical risks.[74] Can a corporation fail its *Caremark* oversight duties for overlooking mission-critical risks, even absent explicit legal violations?

*Marchand* can help only to some extent because the facts were damning. The company in question was a monoline firm, an ice cream maker that failed to monitor food safety, and people died from listeria.[75] Subsequent cases ruling for plaintiffs, like the one involving *Boeing*, further emphasized board failure to oversee mission-critical risks, but again with damning facts: absence of plane safety risk management, several casualties over *two* plane crashes, attempts to deflect responsibilities, large out-of-pocket damages paid by the corporation as settlement to the victims' families, and possibly even larger reputational harm.[76]

Prior to *Marchand*, some scholars contested the doctrinal validity of distinguishing between failure of oversight of legal as opposed to business risk.[77] However, for a series of reasons, Delaware courts may be cautious about broadly expanding *Caremark* to encompass political risks without a conscious disregard for legal or regulatory obligations or clear mission-critical risk(s).[78] First, recall, the business judgment rule gives directors significant discretion in their decisions.[79] In the *Citigroup* case, the Court of Chancery did not extend oversight duties to general business risk management, as it distinguished it from the obligation to monitor legal and regulatory compliance.[80] The *Citigroup* court effectively emphasized that *Caremark* should not be misused as a backdoor challenge to the business judgment rule.[81] The Target hypothetical falls under this category: rather than a typical *Caremark* omission, its management made a deliberate decision to display Pride

72 Roy Shapira, *Conceptualizing Caremark*, 100 IND. L.J. 467, 470 (2025).

73 *See* Stone v. Ritter, 911 A.2d 362, 370 (Del. 2006) (clarifying that *Caremark* requires a showing of bad faith in failing to oversee legal risks).

74 Marchand v. Barnhill, 212 A.3d 805 (Del. 2019).

75 *Id.* at 809–810.

76 In re Boeing Co. Deriv. Litig., No. 2019-0907-MTZ, 2021 WL 4059934 (Del. Ch. Sept. 7, 2021).

77 Stephen M. Bainbridge, *Caremark and Enterprise Risk Management*, 34 J. CORP. L. 967, 968 (2009).

78 Omari Scott Simmons, *Political Risk Management*, 64 WM. & MARY L. REV. 707, 752 (2023) (noting that post-*Marchand* "Delaware decisions have expressed reluctance to extend *Caremark* liability for mission-critical risks in the absence of an overlapping legal or regulatory requirement.").

79 See *supra* Sections B.2 and B.3.

80 In re Citigroup Inc. Shareholder Derivative Litigation, 964 A.2d 106, 131 (Del. Ch. 2009).

81 Scott Simmons, *supra* note 78, at 749–50.

merchandise without violating any laws – it would be hard to distinguish it from *Simeone*.[82] Thus, whenever corporations engage in deliberative processes sufficient to invoke the business judgment rule, it is difficult to see how a plaintiff could plausibly establish bad faith.

Second, absent a legal or regulatory violation, the only potential claim is for failure to oversee *mission-critical* risks.[83] While certain industries – like defense or others depending on government contracts – may face political risks severe enough to qualify as such (e.g., being blacklisted by the Department of Defense), ordinary boycotts or employee backlash over corporate decisions or statements rarely meet the mission critical threshold. Unless the circumstances are exceptionally egregious,[84] such risks are typically transient. Without more, steep drops in stock prices should not be sufficient as the type of claim is derivative, and the harm must affect the corporation first and only indirectly the shareholders.[85]

This brings us to a third point. Given the entrepreneurial nature of the Delaware plaintiff bar, it remains unclear whether non-political plaintiffs would see any upside in pursuing cases where there is no clear regulatory or legal breach – and no immediate out-of-pocket loss, such as a regulatory fine or a settlement payment to tort victims.[86] In the absence of such triggers, the cases most likely to emerge may be ideologically motivated and less likely to succeed, as in *Simeone*, which involved an inspection request that the Chancery Court ultimately denied.[87]

In sum, despite some calls for expanding *Caremark* to address material political risks,[88] the current legal landscape primarily focuses on mission-critical

82 *See supra* Section C.3.

83 Scott Simmons, *supra* note 78, at 753 (arguing that failure to have an enterprise risk management system in place may amount to a *Caremark* breach, but only so long as such a failure can be characterized as mission-critical). *See* In re Clovis Oncology, Inc. Derivative Litig., No. 2017-0222, 2019 WL 4850188, at *13 (Del. Ch. Oct. 1, 2019). For an analysis of how *Caremark* can address failure to address ESG risk, see Roy Shapira, *Mission Critical ESG and the Scope of Director Oversight Duties*, 2022 COLUM. BUS. L. REV. 732.

84 Imagine, by mere example, a durable and significant drop in sales stemming from a massive worldwide boycott generated by controversial political actions and statements of a CEO. A malicious reader may think about the CEO of a certain car corporation that was recently reincorporated in Texas; however, *Caremark* hardly applies outside of Delaware. Itai Fiegenbaum, *Caremark's Fractured State*, 80 BUS. LAW. 59, 63 (2024–2025) (noting that "*Caremark* functions differently outside of Delaware ...[:] the absence of Delaware's ancillary litigation rules makes successful *Caremark* claims substantially less likely, even in jurisdictions with exculpation provisions similar to Delaware.").

85 *See* Tooley v. Donaldson, Lufkin & Jenrette, 845 A.2d 1031 (Del. 2004) (clarifying that the derivative claim must belong to the corporation).

86 Luca Enriques, Matteo Gatti & Roy Shapira, *How the EU Sustainability Due Diligence Directive Could Reshape Corporate America*, Eur. Corp. Governance Inst. Law Working Paper, No. 817/2025 (2025), forthcoming STAN. L. REV. (2026) at 33, https://papers.ssrn.com/sol3/papers.cfm?abstract_id=5083571.

87 *See supra* Section C.3.

88 Some have called for an expansion of *Caremark* to cover broader corporate responsibilities, including political risk management and ESG-related oversight failures. *See, e.g.*, Alexandra Mothner, *Targeting Corporate Political Activity through Caremark*, 2024 COLUM. BUS. L. REV. 1014, 1045 (advocating for *Caremark* expansion to cover political risk management). But such a move would

risks, which tend to overlap with legal or regulatory compliance, and when they do not, they must be of some egregious nature. Therefore, *Caremark* does not alter the legal analysis: Risks of director liability for corporate governing activity remain remote.

## E AREAS OF LEGAL RISK BEYOND CORPORATE LAW

This chapter argues that the legal risks associated with corporate governing are largely trivial, at least with respect to fiduciary duties. However, this does not imply that corporations can operate without encountering legal challenges. Two areas remain particularly vulnerable: securities fraud, on the one hand, and compliance on the ESG and DEI front, on the other hand.[89]

### 1 *Securities Fraud*

Director fiduciary duties should not be a corporate counsel's only worry. Federal securities litigation has become a battleground, with conservative plaintiffs suing companies they consider too "woke," alleging securities fraud.[90] For example, the lawsuit against Target over its 2023 Pride campaign,[91] which survived a motion to dismiss,[92] raises important questions about corporate governing and associated disclosures. The plaintiffs, including Stephen Miller's AFL, alleged that Target misled investors by failing to disclose the potential risks associated with the campaign, which led to consumer boycotts and a subsequent decline in stock value.[93] Target's 2021 Annual Report included risk factors acknowledging potential adverse publicity and consumer boycotts related to its positions on ESG matters, such as DEI.[94] At issue was whether Target adequately addressed the reputational and financial risks of potential backlash and boycotts stemming from its 2023 Pride campaign, and the

stretch *Caremark* beyond its intended function – shifting it from a compliance standard to a vehicle for policing corporate strategy, without clear evidence that corporate governing is, in the aggregate, harmful. As Chapter 4 illustrates, no such evidence exists. This policy shift would not only exceed *Caremark*'s intended function but also risk judicial overreach into areas traditionally reserved for business judgment. *See, e.g.*, *Citigroup*, 964 A.2d 106 (not extending *Caremark* to business risk oversight).

89 *See supra* Section B.4.

90 *See supra* Chapter 1, Section C.2.

91 *See supra* Chapter 1, Section B.3.

92 Brian Craig, et al. v. Target Corporation, et al., No. 2:23-cv-599-JLB-KCD (M.D. Fla. Dec. 4, 2024) (denying defendants' motion to dismiss securities fraud claims, holding that plaintiffs adequately pleaded material misrepresentations, scienter, and loss causation regarding Target's alleged failure to disclose risks associated with ESG/DEI initiatives and a 2023 Pride Month campaign).

93 *Id.* at 2.

94 *Id.* at 8.

court found that the plaintiffs sufficiently pleaded material misstatements, scienter, and loss causation, enabling the case to move forward.[95]

While the outcome remains uncertain – especially if the case settles – the Target litigation underscores an unresolved legal question at the intersection of securities fraud and ESG.[96] This uncertainty may influence board approaches to corporate governing, prompting directors to balance litigation risks with strategic priorities and potentially adjust their focus until, at the very least, their lawyers fine-tune disclosure language that mitigates such risks.[97] As noted in Chapter 1, Target is among the corporations that scaled back DEI initiatives – only to face a new wave of consumer boycotts, this time from the opposite side of the political spectrum.[98]

## 2 *Compliance: DEI and ESG Matters*

A combination of forces – outlined in Chapter 1, Section C – has brought DEI and ESG to the center of corporate governing. A wave of lawsuits, new legislation, and regulatory shifts have made compliance an urgent concern. While ESG backlash has largely targeted the investment sector, anti-DEI efforts have struck corporations directly – through litigation and policy changes. With the broader legal and political landscape already mapped in Chapter 1,[99] this section focuses on the key legal risks associated with corporate DEI initiatives, a recurring form of government substitution.

Assessing the legality of DEI initiatives in the abstract is of limited value; context matters. The label itself covers a wide range of practices that resist one-size-fits-all analysis. Amid growing political backlash, many companies have rebranded their efforts – quietly – but continue to pursue what they view as aligned with long-term business interests.[100]

[95] *Id.* at 43. A key aspect of the ruling was the court's view that Target's general ESG-related risk disclosures may not have adequately accounted for the specific risks linked to the campaign's heightened visibility. For a critique, see Benjamin P. Edwards, *Merchandise Placement as Securities Fraud*, Bus. L. Prof Blog (Dec. 5, 2024), www.businesslawprofessors.com/2024/12/merchandise-placement-as-securities-fraud/.

[96] For a broader description of the issues ESG raises in relation to securities fraud, see *infra* Chapter 6, Section B.2.

[97] Benjamin Edwards argues that Target's prior disclosures on boycott risks were likely sufficient and cautions that the decision could establish a precedent requiring granular risk disclosures for routine business choices, such as product placement. He suggests that such an interpretation might expand securities fraud liability, complicating corporate decision-making, particularly concerning ESG and DEI initiatives. *See* Edwards, *supra* note 95.

[98] Wyatte Grantham-Philips, *A 40-Day Target Boycott Began This Week. What to Know about the Protest and Its Potential Impact*, ABC News (Mar. 6, 2025), https://abcnews.go.com/US/wireStory/40-day-target-boycott-began-week-protest-potential-119530495 (reporting on a boycott organized during Lent to protest Target's potential rollback of DEI initiatives).

[99] *See supra* Chapter 1, Section C.3.

[100] Diane Brady, *Ditching DEI in Name Only*, Fortune (Feb. 24, 2025), https://fortune.com/2025/02/24/ditching-dei-in-name-only/ (reporting that Conference Board CEO Steve Odland stated many CEOs

No federal statute explicitly governs DEI initiatives. Title VII prohibits employment discrimination based on race, color, religion, sex, or national origin and serves as the primary legal framework in challenges to such programs.[101] President Trump's EO 14173, signed on January 21, 2025, called for scrutiny of DEI practices across the private sector.[102] The order directs the Attorney General to propose enforcement measures against "illegal discrimination and preferences, including DEI,"[103] signaling an intensified focus on corporate diversity efforts. Shortly after, ten state attorneys general sent letters to major financial institutions, alleging their DEI and ESG programs promoted unlawful employment, board, and supplier quotas and violated fiduciary duties.[104]

While the Supreme Court has yet to rule on workplace DEI policies outside higher education, on several occasions lower courts upheld specific initiatives, particularly those unrelated to direct employment decisions, such as diversity statements or expanded recruitment efforts.[105] As to the former, diversity statements are unlikely to constitute unlawful discrimination unless there's a direct link between the statement and the challenged action.[106] As to the latter, these efforts have been found to fall short of satisfying the minimal burden of proof under Title VII.[107] Expanded recruitment efforts aimed at broadening the talent pool – by bringing in a wider range of skills, experiences, and backgrounds – have not triggered legal liability.[108]

are dropping the term "DEI" due to its political baggage while retaining the underlying policies and avoiding rhetoric that could provoke reactions from conservative activists).

101 *Employment, Checklist – Diversity, Equity, and Inclusion (DEI) Legal Considerations*, Bloomberg Law (last visited Feb. 13, 2025), www.bloomberglaw.com/external/document/X6158UVC000000/employment-checklist-diversity-equity-and-inclusion-dei-legal-co?showContactExchangeForm=true.

102 *Ending Illegal Discrimination and Restoring Merit-Based Opportunity*, The White House (Jan. 21, 2025), www.whitehouse.gov/presidential-actions/2025/01/ending-illegal-discrimination-and-restoring-merit-based-opportunity/.

103 *Id.*

104 Michael R. Hatcher et al., *Ten State Attorneys General Launch Inquiry into Major Financial Institutions' DEI & ESG Programs*, JacksonLewis (Jan. 29, 2025), www.jacksonlewis.com/insights/ten-state-attorneys-general-launch-inquiry-major-financial-institutions-dei-esg-programs; Evan M. Piercey & Jennifer B. Rubin, *State Attorneys General Take Aim at DEI Policies at Six Major Financial Institutions*, Mintz (Feb. 10, 2025), www.mintz.com/insights-center/viewpoints/2226/2025-02-10-state-attorneys-general-take-aim-dei-policies-six-major.

105 Stacy Hawkins, *How to Deliver Effective Programs to Employees on Diversity, Equity, and Inclusion*, *in* Championing Diversity, Equity, and Inclusion: Effective Strategies for Organizations and Institutions (Volume 1) (Oscar Holmes, IV, ed., forthcoming 2025) (manuscript on file with author), at 21.

106 *Id.* (citing Johnson v. Metro. Gov't of Nashville, 502 F. App'x 523, 535 (6th Cir. 2012); Jones v. Bernanke, 493 F. Supp. 2d 18, 29 (D.D.C. 2007); Crabtree v. Nat'l Steel Corp., 261 F.3d 715 723 (7th Cir. 2001)).

107 Bullen v. Chaffinch, 336 F. Supp. 2d 342, 348 (D. De. 2003) ("[A] generalized effort to achieve more minority representation ... does not prove ... that a quota was established. In fact, under certain circumstances such an effort may be admirable.")

108 Hawkins, *supra* note 105, at 27.

Courts have also been reluctant to second-guess a company's legitimate or non-discriminatory business reasons for the challenged action.[109]

Executive orders cannot override federal anti-discrimination laws, and Trump's EO 14173 does not impose new legal obligations[110] – only mandates investigations into "illegal discrimination and preferences."[111] DEI initiatives remain governed by existing law, and in today's environment, careful compliance with federal, state, and local anti-discrimination statutes is essential. Yet, as legal and political battles continue, the future of corporate DEI programs remains uncertain.

As previously noted, despite the legal and political uncertainty, a 2025 survey of 350 C-suite executives conducted by employment law firm Littler found that most companies still intend to maintain their DEI commitments.[112] Some even expanded their efforts in 2024.[113] That said, the percentage of companies scaling back grew significantly – from 6 percent to 24 percent in 2025 – with the most legally vulnerable initiatives seeing the sharpest reductions.[114] These findings underscore a corporate landscape in flux, where DEI remains integral to business strategy but is increasingly constrained by external pressures.

109 McCone v. Pitney Bowes, Inc., 582 F. App'x 798, 800 (11th Cir. 2014) ("Title VII was not designed to make federal courts second-guess the business judgment of employers."); Maples v. City of Columbia, No. 3:07-3568-CMC-JRM, 2009 WL 483818, at *6 n.6 (D.S.C. Feb. 23, 2009) (finding that, where a plaintiff asserts job qualifications that are similar or only slightly superior to those of the person eventually selected, the promotion decision remains vested in the sound business judgment of the employer); Mlynczak v. Bodman, 442 F.3d 1050, 1054 (7th Cir. 2006). ("Race or sex may be considered only in the unlikely event that two candidates are so equally qualified that there is no other meaningful distinction between them."); Kidd v. Mando Am. Corp., 731 F.3d 1196, 1207 (11th Cir. 2013) ("As we've repeatedly stressed, in enacting Title VII Congress did not intend to transform federal courts into a 'super-personnel department that reexamines an entity's business decisions.' Our job is instead to determine 'whether the employer gave an honest explanation' to justify its hiring decisions. If the employment gives one, we're not in a position to 'second-guess its business judgment.'" (quoting Chapman v. Al Transp., 229 F.3d 1012, 1030 (11th Cir. 2000)).

110 Stacy Hawkins, *An Executive Order Explainer: Why the Courts Will Have the Final Say on Trump's Anti-DEI actions*, Brookings (Feb. 27, 2025), www.brookings.edu/articles/an-executive-order-explainer-why-the-courts-will-have-the-final-say-on-trumps-anti-dei-actions/ ("In spite of what appear to be serious threats and corresponding obligations in these Eos, it is important to remember that Eos do not have the force of law.").

111 *Ending Illegal Discrimination and Restoring Merit-Based Opportunity*, *supra* note 102. *See* Hawkins, *supra* note 110(noting that the executive orders merely direct federal agencies on how to exercise their enforcement authority under the law).

112 *See* Littler Mendelson P.C., *Littler's Inclusion, Equity and Diversity C-Suite Survey Report 2025* (Feb. 26, 2025), www.littler.com/publication-press/publication/littler-csuite-survey-report-2025.

113 *Id.*

114 *Id.*

# 4

# Normative Foundations for Assessing Corporate Governing

This chapter explores the normative foundations of corporate governing, examining its value from various perspectives. The analysis is divided into four key questions: Whether there is a business case for corporate governing, whether it is strategically savvy to engage in it, whether it benefits social activists and society, and whether there are implications for our democracy.

The first question addresses whether corporate governing positively impacts firm value. Given its empirical nature, the answer depends upon factors such as a firm's authenticity, alignment with stakeholder expectations, and understanding of dynamics in product, labor, and capital markets.

The second question delves into the strategic considerations of corporate governing, questioning whether it may lead to longer-term risks. The analysis suggests that even if there is a business case for corporate governing, strategic mistakes may occur, potentially resulting in backlash. However, the response maintains that well-informed corporations with risk mitigation strategies can navigate such challenges. Like any initiative, corporate governing is risky but potentially profitable, and most companies plan for these risks. Importantly, corporate governing initiatives are voluntary, shaped by a firm's strategic choices rather than legal mandates. Companies embrace them when they perceive value or advantage – some have thrived as a result, while others have not. Without clear evidence of widespread harm, limiting these initiatives on business grounds becomes a challenging case to make.

The third question explores whether corporate governing effectively advances social causes and is overall beneficial for society. As discerning adults, social activists grasp the risks of corporate co-optation and can decide whether to collaborate or discontinue collaborations that might prove counterproductive. As to societal benefits, while I acknowledge that determining what is preferable for society is inherently elusive and likely to generate dissent, the evaluation of corporate governing's effectiveness should be based on past achievements.

The final dimension examines the political implications of corporate governing on democratic institutions. It raises concerns about unelected corporate decision-makers wielding political power and the influence of corporate money in politics.

The discussion highlights the risk of eroding democratic principles and accountability when corporations assume roles traditionally reserved for government bodies.



While Chapter 3 posits that corporate governing is broadly permissible within existing corporate law frameworks, it remains an open question whether it is valuable from a normative standpoint. Even if directors avoid legal liability, corporate governing can still have serious negative consequences not only for corporate strategy and value but also for society and democratic institutions.

To assess whether corporate governing is sound for both corporations and society, one must examine the issue from multiple angles. Accordingly, I structure the normative discussion around four key questions. The first two focus on corporate considerations: Is there a business case for corporate governing – does it enhance firm value? Even so, is it strategically sensible for a corporation to engage in it? The latter two questions address broader societal and political implications: Does corporate governing advance the goals of social activists and benefit society at large? Does corporate governing, in turn, pose a risk to democratic institutions?

Raising these normative questions is essential for the analysis in Chapter 5, which examines promises and risks of corporate governing. This chapter addresses each question in turn.

## A THE BUSINESS CASE FOR CORPORATE GOVERNING: DOES IT ENHANCE FIRM VALUE?

The analysis of the merits of corporate governing starts with the business case: Are corporate governing initiatives good for firm value?

This is an empirical question that the literature in various disciplines, including marketing, management, and corporate finance, has been addressing for years. I survey the most critical findings in the following pages.

### 1 *Patagonia and Apple versus Anheuser-Busch and Procter & Gamble*

The empirical literature does not reach an unequivocal conclusion on the desirability of corporate engagement with broader socioeconomic issues. What emerges instead is that the economics of corporate governing are case-specific: some corporate governing may benefit, and some may hurt. For every Patagonia and Apple – companies that have successfully led the way in political engagement, navigating backlash while maintaining strong performance – there are companies like Anheuser-Busch and Procter & Gamble (P&G), which have miscalculated the risks and benefits of a corporate governing initiative. These examples underscore the complexities and potential pitfalls of corporate political engagement.

On the one hand, Patagonia has built a market reputation as a *values*-driven company that adopts practices advancing social change in sustainability, equity, and transparency. It is often cited as a model for balancing these commitments with strong financial success.[1] Similarly, Apple's sociopolitical engagement is widely perceived as authentic, which has, in turn, benefited its bottom line.[2]

[1] *See* Jessica Vredenburg, Sommer Kapitan, Amanda Spry & Joya A. Kemper, *Brands Taking a Stand: Authentic Brand Activism or Woke Washing?*, 39 J. PUB. POL'Y & MARKETING 444, 450 (2020); Ron Carucci, *How Patagonia's Purpose Is Once again Raising the Bar on Doing the Right Thing*, FORBES (Apr. 21, 2021), www.forbes.com/sites/roncarucci/2021/04/21/how-patagonias-purpose-is-once-again-raising-the-bar-on-doing-the-right-thing/?sh=7d0e110f777c.

[2] A study found that consumers exposed to Tim Cook's public advocacy were more likely to purchase Apple products, suggesting that CEO activism can shape brand perception and consumer behavior. Aaron K. Chatterji & Michael W. Toffel, *Assessing the Impact of CEO Activism*, 32 ORG. & ENVIRONMENT 159, 161 (2019). Companies fitting this paradigm include Ben & Jerry's. *See* Joon S. Lim & Cayley Young, *Effects of Issue Ownership, Perceived Fit, and Authenticity in Corporate Social Advocacy on Corporate Reputation*, 47.4 PUB. REL. REV. (2021); Jordyn Holman & Thomas Buckley,

On the other hand, Anheuser-Busch faced backlash from conservative groups and calls for boycotts when Bud Light partnered with transgender influencer Dylan Mulvaney, with a personalized beer can to celebrate Mulvaney's first year of transitioning as part of a social media promotion during Pride Month.[3] The backlash affected Anheuser-Busch's stock price, prompting some analysts to downgrade the company's rating.[4] In the end, the company alienated both conservatives and the trans community: After a significant drop in sales,[5] Mulvaney criticized Anheuser-Busch for lack of public support and not reaching out following the controversy.[6] Florida Governor Ron DeSantis even threatened to sue Anheuser-Busch's board through one of the Florida state pension funds.[7] P&G experienced similar criticism when Gillette released an ad to address toxic masculinity, replacing the brand's tagline "The Best a Man Can Get" with "The Best a Man Can Be." Protests on social media ensued immediately, with twice as many "dislikes" than "likes" on YouTube; angered consumers launched boycott campaigns, and representatives of the ad agency even received death threats.[8] While the CEO defended the campaign, this episode is a textbook example of failed brand messaging – the key to the failure, according to marketing experts, was the sharp departure from the brand's traditional product-focused and men-centered advertising.[9]

*How Ben & Jerry's Perfected the Delicate Recipe for Corporate Activism*, BLOOMBERG (July 22, 2020), www.bloomberg.com/news/features/2020-07-22/how-ben-jerry-s-applied-its-corporate-activism-recipe-to-blm#xj4y7vzkg; Alison Beard, *Why Ben & Jerry's Speak Out*, HARV. BUS. REV. (Jan. 13, 2021), https://hbr.org/2021/01/why-ben-jerrys-speaks-out.

3 Christina Chaddar Berk, *Boycotts hit stocks hard. Here's what might be next for Bud, Target and others caught in the anti-Pride backlash*, CNBC (June 3, 2023), www.cnbc.com/2023/06/03/anti-pride-backlash-what-target-anheuser-busch-and-others-should-expect-next-.html.

4 *See* Kristopher J. Brooks, *Bud Light Gets Stock Downgrade Just Weeks after Dylan Mulvaney Fallout*, CBS NEWS (May 12, 2023), www.cbsnews.com/news/bud-light-dylan-mulvaney-stock-downgrade-anheuser-busch-sales/.

5 Julie Creswell, *Cheaper than Water? Retailers Try to Unload Bud Light.*, N.Y. TIMES (May 31, 2023), www.nytimes.com/2023/06/29/business/bud-light-sales.html.

6 Carlos De Loera, *Dylan Mulvaney Says Bud Light Never Contacted Her after Anti-trans Backlash*, L.A. TIMES (June 30, 2023), www.latimes.com/entertainment-arts/story/2023-06-30/dylan-mulvaney-bud-light-transphobic-backlash-trans-rights. Mulvaney pointed out that hiring a trans person for marketing while failing to publicly support them in the face of backlash can reinforce transphobia and expose individuals to real harm. The controversy played out against a wider backdrop of escalating attacks on trans rights.

7 While Anheuser-Busch miscalculated consumer response and mishandled messaging, I do not suggest its actions violated corporate law, as that would be a matter of Belgian law, on which I do not opine (Bud Light's parent company, AB InBev, is incorporated in Belgium and governed by its corporate law). *See* Benjamin Edwards, *Ron DeSantis' Legal Threats against Bud Light's Parent Company Are Dumb and Bad for Florida*, THE DAILY BEAST (updated July 24, 2023, 4:13 PM EDT), www.thedailybeast.com/ron-desantis-legal-threats-against-bud-lights-parent-company-are-dumb-and-bad-for-florida.

8 *See* Susan Fournier, Shuba Srinivasan & Patrick Marrinan, *Turning Socio-Political Risk to Your Brand's Advantage*, 13.2 NIM MARKETING INTEL. REV. 18, 24 (2021).

9 *Id.*

Corporations elicit different reactions from their engagement in social policies. Yet, this is not something to be particularly surprised by. An article by Yashoda Bhagwat, Nooshin Warren, Joshua Beck, and George Watson frames what I describe as corporate governing in risk/reward terms; corporate governing is more of a feature than a bug of running a business: "while … a risky marketing strategy that investors are generally wary of, [corporate governing] may also be advantageous."[10] This is why it works for some companies and brands but not for others.[11]

### 2 *Indicators from the Empirical Literature: Divisiveness of the Issue, Firm Priors, and Authenticity*

The empirical literature is mixed at best and it is hard to establish whether, even on average, corporate governing is positive or negative. But even if it is impossible to establish whether corporate governing is, in the aggregate, advantageous, the literature suggests that certain variables matter. Such variables include the divisiveness of the issue at stake, the corporation's history, firm authenticity, firm message, and the type of intervention.

#### a Divisiveness

The extent to which an issue is divisive impacts firm value: Taking a public stand on a broadly supported issue is unlikely to be detrimental and can, in fact, create value. On the one hand, a study by Tommaso Bondi, Vanessa Burbano, and Fabrizio Dell'Acqua finds that "when opinion is symmetrically divided, firms are better off being non-political … [; but] when opinion about an issue is (sufficiently) asymmetric, firms can potentially benefit from taking the ideological stance aligned with the (overwhelmingly) popular (and strongly felt) opinion."[12] On the other hand, how closely the underlying issue relates to the business or the workplace is a

[10] *See* Yashoda Bhagwat, Nooshin L. Warren, Joshua T. Beck & George F. Watson, IV, *Corporate Sociopolitical Activism and Firm Value*, 84:5 J. MARKETING 1, 16 (2020):

> Investors on average react negatively to [corporate social activism or] CSA, especially when it deviates from the values of key stakeholders and signals the firm's resource-intensive commitment to activism. However, they also reward activism when it closely aligns with stakeholders. In addition, … customers reward CSA when it resonates with their personal values and attest that it can be an effective means for firms to appeal to their target markets.

*See also* Omari Scott Simmons, *Political Risk Management*, 64 WM. & MARY L. REV. 707, 713–14 (2023) (framing corporate governing as a risk management issue).

[11] *Cf.* Hajin Kim, *Expecting Corporate Prosociality*, 53 J. LEGAL STUD. 267, 271 (2024) (noting "a diversity of firms and stakeholders[]" when it comes to stakeholder expectations on prosocial firm behavior).

[12] Tommaso Bondi, Vanessa C. Burbano & Fabrizio Dell'Acqua, *When (Not) to Talk Politics in Business: Experimental Evidence*, STRATEGIC MGMT. J., 1, 112–13 (2025), https://doi.org/10.1002/smj.3684.

determinant of the success of the initiative: Some research suggests that favorable employee reactions to CEO activism are predominantly associated with positions taken on workplace-related issues, such as diversity and pay equality; conversely, CEO stances on topics like politics, the environment, or other social issues generally result in an employee response considered insignificant.[13]

Determining what divides society (and by how much) isn't always easy because society's political beliefs derive from historical context and constantly evolve (and only sometimes resolve) through time.[14]

In any event, if well played, *some* degree of controversy can help a brand:

> an essential feature of political activism is the partisan nature of the issue on which the activities are focused. This means there will be firm stakeholders – consumers, partners, employees, policy makers, and so on – who want to maintain the status quo on these issues and those who seek a changed world. As a result, when brands engage on these topics, they need to pick a side and either challenge or defend the status quo.[15]

### b Firm Priors, Goals, and Authenticity

The specific history of the corporation and its broader goals matter significantly, as the Patagonia, Apple, Anheuser-Busch, and Procter & Gamble stories illustrate.[16] Studies by scholars in the marketing and management disciplines posit that the public must perceive the corporation's message as authentic. A study by Henry Sarvaes and Ane Tamayo finds that firms that successfully translate CSR initiatives into financial value enjoy good market reputation, whereas firms with poor reputations often fail to benefit from CSR and may even see negative effects on shareholder value.[17] Aaron Chatterji and Michael Toffel similarly argue that, to be value enhancing, corporate activism must be perceived as authentic and aligned with both the leader and the business to influence public policy.[18] Empirical studies further support the role of corporate reputation and CEO integrity in shaping

[13] Anahit Mkrtchyan, Jason Sandvik & Da Xu, *Employee Responses to CEO Activism*, 78 J. Acct. & Econ., no. 1, 2024, at 101701, 34. *See also See also* Anna Toniolo, *Corporate Participation in Social Debates*, 3 U. Chi. Bus. L. Rev. 361, 364 (2024) (mentioning that PR firm Zeno advised corporate clients against making statements on abortion, arguing it to be a "no-win" scenario where any position taken could risk alienating 15 percent to 30 percent of stakeholders).

[14] Bhagwat, Warren, Beck & Watson, *supra* note 10, at 2.

[15] Christine Moorman, *Commentary: Brand Activism in a Political World*, 39 J. Pub. Pol'y & Marketing 388, 389 (2020).

[16] *See supra* Section A.1.

[17] Henri Servaes & Ane Tamayo, *The Impact of Corporate Social Responsibility on Firm Value*, 59 Management Science 1045, 1058–59 (2013).

[18] Aaron K. Chatterji & Michael W. Toffel, *The New CEO Activists*, Harv. Bus. Rev. (Jan.-Feb. 2018), https://hbr.org/2018/01/the-new-ceo-activists, at 14 (noting that "[t]here should be a compelling narrative for why *this* issue matters to *this* CEO of *this* business at *this* time." (emphasis in original)).

financial outcomes.[19] More broadly, stakeholder ability to "distinguish genuine dedication from marketing slogans"[20] can create value for a firm that commits not to exploit its stakeholders.[21]

Thus, Nike's bold political stances attract less attention than other companies because of the company's long history of tackling hot-button issues.[22] A study shows that for the period following Blackout Tuesday in June 2020 – when social media users (including brands) posted black screens to protest racism and police brutality – "true ally" brands performed better than "performative ally" brands and neutral brands that stayed silent.[23] According to another study, while more than half of consumers believe involvement in social issues is, for the most part, a marketing ploy, if consumers trust the brand on social issues, they will buy the products – seven out of ten will even advocate for the brand.[24] Other studies show similar results. While market-driven companies are better off abstaining from taking a stand, for companies generally considered *values*-driven, the opposite occurs: Staying silent on a pressing social issue is riskier for market perception purposes.[25] I argue that staying quiet on a pressing issue is a de facto statement – I call this "passive corporate governing."[26]

[19] *See* Hanh Song Thi Pham, Hien Thi Tran, *CSR Disclosure and Firm Performance: The Mediating Role of Corporate Reputation and Moderating Role of CEO Integrity*, 120 J. Bus Res. 127, 135 (2020) (finding that firm reputation and CEO integrity respectively mediates and moderates the effect of CSR disclosure on financial performance); Vredenburg, Kapitan, Spry & Kemper, *supra* note 1; Joon S. Lim & Cayley Young, *Effects of Issue Ownership, Perceived Fit, and Authenticity in Corporate Social Advocacy on Corporate Reputation*, 47.4 Pub. Rel. Rev. (2021) (describing Ben & Jerry's social media strategy and its perception by the public); Holger J. Schmidt, Nicholas Ind, Francisco Guzmán & Eric Kennedy, *Sociopolitical Activist Brands*, 31 J. Prod. & Brand Mgmt 40 (2022); Jie Jin, Renee Mitson, Yufan Sunny Qin, Marc Vielledent & Linjuan Rita Men, *Enhancing Young Consumer's Relational and Behavioral Outcomes: The Impact of CEO Activism Authenticity and Value Alignment*, 49 Pub. Rel. Rev. 49 102312 (2023).

[20] Holger Spamann & Jacob Fisher, *Corporate Purpose: Theoretical and Empirical Foundations/Confusions*, Eur. Corp. Governance Inst. Law Working Paper, No. 664/2022 (2022), at 8, http://ssrn.com/abstract_id=4269517.

[21] For this argument, see *id.*

[22] Susan Fournier, Shuba Srinivasan & Patrick Marrinan, *Turning Socio-Political Risk to Your Brand's Advantage*, 13.2 NIM Marketing Intel. Rev. 18, 22–24 (2021).

[23] Nathalie Spielmann, Susan Dobscha, & L. J. Shrum, *Brands and Social Justice Movements: The Effects of True versus Performative Allyship on Brand Evaluation*, 8 J. Association Consumer Res. 83 (2023).

[24] *See* Abas Mirzaei, Dean C. Wilkie & Helen Siuki, *Woke Brand Activism Authenticity or the Lack of It*, 139 J. Bus. Res. 1, 1 (2022) (citing Edelman research and noting that advocating for the brand is more than 20 percentage points higher than just trusting the brand on product quality (five out of ten)).

[25] Daniel Korschun, Hoori Rafieian, Anubhav Aggarwal & Scott D. Swain, *Taking a Stand: Consumer Responses When Companies Get (or Don't Get) Political* 34, Working Paper (2019), https://papers.ssrn.com/sol3/papers.cfm?abstract_id=2806476.

[26] *See* Matteo Gatti, *Corporate Governing: Understanding Corporations as Agents of Socioeconomic Change*, Eur. Corp. Governance Inst. Law Working Paper, No. 730/2023 (2023), at 36. *See also* Lisa M. Fairfax, *Racial Rhetoric or Reality? Cautious Optimism on the Link between Corporate #BLM Speech and Behavior*, 2022 Colum. Bus. L. Rev. 118, 137 (describing corporate statements in the aftermath of the murders of George Floyd and Breonna Taylor and noting that such statements serve as a rejection of silence, which many interpret as complicity in systemic racism).

To be sure, authenticity matters not only to consumers but also to retail investors: a study finds that "retail investors' reactions depend on the credibility of the [corporate social advocacy] engagement and on the credibility of the company itself [and] … that the positive reaction of retail investors to [such engagement] is more likely to be influenced by moral sentiment rather than by fundamentals or attention bias."[27] Unsurprisingly, the perceived authenticity of CEO activism positively influences young consumers' relationships with the organization and their intent to purchase.[28]

Some brands match activist messaging, purpose, and values with prosocial corporate practice and engage in authentic brand activism, thus creating potential for social change and gains in brand equity; in contrast, performative brands that detach their activist messaging from their purpose, values, and practice, enact inauthentic brand activism through the practice of "woke washing."[29]

Thus, while some firms are better positioned than others in translating initiatives into wealth creation, "firms with poor reputations are unlikely to reap any immediate benefits (in terms of shareholder value creation) from engaging in [corporate social responsibility] … [and i]n fact, such activities may appear disingenuous and may well have the opposite effect."[30] Unsurprisingly, many PR fallouts stem from initiatives perceived as opportunistic.[31] One example is the 2017 Pepsi ad featuring Kendall Jenner, which was widely criticized for trivializing the Black Lives Matter movement by suggesting a protest could be resolved with a can of soda.[32]

### 3 *Indicators from the Empirical Literature: Understanding the Markets in Which the Corporation Operates*

Another theme in the literature is that corporate governing creates value only when it aligns with the expectations and political views of the corporation's stakeholders.[33]

27 Ruby Brownen-Trinh & Ajan Orujov, *Corporate Socio-political Activism and Retail Investors: Evidence from the Black Lives Matter Campaign*, 80 J. Corp. Fin. 102417 (2023).

28 Jin, Mitson, Qin, Vielledent & Men, *supra* note 17.

29 Vredenburg, Kapitan, Spry & Kemper, *supra* note 1. *See also* Mirzaei, Wilkie & Siuki, *supra* note 24, at 1; Gaia Melloni, Andrea Patacconi & Nick Vikander, *Cashing in on the Culture Wars? CEO Activism, Wokewashing, and Firm Value*, 44 Strategic Mgmt J. 3098 (2023); Andrew C. Baker, David F. Larcker; Charles G. McClure, Durgesh Saraph & Edward M. Watts, *Diversity Washing*, 62 J. Acct. Res. 1661 (2024), https://doi.org/10.1111/1475-679X.12542. For an account of left-side, "greenwashing" critiques of corporate engagement in prosocial issues, see Stavros Gadinis & Chris Havasy, *The Quest for Legitimacy: A Public Law Blueprint for Corporate Law*, 57 U.C. Davis L. Rev. 1581, 1610–12 (2024).

30 Henri Servaes & Ane Tamayo, *supra* note 17, at 1058–59.

31 *Id. See also* Melloni, Patacconi & Vikander, *supra* note 29, at 3103.

32 Daniel Victor, *Pepsi Pulls Ad Accused of Trivializing Black Lives Matter*, N.Y. Times (Apr. 5, 2017), www.nytimes.com/2017/04/05/business/kendall-jenner-pepsi-ad.html (reporting that the backlash prompted the company to pull the ad and issue a public apology).

33 Hajin Kim argues that stakeholders' expectations about whether corporations should prioritize societal impacts influence their willingness to reward or punish firms, thereby shaping corporate incentives for prosocial behavior. *See generally* Kim, *supra* note 11 (showing that stakeholders who expect firms to

In this latter regard, on several occasions, corporations have intervened *precisely* because of bottom-up pressures from their stakeholders: typically their employees (see the Disney/DeSantis feud)[34] and customers (see the long history of consumer boycotts from LGBTQ+ groups).[35] Indeed, leading scholars on ESG investing note that such a phenomenon "[i]s a product of social demand."[36]

Directors and managers evaluating a corporate governing initiative through a firm-value lens must understand the company's position across its key markets – product, labor, and capital – and how stakeholder expectations play out in each.

### a Product Market

A study by Scott Hirst, Kobi Kastiel, and Tamar Kricheli-Katz finds that "on average individuals – as investors and consumers – are willing to forgo some monetary gains to promote social interests … [and] are willing to forgo greater amounts when consuming … than when investing."[37] Yashoda Bhagwat, Nooshim Warren, Joshua Beck, and George Watson echo that "[c]ustomers pay attention to and make long-lasting purchase decisions based on [corporate sociopolitical activism]").[38] For instance, a field study by Aaron Chatterji and Michael Toffel finds that consumers were more inclined to buy Apple products among participants

prioritize societal impacts reward prosocial actions and punish harmful ones, whereas those who view profit maximization as the sole goal are less likely to hold firms accountable, weakening incentives for corporate prosociality).

34 For instance, Disney's initial reaction to the "Don't Say Gay" bill was silence, until it got pressured to speak by workers and its creative partners. *See supra* the description in the Introduction.

35 LGBTQ+ rights are among the first that got bolstered by corporate governing. *See* Carlos A. Ball, The Queering of Corporate America: How Big Business Went from LGBTW Adversary to Ally 95–125 (2019) (describing the expansion of corporate health benefits to domestic partners in the 1990s). After decades of being called out by various activists' campaigns, corporations took the initiative. *Id.* at 31–58 (chronicling boycotts and other actions in the 1970s against phone companies for their discriminatory hiring, TV networks for their depiction of queer people, and Coors for their discriminatory and anti-union positions).

36 Michal Barzuza, Quinn Curtis & David H. Webber, *Shareholder Value(s): Index Fund ESG Activism and the New Millennial Corporate Governance*, 93 S. Cal. L. Rev. 1243, 1250 (2020). *See also* Gadinis & Havasy, *supra note* 29, at 1604 ("To the extent that corporations must compete in labor markets, appeal to consumers, and coexist with other impacted parties, they need to ensure that their decisions are not only economically efficient, but also justifiable to a broader set of stakeholders.").

37 Scott Hirst, Kobi Kastiel & Tamar Kricheli-Katz, *How Much Do Investors Care about Social Responsibility?*, 2023 Wis. L. Rev. 977, 1024 (2023).

38 Bhagwat, Warren, Beck & Watson, *supra* note 10, at 16. *See also* Elena-Mădălina Vătămănescu, Dan-Cristian Dabija, Patrizia Gazzola, Juan Gabriel Cegarro-Navarro & Tania Buzzi, *Before and After the Outbreak of Covid-19: Linking Fashion Companies' Corporate Social Responsibility Approach to Consumers' Demand for Sustainable Products*, J. Cleaner Prod. 321 (2021) 128945 (presenting survey data relating to Italian consumers' reactions to social and environmental sustainability practices of fashion companies in the aftermath of Covid-19 and finding that consumers attach great importance to such practices).

exposed to Cook's CEO activism than those not.[39] They show that individuals supporting same-sex marriage were the driving force behind this effect, and there was no indication that Cook's statements influenced the purchase intent of those opposing same-sex marriage.[40]

To avoid fiascos like those experienced by P&G and Anheuser-Busch, executives must understand the value alignment between the company and its consumer base. As noted already, consumers are relatively tolerant of political stands by values-driven companies (like Patagonia) instead of market-driven ones (like P&G).[41] Also, some evidence suggests adverse reactions are more memorable than positive ones. According to a 2018 survey by the Rock Center for Corporate Governance at Stanford University, the public is "significantly more likely to remember products they stopped using or use less because of the position the CEO took than products they started using or use more."[42]

But how significant is the penalization if corporations aggravate non-likeminded consumers? It is neither too big nor persistent.

A study by Young Hou and Christopher Poliquin found that corporate gun control initiatives following a mass shooting led to a modest – but potentially meaningful – drop in in-store visits, particularly in conservative counties.[43] Liberal counties showed no significant change. The reputational effects, however, proved short-lived, fading within three to four weeks.[44]

A similar study by Hengda Jin, Keneth Merkley, Anish Sharma, and Karen Ton analyzes consumer reactions to firms' stands against Georgia's voting reform laws[45] and finds that customer visits, visitors, and consumer spending decreased at stores of companies that spoke out (relative to stores of other companies).[46] Yet, their results show that the decrease in traffic, which they attribute to less-frequent customers who spend less time shopping, is offset by loyal customers who increase

39 *See* Chatterji & Toffel, *supra* note 2, at 161.

40 *Id.* (noting that CEO activism can function as a signal, informing consumers about where a company leader stands on a controversial issue and potentially mobilizing support and fostering positive sentiments for the company, particularly among those who already align with the CEO's perspective).

41 Korschun, Rafieian, Aggarwal & Swain, *supra* note 25, at 32.

42 David F. Larcker, Stephen A. Miles, Brian Tayan & Kim-Wright-Violich, *The Double-Edged Sword of CEO Activism*, Rock Center for Corporate Governance at Stanford University Closer Look Series: Topics, Issues and Controversies in Corporate Governance No. CGRP-74 (2018), at 4, www.ssrn.com/abstract=3283297 (noting that "35 percent of the public could think of a product or service they use less, while only 20 percent could think of a product they use more.").

43 Young Hou & Christopher W. Poliquin, *The Effects of CEO Activism: Partisan Consumer Behavior and Its Duration*, 44 STRATEGIC MGMT. J. 672, 697–98 (2022).

44 *Id.*

45 *See supra* Chapter 1, Section B.5.

46 Hengda Jin, Keneth Merkley, Anish Sharma & Karen Ton, *Customers' Response to Firms' Disclosure of Social Stances: Evidence from Voting Reform Laws*, 30 REV. ACCT. STUD. 202, 205 (2025), https://doi.org/10.1007/s11142-023-09816-2 (finding that the decrease in customer traffic is stronger for stores in the state of Georgia, in Republican counties, and for corporations that got targeted by conservative media).

their shopping time.[47] According to the authors, this offsetting effect also explains the lack of evidence of changes in firm-level financial performance or stock market reactions.[48]

However, a study by Swarnodeep Homroy & Shubhashis Gangopadhyay reviewing consumer reactions to activism statements by CEOs of S&P 500 corporations in the 2014–2019 period reaches different findings.[49] Drawing on information from 190,000 stores of more than 200 corporations (81 of which made a social statement with their CEO), the authors find "that store visits increased by 3% in the month after CEO activism relative to otherwise identical stores of non-announcing firms."[50] The authors conclude that CEOs engage in activism not because of political belief but for strategic reasons to gain market share in consumer markets characterized by political polarization and identity-based consumption.[51]

If corporations match well with the values of their consumer base, they can benefit significantly. For instance, Nike's Kaepernick ad is said to have generated sales of more than $163 million before the ad was even aired.[52] As pointed out by Tom Lin, initiatives at Walmart and JPMorgan Chase allowed the two companies to expand into new markets:

> Walmart's partnership with the Environmental Defense Fund to tackle environmental issues has helped the company launch new sources of revenue via environmentally-friendly products and cost-savings via smarter energy practices, while simultaneously furthering the objectives of environmentalists. Similarly, in 2015, JPMorgan Chase committed to investing one hundred million dollars into Detroit, Michigan to help jumpstart a faltering, once-great American city, while at the same time creating a new market of clients for JPMorgan Chase.[53]

Notably, JPMorgan Chase opposed backtracking on DEI, with CEO Jamie Dimon emphasizing the firm's continued commitment to diverse communities.[54]

47 *Id.*

48 *Id.* at 206.

49 Swarnodeep Homroy & Shubhashis Gangopadhyay, *Strategic CEO Activism in Polarized Markets*, J. Fin. & Quantitative Analysis 1 (2023), doi:10.1017/S0022109023001382.

50 *Id.* at 7–8 (noting that the "increase is driven by higher consumer visits to Democrat-county stores (share of votes to Donald Trump less than 40%), while consumer visits to Republican counties show a significantly smaller decline" and that "store visits in Republican counties almost fully recovered to pre-activism levels within 8 weeks, but store visits in Democrat counties continued to be elevated."). Their study also shows that "sales turnover of firms increases in the first two quarters following CEO activism, but the effect subsides thereafter." *Id.* at 9.

51 *Id.* at 45.

52 Melloni, Patacconi & Vikander, *supra* note 29, at 3103 (citing Apex Marketing calculations).

53 *See* Tom C.W. Lin, *Incorporating Social Activism*, 98 B.U. L. Rev. 1535, 1580 (2018).

54 Kiara Alfonseca, *These Companies Are Standing by Their DEI Policies amid Backlash*, ABC News (Jan. 23, 2025), https://abcnews.go.com/Business/companies-sticking-dei-amid-backlash/story?id=118037109. *See supra* Chapter 1, Section C.4.

The upside of getting the corporate governing initiative right can be significant. According to data from the US Bureau of Labor Statistics, ninety million Americans self-identify as "conscious consumers," with the overall conscious consumer market in the United States reaching $3.2 trillion in 2017.[55]

### b Labor Market

On the labor market front, where corporations compete to attract and retain talent, corporate governing issues matter.[56] Corporate governing can enhance employees' connection to their organizations and reinforce shared beliefs within the workforce. Empirical studies find that employee satisfaction predicts positive returns. A study by Alex Edmans finds that companies making the list for "Best Companies to Work for in America" enjoyed superior long-term shareholder returns and earnings surprises over a twenty-eight-year period from 1984 to 2011 and suggests that the dimensions captured by the list are financially material.[57] Subsequent studies show that this outperformance persisted through 2020.[58]

A study by Anahit Mkrtchyan, Jason Sandvik, and Da Xu finds that employee satisfaction increases when CEOs actively advocate for diversity and pay equality.[59] Additionally, companies with CEOs engaged in activism tend to attract more productive inventors, signaling an enhanced reputation in the labor market.[60] A 2023 Pew Research Center study shows that most US workers view DEI initiatives positively, with more substantial support among females, younger employees, and racial minorities.[61] Yet, attitudes are divided along ideological lines: 78 percent of Democrats see DEI as beneficial, compared to 30 percent of Republicans.[62]

Assessing polarization is key: If the corporation's stance clashes with employees' ideologies, it could lead to alienation. A study by Vanessa Burbano finds an

[55] *See* Jennifer S. Fan, *Woke Capital: The Role of Corporations in Social Movements*, 9 HARV. BUS. L. REV. 441, 454 (2019). On conscious consumerism, see Sarah Dadush, *Identity Harm*, 89 U. COLO. L. REV. 863, 869–73 & 881–82 (2018) (citing DAVID VOGEL, THE MARKET FOR VIRTUE 3–4 (2005)).

[56] Michal Barzuza, Quinn Curtis & David H. Webber, *The Millennial Corporation: Strong Stakeholders, Weak Managers*, 28 STAN. J.L. BUS. & FIN. 255, 276 (2023) (discussing ESG).

[57] Alex Edmans, *Does the Stock Market Fully Value Intangibles? Employee Satisfaction and Equity Prices*, 101 J. FIN. ECON. 621 (2011).

[58] Hamid Boustanifar & Young Dae Kang, *Employee Satisfaction and Long-Run Stock Returns, 1984–2020*, 78 FIN. ANALYSTS J. 129 (2022).

[59] Mkrtchyan, Sandvik & Xu, *supra* note 13.

[60] *Id. See also* M.V. Lee Badgett, Laura E. Durso, Angeliki Kastanis & Christy Mallory, *The Business Impact of LGBT-Supportive Workplace Policies* (2013), https://escholarship.org/uc/item/3vt6t9zx (finding strong evidence that LGBTQ-supportive policies create openness amongst LGBTQ+ employees and relatively strong evidence that these policies lead to less discrimination in the workplace, augment health results, improve job satisfaction, and more significant job commitment.).

[61] Rachel Minkin, *Diversity, Equity and Inclusion in the Workplace*, PEW RSCH. CTR. (May 17, 2023), www.pewresearch.org/social-trends/2023/05/17/diversity-equity-and-inclusion-in-the-workplace/.

[62] *Id.*

asymmetrical response from the workforce: "a significant demotivating effect if the employer takes a stance with which the employee disagrees but no statistically significant motivating effect if the employer takes a stance with which the employee agrees, compared with the employer not taking a stance."[63] In Burbano's field experiment, the demotivating effect resulted in less quality and quantity of work for the employer.[64] Burbano argues that this asymmetrical effect is attributable to the fact that "individuals tend to perceive a 'false consensus' with regard to the relative commonness of their own opinions and to overestimate the degree to which others share their beliefs[;] … if workers already expect their colleagues and employers to share their views because of a false consensus effect, no updating takes place when it is revealed that the employer shares their perspective."[65]

A study by Adam Wowak, John Busenbark, and Donald Hambrick focusing on employee reactions to CEOs' political messaging following North Carolina's "Bathroom Bill"[66] reaches partially similar results. Unlike Burbano, the authors find that when the employee population is aligned with a CEO's politics, the response to CEO activism is generally positive and strengthens the employee's affiliation to the underlying political cause.[67] However, similar to Burbano, they find that when employees are not aligned – such as when a CEO is more liberal than the workforce – organizational commitment can decline.[68]

Yet, even when CEO activism leads to employee misalignment, the outcome isn't necessarily detrimental. Over time, such misalignment can drive self-selection, leading to a workforce that better reflects the company's cultural identity.[69] In this way, CEO activism can serve a strategic function. According to Mkrtchyan, Sandvik, and Xu, it "may help reduce the information asymmetry and search costs that job-seekers bear in learning about an organization's less observable characteristics,"[70] facilitating the attraction–selection–attrition process and fostering a more like-minded and cohesive workforce.[71]

[63] Vanessa C. Burbano, *The Demotivating Effects of Communicating a Social-Political Stance: Field Experimental Evidence from an Online Labor Market Platform*, 67 Mgmt. Science 1004, 1005 (2021).

[64] *Id.* at 1020. Workers were surveyed on sociopolitical topics at the end of each of two translation jobs on online work platform Upwork. Only at the end of the second job, they were told of the employer's own positions on such topics.

[65] *Id.* at 1019.

[66] *See supra* Chapter 1, Section B.3.

[67] Adam J. Wowak, John R. Busenbark & Donald C. Hambrick, *How Do Employees React When Their CEO Speaks Out? Intra- and Extra-Firm Implications of CEO Sociopolitical Activism*, 67 Administrative Science Quarterly 553, 574–75 & 580–81 (2022).

[68] *Id.* at 574 ("the more conservative the employee population, the greater the decrease in organizational commitment.").

[69] Minkin, *supra* note 61.

[70] Mkrtchyan, Sandvik & Xu, *supra* note 13, at 4.

[71] *See generally* Donald C. Hambrick & Adam J. Wowak, *CEO Sociopolitical Activism: A Stakeholder Alignment Model*, 46 Academy Mgmt. Rev. 33 (2021). *See also* Toniolo, *supra* note 13, at 365 (mentioning that Melissa Hobley, Match Group's global chief marketing officer, emphasized the

This workforce alignment may be reinforced by broader demographic and ideological shifts. A study by Reilly Steel finds a leftward shift among senior managers, driven largely by increased diversity – more women, people of color, and leaders from liberal regions.[72] In fact, Steel's findings may reflect ideological realignment across all employees, not just senior managers. To be fair, his research focuses specifically on directors and senior management, and it does not automatically imply that the entire workforce has moved in the same direction. Nonetheless, this shift could indicate a broader trend in which many Americans – including many in the workforce – have adopted more progressive views. Steel's methodology assesses executives' ideologies based on the political leanings of their campaign contribution recipients, showing that senior managers have increasingly supported politicians like Bernie Sanders and Alexandria Ocasio-Cortez.[73] Whether a part of the country has shifted leftward because these politicians led the way or tapped into existing public sentiment can be up for debate. What seems implausible is that this leftward shift was driven by senior executives themselves, with politicians and segments of the country following suit. More likely, it reflects an organic, society-wide phenomenon in which senior executives participate. If that is the case, corporate governing may increasingly align with the expectations of a more diverse and progressive workforce.[74]

### c Stock Market

The stock market may reward corporations that pick the fitting corporate governing strategy and punish those that pick the wrong one. To begin, studies show that investors are drawn to firms with strong sustainability profiles.[75] Yet, the main question is whether good social performance impacts or at least correlates with good financial performance.

economic and competitive implications of speaking out against the *Dobbs* decision, particularly for industries like tech, law, and finance, which rely heavily on competing for female professionals).

[72] Reilly Steel, *The Political Transformation of Corporate America, 2001–2022*, at 24–25, forthcoming Am. Pol. Sci. Rev. (working draft Mar. 29, 2025), https://static1.squarespace.com/static/6019c4d665a1bd185288d428/t/67e7648118c6d849a51480da/1743217798724/Steel_Political_Transformation_of_Corporate_America_3-28-25.pdf.

[73] *Id.* at 11–12 & 17–18.

[74] Executives may also infer workforce preferences from employees' influence on corporate political spending. *See* Zhao Li, *Can Employees Shape Corporate Political Spending in an Era of Democratic Backsliding? Evidence from the Capitol Insurrection* 4–5 (2025) (manuscript on file with author) (noting that firms with employees favoring pro-certification legislators reduced contributions to election objectors following January 6, illustrating how corporate political spending may reflect workforce sentiment).

[75] Samuel M. Hartzmark & Abigail B. Sussman, *Do Investors Value Sustainability? A Natural Experiment Examining Ranking and Fund Flows*, 74 J. Fin. 2789, 2831–32 (2019) (looking at mutual funds and finding that "funds with the highest globe ratings receive more than $24 billion greater fund flows, while those with the lowest globe ratings face a reduction in fund flows of more than $12 billion").

## I STUDIES FINDING POSITIVE CORRELATION

Although no studies, to my knowledge, establish causation between social and financial performance, several document a correlation. In his 2022 book "Grow the Pie," Alex Edmans surveys empirical studies that show a correlation between the two variables.[76] Similarly, Allen Ferrell, Hao Liang, and Luc Renneboog find a correlation between social responsibility scores and firm valuation.[77] Some studies focusing on specific corporate initiatives have found that firms with supportive sexual orientation equality policies tend to have a lower cost of equity capital.[78]

Another set of studies takes a different approach, tracking cumulative abnormal returns – stock performance adjusted for overall market movement – following corporate actions or announcements with prosocial goals. These studies find a correlation between such actions and positive stock returns. An article by Anahit Mkrtchyan, Jason Sandvik, and Vivi Zhu tests stock reactions following "CEO activism" and finds, on average, that such activism is associated with positive market returns[79] and "an increase in institutional ownership, especially among investors with a higher Democratic leaning and greater inequality aversion, who rebalance their portfolios to place greater weight on firms with activist CEOs."[80] They suggest that a company's activist position on social responsibility and sustainability can capture the interest of institutional investors and influence equity valuations by leveraging investor demand as a conduit.[81]

Other studies reach similar findings. Swarnodeep Homroy & Shubhashis Gangopadhyay analyze activism statements by CEOs of S&P 500 corporations in the 2014–2019 period and show that investors react positively to CEO activism: "[I]n the three-day event windows around CEO social activism, the average cumulative abnormal return is 0.12%."[82] The study also finds that firms that speak out face a lower risk of shareholder activism on ESG issues than the other firms.[83] Similarly, Jens Dammann and Daniel Lawrence explore price reaction to the Statement on

[76] Alex Edmans, Grow the Pie: How Great Companies Deliver Both Purpose and Profit 105–06, 112 (2022).

[77] Allen Ferrell, Hao Liang & Luc Renneboog, *Socially Responsible Firms*, 122 J. Fin. Econ. 585, 586 (2016).

[78] Mostafa Monzur Hasan, Adrian (Wai Kong) Cheung & Trevor Marwick, *Corporate Sexual Orientation Equality Policies and the Cost of Equity Capital*, 34 J. Behav. & Experimental Fin. (2022) 100664.

[79] Anahit Mkrtchyan, Jason Sandvik & Vivi Zhu, *CEO Activism and Firm Value*, Mgmt. Science (2023), https://pubsonline.informs.org/doi/10.1287/mnsc.2023.4971.

[80] *Id.* at 31.

[81] *Id.* (noting, however, that the price reaction is quite modest).

[82] Homroy & Gangopadhyay, *supra* note 49, at 9 (finding that "[a]bnormal returns to CEO activism are higher for companies operating in polarized environments and when the CEO statements are Democrat leaning").

[83] *Id.*

Corporate Purpose by the Business Roundtable[84] and find that signatories to the Statement experienced abnormal returns compared to other corporations.[85]

#### II STUDIES NOT FINDING POSITIVE CORRELATION

However, other studies reach opposite conclusions. Bhagwat, Warren, Beck, and Watson find that, on average, corporate sociopolitical activism elicits an adverse short-term reaction from investors – though they concede that in some instances, such activism proves advantageous.[86] Michael Durney, Joseph Johnson, Roshan Sinha, and Donald Young ran an experiment showing that investors purchase more stock when they agree with the CEO's activism and less when they disagree.[87] A.J. Chen, Patricia Dechow, and Samuel Tan find that firm activism surrounding Black Lives Matter had little impact on shareholder value.[88]

A meta-analysis of studies between 2015 and 2020 on ESG investing covering thousands of underlying studies displays mixed results: The survey finds that "the financial performance of ESG investing has on average been indistinguishable from conventional investing (with one in three studies indicating superior performance)."[89] Relatedly, a survey of 509 equity portfolio managers – both from traditional and sustainable funds – finds that while ESG factors influence stock selection, engagement, and voting for over three-quarters of investors, financial considerations remain the primary driver.[90]

The vast and evolving literature on the effects of DEI on firm value is also as inconclusive either way.[91] For one, DEI impact is difficult to assess, not least because its

84 *See supra* Chapter 2, Section A.2.

85 Jens Dammann & Daniel Lawrence, *CEOs' Endorsements of Stakeholder Values: Cheap Talk or Meaningful Signal? An Empirical Analysis*, 49 J. CORP. L. 577 (2024).

86 Bhagwat, Warren, Beck & Watson, *supra* note 10, at 11–12, 16.

87 Michael T. Durney, Joseph A. Johnson, Roshan K. Sinha & Donald Young, *CEO (In)Activism and Investor Decisions*, Working Paper (June 2022), https://ssrn.com/abstract=3604321 (finding also that CEO activism causes participants to focus more on the CEO and the CEO's position and less on the firm's financial performance).

88 A.J. Chen, Patricia M. Dechow & Samuel T. Tan, *Beyond Shareholder Value? Why Firms Voluntarily Disclose Support for Black Lives Matter* Working Paper (2021), https://ink.library.smu.edu.sg/soa_research/1952 (finding that the activism is driven less by "woke-washing" than by managers who are acting in the interests of a broader set of stakeholders).

89 Ulrich Atz, Tracy Van Holt, Zongyuan Zoe Liu & Christopher C. Bruno, *Does Sustainability Generate Better Financial Performance? Review, Meta-Analysis, and Propositions*, 13 J. SUSTAINABLE FIN. & INV. 802 (2022), https://doi.org/10.1080/20430795.2022.2106934 (reviewing 1,141 primary peer-reviewed papers and 27 meta-reviews based on around 1,400 underlying studies).

90 Alex Edmans, Tom Gosling & Dirk Jenter, *Sustainable Investing: Evidence from the Field*, ECGI Fin. Working Paper No. 1028/2025 (Jan. 2025), https://ssrn.com/abstract=4963062 (finding that even among sustainable funds, few investors are willing to sacrifice returns for ESG performance, largely due to fiduciary duty concerns).

91 The debate on DEI's effects and effectiveness – whether or not it is a good policy on business or moral grounds – remains open. For a synthesis, see *generally* Veronica Root Martinez, *Reframing the DEI Case*, 46 SEATTLE U. L. REV. 399 (2023) (summarizing various studies).

definition is challenging due to its shifting terminology, varying interpretations, and the broad scope of initiatives it encompasses.[92] A study by Alex Edmans, Caroline Flammer, and Simon Glossner distinguishes between demographic diversity (gender, race, and socioeconomic background) and cognitive diversity (differences in perspectives and problem-solving).[93] They find that cognitive diversity enhances employee satisfaction and future accounting performance but does not affect stock returns.[94]

## III ASSESSMENT

The mixed signals from the empirical literature on stockholder returns may be confusing. While there is no clear consensus on whether corporate governing enhances shareholder value, the prevailing evidence does not suggest a negative impact. At some firms, corporate governing enhances value when carefully planned and executed. As I mentioned, this follows a basic risk/reward proposition: While some firms succumb to the backlash, others successfully create value through corporate governing.[95] Nike benefits from endorsing anti-racist messaging that resonates with younger generations and racial minorities (key segments of its consumer base), just as tech companies attract, or at least used to attract, LGBTQ+ talent by signaling support for their causes. Conversely, it makes less business sense for brands with a heavily conservative consumer base (e.g., Bud Light) to adopt similar strategies.

That said, a crucial nuance deserves emphasis: ESG, DEI, and other corporate governing initiatives remain *voluntary*. While firms may be responsive to stakeholder input, the final word rests with directors and managers – no one else. As corporate governing is a matter of choice, firms adopt these initiatives when they see value or convenience. Some benefit, others do not. Without clear evidence

[92] *See generally* Lisa M. Leslie & Evan Flynn, *Diversity Ideologies, Beliefs, and Climates: A Review, Integration, and Set of Recommendations*, 50 J. MGMT. 849 (2024). While often associated with demographic diversity, Leslie and Flynn posit DEI also includes less tangible factors such as workplace climateand employee perceptions and note that different diversity cognitions – such as ideologies, beliefs, and climates – are frequently studied in isolation, creating conceptual ambiguity, and limiting a comprehensive understanding of their effects.

[93] Alex Edmans, Caroline Flammer & Simon Glossner, *Diversity, Equity, and Inclusion*, NBER Working Paper 31215 (2024), www.nber.org/papers/w31215) (gathering information on cognitive diversity from thirteen questions in the *Great Place to Work* questionnaire).

[94] *Id.* Still, even assuming cognitive diversity should be prioritized over demographic diversity, the latter may still serve as a proxy for the former, as diverse backgrounds often translate into different perspectives. Moreover, neglecting demographic diversity risks reinforcing systemic barriers, as Scott Page argues in his work on diversity's role in organizational success See SCOTT E. PAGE, THE DIFFERENCE: HOW THE POWER OF DIVERSITY CREATES BETTER GROUPS, FIRMS, SCHOOLS, AND SOCIETIES (2007).

[95] *Cf.* Simmons, *supra* note 10, at 714. *Cf. also* Stavros Gadinis & Amelia Miazad, *Corporate Law and Social Risk*, 73 VAND. L. REV. 1401, 1401 (2020) (arguing that "ESG serves shareholders' interests, not because of its upside potential to increase profits, but because it helps companies identify and manage social risks to their business.").

of widespread harm, restricting such initiatives on business grounds is hard to justify.[96] True, empirical studies in this charged space warrant careful interpretation,[97] but the burden should rest on critics to provide tested, data-driven arguments for *curbing* voluntary corporate initiatives.[98]

Without political polarization and the politicization of corporate law, this should be uncontroversial.[99] As Alex Edmans pointed out:

> Finance 101 has always stressed how a company's worth is the present value of all its cash flows, including those in the very distant future. A company's relationships with its employees, customers, communities, suppliers, and the environment are highly value relevant; there's nothing particularly cultish, liberal, or – dare I say it – "woke" in considering them.[100]

## 4 *Objections*

While corporate governing can make business sense in many circumstances, it remains subject to two recurring objections. First, executives may use corporate funds to advance personal political agendas. Second, engaging in corporate governing arguably implies a commitment to stakeholderism or enlightened shareholder value, both of which are often critiqued as conflicting with shareholder primacy.

### a The Use of Corporate Funds

Critics often argue that corporate political activity is problematic because shareholders cannot always access full information or prevent their capital from funding

[96] By contrast, when policies become mandatory – such as board diversity quotas, for example – the need for a strong business or moral case becomes more pressing. With regulatory requirements applying across the board, empirical validation becomes essential to assessing their broader economic impact.

[97] *See* Spamann & Fischer, *supra* note 20, at 16 (discussing factors contributing to the "widespread awareness of a credibility problem in empirical research in the social sciences").

[98] *Cf. id.* at 17 (hypothesizing that policies like purpose statements may only work for the firms that have adopted them voluntarily).

[99] *But see*, for a reframing of the debate around the business case for ESG, Ann M. Lipton, *Book Review, Will the Real Shareholder Primacy Please Stand Up? The Profit Motive: Defending Shareholder Value Maximization*, by Stephen M. Bainbridge, Cambridge: Cambridge University Press, 2023. Pp. 223. $34.99., 137 HARV. L. REV. 1584, 1606 (2024) (emphasis in original):

> it is almost certainly the case that activists who *in fact* favor nonfinancial ESG mask their true intentions with spurious claims of a business case for their preferred corporate social behavior. That is, precisely because corporations are so efficiently constructed to seek profits, those who seek to channel corporate behavior in a particular direction frequently try to make a financial case for it, the strength of which may be less than robust.

[100] Alex Edmans, *The End of ESG*, 52 FIN. MGMT. 3, 5 (2023).

speech they oppose.[101] This concern is valid in the abstract – but it does not alter the present analysis. Shareholders routinely lack full insight into core business decisions: whether to enter a new market, launch a product line, or recruit talent for a marketing campaign.[102] Yet these gaps do not invalidate managerial discretion.[103] The same logic applies in the political sphere.

To be sure, political speech raises more delicate concerns than traditional business choices – especially when executive preferences diverge from those of shareholders.[104] But these tensions implicate broader questions about democratic legitimacy and institutional design, which are taken up in Section D and Chapter 6.[105] They do not, on their own, undermine the corporate governing rationale or the firm's ability to create value.

Besides, empirical evidence further complicates this critique. A study of CEO activism across S&P 500 firms from 2014 to 2019 found that although 67% of CEOs were Republican donors, 97% of the 1,188 activism statements aligned with Democratic causes.[106] The authors attribute this asymmetry not to personal ideology, but to strategic calculation.[107] In an era of polarization and identity-based consumption, activism increased store visits in Democratic-leaning counties without

[101] John C. Coates et al., Brief of Corporate Law Professors as Amici Curie in Support of Respondents, *Friedrichs v. California Teachers Ass'n* No. 14-915 (U.S. Nov. 2015), at 8 https://scholarship.law.duke.edu/faculty_scholarship/3546 ("most individual shareholders cannot obtain full information about corporate speech or political activities, even after the fact, nor can they prevent their savings from being used to speak in ways with which they disagree."). To be fair, the Brief by John Coates and other corporate law professors is less about advocating against the use of corporate funds for political goals than about confuting the idea – stemming from Citizens United v. Fed. Election Comm'n, 558 U.S. 310, 370 (2010) – that investors currently have tools to resist such initiatives, which is in fact a sensible critique that I address in Chapter 6 where I sketch some policy avenues to minimize the risks raised by corporate governing.

[102] *Cf.* Robert H. Sitkoff, *Corporate Political Speech, Political Extortion, and the Competition for Corporate Charters*, 69 U. Chi. L. Rev. 1103, 1105 (2002).

[103] This is true also with respect to all stakeholders. For the argument that employees disagree with management on several issues, see *infra* Chapter 5, Section B.2.b.ii.y. For the shareholder/management divide see Gatti, *supra* note 25, at 43; Lisa M. Fairfax, *Reframing the Corporate Political Speech Debate*, Working Paper (2025) (unpublished manuscript on file with author), at 4 (noting that "concerns around investor representation permeate all business activity – and thus such concerns do not make corporate political speech significantly distinguishable from other forms of corporate speech."). Fairfax correctly points out that shareholders often hold strong, divergent views on economic decisions – especially those with social implications – challenging the assumption that such decisions warrant unquestioned deference. *Id.* at 5.

[104] Lucian A. Bebchuk & Robert J. Jackson, Jr., *Corporate Political Speech: Who Decides?*, 124 Harv. L. Rev. 83, 90 (2010) (noting that, compared to straight lobbying, in which corporations and shareholders are aligned in seeking rules that would benefit the business, with some political spending and speech a divergence of interests may arise with respect to the political issues that corporations may choose to influence). *See also id.* at 96 (noting that "shareholders may attach expressive significance to corporate political speech that goes far beyond the amount spent.").

[105] *See* Chapter 6, Section B.3, which describes the challenges in finding truly disinterested decision-makers.

[106] *See* Homroy & Gangopadhyay, *supra* note 50, at 3–4.

[107] *Id.* at 45.

comparable losses in Republican ones – results that were reflected in firm share prices.[108] In this light, corporate political engagement appears less as a vehicle for personal views than as a calculated market response.[109]

### b Is Being Prosocial Consistent with Shareholder Wealth?

Some may argue that making a business case for corporate governing means endorsing stakeholderism or enlightened shareholder value[110] – frameworks often criticized for creating confusion, masking trade-offs, and producing limited impact in practice.[111] The critique isn't wrong.[112] Trade-offs are real, but they're not new to management. Balancing competing pressures is part of the executive function. It reflects the structural reality of doing business in contested markets, where dealing with stakeholder demands – on social, political, and economic fronts – is unavoidable.[113]

"Stay out of politics and focus on the business," the refrain goes.[114] But this *is* the business.[115] Corporate governing is a response to a business risk/opportunity that firms *must* navigate in the 2020s.[116] To ignore this is to misread today's environment. Stephen Bainbridge observes that business decisions increasingly resemble political decisions

108 *Id.*

109 To be sure, Reilly Steel finds a leftward ideological shift among senior managers, largely tied to greater diversity and regional backgrounds. However, as mentioned above, while the data focus on executives, they may signal broader workforce trends. Rather than executives leading public sentiment, it's plausible they reflect evolving societal values – suggesting corporate governing may increasingly align with a more diverse, progressive employee base. *See supra* notes 72–74 and accompanying text.

110 Lucian A. Bebchuk, Kobi Kastiel & Roberto Tallarita, *Does Enlightened Shareholder Value Add Value?*, 77 Bus. Law. 731, 735 (2022) (citing Virginia Harper Ho, *Enlightened Shareholder Value: Corporate Governance Beyond the Shareholder-Stakeholder Divide*, 36 J. Corp. L. 59 (2010)). For an endorsement of enlightened shareholder value, see Robert P. Bartlett & Ryan Bubb, *Corporate Social Responsibility Through Shareholder Governance*, ECGI Law Working Paper No. 682/2023 (2023), https://ssrn.com/abstract=4354220.

111 Bebchuk, Kastiel & Tallarita, *supra* note 110 at 733–34.

112 *See* Matteo Gatti & Chrystin Ondersma, *Can a Broader Corporate Purpose Redress Inequality? The Stakeholder Approach Chimera*, 46 J. Corp. L. 1, 9–10 (2020) (criticizing a stakeholderist corporate law reform as ineffective and potentially perilous for weaker constituencies).

113 *See generally* Bartlett & Bubb, *supra* note 110; Simmons, *supra* note 10; Gadinis & Miazad, *supra* note 95.

114 *See for example*, Leo E. Strine, Jr., *Good Corporate Citizenship We Can All Get Behind? Toward a Principled, Non-Ideological Approach to Making Money the Right Way*, 78 Bus. Law. 329, 353 (2023) (noting that "[w]hen, rather than making a decision based on profit, a board uses the corporation's resources to advance a social or a political cause, conservative thinkers balk … because there is no basis on which to presume a convergence of social and political beliefs on the part of investors, or that they invested to advance those beliefs.").

115 *See* Gatti, *supra* note 26, at 27 & 34 (corporate governing is part of running a business); Gadinis & Havasy, *supra* note 29, at 1660–63 (same).

116 *See generally* Simmons, *supra* note 10 (arguing that political risk is a crucial function of enterprise risk management); Gatti, *supra* note 26, at 34 (arguing that corporate governing is one of many risks); Fairfax, *supra* note 103, at 6 (noting that "risk is an inescapable part of any corporate activity, including corporate speech, and risk cannot be eliminated.").

and managers are asked to juggle growing demands from multiple constituencies.[117] From the opposite ideological end, Robert Reich argues that executives now mediate societal conflict in place of political institutions – a role they were never trained for.[118] Both are right, though they decry this new state of the art. But this is what business leadership looks like today; prosocial engagement is what the marketplace at times might demand.[119] The idea that firms can simply opt out is unrealistic.

Consumer expectations reinforce this shift. A 2018 Stanford Rock Center survey found that 65 percent of Americans wanted CEOs to speak out on major social issues.[120] While support has declined in recent years,[121] expectations remain high among certain demographics[122] – particularly those relevant to values-driven companies. If Section A illustrates anything, it is that corporate governing is deeply idiosyncratic: For some firms, silence carries more risk than engagement.[123] This shift explains the surge in corporate advocacy – between 2011 and 2019, the share of US corporations engaging in such activity rose from just 1 percent to 38 percent.[124]

What followed was not a moral awakening, but a strategic adaptation to a changing political economy. Even critics of stakeholderism concede that, under a shareholder value model, stakeholder concerns cannot be ignored.[125] Corporate governing often reflects this logic: aligning stakeholder expectations with long-term business strategy.

[117] Stephen M. Bainbridge, The Profit Motive: Defending Shareholder Value Maximization 96 (2023).

[118] Robert B. Reich, *The Case Against Corporate Social Responsibility*, Goldman School Working Paper Series GSP08-003 (Aug. 1, 2008), at 23 & 42, https://papers.ssrn.com/sol3/papers.cfm?abstract_id=1213129.

[119] Sometimes silence may in fact be riskier than being vocal. *See* Chatterji & Toffel, *supra* note 18, at 9 (noting that corporations that stayed silent in the aftermath of Charlottesville and the Trump immigration ban were exposed by news outlets like the New York Times, CNBC, and USA Today). Similarly, in a study analyzing employee reactions to their CEOs signing a letter in opposition to North Carolina's Bathroom Bill, the authors point out that "the decision not to sign the letter carried its own implications, as CEOs who chose to stay silent ran the risk of disappointing stakeholders who opposed the bill and wanted to see their CEOs take a stand against it." Wowak, Busenbark & Hambrick, *supra* note 67, at 554.

[120] *See* Larcker, Miles, Tayan & Violich, *supra* note 42, at 4.

[121] Bentley Univ. & Gallup, *Business in Society 2024 Report* (2024), at 6, www.gallup.com/file/analytics/649841/bentley-university-gallup-business-society-2024-report.pdf (reporting that only "38% of Americans say businesses should take a public stance on current events, down from 41% in 2023 and 48% in 2022.").

[122] *Id.* at 15 (finding that younger Americans most likely to want to hear from corporations about issues like diversity, mental health, and climate change).

[123] Korschun, Rafieian, Aggarwal & Swain, *supra* note 25, at 30.

[124] Homroy & Gangopadhyay, *supra* note 50, at 2.

[125] Bebchuk, Kastiel & Tallarita, *supra* note 110, at 744 (mentioning that this was also the approach by Milton Friedman, *The Social Responsibility of Business is to Increase Its Profits*, NY Times Mag. 32, Sept. 13, 1970, whom they quote: "providing amenities to [the local] community or to improving its government … may make it easier to attract desirable employees, it may reduce the wage bill or lessen losses from pilferage and sabotage or have other worthwhile effects.").

### 5 Summary

Whether corporate governing benefits, a corporation's business cannot be determined in the abstract. Its impact depends on how a specific firm engages with a given societal issue and the expectations in its key markets – particularly product, labor, and capital markets. Some firms may gain advantages, such as stronger recruitment, employee commitment, and consumer loyalty, while others may not. However, corporations operating in this space are not blind to the risks. As a study noted, "CEO activism – which is often viewed as an act of self-indulgence or an agency cost – can, in the right context, be a highly effective leadership behavior that serves shareholders well."[126]

While this analysis addresses the business rationale, political backlash presents an additional challenge. The strategic implications of navigating these risks warrant further examination, which I take up below.

## B THE STRATEGIC CASE FOR CORPORATE GOVERNING: DOES IT GIVE RISE TO STRATEGIC RISK?

Despite a business case, could there still be a downside? One could argue that even when there is *potentially* a business case, some initiatives may result in a strategic mistake. Some actions might backfire and generate resentment from a segment of the consumer, employee, or investor bases. The risk is that corporate governing may result in a short-lived gain but backfire in the long term.[127] Such a risk is very much apparent to anyone observing the recent conservative backlash, which culminated in litigating corporate initiatives and passing legislation of various sorts to thwart efforts in those spheres.[128] Also, as I illustrate below, cases such as Disney, Bud Light, and Target, not to mention backlash to corporate responses in the aftermath of October 7 and the war in Gaza, show how long negative repercussions can go – in some cases, they can tarnish brand reputation.

[126] Wowak, Busenbark & Hambrick, *supra* note 67, at 581.

[127] In a way, the distinction between the business and the strategic cases echoes the short- and long-term dichotomy, which is well-known to corporate governance scholars. *See generally* MARK. J ROE, MISSING THE TARGET: WHY STOCK-MARKET SHORT-TERMISM IS NOT THE PROBLEM (2022) (debunking the short-termism critique).

[128] *See generally* Lisa M. Fairfax, *For Corporate Hypocrisy*, 50 J. CORP. L. 287 (2025) (arguing that a company's decision to remain silent on social and political issues reflects a calculated cost–benefit analysis, deeming the risks of backlash too significant to justify taking a stance). *See also* Fairfax, *supra* note 25, at 201–202 (noting that a political and cultural backlash against diversity and equity initiatives, including opposition to critical race theory and DEI policies, has created significant challenges for corporations in sustaining their commitments to racial equity and inclusion). For a description of litigation and legislative efforts against ESG and DEI, see *supra* Chapter 1, Sections C.2 and C.3, and Chapter 3, Section E.2.

Often, the reaction is orchestrated by those sitting on the opposite side of the ideological spectrum,[129] as with the Disney/DeSantis quarrel.[130] Backlash can be overt and of a regulatory nature, as the flurry of anti-ESG/DEI measures can attest.[131] When politicians perceive that corporations are invading their lane, they react, especially against corporate socioeconomic advocacy that criticizes measures passed by legislatures controlled by their party.

Ultimately, like any new phenomenon, corporate governing is not immune to political backlash – quite the opposite. Even when market forces – shaped by investors, workers, corporate leaders, and broader societal pressures[132] – drive firms toward change, these shifts can provoke resistance. As Mark Roe theorized, political actors who mobilize dissent against such changes may respond forcefully, overriding the latest adjustments and entrenching older structures.[133] Firms then must make judgment calls.

Thus, some gains from a seemingly sound corporate governing initiative may ultimately reveal illusory. Even when executives believe it makes business sense for a company to take a stand on an issue, (a) political backlash can erase benefits and provoke harm (think of increased regulatory fervor fueled by opposing politicians),[134] and (b) the very policy goal pursued via corporate governing may be jeopardized because of the distraction generated by the corporation pursuing it and politicians fighting against it.

Take the Bud Light and Target episodes, which spurred boycotts and violent threats. The brands are among the many that faced backlash and calls for boycotts from conservative groups for their support of the LGBTQ+ community.[135] They were criticized for partnering with trans influencers (Bud Light) and offering Pride merchandise (Target).[136] Such attacks impacted stock prices.[137] And this was only

[129] For a description of the risks associated with alienating politicians, especially state governments and legislatures, see Bhagwat, Warren, Beck & Watson, *supra* note 10, at 5. *See also* Jill E. Fisch & Jeff Schwartz, *How Did Corporations Get Stuck in Politics and Can They Escape?*, 3 U. Chi. Bus. L. Rev 342, 344–45 (2024).

[130] *See supra* Introduction.

[131] *See supra* Chapter 1, Section C.3.

[132] This is what Chapter 2 posits.

[133] For an analysis of how backlash operates and can alter efficient or otherwise market-led equilibria, see *generally* Mark J. Roe, *Backlash*, 98 Colum. L. Rev. 217 (1998).

[134] Florida retaliated against Disney by revoking special tax and other benefits the company had been enjoying for over fifty years. A Section 220 DGCL claim ensued, lamenting, among other things, that the company "fail[ed] to appreciate the known risk that [its] political stance would have on its financial position and the value of Disney stock." Simeone v. Walt Disney Co., 302 A.3d 956, 963 (Del. Ch. 2023).

[135] Christina Chaddar Berk, *Boycotts Hit Stocks Hard. Here's What Might Be Next for Bud, Target and Others Caught in the Anti-Pride Backlash*, CNBC (June 3, 2023), www.cnbc.com/2023/06/03/anti-pride-backlash-what-target-anheuser-busch-and-others-should-expect-next-.html.

[136] *Id.*

[137] *See* Nick Halter, *Target, in the Crosshairs, Is Taking a Beating on Wall Street*, AXIOS (June 2, 2023), www.axios.com/local/twin-cities/2023/06/02/target-stock-prices-tumble-pride-boycotts; Kristopher J.

the conservative backlash; the LGBTQ+ community also criticized the companies for not standing by them.[138] These cases show how this type of risk is potentially more significant than the one concerning the business case. As Jill Fisch and Jeff Schwartz pointed out,

> politics is a high risk branding strategy precisely because it appeals to stakeholders who are particularly sensitive to political signaling and therefore more likely to turn on a company if they are not satisfied with its political position than those who are drawn by a corporation's workplace practices or product quality.[139]

In addition, while corporations and executives may have a good handle on what happens in their (and stakeholders') spheres, they may not foresee broader societal changes, especially regarding sentiment toward specific causes.[140] The Israel/Gaza war highlighted the strategic risk for corporations to get involved in complex geopolitical disputes.[141]

Brooks, *Bud Light Gets Stock Downgrade Just Weeks after Dylan Mulvaney Fallout*, CBS NEWS (May 12, 2023), www.cbsnews.com/news/bud-light-dylan-mulvaney-stock-downgrade-anheuser-busch-sales/. To be sure, during the drop of Target's stock, the whole retail sector experienced losses. *See* Michael King, *The Real Reason Target's Stock Is Dropping Has Nothing to Do with Right-Wing Protests Over Pride*, CBS NEWS (June 2, 2023, 11:53 AM), www.cbsnews.com/atlanta/news/the-real-reason-targets-stock-is-dropping-has-nothing-to-do-with-right-wing-protests-over-pride/.

[138] Target faced further criticism for moving Pride merchandise due to concerns for worker safety, a decision that ended up offending LGBTQ+ advocates. Emily Stewart, *Target Giving in to Conservative Pressure on Pride Is Not a Great Sign*, VOX (May 25, 2023, 11:22 AM), www.vox.com/politics/2023/5/25/23737338/target-abprallen-pride-boycott-bud-light-trans-controversy-stock-price. Anheuser-Busch experienced a sizeable drop in sales (Julie Creswell, *Cheaper than Water? Retailers Try to Unload Bud Light.*, N.Y. TIMES (May 31, 2023), www.nytimes.com/2023/06/29/business/bud-light-sales.html) and was called out by Dylan Mulvaney, the trans influencer with whom Bud Light had partnered, for neither standing by her publicly nor reaching out after the backlash. Carlos De Loera, *Dylan Mulvaney Says Bud Light Never Contacted Her after Anti-Trans Backlash*, L.A. TIMES (June 30, 2023), www.latimes.com/entertainment-arts/story/2023-06-30/dylan-mulvaney-bud-light-transphobic-backlash-trans-rights.

[139] Fisch & Schwarz, *supra* note 129, at 344. *But see*, for a counter, *infra* text accompanying notes 144–148.

[140] *Cf.* Bridget Bowman, *"A Country on Fire": New Poll Finds America Polarized over Culture, Race and "Woke,"* NBC NEWS (Apr. 26, 2023), www.nbcnews.com/meet-the-press/first-read/-country-fire-new-poll-finds-america-polarized-culture-race-woke-rcna81592.

[141] After October 7, many businesses expressed solidarity with Israel and the victims of the attack, drawing backlash from those who felt this support ignored the suffering of Gazans. As Israel's military response in Gaza unfolded, brands operating in or with Israel faced boycotts, while those supporting the Palestinian cause were criticized by Israel and its political allies. Meanwhile, businesses that remained silent were accused of hypocrisy by both sides, given their past public stances on political issues. *See The controversies of company activism: How are businesses responding to the Israel Hamas war?*, EURONEWS (Nov. 1, 2023), www.euronews.com/business/2023/11/01/the-controversies-of-company-activism-how-are-businesses-responding-to-the-israel-hamas-wa; Andrew Ross Sorkin, Ravi Mattu, Bernhard Warner, Sarah Kessler, Michael J. de la Merced, Lauren Hirsch & Ephrat Livni, *Companies Are Caught in the Israel-Hamas War's Crossfire*, N.Y. TIMES (Oct. 23, 2023), www.nytimes.com/2023/10/23/business/dealbook/companies-israel-hamas-war-statements.html; Caroline O'Donovan, Taylor Telford & Gerrit De Vynck, *Israel-Gaza War Prompts U.S. Employees to Demand Companies Take a Side*, WASH. POST (Oct. 22, 2023), www.washingtonpost.com/technology/2023/10/22/google-amazon-meta-gaza-israel-contracts/. *See* Paul Musgrave, *Brands Are*

Despite all this, the strategic case for corporate governing still tracks the broader business case: When done right, it can create value, manage risk, and reinforce a firm's long-term positioning. The fact that *some* initiatives may trigger political backlash or long-term reputational risk does not mean the practice is inherently flawed – or that any given corporation doesn't know what it's doing. Issues differ: Some are deeply divisive and carry meaningful exposure; others are more straightforward and less likely to provoke controversy. So do firms. Some are simply better positioned – organizationally, reputationally, or culturally – to take on corporate governing than others.

Besides, even when controversy follows, it is plausible that corporations have already accounted for the associated risk. In some cases, the controversy may even be part of the strategy. Gaia Melloni, Andrea Patacconi, and Nick Vikander argue that a certain degree of polarization is essential for credibility; without it, firms risk being seen as wokewashing.[142] In their view, CEO activism has gained traction for three reasons: growing polarization, the rising salience of sociopolitical values for consumers, and thin profit margins.[143] In such an environment, appealing to the middle ground offers diminishing returns. Provoking strong reactions – both awe and outrage – can be an effective way to capture attention.[144]

As Ann Lipton noted in response to the backlash against Nike's Kaepernick ad, it is "difficult to believe that [Nike founder and then-CEO Phil] Knight was unaware this [was] a controversial move; it seems designed to be controversial."[145] In fact, the politicization of consumer markets is a feature, not a bug.[146] None of this suggests it works for every firm – but for some, it probably does.

Moreover, it is plausible – and normatively preferable – that corporations prepare counternarratives and contingency plans. Corporate leaders should possess the expertise, or at least the judgment to rely on those who do, to assess the risks and benefits of corporate governing initiatives. While some may view these moves as rushed attempts to score political points, they are often structured deliberately – if only to withstand potential legal challenges.[147] Given their deep industry knowledge,

*the First Causality of War*, FOREIGN POLICY (Nov. 24, 2023), https://foreignpolicy.com/2023/11/24/war-coke-brands-mcdonalds-palestine-israel/.

142 Melloni, Patacconi & Vikander, *supra* note 29, at 3116.

143 *Id.*

144 *Id.* at 3116–17 (noting that "in industries where profit margins are lower, such as the apparel or food industries, sociopolitical differentiation may pay off").

145 *See for example*, Ann Lipton, *The Revolution Will Be Marketed*, BUSINESS LAW PROF. BLOG (Sept. 8, 2018), https://lawprofessors.typepad.com/business_law/2018/09/therevolution-will-be-marketed.html. *See supra* text accompanying note 52.

146 VOGEL, *supra* note 55, at 3–4 (challenging the notion that markets are apolitical, arguing that consumer preferences inherently introduce political dimensions into market behavior).

147 Simmons, *supra* note 10, at 734. Even when politicians at the highest office decide to retaliate, businesses might avoid significant repercussions. *See* Chatterji & Toffel, *supra* note 18, at 15 (describing

corporations are expected to understand their operations and the market dynamics that shape these decisions, and failure to do so may expose them to scrutiny.

Of course, corporate governing initiatives often face criticism – whether political or commercial. Like any strategic decision, they can backfire.[148] But when firms take a stance, they should be given the benefit of the doubt that the move follows a deliberative process. In a field as charged as this, it is difficult to imagine executives inviting scrutiny without first conducting a risk assessment. The most plausible explanation is that they act when the expected payoff – financial, reputational, or both – outweighs the downside. Mistakes happen. But corporations, more than outside observers, are positioned to evaluate the strategic tradeoffs. After all, managing stakeholder expectations and reputational risk already falls squarely within the scope of executive responsibility.

Disney CEO Bob Iger captured this reality well during the company's 2023 annual shareholder meeting, when asked why Disney engaged in cultural and social disputes rather than focusing solely on entertainment:

> I think my job is to strive to do what I think is best for our business, and that includes doing what's best for our cast members – our employees – and what will enable both to flourish. I don't think we should or can weigh in on every issue, and I also understand there are going to be gray areas. There are going to be times when we decide to weigh in on an issue that we believe is worthy of debate because of its relevance and importance to our business or to our employees. And there are times when I actually believe we shouldn't. But I strongly feel that we alone have to determine whether, when, or how to weigh in on an issue, whether it's private or public, of course with the standard that, when we take a position on those matters, there's a true reason why we have. And in almost all cases, it has to be because it directly affects our business or our people.[149]

Ultimately, assessing the business and strategic merits of corporate governing requires analyzing the specific circumstances, intended outcomes, and expertise of decision-makers. In this context, the potential risks and rewards of corporate governing can be properly evaluated – not through broad generalizations, but through a case-by-case assessment.

Therefore, commentators should be wary of calling for blanket constraints simply because corporate governing alienates some politicians.[150] As noted, provoking

Merck's CEO's fallout with Trump in the aftermath of Charlottesville and noting "there's no evidence that this has hurt Merck's business.").

[148] *See infra* Section B.

[149] Quoted in Doug Chia, *Guardians of the VSM Galaxy, Vol. 2*, SOUNDBOARD GOVERNANCE (May 2023), www.soundboardgovernance.com/post/guardians-of-the-vsm-galaxy-vol-2 (emphasis added).

[150] Unsurprisingly, some politicians proposed bills endorsing wholesale approaches. Florida Senator Marco Rubio introduced the Mind Your Own Business Act of 2021 (S. 2829, *117th Cong.* § 1 (2021)), proposing an amendment to the Securities Exchange Act of 1934 granting shareholders the right to sue a company for promoting "divisive concepts" unrelated to its financial interests. Gadinis & Havasy, *supra* note 29, at 1613 n.124.

political backlash may well be part of the strategy.[151] At times, corporations seize an opportunity; at others, they respond to pressure. Disney's conflict with Governor DeSantis, for example, was not only a matter of corporate initiative – it was a reaction to mounting stakeholder demands.[152] In some cases, silence is not even an option, or at least not a neutral one: Saying nothing can function as a position in itself, a form of *passive corporate governing*.[153] Finally, the politicization of corporate action is often not of the corporation's own making – it's imposed from the outside, shaped by media cycles, activist pressure, and a political landscape eager to seize on brand behavior. As Lisa Fairfax observes, corporate political speech now encompasses nearly any issue that has been politicized – whether by political actors or through public discourse – resulting in an ever-expanding and unpredictable range of topics.[154] What is seen as ordinary one day may be cast as political the next, often catching companies off guard.[155] Yet in this volatile landscape, it is still corporations – not courts, not legislatures – that are best positioned to assess the stakes and navigate the fallout.[156]

## C THE SOCIAL ADVOCACY CASE FOR CORPORATE GOVERNING: DO SOCIAL ACTIVISTS AND SOCIETY ULTIMATELY BENEFIT?

The merits of corporate governing become more challenging to decipher when one considers its impact on society, a vast topic beyond the traditional confines of corporate governance. Because corporate governing is geared to make an impact on society, it is essential to understand its normative implications for social activists, on the one hand, and for civil society, on the other hand.

### 1 *Social Activists*

The implications for social activists are more straightforward to address. If they decide to partner up with corporations, it is because they expect to make progress

151 *See supra* note 145 and accompanying text.

152 Disney's initial approach to the "Don't Say Gay" bill was to stay silent. Its stakeholders did not take it well:

> [Disney CEO]'s memo was met with pervasive disappointment and frustration from Disney employees and creative partners. Some – including actors, directors, writers, and animators – called the memo "weak" and "unacceptable." Others demanded that Disney take a public stand against HB 1557.

*Simeone*, 302 A.3d 956, *at* 960 *(footnotes omitted)*.

153 *See supra* note 26 and accompanying text.

154 Fairfax, *supra* note 103, at 2.

155 *Id.* (noting that efforts to clearly distinguish corporate political speech are understandable, but ultimately illusory, making consistent policy development challenging in this fluid environment.).

156 Matteo Gatti, *Corporate Governing: Understanding Corporations as Agents of Socioeconomic Change*, 50 J. Corp. L. 149, 189–90 (2024); Fairfax, *supra* note 103, at 2 (arguing that corporations should address corporate political speech via effective risk management).

they would not otherwise achieve alone.[157] From their perspective, corporate governing is a strategic partnership to get results in high-stakes issues.[158] So long as they perceive the bargain is advantageous, they will engage with corporations and solicit their involvement. If social activists find corporate governing counterproductive, they can stop collaborating with the corporation. While corporations routinely engage in fake grassroots movements to build misleading narratives,[159] "true" social activists can keep corporations honest and disavow initiatives they consider misaligned with their mission. It takes two to tango. If social activists don't stop the dance, it's because, in their strategic calculous, corporate governing works.

Whether corporate governing works for social activism is something to test based on its effectiveness by looking at the solutions corporations managed to offer to pressing policy issues. Some corporations have demonstrated a commitment to social causes and their ability to deliver results. Observing tangible past achievements strengthens the case for corporations as potential allies in addressing societal concerns. Assessing the track record of corporate governing thus offers insight into its ability to drive meaningful change. Past experience suggests that corporate governing has helped social activists gain public support for policy initiatives on LGBTQ+ rights[160] and gun control.[161]

True, some issues are so politically charged that corporate governing risks limited traction.[162] While companies often aim to address societal problems, their actions can fall short – whether due to political risk, strategic calculation, or both.[163]

[157] *See* Lin, *supra* note 53, at 1574 ("By using the resources and expertise of businesses, activists can have a broader, more diverse reach and a more effective impact than they otherwise could on their own").

[158] Corporations and their CEOs help social causes make headlines, which is valuable to social activists. *See* Chatterji & Toffel, *supra* note 2, at 161: "Because the media often widely report CEO statements … – especially on contentious topics – our results imply that when CEOs frame public discourse, they have the potential to shape public policy." (citation omitted). In addition, CEO's help persuade the public, which is also valuable to social activists: "We find that exposure to [Apple CEO Tim] Cook's statement that [Indiana's Religious Freedom Restoration Act] may allow discrimination resulted in 40% of respondents supporting the law, substantially less than the 50% support reported by respondents who were not prompted with this statement; this was a statistically significant difference." *Id.*

[159] *See* John Braithwaite & Peter Drahos, Global Business Regulation 489 (2000) (citing Consumers for World Trade, a pro-GATT industry coalition, Citizens for Sensible Control of Acid Rain, a coal and electricity industry coalition, and the National Wetlands Coalition, a coalition of US oil companies and real estate developers); *see also generally* Melissa J. Durkee, *Astroturf Activism*, 69 Stan. L. Rev. 201 (2017) (discussing the ways in which businesses imitate grassroot organizations).

[160] *See for example*, Ball, *supra* note 35, at 95–125 (describing the extension of corporate benefits to domestic partnership in the 1990s); Fan, *supra* note 55, at 476–83; Sanjukta Brahma, Konstantinos Gavriilidis, Vasileios Kallinterakis, Thanos Verousis, Mengyu Zhang, *LGBTQ and Finance*, 86 Int'l. Rev. Fin. Analysis 8–9 (2023) 102547. *See also* Chatterji & Toffel, *supra* note 18, at 7 (citing various initiatives to thwart religious bills in various states).

[161] *See supra* Chapter 1, Section B.6.

[162] *Cf.* Dorothy S. Lund, *Asset Managers as Regulators*, 171 U. Pa. L. Rev. 77, 138–40 (2023) (discussing "policymaking" efforts by asset managers).

[163] *Id.*

Especially in an age of overt "anti-woke" sentiment,[164] corporations might prefer to play it safe to avoid attracting the ire of politicians and their electorate – corporate silence at the start of the second Trump administration confirms this.[165]

This limitation raises questions about the sufficiency of corporate efforts to bring about meaningful change and whether relying on corporate governing is adequate to address complex social challenges,[166] which I address in Chapter 5.[167] For current purposes, I note that social activists can decide for themselves if they want to collaborate with corporations to achieve socioeconomic change.

### 2 *Civil Society and the Dissenter Rights Issue*

Evaluating the benefits of corporate governing for civil society is far more complex due to challenges in (a) precisely defining the scope – should it include only immediate stakeholders or broader segments of the population? – and (b) measuring its impact in real time – how can the effects of a corporate governing initiative on civil society be accurately assessed?

One's political views inevitably influence the perception of corporate governing in society. As former Chief Justice Leo Strine wrote, people tend "to like corporate conduct that echoes their beliefs and to call corporate conduct discordant with their beliefs illegitimate."[168] Also, one's philosophy as to the role of corporations in society matters. On the one hand, advocates of market-based solutions may view corporate governing as an effective means to address societal issues without pervasive governmental intervention.[169] On the other hand, critics of corporate political expression may rebut that shareholders have no opt-out mechanisms when they disagree with the corporation's political orientation.[170]

Of course, some in society will inevitably raise concerns about a corporate governing initiative,[171] no matter how popular it may be – after all, unanimity is

164 *See supra* Chapter 1, Section C.

165 *See supra* Chapter 2, Section B.2.

166 I address these concerns in Chapter 6.

167 *See infra* Chapter 5, Section B.2.

168 Strine, *supra* note 114, at 346.

169 *See for example*, Martin Lipton, *Corporate Governance: The New Paradigm*, HARV. L. SCH. F. ON CORP. GOVERNANCE (Jan. 11, 2017), https://corpgov.law.harvard.edu/2017/01/11/corporate-governance-the-new-paradigm/#1. (supporting stakeholderism as a recipe to avoid more pervasive governmental regulation).

170 *See for example*, Coates et al., *supra* note 101; Bebchuk & Jackson, *supra* note 104.

171 *See for example*, Stephen Bainbridge, *Woke Business: Putting the Nike-Kaepernick Ad Controversy into Context: The Problem of Social Justice Warrior CEOs*, PROFESSORBAINBRIDGE.COM (Sept. 5, 2018), www.professorbainbridge.com/professorbainbridgecom/2018/09/woke-business-putting-the-nike-kaepernick-ad-controversy-into-context-the-problemof-social-justice-.html (lamenting that "it simply would not occur to [social justice warriors] … like [Nike CEO Phil] Knight that there are folks who would take offense from the Kaepernick ad.").

impossible to achieve.[172] This problem arises from what political theorists call "moral pluralism," that is, societies must grapple with many opinions to bring together.[173] The concerns are understandable; I dub this as the "dissenter rights" issue. For any corporate governing action or message, some in the shareholder base, workforce, or broader society will disagree with it and feel uncomfortable with the corporation's using its levers to achieve the underlying sociopolitical goal.[174] To exemplify, I use the following roadmap to track the impact of corporate governing on various members of society.

### a Investors

The analysis in Sections A and B has mainly focused on shareholders (particularly those who prioritize wealth maximization)[175] and indicates that, though no firm answer can be offered in the abstract, there are circumstances in which shareholders can be well-served by corporate governing.[176] Still, even with an action that results in some verifiable financial gain, some in the shareholder base might object based on political or religious beliefs. Corporate scholarship has elucidated that beneficial owners like investors in a 401(k) plan cannot use the Wall Street rule and sell the stock to invest in an issuer more aligned with their

[172] *See* Strine, *supra* note 114, at 334:

> Encouraging corporations to act on society when you like the policies they support but arguing that they should not act when you oppose the policies is a natural human tendency, of course. But, until the world is comprised solely of people and thus corporations exactly like you, it does not chart a principled path forward.

[173] For a description, see Gadinis & Havasy, *supra* note 29, at 1594 (citing political theory literature and noting that moral pluralism makes "reaching consensus on most policy outcomes exceedingly difficult."). To solve this impasse, they believe the system must find solutions entrusting corporate choices with both sociological and moral legitimacy, as legal legitimacy alone may create much discontent among stakeholders and citizens. *Id.* at 1596–97 & 1599 (arguing that administrative law offers ways to justify such choices to stakeholders and citizens). Some in the literature discuss requiring unanimous shareholder approval for political speech, see Bebchuk & Jackson, *supra* note 104, at 115. *See infra* Chapter 6.

[174] For an analysis of the risks for a pluralistic society when corporations push a policy agenda to its various stakeholders and employees, see Strine, *supra* note 114, at 355–60.

[175] However, there are also shareholders, such as the shareholders described by Hart & Zingales who are interested in "values" and seek to balance financial and non-financial goals. For the latter group, corporate governing may be seen as a way to align corporations with the broader societal objectives they care about. *See* Oliver Hart & Luigi Zingales, *Companies Should Maximize Shareholder Welfare Not Market Value*, 2 J.L. FIN. & ACCT. 247 (2017); Caleb N. Griffin, *Humanizing Corporate Governance*, 75 FLA. L. REV. 689 (2023). *See also* Lipton, *supra* note 99, at 1599–1602.

[176] *See supra* Sections A (discussing the business case) and B (discussing the strategic case). *Cf.* Saura Masconale & Simone M. Sepe, *Citizen Corp. – Corporate Activism and Democracy*, 100 WASH. U. L. REV. 257, 305 (2022) ("Corporate activism increases, rather than reduces, shareholder value.").

beliefs.[177] This is fundamentally a corporate governance issue, widely discussed in the literature[178] and further examined in Chapter 6.

### b Employees and Stakeholder Communities

Similarly, while Sections C.1 and C.2 describe how corporate governing can positively impact employees and similar stakeholder communities (such as business partners or gig workers),[179] a similar dissenter issue arises: The typical example is that of a conservative who works at a corporation whose CEO publicly embraces one or more liberal causes (but of course examples can go in the opposite direction – think of Tesla employees not aligned with Elon Musk's politics). The concern is that non-aligned employees would feel less free when they perceive they are expected to conform to the employer's view.[180] For employees, who are typically dependent on the corporation for their livelihood and may lack viable exit strategies, this is considered a far more significant risk than those suffered by dissenting shareholders.[181]

### c Broader Society

The analysis above is also helpful if we look at broader society. Corporate governing can reverberate outside the corporation and impact citizens and society. Effective corporate governing can contribute to a more sustainable and inclusive economic system in ways that politics may not have as effectively achieved.[182] Additionally, corporations that embrace social responsibility through their initiatives can influence societal values, norms, and, ultimately, policymakers.[183] But again, some

[177] *See for example*, Coates et al., supra note 101.

[178] *See generally* Bebchuk & Jackson, *supra* note 104 (discussing corporate political spending and proposing various measures including disclosures, independent director approval, and shareholder approval); Strine, *supra* note 114 (proposing a series of measures as guardrails against executive abuses); Fisch & Schwarz, supra note 129, at 355 (proposing that corporations collectively take a pledge never to take political postures); Gadinis & Havasy, *supra* note 29, at 1589–90 (suggesting to borrow from the administrative law toolkit).

[179] Lin, *supra* note 53, at 1573. *See also* the literature cited *supra* in Section A.3.B. For a description of selected initiatives that benefit such categories, see *supra* Chapter 1, Section B.

[180] Fisch & Schwarz, *supra* note 129, at 349; Masconale & Sepe, *supra* note 176, at 265.

[181] *Id. See also* Strine, *supra* note 114, at 356–57. *See generally* ELIZABETH ANDERSON, PRIVATE GOVERNMENT: HOW EMPLOYERS RULE OUR LIVES (AND WHY WE DON'T TALK ABOUT IT) (2017) (arguing that Americans who are employed in the private sector lose their fundamental freedoms not only when they are at work but also off-work).

[182] Lin, *supra* note 53, at 1574–79 (mentioning the deeper social impact that corporations could help attain, along with improving operations and funding at social activist organizations); Fan, *supra* note 55, at 490 (noting that corporations have the ability to, among other things, "increase public attention on particular social issues" and "provide funding to the social movement organization").

[183] *Cf.* Marcel Kahan & Edward Rock, *The Emergence of Welfarist Corporate Governance* (Eur. Corp. Governance Inst. Law Working Paper, No. 683/2023), Draft December 22, 2022 (on file with author), at 53:

citizens will be outraged by corporations for using their powers to impact society in this manner.[184]

I address the dissenter rights objection in Chapter 5.[185]

## D THE POLITICAL CASE FOR CORPORATE GOVERNING: DOES IT IMPERIL DEMOCRATIC INSTITUTIONS?

Finally, a critical dimension of the normative analysis revolves around the implications of corporate governing on our democratic institutions. The overarching question one should ask is how imperiled society is by corporations being active on the political front and becoming crucial catalysts for social change. As an observer put it, "[t]he fact that companies, rather than Congress or the courts, are shifting in response to political activism in the United States says something profound – about American tribalism, the demise of political cooperation, and the rise of a sort of liberal corporatocracy."[186]

Before examining the risks associated with this issue in Chapter 5, it is important to first outline key aspects that will help frame the analysis. First, the presence of unelected policymakers raises concerns. Echoing the fund literature,[187] several scholars point to the potential risks arising from the significant political power of unelected actors such as corporations and their ultimate decision-makers.[188] This phenomenon challenges democratic principles by concentrating authority on individuals who lack the legitimacy that elected representatives possess and are not representative of society.[189]

Second, corporate money in politics and corporate influence in policymaking go hand in hand. The impact of corporate contributions and lobbying efforts on political campaigns and policymaking processes is a hotly debated topic, not just

> we see the promise of welfarism as playing out in the political realm by potentially changing the political economy of social regulation and thereby facilitating needed regulatory change. While welfarism looks to the corporate sector to make up for the regulation of externalities that political dysfunction blocks, it may, somewhat ironically, ultimately have a greater impact on improving our politics than on changing private enterprise.

[184] The corporate literature has shown unease not only in finding satisfactory solutions but also in participating to the discussion. Leo Strine described the underlying debate as "rancorous." Strine, *supra* note 114, at 329 & 344.

[185] *See infra* Chapter 5, Sections B.2.a.ii and B.2.b.ii.y.

[186] Derek Thompson, *Why Are Corporations Finally Turning against the NRA?*, ATLANTIC (Feb. 26, 2018), www.theatlantic.com/business/archive/2018/02/nra-discounts-corporations/554264/ (cited by Fan, *supra* note 55, at 471).

[187] John C. Coates, IV, *The Future of Corporate Governance Part I: The Problem of Twelve*, 1, 5–6 (Harv. Pub. L. Working Paper No. 19-07, Sept. 20, 2018), https://papers.ssrn.com/sol3/papers.cfm?abstract_id=3247337; Lund, *supra* note 162, at 140–42.

[188] *See for example*, Lin, *supra* note 53, at 1588 (mentioning corrosion of democratic values); Masconale & Sepe, *supra* note 176, at 305–11; BAINBRIDGE, *supra* note 119, at 150; Fisch & Schwartz, *supra* note 129, at 343–46.

[189] *See infra* Chapter 5, Section B.2.a.i.

in scholarly circles.[190] The substantial financial resources at the disposal of corporations distort the democratic decision-making process, favoring the interests of those with significant economic power over the broader public interest.[191] The 2024 elections not only reinforced this trend but also escalated it to an unprecedented level.[192]

In this regard, the concept of "supercitizens" introduced by Saura Masconale and Simone Sepe inserts another layer to the normative analysis.[193] It highlights the increasing influence of corporations (and, one would add, the superwealthy[194]) to pick and choose areas of policy intervention – a game ordinary individual citizens play in much lower leagues. This power asymmetry can undermine democratic foundations and potentially diminish the ability of ordinary citizens to shape public policy outcomes.

Finally, delegating too much to corporations while giving up on traditional politics is a big hazard. If corporations increasingly take on roles traditionally reserved for government bodies, accountability and transparency mechanisms inherent to democratic governance will be eroded. Chapter 5, which analyzes the trade-offs associated with corporate governing, delves deeply into this issue.[195]

## E SUMMARY

This chapter has analyzed corporate governing through multiple lenses. While traditional corporate governance concerns – such as shareholder value maximization – frame parts of the discussion (Sections A and B), corporate governing extends beyond business strategy. It raises deeper questions about its role in social advocacy and its potential risks to democratic institutions.

Corporations engage in these initiatives as both risk management and opportunity, yet their societal and political implications are far more complex. If corporate governing proves ineffective or counterproductive, stakeholders like social activists may withdraw support. But the broader impact on civil society and democratic institutions requires closer scrutiny. This chapter outlines core tensions; the next two take a deeper dive – Chapter 5 explores promises and risks of corporate governing; Chapter 6 turns to possible policy responses.

190 *See supra* Chapter 2, Section A.3.

191 *See for example*, Bebchuk & Jackson, *supra* note 104; Strine, *supra* note 114.

192 Alan Kronenberg, *The Biggest Political Donors of the 2024 Election*, U.S. News & World Report (Nov. 5, 2024), www.usnews.com/news/elections/articles/2024-11-05/the-biggest-political-donors-of-the-2024-election (mentioning that major donors like Moskovitz, Hoffman, Mellon, and Adelson poured tens to hundreds of millions into political campaigns). Sarah E. Needleman & Anthony DeBarros, *Elon Musk Donated over $250 Million to Pro-Trump Super PACs*, Wall St. J. (Dec. 6, 2024), www.wsj.com/politics/elections/elon-musk-trump-republican-super-pac-investment-78a725cb (reporting that Elon Musk alone gave nearly $250 million to PACs backing Donald Trump).

193 *See* Masconale & Sepe, *supra* note 176, at 282–85.

194 *See* Benjamin I. Page, Jason Seawright & Matthew J. Lacombe, Billionaires and Stealth Politics 86–87 (2019). *See infra* Chapter 5, Section B.2.a.vi.

195 *See infra* Chapter 5, Sections B.2.a.vii and B.2.b.ii.z.

# 5

# The Promises and Risks of Corporate Governing

This chapter analyzes the trade-offs associated with corporate governing. From a corporate perspective, effective corporate governing can positively impact employee recruitment, morale, marketing endeavors, and overall profitability. However, corporations risk alienating stakeholders with divergent political views, including shareholders uncomfortable with their investments endorsing causes that conflict with their beliefs. From a societal standpoint, the issue is even more complex. While corporate governing holds promise for positive societal change, particularly in areas where traditional politics may fall short, it introduces inherent risks. These risks span concerns over accountability, representativeness, divisiveness, and the partial reach of corporate influence. Corporations might act opportunistically, become disengaged, or even adopt antagonistic stances toward prosocial aspirations. The abandonment of traditional politics in favor of corporate governing is fraught with risks, jeopardizing the effective resolution of critical societal issues and potentially weakening democratic institutions.

Ultimately, I identify two fundamental issues with corporate governing. First, it fails genuine social progress in areas where corporate interests clash with broader society needs, such as worker rights, antitrust, privacy, financial regulation, AI, taxes, and many more. This caution is a reminder for policymakers contemplating stakeholderist reforms that might grant corporate executives expanded mandates. Second, the book highlights the potentially undemocratic nature of corporate governing, where dissenting voices may be marginalized, and corporations increasingly shape public policy in ways that sideline traditional democratic institutions. As politics cedes ground to the private sphere, there is a growing risk that public deliberation and institutional policymaking will be replaced by corporate decision-making, further accelerating the erosion of democratic governance.

With the groundwork laid in Chapter 4, this chapter examines the promises and risks of corporate governing. The analysis is structured around two perspectives: corporations (Section A) and society (Section B). As this chapter illustrates, while the benefits to corporations are highly context-dependent, the broader societal implications are more complex, making them harder to navigate and regulate.

## A THE PROMISES AND RISKS OF CORPORATE GOVERNING FOR CORPORATIONS

### 1 *Promises to Corporations (Advantages in Product, Labor, and Capital Markets)*

Chapter 4 posits that, under certain conditions, corporate governing can create advantages across product, labor, and capital markets. Whether these benefits materialize, however, is an empirical question – one that depends on context and is often only clear in hindsight. From a corporate standpoint, corporate governing is a strategic risk that can yield positive or negative outcomes, depending on how effectively it is managed.[1]

In product markets, social initiatives that align with the values of current and potential customers can enhance loyalty and expand the customer base. While companies such as Patagonia and Apple are the first that generally come to mind,[2] many other companies have, at times, benefited from positioning themselves as virtuous actors on key social issues: Walmart's partnership with the Environmental Defense Fund helped the company launch new sources of revenue via environmentally friendly products and cost saving through new energy practices;[3] the Big Three asset managers lured younger generations into investing;[4] Lyft swayed clients from Uber in the immediate aftermath of Trump's Muslim ban;[5] Nike's market share and capitalization soared after offering an endorsement deal to Colin Kaepernick.[6]

Consumers generally respond well to corporate initiatives they see as "values-driven."[7] This explains Nike's disproportionate success in addressing race[8] compared to other more performative companies, like Pepsi.[9] Notably, "true ally" brands have less downside when tackling these issues,[10] as even consumers who disagree with a given initiative are less likely to protest when the company has a history of engaging in hot-button issues.[11]

1 *See* Omari Scott Simmons, *Political Risk Management*, 64 Wm. & Mary L. Rev. 707 (2023) (framing corporate governing as a risk management issue); Matteo Gatti, *Corporate Governing: Understanding Corporations as Agents of Socioeconomic Change*, 50 J. Corp. L. 149, 157 (2024).

2 *See supra* Chapter 4, Section A.1.

3 Tom C.W. Lin, The Capitalist and the Activist: Corporate Social Activism and the New Business of Change 113–14 (2022).

4 *See generally* Michal Barzuza, Quinn Curtis & David H. Webber, *Shareholder Value(s): Index Fund ESG Activism and the New Millennial Corporate Governance*, 93 S. Cal. L. Rev. 1243 (2020).

5 Marisa Kendall, *In Trump Backlash, Lyft Ends Up on Top*, Mercury News (Jan. 31, 2017), www.mercurynews.com/2017/01/31/lyft-scores-first-ever-app-store-win-over-uber/.

6 *See* Aneil Kovvali, *Stark Choices for Corporate Reform*, 123 Colum. L. Rev. 693, 742 (2023); Kate Gibson, *Colin Kaepernick Is Nike's $6 Billion Man*, CBS News (Sept. 24, 2018), www.cbsnews.com/news/colin-kaepernick-nike-6-billion-man/.

7 Daniel Korschun, Hoori Rafieian, Anubhav Aggarwal & Scott D. Swain, *Taking a Stand: Consumer Responses When Companies Get (or Don't Get) Political* 34, Working Paper (2019), https://papers.ssrn.com/sol3/papers.cfm?abstract_id=2806476.

8 *See* Susan Fournier, Shuba Srinivasan & Patrick Marrinan, *Turning Socio-Political Risk to Your Brand's Advantage*, 13.2 NIM Marketing Intel. Rev. 18, 22–24 (2021) (mentioning Nike's extensive history in advocating for social change, especially on racial matters in America). Kovvali, *supra* note 6.

9 Daniel Victor, *Pepsi Pulls Ad Accused of Trivializing Black Lives Matter*, N.Y. Times (Apr. 5, 2017), www.nytimes.com/2017/04/05/business/kendall-jenner-pepsi-ad.html.

10 Nathalie Spielmann, Susan Dobscha, & L. J. Shrum, *Brands and Social Justice Movements: The Effects of True versus Performative Allyship on Brand Evaluation*, 8 J. Association Consumer Res. 83 (2023).

11 *See* Fournier, Srinivasan & Marrinan, *supra* note 8, at 22–24.

Likewise, in labor markets, initiatives promoting sustainability or DEI can impress job candidates, facilitate talent recruitment, and improve productivity within the workforce.[12] Such initiatives boost morale among existing like-minded employees, who, in some cases, are those whose activism has ignited the corporate initiative.[13] Studies have shown that social advocacy can enhance the existing employees' connection to their employer or organization.[14] In turn, employee satisfaction and commitment to their organization predict positive returns.[15] By advocating for issues in which an organization's employees are united in support, an organization can benefit from a more productive and committed workforce, leading to financial gain.[16]

A reputation for a committed and productive workforce may also attract investors, as these companies are more likely to have a strong workforce and be more competitive in the labor markets.[17] As empirical studies suggest, the above advantages may reverberate in the corporation's results for the benefit of shareholders: While there is no evidence that the above advantages *cause* improved financial performance, some studies show a correlation.[18] A study shows that companies with an "activist CEO" tend to have positive market returns.[19] The authors suggest that socially responsible corporate governance can attract institutional investors and bolster equity valuation via increased investor demand.[20]

### 2 *Risks to Corporations (for Shareholders and Other Stakeholders)*

While corporate governing may have advantages, businesses also face risks, as Chapter 4 indicates. One of the primary risks is the alienation of stakeholders, particularly those whose political views conflict with the corporation's stance.[21] This can lead to dissatisfied employees and backlash from consumers, investors, and

12 Justin McCarthy, *Environmental Record a Factor for Most U.S. Job Seekers*, GALLUP (Apr. 13, 2021) https://news.gallup.com/poll/346619/environmental-record-factor-job-seekers.aspx; DELOITTE, 2023 GEN Z AND MILLENNIAL SURVEY 7, www.deloitte.com/global/en/issues/work/content/genzmillennialsurvey.html. *See supra* Chapter 4, Section A.3.b.

13 *See supra* Chapter 2, Section A.1.a.

14 *See* the literature cited *supra* Chapter 4, Section A.3.b. *See also* Alex Edmans, *Does the Stock Market Fully Value Intangibles? Employee Satisfaction and Equity Prices*, 101 J. FIN. ECON. 621 (2011).

15 *Id.*

16 *See* Adam J. Wowak, John R. Busenbark & Donald C. Hambrick, *How Do Employees React When Their CEO Speaks Out? Intra- and Extra-Firm Implications of CEO Sociopolitical Activism*, 67 ADMINISTRATIVE SCIENCE QUARTERLY 553, 574–75 & 580–81 (2022).

17 Anahit Mkrtchyan, Jason Sandvik & Da Xu, *Employee Responses to CEO Activism*, 78 J. ACCT. & ECON., no. 1, 2024.

18 *See* the literature cited *supra* Chapter 4, Section A.3.c. ALEX EDMANS, GROW THE PIE: HOW GREAT COMPANIES DELIVER BOTH PURPOSE AND PROFIT 105–06, 112 (2022).

19 Anahit Mkrtchyan, Jason Sandvik & Vivi Zhu, *CEO Activism and Firm Value*, MGMT. SCIENCE (2023), https://pubsonline.informs.org/doi/10.1287/mnsc.2023.4971.

20 *Id.*

21 Stavros Gadinis & Chris Havasy, *The Quest for Legitimacy: A Public Law Blueprint for Corporate Law*, 57 U.C. DAVIS L. REV. 1581, 1609–10 (2024).

policymakers. Examples abound, ranging from conservative backlash at Bud Light and Target[22] to progressive backlash against companies whose executives took advisory roles during Trump's first term.[23] This risk has only intensified as conservative groups increasingly target corporations they deem too "woke."[24] Boycotting has indeed become a persistent feature of our political landscape and a risk for corporations, with a 2020 survey showing that 38 percent of Americans were actively boycotting a company.[25]

Among the various stakeholders that can be affected, shareholders are historically on top of policymakers' concerns. Some shareholders may be reluctant to see "their money" spent on causes they do not support.[26] Some others may be wary of actions that carry strategic risks and might ultimately backfire, as illustrated in Section B of Chapter 4. These shareholders may argue that it is not in the corporation's best interest to be distracted by politics,[27] let alone to make enemies among politicians, as this could result in increased regulatory scrutiny, investigations, and counter-activism. As Tom Lin put it, "Politicians could subject businesses that take social positions adverse to their political interests to greater scrutiny, negative commentary, and possibly punitive actions, like cancellations of tax subsidies and government contracts."[28] The Disney/DeSantis feud is an example of the risk of becoming a prominent target for regulation and counter-activism. After Disney took a stand against the "Don't Say Gay" law, Florida retaliated by revoking Disney's self-governance rights and seeking payment of prior taxes and debts, and Disney's stock price significantly

[22] *See supra* Chapter 1, Section B.3.

[23] Tanya Dua, *Under Armour Is The Latest Brand Facing Backlash after Ceo Praises Trump*, DIGIDAY (Feb. 8, 2017), https://digiday.com/marketing/armour-latest-brand-facing-backlash-ceo-praises-trump/ (mentioning backlash at Under Armour, L. L. Bean, and New Balance for their CEOs' associations with Trump).

[24] *See supra* Chapter 1, Section C.1 and Chapter 4, Section B.

[25] Jill E. Fisch & Jeff Schwartz, *How Did Corporations Get Stuck in Politics and Can They Escape?*, 3 U. CHI. BUS. L. REV 342, 343–44 & n.99 (2024) (citing Julie Sherrier, *38% of Americans Are Currently Boycotting a Company, and Many Cite Political and Coronavirus Pandemic-Related Reasons*, LENDINGTREE.COM (July 20, 2020), www.lendingtree.com/credit-cards/study/boycotting-companies-political-pandemic-reasons/ (reporting results of survey about customer boycotts)).

[26] See, *for example*, Milton Friedman, The Social Responsibility of Business is to Increase Its Profits, NY TIMES MAG. 32, Sept. 13, 1970; Victor Brudney, *Business Corporations and Stockholders' Rights Under the First Amendment*, 91 YALE L.J. 235, 237–39 (1981); Lucian A. Bebchuk & Robert J. Jackson, Jr., *Corporate Political Speech: Who Decides?*, 124 HARV. L. REV. 83, 112 (2010); John C. Coates et al., Brief of Corporate Law Professors as Amici Curie in Support of Respondents, Friedrichs v. California Teachers Ass'n No. 14–915 (U.S. Nov. 2015), at 4–5 https://scholarship.law.duke.edu/faculty_scholarship/3546; Leo E. Strine, Jr., *Good Corporate Citizenship We Can All Get Behind? Toward a Principled, Non-Ideological Approach to Making Money the Right Way*, 78 BUS. LAW. 329, 331 (2023); STEPHEN M. BAINBRIDGE, THE PROFIT MOTIVE: DEFENDING SHAREHOLDER VALUE MAXIMIZATION 92 (2023); Fisch & Schwartz, supra note 25.

[27] *Id.*

[28] *See* Tom C.W. Lin, *Incorporating Social Activism*, 98 B.U. L. REV. 1535, 1582–83 (2018) (mentioning that "politicians could heap favors onto those that adhere to social positions aligned with their own in a corrupt manner, leading to cronyism in the marketplace.").

declined.[29] Delta also fell victim to political backlash when losing a $35 million tax break for opposing a new Georgia voting law.[30]

In sum, corporations encounter multi-faceted risks when they engage in corporate governing. They risk alienating stakeholders with contrasting political views, shareholders may be uneasy with their firm funding causes they disagree with, and the current corporate governance framework may not be equipped to effectively manage broader agendas that may conflict with shareholder and stakeholder desires.

## B THE PROMISES AND RISKS OF CORPORATE GOVERNING FOR SOCIETY

Viewing corporate governing through a corporate lens suggests, at the very least, withholding immediate judgment. However, given the stakes, reducing it to a mere corporate governance issue would be shortsighted – it is essential to examine its broader societal implications.

### 1 *Promises to Society*

Compared to traditional political action, corporate governing offers distinct advantages in the pursuit of socioeconomic goals. Some relate to its ability to drive change – feasibility, flexibility, speed, and a direct path to policy reform. In some cases, corporations are the only viable force for certain reforms. Other advantages stem from the unique role of corporations in advocacy, including their expertise and the private sector's influence in America. Finally, from a social advocacy perspective, corporations can play a key role in amplifying grassroots activism. I explore each of these advantages below.

#### a Corporate Governing Facilitates Change

##### I FEASIBILITY

Corporate governing offers a feasible avenue for addressing pressing policy issues when the government is dysfunctional or unwilling to act due to political constraints. As illustrated in Chapter 2, it is increasingly difficult for politics to pass meaningful reforms due to several factors, including polarization, the influence of money in politics, and structural challenges like the filibuster. Political gridlock has prevented the implementation of policies that, according to polls, are supported by a majority of citizens: The long list includes labor reform, minimum wage, gun control, and climate change.[31] In this vacuum, and driven by workforce pressure, investor demands, and stakeholder expectations, corporations often step in to address socioeconomic issues and act as alternative agents

[29] Simeone v. Walt Disney Co., 302 A.3d 956, 961–963 (Del. Ch. 2023) (mentioning that the "stock price fell during the summer [of 2022] from $145.70 per share on March 1 to $91.84 on July 14. On November 9 – the day after Governor DeSantis was reelected – Disney's stock fell to $86.75 per share.").

[30] Fisch & Schwartz, *supra* note 25, at 345.

[31] *See supra* Chapter 2, Section B.3.

of change, especially in areas like climate action, social justice, and economic inequality, where they fill the void left by the government.[32]

## II FLEXIBILITY AND SPEED

In addition, corporations have the advantage of being nimble and adaptable in their decision-making processes. Unlike politics, which are often slow and bureaucratic, corporate entities can quickly respond to emerging issues and adjust their strategies accordingly. They do not need to start a movement or convince a large group of people that their stance is, in fact, correct.[33] This flexibility enables them to address pressing concerns with agility, bypassing the delays often associated with legislative and regulatory processes. Timely responses to societal demands ensure that pressing issues are addressed.[34]

## III CONDUIT TO ACTUAL REFORM

Not only can corporate governing provide an alternative to political reform, but corporations' initiatives should also be seen as the first and almost necessary steps to get to such a reform.[35] Corporations act as first movers in fields like climate action or abandoning mandatory arbitration because they expect legislatures to level the playing field eventually. By establishing new norms, these corporations hope lawmakers will introduce regulations to compel their competitors to adopt similar standards, ensuring a fair, competitive environment. For example, Marcel Kahan and Ed Rock argue that, as corporations increasingly engage in ESG practices, they will push lawmakers to adopt ESG reforms that ensure all companies, including those resistant to change, adhere to similar standards.[36] This creates consistency between companies prioritizing ESG and those not yet embracing these practices.[37] In addition, multinational companies can even bypass the challenges

[32] Many authors describe, and some even praise, corporate reforms as more feasible. *See, for example*, Lin, *supra* note 28, at 1574–75; Jennifer S. Fan, *Woke Capital: The Role of Corporations in Social Movements*, 9 HARV. BUS. L. REV. 441, 471 (2019); Kovvali, *supra* note 6, at 717–23. *See also* Marcel Kahan & Edward Rock, *The Emergence of Welfarist Corporate Governance* (Eur. Corp. Governance Inst. Law Working Paper, No. 683/2023), Draft December 22, 2022 (on file with author), at 52; Leo E. Strine, Jr., *Restoration: The Role Stakeholder Governance Must Play in Recreating a Fair and Sustainable American Economy: A Reply to Professor Rock*, 76 BUS. LAW. 397, 434 (2021). *But see*, for a progressive voice skeptical of the efficacy of corporate intervention, Robert B. Reich, *The Case against Corporate Social Responsibility* 3, Goldman School Working Paper Series GSP08-003 (Aug. 1, 2008), https://papers.ssrn.com/sol3/papers.cfm?abstract_id=1213129.

[33] Kovvali, *supra* note 6, at 701.

[34] *See id.* at 720.

[35] Kahan & Rock, *supra* note 32, at 52 (noting that "[welfarism] may ultimately have a greater impact on improving our politics than on changing private enterprise").

[36] *Id.*

[37] Aneil Kovvali speculates that once corporations move in a certain direction, opposing politicians will take notice and recalibrate their priors. *See* Kovvali, *supra* note 6, at 728–29. Based on recent experience, at least on the ESG front, this has not materialized. Not only have Republican politicians not budged, but they have unleashed significant counterattacks against ESG. *See supra* Chapter 1, Section C.

of international coordination in policymaking and establish transnational practices, potentially fostering convergence on key themes at the global level.[38]

Corporate governing has, in fact, driven meaningful reform. In response to the #MeToo movement, companies like Microsoft, Uber, and Google ended forced arbitration for sexual harassment claims, revamped reporting procedures, and strengthened internal policies.[39] The momentum culminated in Congress banning mandatory arbitration for such claims in 2022.[40] Similarly, corporate recognition of Juneteenth as a paid holiday – led by Nike, Twitter, Target, General Motors, and Lyft, with banks like JPMorgan Chase and Capital One adjusting their hours[41] – helped pave the way for Congress to establish it as a federal holiday.[42] Though initially stayed by federal courts and ultimately rescinded by the Trump SEC,[43] the Biden-era SEC climate disclosure rules were designed, in part, to standardize the fragmented and inconsistent ESG disclosures that corporations had been voluntarily producing.[44]

## IV ONLY GAME IN TOWN

Finally, for liberals and progressives, corporations may represent the only viable path to prosocial reform in conservative states or when national politics lean right. When political backing is absent, aligning with Corporate America can become a way for underrepresented groups to safeguard – or even advance – their rights. For example, as illustrated in Chapter 2, corporations frequently opposed controversial policies during the Trump presidency, including the Muslim Ban and the withdrawal from the Paris Climate Agreement, with responses ranging from amicus briefs and public statements to executive resignations.[45] Past corporate efforts led to tangible successes, such as the backlash against North Carolina's HB2 which contributed to its partial repeal in 2017.[46] A study by Dorothea Roumpi, Panagiotis Giannakis, and John Delery finds that corporations with liberal CEOs operating in states that do not have laws protecting LGBTQ+ employees are more likely to adopt LGBTQ+-friendly practices.[47]

38 For this insight, see Dorothy S. Lund, *Asset Managers as Regulators*, 171 U. PA. L. REV. 77, 135–36 (2023) (making this point with respect to the influence of large asset managers on corporations).

39 *See supra* Chapter 1, Section B.2.

40 Deborah A. Widiss, *New Law Limits Mandatory Arbitration in Cases Involving Sexual Assault or Sexual Harassment*, 50 A.B.A. LAB. & EMP'T L. NEWS, no. 13, Fall 2022, at 13.

41 *See supra* Chapter 1, Section B.1.

42 *See* Lexi Lonas, *Biden Signs Bill Establishing Juneteenth as Federal Holiday*, THE HILL (June 17, 2021), https://thehill.com/changing-america/respect/equality/559079-biden-signs-bill-establishing-juneteenth-as-federal-holiday/.

43 *See supra* Chapter 1, Section B.4.

44 Lisa M. Fairfax, *Dynamic Disclosure: An Expose on the Mythical Divide between Voluntary and Mandatory ESG Disclosure*, 101 TEX. L. REV. 273, 296 (2022) (mentioning that "the 2022 climate rule proposal indicated that concerns around accuracy served as an important impetus for the rule.").

45 *See supra* Chapter 2, Section B.2.

46 *See supra* Chapter 1, Section B.3.

47 *Cf.* Dorothea Roumpi, Panagiotis Giannakis & John E. Delery, *Adoption of Lgbt-Friendly Practices: The Effect of Institutional Pressures and Strategic Choice*, 30 HUM. RESOUR. MANAG. J. 604, 617 (2019).

### b The Qualities of Corporate Governing

#### I KNOWLEDGE

Compared to the public sector, corporations are said to have superior expertise and greater data in certain areas, especially technology.[48] They can repurpose that knowledge through powerful advertising arms to shape public opinion.[49] Moreover, corporations benefit from having diverse teams, bringing together people with different backgrounds, skills, and perspectives, many of whom are knowledgeable or support social and economic causes.[50] This collective knowledge, which is often supplemented by experts the corporation hires to navigate the issues,[51] helps companies address modern social issues and improves the effectiveness of their governing efforts.[52]

#### II PRIVATE SECTOR IN AMERICA

In the United States, the private sector is perceived as a more fertile avenue for change than traditional politics. This perception stems from a combination of factors, including the ideology of a more individualistic society and a changing workforce composition, particularly in high-profile industries like technology.[53] Of course, some policy advocates have a vested preference for the private sector to take the lead: Martin Lipton and others who support stakeholder-oriented governance believe that businesses can address and manage social and economic concerns through self-regulation, thus reducing the need for legislative intervention.[54]

### c Appeal to Social Activists: Amplifying Grassroots Activism

For social activists, engaging with corporations can effectively exert "prime time" pressure and gain media coverage for their causes.[55] By partnering with corporations,

48 Omari Scott Simmons, *Political Risk Management*, 64 WM. & MARY L. REV. 707, 766 (2023).

49 *Id.*

50 *Cf.* Michal Barzuza, Quinn Curtis & David H. Webber, *The Millennial Corporation: Strong Stakeholders, Weak Managers* 21–22, Eur. Corp. Governance Inst., Law Working Paper No. 687/2023 (2023), http://ssrn.com/abstract_id=3918443;DELOITTE, 2023 GEN Z AND MILLENNIAL SURVEY 7, www.deloitte.com/global/en/issues/work/content/genzmillennialsurvey.html.

51 Gadinis & Havasy, *supra* note 21, at 1639–40.

52 Lin, *supra* note 28, at 1574–78. However, these claims have limits. Corporations surely know their markets – but that doesn't mean they're equipped to govern the public sphere, which demands solving different problems for different constituencies.

53 *See* Jennifer S. Fan, *Employees as Regulators: The New Private Ordering in High Technology Companies*, 2019 UTAH L. REV. 973, 1008–14 (2020).

54 Martin Lipton, *Corporate Governance: The New Paradigm*, Harv. L. Sch. F. on Corp. Governance (Jan. 11, 2017), https://corpgov.law.harvard.edu/2017/01/11/corporate-governance-the-new-paradigm/#1 [https://perma.cc/D686-D7GK] ("corporations and investors should band together to resist legislation and regulation that may discourage long-term investment or that presumes that the long-term health of society is not aligned with the long-term interests of business"). On the flip side, it is when private ordering fails that actual reform may kick in. *See* Gadinis & Havasy, *supra* note 21, at 1652–53.

55 Lin, *supra* note 28, at 1575–76.

activists can draw attention to specific issues and amplify their voices, benefiting from corporate influence and reach. They can achieve goals that would be prohibitive without the resources and reach of a large corporation. This, of course, goes both ways. Because one of the most critical factors in the success of a corporate governing initiative is authenticity,[56] activists can supply authenticity in exchange for getting the necessary thanks to corporations.

### d Assessment

In general, corporate governing aims to address societal issues that politics cannot or will not resolve. From a societal standpoint, it helps tackle critical policy challenges where government action is delayed or absent. Significant progress has been made: LGBTQ+ rights,[57] Detroit's revitalization,[58] changing perceptions of the gun industry,[59] corporate pledges following George Floyd's murder,[60] and increased board diversity[61] are notable examples. While these actions alone may not solve systemic problems, some can plausibly argue that incremental improvements are preferable to stagnation.[62] However, as Section B.2 highlights, such initiatives also carry substantial societal risks.

## 2 *Risks to Society*

At a societal level, corporate governing raises several concerns. Critics argue it is undemocratic, lacks accountability, and often excludes diverse viewpoints. Its impact can be limited and inconsistent, with corporations potentially losing interest or acting opportunistically against societal goals. Corporate influence can contribute

56 *See supra* Chapter 4, Section A.2.

57 *See generally* CARLOS A. BALL, THE QUEERING OF CORPORATE AMERICA: HOW BIG BUSINESS WENT FROM LGBTQ ADVERSARY TO ALLY (2019) (chronicling how big business became an important ally to promote marriage equality and rebuke discriminatory laws and regulations). *See also* the partial repeal of North Carolina's HB2. *See supra* Chapter 1, Section B.3.

58 LIN, supra note 3, at 110–13 (citing data collected by the Chicago Fed and noting that JPMorgan Chase's commitment to revitalize Detroit resulted in increases in real per capita income and "gross city product").

59 *Id.* at 3–4 (noting that Corporate America's response to Parkland and subsequent shootings represented a sea change on the overall perception of the gun industry not just in public opinion but within the capitalist establishment).

60 Whether the pledges translated into real progress is unclear given the lack of transparency on the implementation of the various initiatives; also, the bulk of the pledged money (around $45 billion) is for home ownership programs at JPM Morgan Chase and Bank of America, which non-Black citizens can apparently tap into. *See* Tracy Jan, Jena McGregor & Meghan Hoyer, *Corporate America's $50 Billion Promise*, WASH. POST (Aug. 23, 2023), www.washingtonpost.com/business/interactive/2021/george-floyd-corporate-america-racial-justice/.

61 Lisa M. Fairfax, *Racial Rhetoric or Reality? Cautious Optimism on the Link between Corporate #BLM Speech and Behavior*, 2022 COLUM. BUS. L. REV. 118, 166–68 (2022).

62 *See* the literature cited *supra* note 32.

to political gridlock, and shifting from traditional politics to corporate governing is risky and may leave critical issues unaddressed. Section B.2.a showcases these risks, while Section B.2.b takes a deeper look at the most concerning among them.

### a Showcasing the Societal Risks of Corporate Governing

#### I UNDEMOCRATIC: LACK OF ACCOUNTABILITY AND REPRESENTATIVENESS

One of the most recurring concerns in the literature is the lack of political accountability of the executives and managers who make policy choices. Some critics see this as fundamentally undemocratic because the decision-makers are not elected by the polity.[63] Those who want to make a policy impact should run for office, the argument goes. Surreptitiously passing what detractors call divisive policies defies the rules of the democratic game. This line of criticism is a staple of Milton Friedman's famous opposition to corporate social responsibility:[64] "those who favor the taxes and expenditures in question have failed to persuade a majority of their fellow citizens to be of like mind and … are seeking to attain by undemocratic procedures what they cannot attain by democratic procedures."[65]

A related criticism points out that the corporate decision-makers are not representative of society at large, because they mostly come from privileged backgrounds and skew white and male.[66] Given that the majority of corporate decision-makers are wealthy, some argue that corporate social agendas have promoted a pseudo-plutocracy.[67]

#### II DIVISIVENESS AND LACK OF PLURALISM

Corporate initiatives often divide. As discussed earlier, choosing the wrong political stance risks alienating key stakeholders, posing a significant challenge at the corporate level.[68] Moreover, these actions can have broader societal repercussions.

63 *See, for example*, Saura Masconale & Simone M. Sepe, *Citizen Corp.- Corporate Activism and Democracy*, 100 WASH. U. L. REV. 257, 305–11 (2022); John Coates IV, *Corporate Speech and the First Amendment: History, Data, and Implications*, 30 CONST. COMMENT. 223 (2015) (discussing the implications of *Citizens United*); Gadinis & Havasy, *supra* note 21, at 1616. Similar concerns are raised with respect to the related issue of the influence exerted by large asset managers on corporations. *See* John C. Coates, IV, *The Future of Corporate Governance Part I: The Problem of Twelve*, 1, 5–6 (Harv. Pub. L. Working Paper No. 19–07, Sept. 20, 2018), https://papers.ssrn.com/sol3/papers.cfm?abstract_id=3247337; Lund, *supra* note 38, at 1381.

64 *See* Friedman, *supra* note 26.

65 *Id*. In a similar vein, see Phil Gramm & Mike Solon, *Keep Politics out of the Boardroom*, WALL ST. J. (July 19, 2018), www.wsj.com/articles/keep-politics-out-of-the-boardroom-1531952912 ("Arguments for imposing political and social objectives on business often are little more than rationalizations for forcing businesses to abide by values that have been rejected in Congress and the courts.").

66 *See generally* Jill E. Fisch, *The "Bad Man" Goes to Washington*, 75 FORDHAM L. REV. 1593 (2006); Ronald J. Gilson, *Corporate Governance versus Real Governance*, 34 J. APPL. CORP. FIN. 8, 11 (2022); Strine, *supra* note 26, at 354.

67 Fisch & Schwartz, *supra* note 25, at 349.

68 *See supra* Section A.2.

For example, the fact that corporate governing initiatives may alienate several employees reinforces fears that many Americans lose their fundamental freedoms in the workplace – an issue I refer to as "dissenter rights." Drawing on Elizabeth Anderson's work,[69] former Chief Justice Leo Strine expressed the following concern:

> [A] system that facilitates corporate inculcation of certain political and social values is disadvantageous for workers, because it could make them have to shop for red or blue companies, or just endure working hours in an atmosphere that lacks the pluralism and freedom that represents a key part of being an American.[70]

In many cases, corporations and society face a lose–lose scenario: Speaking out risks alienating some, while staying silent risks alienating even more. This critical dilemma will be explored further in subsection B.2.a.vii.b.

### III PARTIAL REACH OF CORPORATE GOVERNING

Another limitation of corporate governing is the inherent partiality of government substitution – it cannot address society as a whole but primarily benefits a corporation's own stakeholders, those who get to enjoy better treatment than the bare minimum under the law. This voluntary trend is most visible among large, publicly traded firms – often influenced by the personalities and politics of their CEOs.[71] Some might argue that large firms willingly adopt higher self-imposed standards because, unlike their smaller peers, they can absorb the costs and position themselves advantageously for when legislative mandates eventually level the playing field.[72] Additionally, corporate governing may be something only firms in high-margin, low-competition markets can afford.[73]

69 Elizabeth Anderson, Private Government: How Employers Rule Our Lives (And Why We Don't Talk about It) (2017).

70 Strine, *supra* note 26, at 357.

71 *Id.* at 369 (summarizing empirical literature finding that CEOs who are powerful, younger, celebrity figures, narcissistic, or from underrepresented groups (e.g., women, BIPOC, LGBTQ+) are more likely to engage in activism).

72 On the leveling the playing field as a policy rational, see John Braithwaite, Regulatory Capitalism: How It Works, Ideas for Making It Work Better 22 (2008) (discussing self-regulation as a means of creating competitive parity) *and* Luca Enriques, Matteo Gatti & Roy Shapira, *How the EU Sustainability Due Diligence Directive Could Reshape Corporate America*, Eur. Corp. Governance Inst. Law Working Paper, No. 817/2025 (2025), forthcoming Stan. L. Rev. (2026) at 16, https://papers.ssrn.com/sol3/papers.cfm?abstract_id=5083571 (arguing that certain EU harmonization efforts in climate and human rights regulation may function as barriers to entry, favoring large incumbents over smaller competitors). Of course, this concern goes back to George J. Stigler, *The Theory of Economic Regulation*, 2 Bell J. Econ. & Mgmt. Sci. 3, 3 (1971) (observing that large businesses often push for regulation that ultimately benefits them).

73 Mark J. Roe, *Corporate Purpose and Corporate Competition*, 99 Wash. U. L. Rev. 233 (2021) (arguing that only firms operating in noncompetitive settings can afford to pursue a stakeholderist agenda, while those under the pressure of competitive markets might take a more cautious approach).

The flip side is that its voluntary and selective nature creates a hold-out problem: Firms embracing societal values may risk lower returns compared to those that do not; as a result, many might decide to stay out of it.[74] Overall, corporate governing lacks crucial characteristics of state actions, like for instance generality, durability, and enforceability of its measures.[75]

## IV FLAKY OR OPPORTUNISTIC CORPORATE GOVERNING

Even when limited in scope, corporate governing initiatives can still yield incremental benefits for affected groups. The argument goes: It's imperfect, but it's better than nothing. Still, these efforts are vulnerable. Corporations may scale them back over time – often in response to shifting incentives or mounting political pressure.[76]

As self-interested actors,[77] corporations are quick to recalibrate when the risks outweigh the perceived gains. One clear example is the retreat from DEI initiatives in response to growing backlash from conservative groups.[78] In the current political climate, many corporations have chosen to step back.[79]

Another reason is that corporations now face diminished investor pressure to act on ESG matters, a trend that some have already observed in the disengagement of some asset managers.[80] Meanwhile, some activist shareholders – like Bill

74 *Id.*; Matteo Gatti & Chrystin Ondersma, *Stakeholder Syndrome: Does Stakeholderism Derail Effective Protections for Weaker Constituencies?*, 100 N.C. L. Rev. 167, 224 (2021) (discussing stakeholderism and noting that voluntary stakeholderism may be affected by a hold-out problem); Kahan & Rock, *supra* note 32, at 41–43; Holger Spamann & Jacob Fisher, *Corporate Purpose: Theoretical and Empirical Foundations/Confusions*, Eur. Corp. Governance Inst. Law Working Paper, No. 664/2022, at 6, http://ssrn.com/abstract_id=4269517 (discussing substitution effects as a limit to prosocial actions in markets).

75 *See infra* note 119 and accompanying text.

76 *See supra* Chapter 1, Section C.4.

77 David Vogel, The Market for Virtue 4 (2005):

> precisely because CSR is voluntary and market-driven, companies will engage in CSR only to the extent that it makes business sense for them to do so.

78 Jeff Green & Phil Kuntz, *Anti-LGBTQ Backlash Puts a Chill on Corporate America's Rhetoric*, Bloomberg (June 29, 2023), www.bloomberg.com/news/articles/2023-06-29/us-companies-were-less-vocal-on-pride-month-during-anti-lgbtq-protests?leadSource=uverify%20wall&sref=DIvsyJQr#xj4y7vzkg (reporting that mentions of Pride Month were down on earnings calls and in filings for the first time in five years); Jeff Green, *Businesses Are Quietly Rethinking Their DEI Efforts: Equality*, Bloomberg (July 27, 2023), www.bloomberg.com/news/newsletters/2023-07-27/businesses-are-quietly-rethinking-their-dei-efforts-equality; Jeff Green, *US Companies Caught in Diversity Crossfire Are Frozen by Uncertainty*, Bloomberg (July 29, 2023), www.bloomberg.com/news/articles/2023-07-29/us-companies-worry-they-could-face-legal-action-over-dei-initiatives.

79 *See* supra Chapter 1, Section C.4.

80 *See, for example*, William W. Bratton, *Shareholder Primacy versus Shareholder Accountability*, Eur. Corp. Governance Inst. Law Working Paper, No. 726/2023, at 34, http://ssrn.com/abstract_id=4431055 (noting that asset managers have been implementing schemes for passing voting decisions to their clients in response to backlash from red state politicians opposing climate change mitigation). For the argument that achievements in stakeholder governance have been largely driven by shareholders rather than management, see Cathy Hwang & Yaron Nili, *Shareholder-Driven Stakeholderism*,

Ackman – engage corporations in ideological battles, while others intervene with a narrower aim: to improve financial performance. In both cases, corporate governing can end up on the chopping block. In other words, stock markets may pressure corporations to abandon corporate governing – whether due to its potential to alienate politicians and large segments of the electorate or simply as a pretext to justify a strategic shift or boardroom change.[81]

All of this can have detrimental effects on citizens. Not only do they lose trust in corporations and markets but also as corporate activism fades from the spotlight and becomes less appealing to businesses, the resulting instability could also disrupt corporate practices that many individuals have come to expect and some may even depend on.

## V ABSENT OR ANTAGONISTIC CORPORATE GOVERNING: DISTRIBUTIONAL MATTERS

There's worse: If corporations only intervene when it makes business sense,[82] they will *not* intervene in matters where they have a conflicting interest.[83] Whenever the underlying policies advocated by reform advocates are expected to hurt a corporation's bottom line, corporations will not activate.[84]

As a result, we shouldn't expect corporations to coordinate meaningfully around issues that matter most to citizens. Quite the contrary. Consider

U. CHI. L. REV. ONLINE (Apr. 15, 2020), https://lawreviewblog.uchicago.edu/2020/04/15/shareholder-driven-stakeholderism-hwang-nili/ [https://perma.cc/NRC7-M3HB].

81 Even before the current retreat, authors were warning about the opportunistic nature of corporations, which tend to engage selectively, avoiding high-risk issues. *See* Lin, *supra* note 28, at 1586 (noting the reluctance to take on religious or conservative issues); Anna Toniolo, *Corporate Participation in Social Debates*, 3 U. CHI. BUS. L. REV. 361, 367 (2024) (analyzing corporate reactions to *Dobbs* and noting that "corporate leaders are getting more cautious in wading into political matters"). Similar dynamics affect large asset managers. *See* Lund, *supra* note 38, at 84 (noting that "the need to ensure client approval indicates that the Big Three will mandate only tepid changes in corporate behavior, and that their rules are not likely to bring about the sweeping changes that may be necessary to address pressing social problems"); Barzuza, Curtis & Webber, *supra* note 4, at 1305–06 (finding that index funds push low-cost issues like board diversity but hesitate on costly ones like carbon reduction).

82 *See supra* note 77.

83 ADOLF A. BERLE & GARDINER C. MEANS, THE MODERN CORPORATION AND PRIVATE PROPERTY 313 (Routledge ed., 2017) (1932) ("Where its own interests are concerned, [the corporation] even attempts to dominate the state.").

84 Gatti & Ondersma, *supra* note 74, at 229–30. *See also* BAINBRIDGE, *supra* note 26, at 109–111 (quoting Lucian A. Bebchuk, Kobi Kastiel & Roberto Tallarita, *Stakeholder Capitalism in the Time of COVID*, 40 YALE J. REG. 60, (2023) (discussing how corporations did (not) cater to stakeholders in the wake of the Covid-19 pandemic and arguing that "if corporate leaders chose not to protect the environment, employees, or other stakeholders in a time when stakeholders needed extraordinary protection and shareholders enjoyed a booming market, it is not reasonable to expect them to protect stakeholders in normal times.")). For the argument that corporations intervene only when it helps their bottom line, *see* Reich, *supra* note 32, at 51:

> Supercapitalism does not permit acts of corporate virtue that erode the bottom line. No company can "voluntarily" take on an extra cost that its competitors don't also take on.

labor and employment matters,[85] data protection,[86] antitrust,[87] tax,[88] financial reform,[89] corporate reform where management or controlling shareholders have rents to protect (e.g., proxy access, executive compensation, and self-dealing),[90] lobbying and political spending,[91] AI,[92] and so forth.

Not only do corporations fail to help on such matters but they also actively *lobby against* prosocial policies. For example, some businesses that outwardly champion progressive causes through corporate governing have unequivocal anti-union track records.[93] Corporations' union-busting efforts – well documented at the likes of Walmart, Google, Amazon, and Starbucks – underscore the anti-labor stance of big business.[94] Opaque contributions to the US Chamber of Commerce and ALEC,

85 Gatti & Ondersma, *supra* note 74, at 216–19.

86 Karl Evers-Hillstrom & Rebecca Klar, *Corporate lobbying could imperil sweeping data privacy bill*, THE HILL (Aug. 3, 2022), https://thehill.com/lobbying/3585322-corporate-lobbying-could-imperil-sweeping-data-privacy-bill/.

87 Emily Birnbaum, *How Big Tech Defeated the Biggest Antitrust Push in Decades on Capitol Hill*, L.A. TIMES (Dec. 20, 2022), www.latimes.com/business/technology/story/2022-12-20/how-big-tech-defeated-the-biggest-antitrust-push-in-decades-on-capitol-hill (documenting Big Tech's resistance to Biden-era antitrust proposed restrictions).

88 Brian Kelleher Richter, Krislert Samphantharak & Jeffrey F. Timmons, *Lobbying and Taxes*, 53 AM. J. POL. SCIENCE 893 (2009) (finding that firms that spend more on lobbying in a given year pay lower effective tax rates in the next year). *Cf.* Gideon Parchomovsky & Danielle A. Chaim, *The Missing "T" in ESG*, 77 VAND. L. REV. 789 (2024) (arguing that the standard ESG framework is flawed because it ignores corporate tax avoidance, undermining the public goods and social policies that ESG seeks to promote); Reuven S. Avi-Yonah, *ESG Irony: Why Corporate Tax Avoidance Must Be Considered*, 117 TAX NOTES INT'L 739 (2025) (same).

89 Brian Slodysko, Ken Sweet & The Associated Press, *Army of Lobbyists Worked to Water Down Bank Rules That Regulated Svb and Signature: "You Couldn't Throw an Elbow without Running into One,"* FORTUNE (Mar. 21, 2023), https://fortune.com/2023/03/21/army-lobbyists-worked-water-down-bank-rules-regulated-svb-signature-dodd-frank/.

90 Bebchuk & Jackson, *supra* note 26, at 91. With regards to the 2025 overhaul of Delaware corporate law, see, *for example*, Lucian Bebchuk, Kobi Kastiel & Edward B. Rock, *Delaware and the Perils of Small Minority Controllers*, HARV. L. SCH. F. ON CORP. GOVERNANCE (Mar. 5, 2025), https://corpgov.law.harvard.edu/2025/03/05/delaware-and-the-perils-of-small-minority-controllers/ (arguing that Delaware SB 21 seeks to make the state's corporate law more favorable to controlling shareholders by weakening judicial oversight of conflicted transactions and director independence, potentially at the expense of public investors).

91 *See* Lund, *supra* note 38, at 143:

> if the Big Three were to push the government to take steps to limit the influence of corporate spending in politics, and to regulate business to respond to the risk of climate change or improve workplace diversity, there would be less of a need for them to intervene to adopt rules. The fact that they have not done so suggests that they may benefit from playing the role of regulator of last resort.

92 Roberto Tallarita, *AI Is Testing the Limits of Corporate Governance*, HARV. BUS. REV. (Dec. 05, 2023), https://hbr.org/2023/12/ai-is-testing-the-limits-of-corporate-governance (arguing that corporate governance is ill-equipped to contain the externalities of AI expansion).

93 Gatti & Ondersma, *supra* note 74, at 216–19; Strine, *supra* note 26, at 333 n.7 (arguing that "[c]orporations often oppose laws that protect workers, consumers, or the environment" and providing a long list of examples).

94 Gatti & Ondersma, *supra* note 74, at 216–19.

both of which actively obstruct pro-worker policies, further confirm this.[95] What applies to labor and employment legislation extends virtually across any areas of regulation: Corporations invest heavily to resist regulations that could threaten their business.[96]

Perhaps corporate governing is helpful to (at least some) corporations because it lures enough social activists and distracts public opinion from what once was an undisputed assumption: that corporations are generally against prosocial measures. While this book illustrates that this, in fact, may no longer be true in many fields, corporate governing might have perilous side effects in other fields with a greater distributive component. Managers will be cautious about trading off value with *values* when real money is on the table. As Stephen Bainbridge observed, "Managers' incentives are aligned more closely with the shareholders' interest in value maximization than with ESG concerns."[97]

Studies on executives' political affiliation reinforce these concerns: CEOs' political contributions substantially favor Republicans,[98] and voter registration of top executives leans Republican by a seven-to-three ratio.[99] How do we reconcile this with the observation that corporate governing primarily advances liberal goals? Perhaps some corporate governing initiatives benefit business, while others do not. Or maybe certain initiatives are less harmful (or perceived as less harmful) to business than the more distributive policies described above. The literature on billionaires' politics suggests that while most of the ultra-wealthy do not hold socially conservative views, they support Republican candidates due to alignment on economic issues.[100] Certain initiatives may be reconciled with decision-makers' politics because they do not frustrate their economic credo.[101]

95 *See supra* Chapter 2, Section A.3.

96 *See supra* Chapter 2, Section A.3.

97 Bainbridge, *supra* note 26, at 97. *See also* Dorothy S. Lund & Elizabeth Pollman, *The Corporate Governance Machine*, 121 Colum. L. Rev. 2563, 2565–66 (2021) (arguing that "a vast array of institutional players – proxy advisors, stock exchanges, ratings agencies, institutional investors and associations – enshrine shareholder primacy in public markets.").

98 Alma Cohen, Moshe Hazan, Roberto Tallarita & David Weiss, *The Politics of CEOs*, 11 J. Leg. Analysis, 1 (2019). A study by Reilly Steel confirms that CEOs' are the most conservative individuals in the C-suite and the board. *See* Reilly Steel, *The Political Transformation of Corporate America, 2001–2022*, at 4, Reilly Steel, *The Political Transformation of Corporate America, 2001–2022*, at 3, forthcoming Am. Pol. Sci. Rev. (working draft Mar. 29, 2025), https://static1.squarespace.com/static/6019c4d665a1bd185288d428/t/67e7648118c6d849a51480da/1743217798724/Steel_Political_Transformation_of_Corporate_America_3-28-25.pdf.

99 Vyacheslav Fos, Elisabeth Kempfs & Margarita Tsoutsoura, *The Political Polarization of Corporate America* (Working paper June 29, 2022), https://papers.ssrn.com/sol3/papers.cfm?abstract_id=3784969.

100 Benjamin I. Page, Jason Seawright & Matthew J. Lacombe, Billionaires and Stealth Politics 86–87 (2019) (mentioning that both Robert Koch and Sheldon Alston went on record as pro-choice but supported Republicans for their policies on the budget and for their anti-union stance).

101 *Id.*

## VI DO CORPORATIONS CONTRIBUTE TO GRIDLOCK IN DC?

If corporate governing is ultimately constrained by business interests, we must ask whether its influence extends beyond regulatory resistance to shaping the broader political landscape itself. One can push this argument further and speculate that corporations contribute to political gridlock, especially at the federal level.[102] Lobbying and political contributions indicate this is the case: the outsized influence of a small group of wealthy individuals and corporations on the political process can exacerbate gridlock by reinforcing partisan interests and obstructing broader legislative progress.[103] Bill Niskanen, former Reagan economic advisor and former chairman of the Cato Institute, famously praised gridlock on the argument that businesses flourish because of less public spending and fewer chances of new legislation.[104] In other words, corporations prefer to maintain legislative inertia to create a stable regulatory environment that aligns with their interests.[105] Unsurprisingly, most political contributions remain opaque and primarily originate from the extremely wealthy.[106]

Moreover, political gridlock amplifies corporate influence, enabling businesses to steer societal outcomes in their favor while obstructing policies detrimental to their interests. From this perspective, corporate governing can be viewed as corporations both responding to and capitalizing on a crisis they helped create, reaping benefits on multiple fronts.[107] Of course, Elon Musk's tenure at DOGE – though technically a case of individual rather than corporate power – illustrates the troubling dynamics of private interests directly entering the realm of public governance, which I explore more fully below.[108] It suffices to say that these dynamics reinforce

[102] Reich, *supra* note 32, at 4.

[103] *See* Soo Rin Kim, *Just 12 Megadonors Accounted for 7.5% of Political Giving over Past Decade, Says Report*, ABC NEWS (Apr. 20, 2021), https://abcnews.go.com/Politics/12-megadonors-accounted-75-political-giving-past-decade/story?id=77189636. *See also generally* FRED S. MCCHESNEY, MONEY FOR NOTHING: POLITICIANS, RENT EXTRACTION, AND POLITICAL EXTORTION (1997) (arguing that politicians receive contributions and other incentives not only for taking action but also for merely threatening to act and subsequently failing to follow through on those threats).

[104] William A. Niskanen, *Give Divided Government a Chance*, CATO INST. (Oct. 1, 2006), www.cato.org/commentary/give-divided-government-chance#. *See also* Victor Davis Hanson, *Not a State, Broken People*, REALCLEARPOLITICS (July 26, 2010), www.realclearpolitics.com/articles/2010/07/26/not_a_state-broken_people_106463.html.

[105] *Cf.* FRANK R. BAUMGARTNER, JEFFREY M. BERRY, MARIE HOJNACKI, DAVID C. KIMBALL & BETH L. LEECH, LOBBYING AND POLICY CHANGE: WHO WINS, WHO LOSES, AND WHY (2009).

[106] *See generally* PAGE, SEAWRIGHT & LACOMBE, *supra* note 100; BENJAMIN I. PAGE & MARTIN GILENS, DEMOCRACY IN AMERICA? WHAT HAS GONE WRONG AND WHAT WE CAN DO ABOUT IT 3 (2017). *See also supra* Chapter 2, Section A.3.

[107] For a similar point, but with respect to asset managers, see Lund, *supra* note 38, at 125 (noting that the Big Three "appear to enjoy exercising regulatory heft as a result of government dysfunction. Rather than using their power to alleviate rent-seeking by industry (which they also engage in), they choose to maintain the status quo, which positions them to attract new clients and satisfy existing ones." Footnote omitted.).

[108] Despite holding no official elected position, Elon Musk, rapidly amassed significant influence over the federal government under Trump's second administration, leading efforts to slash spending through an executive task force while gaining access to sensitive government systems. While Musk's

the idea that corporate governing is shaped by strategic business considerations rather than a genuine commitment to social responsibility, raising broader questions about its role in creating systemic barriers to legislative and regulatory change.

### VII THE "DEATH" OF POLITICS

Finally, allowing corporations to assume more extensive sociopolitical responsibilities risks sidelining traditional political processes, which could introduce significant long-term uncertainties and challenges. As with Elon Musk's past role in the Trump administration,[109] this type of development blurs the boundaries between private influence and public authority and underscores a broader and more disturbing trend: If corporations or influential private individuals take on roles traditionally reserved for government bodies, the accountability and transparency mechanisms inherent in democratic governance may slowly but surely disappear – often without the public even noticing.[110] This shift signals a quasi-feudal reallocation of power to non-state actors and raises serious questions about the adequacy of corporate governing mechanisms to safeguard the public interest.

This is one of the most severe risks of corporate governing, which I address more thoroughly in the ensuing subsections.

## b Addressing the Most Severe Risks

Assessing the severity of societal risks is a complex task. Some risks are difficult to quantify and compare against corresponding benefits. For instance, how do we

stint in government did not last long, his unchecked power sparked alarm over conflicts of interest, as he installed close associates in key agencies and secures control over federal payment flows, raising concerns about his influence over both government operations and his private business dealings. *See* Jonathan Lemire, *Elon Musk Is President*, ATLANTIC (Feb. 3, 2025), www.theatlantic.com/politics/archive/2025/02/president-elon-musk-trump/681558/; Kyle Chayka, *Techno-Fascism Comes to America*, NEW YORKER (Feb. 26, 2025), www.newyorker.com/culture/infinite-scroll/techno-fascism-comes-to-america-elon-musk (arguing that Musk's DOGE mirrors past regimes that used technology and bureaucratic restructuring to consolidate control while bypassing democratic norms); Dana Hull, *White House Says Musk Will Police His Own Conflicts of Interest*, BLOOMBERG (Feb. 5, 2025), www.bloomberg.com/news/articles/2025-02-05/white-house-says-musk-will-police-his-own-conflicts-of-interest (describing the absolute lack of checks and balances over Musk's conflicts of interests); Eric Lipton & Kirsten Grind, *Elon Musk's Business Empire Scores Benefits under Trump Shake-Up*, N.Y. TIMES (Feb. 11, 2025), www.nytimes.com/2025/02/11/us/politics/elon-musk-companies-conflicts.html (discussing how government investigations into Musk's companies have stalled amid federal shake-ups and resignations).

109 *See supra* note 108.

110 *See* former head of sustainable investing at BlackRock Tariq Fancy, *The Secret Diary of a "Sustainable Investor" – Part 1*, MEDIUM (Aug. 21, 2021), https://medium.com/@sosofancy/the-secret-diary-of-a-sustainable-investor-part-1-70b6987fa139 (discussing ESG investing and warning about the peril that corporate initiatives may lead the public into accepting that business is the best-suited economic policy reformer). *See also* BAINBRIDGE, *supra* note 26, at 92; Lin, *supra* note 28, at 1585–86 (mentioning accounts that warn about plutocracy).

measure whether corporate governing contributes to the decline of traditional politics? Even measurable risks – such as quantifying the stakeholders who oppose a type of corporate intervention by looking at outcomes of shareholder proposals, survey data, and other metrics – do not necessarily reveal the overall societal impact. Pinning down what's objectively best for society is a fool's errand – social scientists, policymakers, let alone the general public cannot even agree on what that means.

Despite the difficulty of achieving precise assessments, careful analysis remains essential for refining the evaluation of these issues. This can help filter out distracting arguments and lead to a clearer understanding of the phenomenon. To explore this further, I categorize the societal risks of corporate governing into two main groups: First, the risk that corporate governing may fall short in effectively addressing the societal issues it seeks to resolve, and second, the fundamental dangers it poses as an alternative to traditional political processes.

### I CORPORATE GOVERNING IS NOT ENOUGH: THE CASE AGAINST A STAKEHOLDERIST REFORM OF DIRECTOR FIDUCIARY DUTIES

Many of the risks listed above describe the inadequacy of corporate governing in attaining socioeconomic change. This is due to a variety of reasons. First, corporate governing has limited scope: for example, government substitution affects only *some* stakeholders of *some* corporations, typically the largest ones.[111] Second, corporate interest in engagement may wane as trends shift cyclically – especially in an era when conservative politicians, including the President himself, actively target political expression and certain policies.[112] Third – and perhaps most importantly – corporations may be indifferent, or even openly resistant, to key societal concerns: equitable taxation, stronger labor and consumer protections, regulation of AI, and other efforts to rein in business externalities.[113] Taken together, these risks suggest that corporate governing is unlikely to foster genuine societal progress, particularly in terms of distributional issues that likely find support from the public.[114]

[111] *See supra* Section B.2.a.iii.

[112] *See supra* Section B.2.a.iv. *See also supra* Chapter 1, Sections C.1 and C.3.

[113] *See supra* Section B.2.a.v. Adam Smith warned us about this almost 250 years ago:

> The interest of the dealers … in any particular branch of trade or manufactures, is always in some respects different from, and even opposite to, that of the public … The proposal of any new law or regulation of commerce which comes from this order, ought always to be listened to with great precaution, and ought never to be adopted till alter having been long and carefully examined, not only with the most scrupulous but also with the most suspicious attention.

ADAM SMITH, THE WEALTH OF NATIONS 372 (Collier ed., 1902) (1776).

[114] As anticipated in Chapter 2, Section B.3, surveys indicate widespread support across demographics for policies such as unionization, a $15 minimum wage, gun control, and climate action, suggesting corporate leaders may simply be responding strategically to changing market demands and not mere personal indulgence. BENJAMIN I. PAGE & MARTIN GILENS, DEMOCRACY IN AMERICA? WHAT HAS GONE WRONG AND WHAT WE CAN DO ABOUT IT 53–54 & 74–88 (2017); Megan Brenan, *At 65%, Approval of Labor Unions in U.S. Remains High*, GALLUP (Sept. 3, 2020), https://news.gallup.com/poll/318980/approval-labor-unions-remains-high.aspx; Amina Dunn, *Most Americans*

This warning primarily addresses citizens who may overlook the risks of relying on corporate initiatives for societal change, rather than social activists who likely already recognize the inherent limitations and pitfalls of partnering with corporations. Policymakers must carefully weigh the risks before implementing reforms that expand corporate mandates and grant executives greater discretion.

In this regard, institutionalizing stakeholderism through explicit expansions of fiduciary duties poses particular dangers, as it risks embedding corporate lobbying within a broader stakeholderist agenda.[115] This, in turn, would enable executives to assert themselves as authoritative voices on socioeconomic issues, claiming a superior ability to achieve societal goals compared to elected legislators or regulators.[116] The risks become even more pronounced in the realm of distributional reforms, where corporate leaders face clear trade-offs on issues such as unionization, mandatory arbitration, and workers' rights.[117] By positioning themselves as arbiters of the public interest, corporations could sideline democratic decision-making and steer policies in ways that ultimately serve their own interests rather than genuine social progress.

*Support a $15 Federal Minimum Wage*, Pew Rsch. Ctr. (Apr. 22, 2021), www.pewresearch.org/fact-tank/2021/04/22/most-americans-support-a-15-federal-minimum-wage/; Sara Burnett, *AP-NORC Poll: Most in US Say They Want Stricter Gun Laws*, AP News (Aug. 23, 2022), https://apnews.com/article/gun-violence-covid-health-chicago-c912ecc5619e925c5ea7447d36808715.

115 *See* Matteo Gatti & Chrystin Ondersma, *Can A Broader Corporate Purpose Redress Inequality? The Stakeholder Approach Chimera*, 46 J. Corp. L. 1, 10–11, 47–57 (2020) [hereinafter Gatti & Ondersma, *Stakeholder Approach Chimera*] (warning that stakeholderism may do more harm than good in pursuing the social goals it purports to achieve, as it could further empower the very actors – executives – who helped create the problems it now seeks to remedy, granting them broad discretion to advance their own interests or block reforms they find unfavorable).

To be clear, this book does not argue that corporate pro-stakeholder reforms are inherently incompatible with external regulation. Several scholars have shown that ESG-driven corporate initiatives need not crowd out public regulation. *See for example*, Hajin Kim, Joshua Macey & Kristen Underhill, *Does ESG Crowd Out Support for Government Regulation?*, Coase-Sandor Inst. for L. & Econ., Univ. of Chi., Rsch. Paper No. 983 (2023), https://ssrn.com/abstract=4521781; Kovvali, *supra* note 6. Indeed, this book embraces that compatibility. Chapter 3 defends the legality of corporate governing, while Chapter 4 (Sections A and B) highlights its potential business and strategic value. And with Chrystin Ondersma, I have previously acknowledged the potential for coexistence between corporate action and robust public policy. See Matteo Gatti & Chrystin D. Ondersma, *The Perils of a Stakeholderist Corporate Law Reform: A Reply to Professor Kovvali*, 123 Colum. L. Rev. F. 229, 239–40 (2023). But that is not the debate here. The concern I raise is narrower and more structural: statutory expansions of fiduciary duties to include stakeholder or ESG interests are misguided, for the reasons outlined in the text. Other reforms may hold promise. For instance, some advocate codetermination on democratic grounds. *See* Jens Dammann & Horst Eidenmüller, *Corporate Law and the Democratic State*, 2022 U. Ill. L. Rev. 1019. *See also* Gatti & Ondersma, *Stakeholder Approach Chimera*, *supra*, at 69–70 & n.409 (identifying codetermination as a distinct reform category). Yet, these are fundamentally different proposals. My critique here is specific to fiduciary duties expansion – not all forms of pro-stakeholder reform.

116 *Id.* at 19. Again, the Musk/DOGE precedent compounds this risk. *See supra* notes 108–109 and accompanying text.

117 *See* Gatti & Ondersma, *supra* note 74, at 216–22 (describing lobbying efforts by corporations in such fields).

Currently, executives avoid actions that disadvantage their firms, because they stand to lose financially if the stock price drops. However, suppose their fiduciary duties were expanded to include certain societal concerns explicitly. In that case, there is a real danger that executives might exploit this broader mandate to co-opt the legislative process altogether.[118] This could lead to corporations wielding even greater influence over policy, often in ways that benefit their interests while undermining regular citizens' rights and social equity. In essence, rather than being held accountable, executives could use these broader responsibilities as a means to further entrench corporate power.

The problem with corporate governing isn't just about trusting executives. It's structural. Private actors and markets are simply not built to tackle society's most complex challenges. Those require responses that are *systemic*, *coordinated*, *enforceable*, and *durable* – capacities that only the state possesses.[119] Corporations, by contrast, are too insular, too constrained, and too self-interested to meet the moment. Coordination across firms risks antitrust violations. Enforcement stops at the edge of firm boundaries. And nothing they do – not even their boldest pledges – carries the durability or signaling power of law. The point became painfully clear when many walked back their public commitments the moment political winds shifted under the second Trump administration.[120]

Thus, without robust state action, corporate-led initiatives risk being fragmented, inconsistent, and ultimately insufficient to address the scale and complexity of system-wide challenges.

Still, the fact that corporate governing can't solve everything doesn't mean it solves nothing. Even if it falls short of systemic change, partial gains are still gains – especially for those who benefit directly. Dismissing these efforts outright makes little sense, so long as we don't elevate corporations to the role of primary problem-solvers. In other words, the real problem lies not in incremental help, but in pretending it's enough.

True, this approach may produce uneven outcomes – corporations will always act selectively, favoring certain causes and, inevitably, their stakeholders over the broader public. But this is something that would happen regardless: disparity of treatment is not a bug in the system; it's how markets function. The alternative – shutting down corporate governing altogether – would be an overcorrection.

118 This would not be the first time executives do that. *See* Gatti & Ondersma, *supra* note 74, at 232–33 (mentioning how arbitration, which was originally conceived to provide citizens with a faster avenue to litigate, was ultimately coopted by private interests). *See also generally* Sarah Staszak, *Privatizing Employment Law: The Expansion of Mandatory Arbitration in the Workplace*, 34 Stud. Am. Pol. Dev. 239 (2020).

119 *Cf.* Daron Acemoglu & James A. Robinson, Why Nations Fail: The Origins of Power, Prosperity, and Poverty 75–76 (2012). Yet, even states sometimes struggle to act effectively, as seen in the context of climate change, where multilateral inertia and domestic political gridlock frequently stall meaningful progress.

120 *See supra* Chapter 1, Section C.4.

Corporations can't solve every problem, but banning them from trying misses the point. A more pragmatic path preserves room for corporate initiative, leaves questions of distribution to the state, and leans on governance tools to curb executive overreach.[121]

## II CORPORATE GOVERNING IS DANGEROUS

The objections above emphasize the inability of corporate governing to achieve meaningful change. Yet, other critiques argue further that corporate governing is not simply insufficient but outright dangerous.

One prominent line of criticism views corporate governing as fundamentally undemocratic. This critique has several variations but generally falls into two main claims, both predominantly advanced by conservative voices. The first is that corporate governing undermines democratic institutions by enabling policies that failed to succeed through traditional political processes.[122] The second highlights that corporate governing infringes upon the rights of dissenting stakeholders.[123]

A third, distinct critique contends that corporate governing threatens to replace genuine democratic politics altogether – a phenomenon this book terms the "death of politics."[124]

I address all three objections below.

### x *Is the Unorthodoxy of Corporate Governing Truly Undemocratic?*

Milton Friedman's influential 1970 article challenged the democratic nature of corporate involvement in the social field. In his famous remark, corporate social responsibility efforts should be rejected because their proponents have "failed to persuade a majority of their fellow citizens to be of like mind and … are seeking to attain by undemocratic procedures what they cannot attain by democratic procedures."[125] Many conservative voices have echoed this concern. More recently, former Vice President Mike Pence wrote a *Wall Street Journal* op-ed in which he attacked ESG as a pernicious political strategy that "allows the left to accomplish what it could never hope to achieve at the ballot box …."[126]

A pragmatic counter to this argument is that, as Chapter 2 shows, the American democratic process faces so many challenges that any approach that might help break through political gridlock should be seriously considered.[127] There's more.

[121] *See infra* Chapter 6.
[122] *See supra* Section B.2.a.i.
[123] *See supra* Section B.2.a.ii.
[124] *See supra* Section B.2.a.vii.
[125] *See* Friedman, *supra* note 26.
[126] Mike Pence, *Republicans Can Stop ESG Political Bias*, WALL ST. J. (May 26, 2022), www.wsj.com/articles/only-republicans-can-stop-the-esg-madness-woke-musk-consumer-demand-free-speech-corporate-america-11653574189.
[127] *See supra* Section B.2. This is a recurring critique to Friedman's position. For an account, see Spamann & Fisher, *supra* note 74, at 4–5.

Drawing on Erwin Chemerinsky's recent critique of the US Constitution,[128] one might question whether Friedman's "democratic procedures" are democratic at all – given structural distortions in the legislative process, including the Electoral College, Senate apportionment, the filibuster, and more.[129] However, critics push back arguing that relying on corporate solutions to fix political dysfunction may backfire – provoking backlash and, in some cases, producing outcomes even more distorted than the politics they aim to replace.[130] After all, corporate decision-makers are unelected, incentive-driven, and structurally unaccountable to the broader public.

Thus, I focus on Friedman's perspective, assuming the US institutional framework as it stands. The late Nobel laureate implicitly suggests that political messaging and action should occur primarily, if not only, through official channels, such as the legislative halls of Capitol Hill or state governments. He emphasizes the importance of maintaining the boundary between economic and political power, arguing that corporations should limit their focus to profit maximization within the constraints of the law, leaving political decision-making to democratically elected bodies.[131]

While the idealistic concern over corporate influence on democracy is valid – especially as the risks of concentrated private power grow more evident – the challenges of our political system may necessitate a more pragmatic approach.

To start, the idea that politics should be confined to traditional, state-centered channels is untenable – even descriptively. Our legal and cultural framework permits a wide range of political expression: citizens voice preferences through protests, rallies, and social media – at times, through corporations.[132] The political speech ecosystem is open-ended, allowing individuals to exert direct pressure on firms and indirect pressure on policymakers via market actors.[133]

128 Erwin Chemerinsky, No Democracy Lasts Forever: How the Constitution Threatens the *United* States 6 (2024) (labeling the U.S. Constitution as "profoundly anti-democratic.").

129 *Id.* at 6–11.

130 Spamann & Fischer, *supra* note 74, at 4–5 (questioning whether wealth-weighted investor decisions, such as votes on carbon costs, are any less problematic than political voting). Still, they argue that Friedman's concern is too broad, as many corporate decisions occur outside regulatory oversight, where inaction by regulators does not imply approval. In such cases, corporations must rely on widely shared moral norms, as ignoring known harms – like dumping toxic chemicals before regulation – would be both inefficient and socially unacceptable. *Id.* at 5–6.

131 *See* Friedman, *supra* note 26. Friedman's worldview rests on political–economic separation: markets and democracies should operate in distinct lanes, with corporations steering clear of political action. *Cf.* Oliver Hart & Luigi Zingales, *Companies Should Maximize Shareholder Welfare Not Market Value*, 2 J.L. Fin. & Acct. 247 (2017) (describing Friedman's assumption). But that clean divide has long eroded. In reality, the spheres bleed into one another – by design and by necessity.

132 *See, for example*, Sergio Alberto Gramitto Ricci & Christina M. Sautter, *Wireless Investors & Apathy Obsolescence*, 100 Wash. U. L. Rev. 1653, 1666–67 (2023) (detailing the use of online venues to organize support for various movements including the Black Lives Matter movement).

133 *Cf.* Roberto Tallarita, *Stockholder Politics*, 73 Hastings L.J. 1697, 1733 (2022) (arguing that corporate governance allows a connection between "shareholders with prosocial and expressive motives on one side and extra-corporate actors (stakeholders, activists, concerned citizens) on the other side.").

Nothing in US law prohibits these dynamics. If anything, Supreme Court jurisprudence has often – if controversially – shielded such forms of expression from restriction.[134] In that light, corporations function as one of many platforms through which citizens can engage in it.

As David Vogel observed nearly thirty years ago:

> [W]hat is least important about citizen pressures has been their direct, substantive effect on corporate decisions. These have been, and are likely to remain, marginal. Their impact on public policy has been more substantial. They have played a relatively important role both in bringing a number of issues before the political process, and in increasing the effectiveness of government controls over business.[135]

The modern landscape allows multiple avenues for citizen engagement, and corporations are increasingly used as political forums where citizens can advocate for change. By viewing corporations as one of many forums for political discourse, I argue that corporate governing represents a pragmatic way for political pressure to be applied in a modern democratic society and suggest that citizens can use this means to push for political outcomes. This perspective offers a counterpoint to Friedman's ideal of clear boundaries between political and corporate spheres, arguing in favor of a flexible, citizen-driven approach to political influence instead.[136]

Despite this, one could still invoke Friedman and argue that a crucial distinction exists between individual citizens – retail investors, employees, or customers – exercising their First Amendment rights through corporate engagement and corporate executives using their official roles to advance personal agendas.

While this objection is well-rooted in corporate literature,[137] studies suggest corporate governing initiatives are not managerial pet projects but primarily aim – though not always successfully – to enhance brand value and business

[134] The Supreme Court significantly expanded corporate political speech in the *Citizens United* and *Hobby Lobby* decisions. *See* Citizens United v. Fed. Election Comm'n, 558 U.S. 310, 336–66 (2010) (prohibiting the government from restricting independent expenditures for political communications by corporations, including nonprofit corporations, labor unions, and other associations, so long as such spending is independent of a party or a candidate) *and* Burwell v. Hobby Lobby Stores, Inc., 573 U.S. 682 (2014) (allowing exemptions for close corporations from a regulation that its owners religiously object to if there is a less restrictive means of furthering the law's interest).

[135] David Vogel, Kindred Strangers: The Uneasy Relationship between Politics and Business in America 189 (1996) (noting also that "citizen challenges … helped increase the visibility and public scrutiny of corporate decisions.").

[136] Sergio Gramitto Ricci and Christina Sautter highlight the growing influence of retail investors in corporate governance, framing corporations as platforms for political and social engagement. They argue that corporate voting mirrors civic participation, with increased investor activism shaping both corporate decisions and broader societal outcomes. See Gramitto Ricci & Sautter, supra note 132, at 1678–86; Sergio Alberto Gramitto Ricci & Christina M. Sautter, *Corporate Governance Gaming: The Collective Power of Retail Investors*, 22 Nev. L.J. 51, 92–96 (2021).

[137] *See, for example*, Bainbridge, *supra* note 26, at 107–08; Fisch & Schwartz, *supra* note 25, at 342. *See supra* Chapter 4, Section A.4.a.

performance.[138] Indeed, the objection overlooks the broader executive–stakeholder dynamic, where leaders are often pressured by shareholders or other stakeholders to take a stand. When executives remain silent on pressing social issues despite stakeholder demands, their inaction itself becomes a form of corporate governing – what I previously described as passive corporate governing.[139] In an era where corporations are expected to take positions – whether voluntarily or under pressure – silence is rarely neutral. It is often interpreted as speech, carrying potential political, business, and financial consequences for the company and its stakeholders.[140] In many instances, it is difficult for executives to avoid taking a side – this is an inherent risk in the current business landscape.[141] As there is no a priori, one-size-fits-all solution to this dilemma, we must rely on an ecosystem in which executives and boards make judgment calls, subject to stakeholder pushback and market reactions. And that need not be cause for undue concern. In our system, judgment-based governance – tempered by external pressures – may well be the most workable model available.

### y *Addressing Dissenter Rights*

The issue of dissenter rights – the concern that corporate governing may alienate segments of a company's stakeholder base – is more complex than it first appears. These initiatives may indeed provoke backlash from stakeholders who oppose their underlying politics, potentially reinforcing "a system that facilitates corporate inculcation of certain political and social values[,]"[142] in tension with "the pluralism and freedom that represents a key part of being an American."[143]

While this concern is valid in principle, it is difficult to operationalize. Its logical corollary would be to act only by unanimity – an impossible standard in any large organization.

More broadly, the argument risks proving too much. Even outside the sociopolitical sphere, many workers and Americans already dissent, implicitly or explicitly, from prevailing corporate practices. The long list of employer–employee disagreements includes wage levels, healthcare and benefits, workplace safety, workplace flexibility, job security, unionization and collective bargaining, workplace equity, burnout and mental health, employee surveillance, and executive compensation. Yet, for better

[138] *See supra* Chapter 4, Section A.3.

[139] *See supra* Chapter 4, Section A.2.b.

[140] For example, Disney initially sought to stay silent on Florida's "Don't Say Gay" law but faced backlash from stakeholders and ultimately took a stand. *See supra* Introduction. In contrast, Wayfair resisted pressure to halt furniture sales to a migrant detention center during the Trump era, triggering an intense fallout. Barzuza, Curtis & Webber, *supra* note 4, at 1296–97.

[141] I am obviously not discussing whether or when corporations *must* speak as a matter of law – they generally do not have such an obligation, yet they normally tend to disclose their lobbying and advocacy efforts. *See infra* Chapter 6, Section B.1.

[142] Strine, *supra* note 26, at 357.

[143] *Id.*

or worse, dissenters often have no choice but to accept such practices because firms operate as hierarchies, as Coase famously explained.[144] When joining a workplace, employees should be prepared to have disagreements of various natures with their employers. While some on the left take issue with this,[145] it is telling that it is cited as a problem by conservatives only when executives embrace liberal or progressive causes.

This hierarchical dynamic also applies to investors in large public corporations, where boards make decisions that may not always align with shareholder preferences.[146] As Chancellor Allen once famously said: "while corporate democracy is a pertinent concept, a corporation is not a New England town meeting; directors, not shareholders, have responsibilities to manage the business and affairs of the corporation …."[147]

In sum, disagreement over how a corporation is managed is a natural and expected part of decision-making processes in large organizations.[148]

To address dissenter rights in the spirit of pluralism, some have suggested excluding highly controversial issues from corporate actions or speech. In an article on corporate social activism, former Chief Justice Leo Strine highlights voting rights, reproductive rights, guns, policing, and criminal codes as issues of "passionate and legitimate disagreement" that are too divisive for corporate involvement.[149] However, these proposed exclusions seem arbitrary and incomplete, omitting politically charged issues like race (except for policing tactics), gender (except for reproductive rights), and sexual orientation, which also provoke profound societal conflict – for one, they are the main targets of the anti-DEI backlash described in Chapter 1.[150] Frankly, any attempt to draw a line based on divisiveness is unworkable; expecting

144 Ronald H. Coase, *The Nature of the Firm*, 4 ECONOMICA 386, 388 (1937).

145 It is certainly true that certain basic freedoms, including the freedom to openly dissent, do not fully extend to the private workplace, where employers have extensive, often unchecked, power over their employees not just with respect to work-related activities but also aspects of employees' personal lives, including their speech, behavior, and even off-duty conduct. For a description and normative critique, see generally ANDERSON, *supra* note 69.

146 *Cf.* Lucian A. Bebchuk, *The Myth of the Shareholder Franchise*, 93 VA. L. REV. 675, 676 (2007) (arguing that shareholder democracy is largely illusory).

147 TW Servs. v. SWT Acq. Corp., 1989 WL 20290, at *8 n.14 (Del. Ch. Mar. 2, 1989). Of course, such power is not unconstrained – there are not only fiduciary duties directors and officers are subject to but also ways for shareholders to exert pressure on directors via appointment rights, for instance. *See for example*, Luca Enriques, Henry Hansmann & Reinier Kraakman, *The Basic Governance Structure: The Interests of Shareholders as a Class*, in THE ANATOMY OF CORPORATE LAW 79, 80–81 (3d ed. 2017). More broadly, the "corporate governance machine" is structurally skewed in favor of shareholders. *See generally* Lund & Pollman, *supra* note 97. This doesn't change the fact that dissent over day-to-day corporate decisions is a normal, even necessary, feature of large enterprise governance.

148 *See* Gatti, *supra* note 1, at 205 (addressing employees). *See also* Lisa M. Fairfax, *Reframing the Corporate Political Speech Debate*, Working Paper (2025) (unpublished manuscript, on file with author), at 4–5 (addressing investors and noting that shareholders' views often strongly diverge with management's on economic decisions – especially those with social implications).

149 Strine, *supra* note 26, at 357.

150 *See supra* Chapter 1, Section C. Besides, disagreement and backlash aren't triggered by advocacy alone – they can stem just as much from corporate actions themselves, as the Target and Bud Light episodes make clear.

corporations to act or speak only on the remaining uncontroversial matters is, in a deeply divided society, unrealistic.[151]

Besides, deeming an issue off-limits for its divisiveness presents further problems. First, as noted earlier, avoiding a pressing issue can be seen as *passive* corporate governing.[152] The public may view this passive approach as divisive and anti-pluralistic, much like taking an active stance on controversial issues.

Second, we must ask whether pluralism is better served by sparing workers or shareholders the discomfort of divisive issues – such as anti-trans sentiment – or by standing with trans employees who face real harm from societal and workplace discrimination. In this context, trans individuals seek dignity, respect, and corporate support for the right to live authentically; by contrast, dissenting stakeholders seek to impose their own, *external* preferences that constrain others' lives. From a utilitarian perspective, it is worth asking how much weight external preferences on other people's lives should carry in policymaking.[153] More broadly, on substance, it is hard to characterize as anti-democratic – or even anti-pluralistic – a corporate intervention aimed at shielding some of its stakeholders from policies that are facially retaliatory and discriminatory.

### *z The Death of Politics*

The growing influence of corporations in policymaking poses significant risks to democratic governance. As corporations exert more influence over policy – whether through corporate governing or direct political spending and lobbying – the balance of power between the state and private actors is shifting.[154] This is the most serious issue raised by corporate governing.

Unlike the issues discussed earlier, this concern primarily involves the demand side of policymaking: the citizens. As corporations take on a more significant role as agents of change, people may increasingly rely on them for societal change,

[151] *See* Gatti, *supra* note 1, at 205–06. *See also* Fairfax, *supra* note 148, at 1–2 (arguing that "the debate about corporate political speech is fundamentally flawed because it is based on the false premise that we can legitimately distinguish corporate political speech from other forms of corporate speech."). Fairfax points out that courts have consistently protected corporate political speech across a range of accepted categories – including routine business communications, commercial advertising, charitable donations, and electoral advocacy – rendering attempts to draw clear lines between political and non-political corporate speech largely illusory. *Id.* at 3.

[152] On passive corporate governing, *see supra* Chapter 4, Sections A.2.b and B.

[153] Ronald Dworkin makes this point, though it remains debated in political philosophy. RONALD DWORKIN, TAKING RIGHTS SERIOUSLY 275–76 (1980). For an assessment, see Howard S. Chang, *A Liberal Theory of Social Welfare: Fairness, Utility, and the Pareto Principle*, 110 YALE L.J. 173, 183–96 (2002).

[154] *Cf.* PAGE & GILENS, *supra* note 106, at 4 (discussing the fundamental concerns regarding the erosion of democratic governance due to, among other things, the increasing power of private interests); JACOB S. HACKER & PAUL PIERSON, AMERICAN AMNESIA: HOW THE WAR ON GOVERNMENT LED US TO FORGET WHAT MADE AMERICA PROSPER 9 (2016) (describing how private interests have been pushing to depart from a mixed economy with strong public institutions and to weaken government action).

losing interest in traditional politics.[155] The growing influence of corporations in policy reform risks normalizing their involvement, which could undermine participatory governance and democratic institutions.[156] By taking on responsibilities traditionally reserved for legislatures or government bodies, non-political entities like corporations may thus lead citizens to disengage from politics, diminishing and reducing the focus on transparency and public interest protections.[157] Over time, corporations could exploit this shift.

Consider, for example, the gradual transfer of risk management from the public to the private sector – an evolution that highlights how private actors have assumed roles once reserved for the state, but with far less accountability. This shift, often described as the "privatization of risk," has weakened the state's ability to offer collective protections against societal risks, instead offloading these burdens onto individuals and families who are often ill-equipped to bear them.[158] Over time, this reconfiguration becomes the new baseline in citizens' expectations – one from which corporations may quietly benefit.

This transformation parallels the broader concern that the de facto transfer of policymaking authority to private actors results in a diminished role for the government. Adolf Berle and Gardiner Means predicted this almost a century ago:

> The state seeks in some aspects to regulate the corporation, while the corporation, steadily becoming more powerful, makes every effort to avoid such regulation. Where its own interests are concerned, it even attempts to dominate the state.[159]

Two key problems arise from this shift. First, as discussed above, it weakens democratic principles that rely on transparency and citizen engagement in policymaking. In such a scenario, corporate interests – primarily motivated by profit[160] – are likely to dominate, prioritizing their objectives over the public good and reducing the

155 *Cf.* Reich, *supra* note 32, at 5 (admonishing that "[c]itizens of … big and powerful nations [in America and Europe] who assume they have more impact pushing corporations to be virtuous than working through the democratic process to require them to be so, are simply wrong").

156 *Cf.* Joseph E. Stiglitz, The Price of Inequality: How Today's Divided Society Endangers Our Future li (2012).

157 For a critique of the limitations of civil society alone in fostering political unity, see Christopher Beem, The Necessity of Politics: Reclaiming American Public Life 218–247 (1999) (arguing for the necessity of political associations that engage in partisan debate to define public values, and insisting that only politics and government can translate moral arguments into moral judgments, with the national government serving as the common moral authority). Beem's analysis of civil society movements suggests that non-governmental entities – whether driven by communal or private interests – cannot effectively substitute for formal political institutions in sustaining democratic governance.

158 Jacob S. Hacker, *Privatizing Risk without Privatizing the Welfare State: The Hidden Politics of Social Policy Retrenchment in the United States*, 98 Am. Pol. Sci. Rev. 243, 243, 245, 252–53 (2004).

159 Berle & Means, *supra* note 83, at 313 (speculating that the future may see the corporation "possibly even superseding [the state] as the dominant form of social organization.").

160 *See generally* Lund & Pollman, *supra* note 97 (showing how the profit motive plays a paramount role in the corporate governance machine); Bainbridge, *supra* note 26 (explaining how both doctrinally and normatively the profit motive is the polestar of a corporation).

political participation of ordinary citizens even further.[161] Second, this shift would deprive citizens of the unique strength of state action: providing systemic, coordinated, durable, and enforceable responses to complex challenges that private actors, by design, cannot resolve on their own.[162] Such capacities are essential to the health of political institutions and the stability of democratic governance.[163]

In sum, the potential consequences of sidelining traditional politics in favor of corporate governing are significant and warrant serious attention. The post-2024 election political landscape – marked by the rise of non-traditional political figures and deepening entanglements between business and state power – amplifies these risks. What's at stake is not just policy substance, but the long-term resilience of democratic institutions themselves. These themes, and the broader implications for democratic renewal, are revisited in Conclusion.

[161] *Cf.* Martin Gilens & Benjamin I. Page, *Testing Theories of American Politics: Elites, Interest Groups, and Average Citizens*, 12 PERSP. ON POL. 564 (2014) (finding that US policymaking is largely dominated by economic elites and organized interest groups, while the views of average citizens have little to no independent impact on public policy); PAGE & GILENS, *supra* note 106, at 70 (noting that "on many important issues, affluent and wealthy Americans seriously disagree with average citizens"); HACKER & PIERSON, *supra* note 154, at 195–97 (discussing the prioritization of interests of the wealthy over public welfare and its detrimental effect on citizen trust in government and engagement in politics).

[162] Fixing market failures and providing public goods are typical cases where state action is generally considered necessary, though there is no consensus on the optimal type and degree of intervention. Spamann & Fischer, *supra* note 74, at 6–7 (arguing that because of substitution effects, "major environmental and other issues are most effectively addressed through regulation." *Id.* at 7).

[163] *Cf.* ACEMOGLU & ROBINSON, *supra* note 119, *at* 75–76 (listing several public constraint-type preconditions to the prosperity of economic institutions) *and generally* HACKER & PIERSON, *supra* note 154 (arguing that government action to create a mixed economy channeled growth and social development).

PART III

# The Way Forward

# 6

# Corporate Governance Safeguards for Sound Corporate Governing

This chapter examines whether the risks of corporate governing can be effectively managed through traditional corporate governance mechanisms. Historically, corporate governance serves managers and shareholders, not external stakeholders. This leaves the broader societal implications of corporate action, including corporate governing, which Chapter 5 identified as particularly severe, largely unaddressed. Corporate law is generally ill-equipped, and policymakers are often reluctant, to regulate corporate externalities, especially in politically charged areas. Efforts to impose direct restrictions face legal and practical hurdles, which include *Citizens United* and the business judgment rule. Given these constraints, policy interventions should better focus on disclosure frameworks and governance mechanisms to ensure oversight and accountability. Disclosure is often proposed as a transparency-enhancing tool for corporate governing, but its effectiveness depends on scope, content, and enforcement. Governance mechanisms – such as internal guidelines, board oversight, disinterested director, and shareholder involvement – could serve as checks on corporate governing, but their effectiveness is mixed.

At the same time, market forces already discipline corporate governing as companies respond to investor expectations, litigation risks, and consumer and other stakeholder sentiment. Shareholder activism, stakeholder pressure, and political backlash all influence corporate governing, often creating a rebalancing effect. Via private ordering or other internal initiatives, corporations can deflect some of the heat by showing they have procedures in place, and offer adequate disclosures, about corporate governing.

To examine how corporate governing plays out in practice, Section D surveys corporate disclosures on advocacy, lobbying, and policy engagement across two subsets of S&P 500 firms. Using data from securities filings and supplementary corporate reports, I evaluate how corporations communicate their advocacy policies, the issues they support, and the interests they claim to represent. The findings reveal the selective and strategic nature of corporate advocacy. Firms in the S&P 100 are far more likely than smaller peers to disclose advocacy policies, particularly on diversity and climate, reflecting heightened scrutiny from investors, regulators, and the public. Even so, disclosure gaps remain striking: many companies that publicize ESG goals refrain from acknowledging related advocacy, and politically charged topics such as democracy and voting rights receive scant attention. Corporate disclosures also frame advocacy chiefly as serving business, industry, or immediate stakeholders, with society at large almost never identified as a beneficiary. A significant number of firms remain silent on advocacy altogether.



## A THE LIMITS OF CORPORATE LAW AND GOVERNANCE

This chapter explores policy options to address the challenges posed by corporate governing. As previously discussed, from a strict corporate governance perspective, corporate governing does not raise insurmountable difficulties. Targeted governance adjustments like those surveyed in this chapter can mitigate corporate-level risks.

However, as Chapter 5 warns, the societal implications of corporate governing are more severe. Also, they are much harder to regulate. This is partly because the tools of conventional corporate governance and finance do not work well to address issues beyond the corporate sphere. Those tools generally give protections to managers and shareholders[1] and, to some extent, to stakeholders who contract, or at least can contract, for protections.[2]

Conversely, *external* stakeholders, and thus society at large, typically lack clout in how governance is set up at the given company. This is for two reasons. First, external stakeholders who do not contract with shareholders and managers have no way to *adjust* in their favor the deal that shareholders and managers agree among themselves.[3] As I noted elsewhere, a pro-stakeholder redesign of corporate governance through private ordering faces significant challenges precisely because stakeholder advocates are absent from the negotiation of key corporate terms.[4] Second, corporate laws have proven incapable to deal with issues transcending the corporate boundaries. This is because of the dynamics of corporate law production in the US, with states mostly in charge and Delaware as the historical de facto monopolist that caters mostly to managers[5] and, more recently, controlling shareholders.[6] Unless the federal government intervenes, which it does *sometimes* but mostly in times of

1 *See* Dorothy S. Lund & Elizabeth Pollman, *The Corporate Governance Machine*, 121 Colum. L. Rev. 2563, 2565–66 (2021) (arguing that corporate decision-making is primarily based on shareholder-centric interests, rather than broader societal concerns, because of the nature of incentives executives and directors respond to within what they call the "corporate governance machine[,]" which they describe as "a vast array of institutional players – proxy advisors, stock exchanges, ratings agencies, institutional investors and associations – [that] enshrine shareholder primacy in public markets.").

2 *See* Henry Hansmann & Reinier Kraakman, *The End of History for Corporate Law*, 89 Geo. L.J. 439, 441–42 (2001).

3 I am borrowing from the taxonomy Lucian Bebchuk and Jesse Fried use to describe how involuntary creditors fare in bankruptcy. *See generally* Lucian Ayre Bebchuk & Jesse M. Fried, *The Uneasy Case for the Priority of Secured Claims in Bankruptcy*, 105 Yale L.J. 857, 864 (1996) (defining as nonadjusting creditors those that do not adjust the terms of their claims to anticipate or take into account the effects of new developments).

4 *See* Matteo Gatti, *What Corporate Governance for AI?*, Jotwell (June 13, 2024) (reviewing Roberto Tallarita, *AI Is Testing the Limits of Corporate Governance*, Harv. Bus. Rev. (Dec. 05, 2023)), https://corp.jotwell.com/what-corporate-governance-for-ai/ and noting that a key concern with private ordering is whether practitioners can fairly represent societal interests at the bargaining table given that corporate lawyers primarily serve paying clients, typically management and investors).

5 Lucian A. Bebchuk & Assaf Hamdani, *Vigorous Race or Leisurely Walk: Re-considering the Competition over Corporate Charters*, 112 Yale L. J. 553, 563–64 (2002). Because states want to appeal to those who decide where to incorporate, many believe that the result of state competition in attracting incorporations is a race to the bottom in terms of protections to shareholders and, by extension, stakeholders. *See, for example*, William L. Cary, *Federalism and Corporate Law: Reflections upon Delaware*, 83 Yale L.J. 663 (1974); Lucian A. Bebchuk, *Federalism and the Corporation: The Desirable Limits on State Competition in Corporate Law*, 105 Harv. L. Rev. 1435 (1992). *But see*, for the opposite view arguing that state competition is a race to the top, Ralph K. Winter, Jr., *State Law, Shareholder Protection, and the Theory of the Corporation*, 6 J. Legal Stud. 251, 254–58 (1977); Frank H. Easterbrook & Daniel R. Fischel, The Economic Structure of Corporate Law, 212–27 (1991); Roberta Romano, The Genius of American Corporate Law 14–31 (1993).

6 Recent statutory corporate law reform in Delaware indicates that controlling shareholders are now a leading interest group in Delaware. *Cf.* Tom Hals, *Delaware Lawmakers Approve Corporate Bill That Critics Call Giveaway to Billionaires*, Reuters (Mar. 25, 2025, 8:39 PM), www.reuters.com/legal/government/delaware-lawmakers-approve-corporate-bill-that-critics-call-giveaway-billionaires-2025-03-25/ (chronicling the passage of SB 21 in Delaware, which critics describe as pro-controlling shareholders).

crisis,[7] it is safe to say that state corporate law won't come to the rescue of weaker constituencies or society at large – one of the few times it purported to intervene in that direction was to ultimately shield managers from hostile takeovers,[8] and it is questionable that weaker constituencies were protected at all.[9]

Thus, given corporate law is not a viable option, we tend to rely on other types of protections for external stakeholders, which are typically offered by external regulation.[10] Ironically, corporate governing often involves proactive actions with the goal – or effect – of preempting, substituting for, or fending off external regulation.[11]

Compounding the difficulty is the political nature of societal issues addressed by corporate governing. Politicians' responses to corporate governing are driven by alignment with the underlying issues corporations address, not on an objective assessment of the merits of corporate governing, that is, whether is desirable that corporations act as political agents.

Moreover, assuming we pass these obstacles and there is political willingness to fix or contain the risks raised by corporate governing, it is unclear what role corporate governance itself would play. In Chapter 5, we concluded that corporate governing faces two major challenges. First, it falls short in critical areas (including labor, antitrust, data privacy, and AI) where corporate interests often conflict with prosocial quests. Second, an overreliance on corporate governing poses significant risks to democratic institutions over time. These issues can't be resolved through corporate governance tweaks alone. What's needed is a broader policy toolkit – external regulations aimed at the critical areas corporate governing tends to avoid due to built-in

7 While US corporate law is generally produced at the state level and Delaware has a predominant position, over the years Congress has enacted a number of measures in corporate law, especially in the aftermath of crisis. *See* Mark J. Roe, *Delaware's Competition*, 117 HARV. L. REV. 588, 610–34 (2003) (discussing examples of federal regulation of corporate law, such as securities and takeover laws). On the reactive nature of business law, see Frank Partnoy, *Why Markets Crash and What Law Can Do about It*, 61 U. PITT. L. REV. 741 (2000); Roberta Romano, *The Sarbanes-Oxley Act and the Making of Quack Corporate Governance*, 114 YALE L.J. 1521 (2005).

8 For the argument that workers were used as pawns to grant more discretion to managers during the takeover era, see Mark J. Roe, *Takeover Politics*, in THE DEAL DECADE: WHAT TAKEOVERS AND LEVERAGED BUYOUTS MEAN FOR CORPORATE GOVERNANCE 321, 330–33 (Margaret M. Blair ed., 1993).

9 *See generally* Lucian A. Bebchuk, Kobi Kastiel & Roberto Tallarita, *For Whom Corporate Leaders Bargain*, 94 S. CAL. L. REV. 1467 (2021) (analyzing the treatment of workers in M&A deals in jurisdictions that passed a constituency statute and noting that employees were not protected by managers).

10 *See also* Ann. M. Lipton, *The Legitimation of Shareholder Primacy*, Eur. Corp. Governance Inst. Law Working Paper, No. 826/2025 (2025), at 6 (arguing that "the elevation of shareholder wealth maximization above all other values … is best read as something like a cry for help, to be provided in the form of generalized acknowledgment that Delaware's corporate law cannot be relied upon to exercise social control over corporations, and in fact, regulation among those lines must occur externally."). In her paper, Lipton further observes that, unsurprisingly, certain federal corporate governance reforms, while ostensibly pro-investor, are sometimes enacted primarily to advance broader societal interests. *Id.* at 22–25 (citing Dodd-Frank and the now-defunct climate disclosure rules).

11 *See supra* Chapter 5, Section B.2.a.v.

conflicts,[12] and reforms to the norms and rules that structure political engagement by citizens themselves. None of this is easy, of course.[13] But acknowledging that corporate governance is largely powerless here is, at the very least, a useful place to start.

Recognizing these limitations, the rest of this chapter explores targeted governance adjustments to manage immediate corporate risks, for shareholders and other stakeholders. Section B outlines potential regulatory interventions, Section C assesses the effectiveness of market-based corporate governance solutions, and Section D presents a survey of disclosures by 200 large corporations (from the S&P 100 and the 401–500 corporations within the S&P 500) regarding their policies and practices in connection with corporate governing.

## B SKETCHING A POLICY INTERVENTION

### 1 *Preliminary Obstacles*

Before sketching some policy options, it is helpful to address two preliminary obstacles to reform: *Citizens United* for corporate socioeconomic advocacy and the business judgment rule for government substitution.

#### a Corporate Socioeconomic Advocacy and *Citizens United*

Regulating corporate socioeconomic advocacy faces an uphill battle because, at a minimum, any policy would have to be consistent with *Citizens United*[14] and its progeny.[15] Even scholars not particularly fond of corporate political spending and speech acknowledge that any reform that seeks to deter corporate speech would unlikely survive a constitutionality challenge.[16] In light of this, among the potential measures to mitigate the risks associated with corporate governing, a flat-out restriction of corporate advocacy is not viable. The *Citizens United* opinion acknowledged the government's legitimate interest in protecting dissenting minority shareholders but argued that the solution lies in exploring alternative regulatory mechanisms rather than restricting speech.[17]

12 *Cf.* Matteo Gatti & Chrystin Ondersma, *Stakeholder Syndrome: Does Stakeholderism Derail Effective Protections for Weaker Constituencies?*, 100 N.C. L. Rev. 167 (2021) (arguing that external regulation is a superior strategy to attain pro-stakeholder goals than reforming corporate law).

13 *See infra* text accompanying notes 40 and 41. *See also infra* Section D.

14 Citizens United v. Fed. Election Comm'n, 558 U.S. 310, 336–66 (2010) (prohibiting the government from restricting independent expenditures for political communications by corporations, including nonprofit corporations, labor unions, and other associations, so long as such spending is independent of a party or a candidate). *See supra* Chapter 2, Section A.3.

15 *See* Burwell v. Hobby Lobby Stores, Inc., 573 U.S. 682 (2014) (allowing exemptions for close corporations from a regulation that its owners religiously object to if there is a less restrictive means of furthering the law's interest).

16 Lucian A. Bebchuk & Robert J. Jackson, Jr., *Corporate Political Speech: Who Decides?*, 124 Harv. L. Rev. 83, 108 (2010).

17 *Id.* at 114 (citing *Citizens United*).

### b Government Substitution and the Business Judgment Rule

Intervening on government substitution poses no constitutional challenges but remains complex. This is because government substitution primarily involves internal corporate actions directly impacting a corporation's ordinary business operations.[18] Any intervention would burden how a corporation runs its business and treats its stakeholders. Policymakers would need to present compelling justifications for departing from standard practice, particularly given the judicial deference that normal business operations receive under the business judgment rule.[19]

To be clear, the business judgment rule is not absolute and is subject to exceptions – for one, it does not apply if the decision-makers are interested.[20] Thus, one argument that could justify a policy intervention in government substitution – and by extension even corporate socioeconomic advocacy – is that directors and executives are not neutral arbiters of corporate governing, but instead pursue pet projects that align with their political ideologies.[21] Some commentators support this narrative, citing it as a potential justification for enhanced oversight or restrictions on corporate political engagement.[22]

If policymakers buy into the interestedness argument, they can craft policies that, to varying degrees, depart from the business judgment rule. Under existing Delaware law, generic political preferences are likely insufficient to justify such a departure and establish a violation of the duty of loyalty.[23] However, even without textbook self-dealing, a conflict can still be problematic. For instance, Delaware takeover law recognizes "the omnipresent specter that a board may be acting primarily in its own interests, rather than those of the corporation and its shareholders[,]"[24] and courts apply a regime of enhanced scrutiny – less taxing than entire fairness, but not as lenient as the business judgment rule.[25]

[18] *See supra* Chapter 3, Section A.

[19] *See supra* Chapter 3, Section B.2.

[20] *See, for example,* AMERICAN LAW INSTITUTE, PRINCIPLES OF CORPORATE GOVERNANCE (1994), Section 4.01(C).

[21] *But see supra* Chapter 4, Section A.4.a.

[22] *See, for example,* STEPHEN M. BAINBRIDGE, THE PROFIT MOTIVE: DEFENDING SHAREHOLDER VALUE MAXIMIZATION 106–09 (2023) (arguing that when some CEOs engage in social activism, they may sacrifice profits to prioritize stakeholder interests).

[23] Delaware courts require plaintiffs challenging director decisions to allege facts that demonstrate a tangible conflict of interest to rebut the presumption of the business judgment rule. To show that a director was "interested," plaintiffs must plead facts indicating the director received a personal financial benefit not equally shared by stockholders or had a competing fiduciary duty to another entity on the other side of the transaction. Similarly, independence may be challenged by alleging facts that demonstrate a director's loyalty to or undue influence by an interested party, undermining the director's ability to act impartially. *See In re McDonald's Corp. S'holder Derivative Litig.*, 291 A.3d 652, 687–88 (Del. Ch. 2023); *Solomon v. Armstrong*, 747 A.2d 1098, 1111–12 (Del. Ch. 1999).

[24] Unocal Corp. v. Mesa Petroleum Co., 493 A.2d 946, 954 (Del. 1985).

[25] Enhanced scrutiny, Delaware's intermediate standard of review, applies to specific and recurring scenarios where potential conflicts of interest may subtly undermine the decision-making process,

Thus, a legitimate question is whether corporate governing presents a conflict as serious – if not more so – than hostile takeovers, warranting a similar departure from the business judgment rule. A related question is whether an analogous regime of enhanced scrutiny should be tailored to corporate governing.

This said, a policy intervention departing from the business judgment rule may risk overreach. While all managers and directors hold political preferences, it would be hard to establish whether their actions reflect those preferences at the expense of the corporation's best interests or are aligned with such interests. As highlighted in Chapter 4, studies show that corporate governing decisions often respond to pressures executives face in various markets (product, labor, and capital).[26] In fact, while some segments of Corporate America, such as senior managers, have shifted leftward, CEOs, on average, remain conservative and can hardly be faulted for picking pet projects.[27] It is plausible that corporate leaders act less out of personal political preferences and more in strategic response to market pressures. In such cases, policy interventions that override the business judgment rule could unintentionally deter corporate actions aligned with consumer and labor market expectations. Penalizing firms for responding to market demands would undermine seeking their best interests.[28]

The remainder of this section surveys traditional corporate governance tools designed to mitigate bias and promote balanced decision-making, including enhanced disclosure (Section B.2), improved process, board centrality, approval by disinterested directors, and shareholder approval (Section B.3). The aim is not to prescribe definitive solutions but rather to outline a modular toolkit for policy and practice experimentation.

## 2 *Disclosure*

One approach to addressing the risks raised by corporate governing is improving disclosure of the underlying initiatives.[29] Better disclosures are a relatively soft and

even when directors appear independent and disinterested. This standard addresses structural and situational conflicts that fall short of necessitating entire fairness review but still require more judicial oversight than the deference typically afforded under the business judgment rule. Under enhanced scrutiny, defendant fiduciaries bear the burden of demonstrating that their motivations were proper and not self-serving, and that their actions were reasonable in advancing a legitimate corporate objective. See *McDonald's*, 291 A.3d 652, at 686; In re Trados Inc. S'holder Litig. (Trados II), 73 A.3d 17, 43 (Del. Ch. 2013); Mercier v. Inter-Tel (Del.), Inc., 929 A.2d 786, 810 (Del. Ch. 2007). In the takeover context, Delaware judges allow directors to adopt antitakeover defensive measures so long as they can meet a two-prong test that requires that: (i) there are "reasonable grounds for believing that a danger or a threat to corporate policy exists" and (ii) "the response taken by the company … [is] reasonable in relation to the threat posed" (the latter is often referred to as the *Unocal* proportionality test). *Unocal*, 493 A.2d 946, at 955. *See infra* note 61.

26 *See supra* Chapter 2, Section A.1 and Chapter 4, Section A.3.

27 *See supra* Chapter 2, Section A.1.a and Chapter 4, Section A.4.a.

28 I explore this conundrum more when I discuss empowering disinterested directors *infra* Section B.3.

29 For a proposal on corporate political spending, see Comm. On Disclosure of Corporate Political Spending, *Letter from Comm. on Disclosure of Corporate Political Spending to Elizabeth M. Murphy, Secretary, U.S. Sec. & Exch. Comm'n* (Aug. 3, 2011), www.sec.gov/rules/petitions/2011/petn4-637.pdf.

straightforward intervention, providing the necessary information to stakeholders without substantive limits on how corporations run their business.[30]

To be sure, many corporate initiatives are already publicly visible; indeed, corporate socioeconomic advocacy fundamentally involves public messaging – that is the whole point of it. The central question is whether the current system – mandatory disclosure accompanied by a liability regime only for information meeting the materiality threshold,[31] and voluntary disclosure otherwise – is sufficient, or if policymakers should impose additional disclosure requirements around corporate governing.[32] If greater transparency is warranted,[33] various policy options emerge, several of which I outline below.

What to Disclose. (A) Mandatory disclosure of *corporate socioeconomic advocacy* can follow four main approaches. The first requires corporations to disclose every initiative, providing comprehensive transparency but potentially overwhelming stakeholders with

30 *See generally* Lucian A. Bebchuk, Robert J. Jackson Jr., James D. Nelson & Roberto Tallarita, *The Untenable Case for Keeping Investors in the Dark*, 10 HARV. BUS. L. REV. 1 (2020) (supporting mandatory disclosure on corporate political spending and addressing various critiques to the proposal).

31 In securities regulation, materiality refers to information that a reasonable investor would consider important in making investment decisions, encompassing facts or events that could significantly affect a company's financial performance, stock price, or operations (see TSC Industries, Inc. v. Northway, Inc., 426 U.S. 438, 449 (1976); Basic Inc. v. Levinson, 485 U.S. 224, 231–232 (1988)). *See infra* note 35.

32 The securities law debate on mandatory vs. voluntary disclosure is immense. *Compare, for example,* Merritt B. Fox, *Retaining Mandatory Securities Disclosure: Why Issuer Choice Is Not Investor Empowerment*, 85 VA. L. REV. 1335, 1338–39 (1999) (arguing voluntary disclosure is suboptimal) *with* Roberta Romano, *The Need for Competition in International Securities Regulation*, 2 THEORETICAL INQUIRIES L. 387, 418 (2001) (arguing issuers have strong incentives to produce information). For a critique to a rigid dichotomy between voluntary and mandatory disclosure, see Lisa M. Fairfax, *Dynamic Disclosure: An Expose on the Mythical Divide between Voluntary and Mandatory ESG Disclosure*, 101 TEX. L. REV. 273 (2022) (arguing these categories are not distinct but rather exist on a continuum). Presciently, Fairfax noted that a clear advantage of voluntary disclosures is their resilience – unlike mandatory regimes, which may never materialize or, if enacted, risk being repealed (*id.* at 313–15). This is precisely what happened with the rollback of the climate disclosure rules introduced by the Biden SEC, which were later dismantled under the Trump SEC. *See supra* Chapter 1, Section B.4.

33 A separate issue is the political feasibility of mandating new disclosures. Given the tortured rollout – and eventual demise – of the SEC's climate disclosure rules, it's hard to imagine the Commission eager to tread a similar path again anytime soon. The only plausible exception would be a pivot toward the conservative goal of restricting prosocial corporate speech. Even then, as discussed in Section B.1.a, such a move would face serious constitutional obstacles. The rulemaking process itself exposed deep divisions – within the SEC, the business community, academia, and Wall Street – underscoring the political volatility surrounding corporate disclosure and ESG. On the institutional and academic front, compare Hester M. Peirce, *We Are Not the Securities and Environment Commission – At Least Not Yet* (SEC Comm'r statement, Mar. 21, 2022), www.sec.gov/news/statement/peirce-climate-disclosure-20220321 (criticizing the SEC climate proposal adopted by the majority of Commissioners) *and* Lawrence Cunningham, Proposal on *Climate-Related Disclosures for Investors*, HARV. L. SCH. F. ON CORP. GOVERNANCE (June 23, 2022) https://corpgov.law.harvard.edu/2022/06/23/proposal-on-climate-related-disclosures-for-investors/ (summarizing the content of academic comment letter against the SEC climate proposal) *with* Jill E. Fisch, *The SEC's Authority to Pursue Climate-Related Disclosure*, HARV. L. SCH. F. ON CORP. GOVERNANCE (June 20, 2022), https://corpgov.law.harvard.edu/2022/06/20/the-secs-authority-to-pursue-climate-related-disclosure/ (summarizing comment letter in support of the SEC climate proposal) *and* John C. Coates, *Proposal on Climate-Related Disclosures Falls within the SEC's Authority*, HARV. L. SCH. F. ON CORP. GOVERNANCE (June 22, 2022), https://corpgov.law.harvard.edu/2022/06/22/proposal-on-climate-related-disclosures-falls-within-the-secsauthority/ (same).

excessive information.[34] The second approach focuses on disclosing only those initiatives that contrast with existing or proposed legislation or regulation, emphasizing areas of tension or conflict with legislatures or regulators and striking a balance between transparency and relevance. The third, which can be implemented alone or combined with the second, is to require corporations to disclose any reversal of their prior positions. The fourth, which reflects the current standard, limits disclosure to *material* advocacy activities,[35] reducing the burden on corporations but potentially leaving stakeholders with an incomplete understanding of the company's broader advocacy footprint, especially when non-material activities may still carry significant public or societal implications.

(B) For *government substitution*, materiality should remain the guiding principle, as imposing disclosure obligations for non-material matters seems overkill; one exception, again, could be when a corporation reverses a prior initiative. In any event, actions initially deemed non-material can become material if they trigger significant backlash or boycotts, leading to declines in sales or stock prices. Consider the lawsuit against Target over its 2023 Pride campaign. Plaintiffs argued that the risk factors in Target's Annual Report, which acknowledged potential negative publicity and consumer boycotts related to its ESG positions, including DEI, were misleading in light of the company's 2023 Pride campaign.[36] As mentioned earlier, the *Target* case survived the motion to dismiss.[37]

*When and Where*. The main choice is between prompt disclosure through an 8-K filing or periodic disclosure, such as in a company's annual 10-K, in quarterly 10-Q filings, or via ad hoc new filings. As I further illustrate in Section D, corporate governing initiatives are currently disclosed primarily through "shadow governance"[38] documents, including sustainability or ESG reports, codes of conduct, political activity reports, and, occasionally, risk factors or descriptions within securities filings.[39]

*Transparency on Rules of Engagement*. Investors have a legitimate interest in understanding the drivers of corporate governing within a corporation – what areas

[34] Fairfax, *supra* note 32, at 291–92 & 295–98 (describing the confusion stemming from the sheer amount of – voluntary – ESG disclosures). While a sensible objection to imposing such requirements is the risk of flooding investors with excessive micro-disclosures, it is worth considering how even small-scale initiatives can grant executives access to politicians, increased exposure, and influence – potentially creating a misalignment with the interests of the corporation and its shareholders.

[35] The SEC mandates limited ESG disclosures under a materiality-based approach. Regulation S-K requires reporting on board composition, executive compensation, board diversity considerations, and the material effects of environmental compliance. Investor pressure has led to modest expansions, including enhanced human capital management disclosures beyond just workforce size. *Id.* at 299.

[36] Brian Craig, et al. v. Target Corporation, et al., No. 2:23-cv-599-JLB-KCD (M.D. Fla. Dec. 4, 2024) (allowing the case to proceed, finding sufficient allegations of material misstatements, scienter, and loss causation over undisclosed ESG/DEI risks and the 2023 Pride campaign.

[37] *See supra* Chapter 3, Section E.1.

[38] Yaron Nili & Cathy Hwang, *Shadow Governance*, 108 CAL. L. REV. 1097 (2020) (highlighting the role of "shadow governance" documents – non-charter, non-bylaw policies that address issues like campaign finance, environmental sustainability, and sexual harassment – in shaping corporate decision-making and behavior); Fairfax, *supra* note 32, at 292 (describing the various types and names of these documents).

[39] *See supra* note 38 and accompanying text.

are prioritized, what goals are pursued, whose interests are fostered, the framework of these initiatives, and who within the corporation holds the authority to act or speak on its behalf. Investors may benefit from disclosure rules that contextualize individual initiatives within a corporation's broader agenda on specific matters. Regulators must determine whether corporations should disclose discrete corporate governing initiatives truthfully and frame these disclosures within their overarching policy agendas to prevent incomplete, selective, or misleading information. Section D examines current corporate efforts to ensure transparency on these issues.

Beneficiaries of the Disclosure Regime. Earlier in Section A, I illustrate how corporate governance is typically protective of equity investors. Yet, whether a corporate disclosure regime, like the modular one sketched above, should be for the protection of shareholders only or a broader set of stakeholders is subject to a vibrant policy debate.[40] The latter option would be more aligned with dealing with a phenomenon that, by its nature, as Chapter 5 shows, transcends intrafirm standard dynamics.

Nevertheless, implementing a system with a broader set of protected actors – for instance, the employees affected by a corporation's reversal of DEI policies, communities impacted by abandoned environmental pledges, or customers misled by corporate socioeconomic advocacy would be no small feat. For one, for the last fifty years, securities regulation has operated with standing rules that select only certain plaintiffs: Under Rule 10b-5, an investor must be a purchaser or seller of the security during the alleged fraud,[41] effectively excluding other stakeholders who may suffer harm from false or misleading statements or omissions.

Liability Rules. In any disclosure regime for corporate governing, a central question is what kind of liability and enforcement framework would apply. This issue is already playing out in real time, as illustrated by securities fraud claims like those in the Target case – where plaintiffs are using disclosure-based theories to challenge prosocial corporate initiatives.[42] Studies indicate that misleading information in this field is widespread.[43]

40 *Compare* Cynthia A. Williams, *The Securities and Exchange Commission and Corporate Social Transparency*, 112 HARV. L. REV. 1197 (1999) (arguing that federal securities law disclosure was intended to promote accountability beyond investors to the broader public) *and* Ann M. Lipton, *Not Everything Is About the Investors: The Case for Mandatory Stakeholder Disclosure*, 37 YALE J. REG. 499 (2019) (arguing for a more expansive disclosure system) *with* Paul G. Mahoney & Julia D. Mahoney, *The New Separation of Ownership and Control: Institutional Investors and ESG 2021*, COLUM. BUS. L. REV. 840 (2021) (arguing to not depart from the SEC's stated mission of protecting Main Street investors and maintaining fair, orderly, and efficient markets).

41 *Blue Chip Stamps v. Manor Drug Stores*, 421 U.S. 723, 731–32 (1975) (holding that only actual purchasers or sellers of securities have standing to bring a private damages action under Rule 10b-5).

42 *See supra* note 37. *See also supra* Chapter 3, Section E.1.

43 *See generally* Federica Balluchi, Arianna Lazzini & Riccardo Torelli, *CSR and Greenwashing: A Matter of Perception in the Search of Legitimacy* 2 (Dec. 15, 2020), https://papers.ssrn.com/sol3/papers.cfm?abstract_id=3721199 (noting "a worrying increase in the amount of misleading information produced by companies, including information on environmental and social aspects");

Rule 10b-5 prohibits materially misleading statements or omissions concerning securities transactions, but its application to corporate governing initiatives like ESG and DEI commitments raises challenges. For instance, a corporation might publicly commit to a "Climate Advocacy Code" that pledges alignment with net-zero goals while secretly funding lobbying efforts against a carbon tax – what happens when a green investor discovers this contradiction? Similarly, a retailer might prominently disclose its support for LGBTQ+ rights and related DEI policies but then quietly abandon those initiatives without informing stakeholders, leading to consumer backlash when the inconsistency is exposed.

These examples expose gaps in the current framework, where materiality – narrowly tied to financial impact – overlooks reputational inconsistencies that may still matter to investors and other stakeholders.[44] As noted above, the current regime also leaves stakeholders without recourse when harmed by misleading statements but unable to satisfy standing requirements under existing law.[45] Moreover, courts have frequently shown leniency toward issuers, allowing them to invoke the puffery defense in Rule 10b-5 cases involving ESG disclosures.[46]

The scenarios described above raise critical questions about whether securities regulation should address significant deviations from advocacy principles, even without clear financial impact, and whether materiality should extend to reputational harm or societal implications. The current regime prioritizes financial materiality, often leaving stakeholders without recourse for inconsistencies that erode trust and reveal governance failures.[47] Some scholars argue that the mismatch between the

Andrew C. Baker, David F. Larcker; Charles G. McClure, Durgesh Saraph & Edward M. Watts, *Diversity Washing*, 62 J. Acct. Res. 1661 (2024), https://doi.org/10.1111/1475-679X.12542.

44 *See supra* note 31 and accompanying text. Renee Jones argues that materiality should not be confined to financial outcomes but should also reflect information investors deem important for voting decisions, particularly on ESG-related matters. *See* Renee M. Jones, *Voting Matters: Materiality Considerations and the Shareholder Vote*, 48 Seattle U. L. Rev. 419 (2025).

45 *See supra* note 41 and accompanying text.

46 The puffery doctrine treats vague or aspirational statements as immaterial as a matter of law, leading to dismissal of claims at the pleading stage. The doctrine has been a primary tool used by courts to dismiss ESG securities fraud claims brought by private plaintiffs, as judges often view broadly worded statements about ESG compliance or risk management as "rosy statements of optimism" or "aspirational statements" that a reasonable investor would not take literally and therefore deem them immaterial. *See* James J. Park, *ESG Securities Fraud*, 58 Wake Forest L. Rev. 1149, 1154 (2023) (citing In re Petrobras Sec. Litig., 116 F. Supp. 3d 368, 281 (S.D.N.Y. 2015)). To address this, Park suggests that courts apply the probability/magnitude test from *Basic v. Levinson*, 485 U.S. at 237, to assess the materiality of ESG risks. While well-established, this test is primarily used in the M&A context and evaluates both the likelihood of an event occurring and its potential impact. *Id.* at 1155. *See also* Kevin S. Haeberle, *Fraud-on-the-Market Liability in the ESG Era*, 98 Tul. L. Rev. 641, 672–74 (2024) (discussing risks of relying on the puffery doctrine).

47 *Cf.* Cynthia A. Williams & Donna M. Nagy, *ESG and Climate Change Blind Spots: Turning the Corner on SEC Disclosure*, 99 Tex. L. Rev. 1453 (2021). Yet, as Hillary Sale and Bob Thompson argue, securities liability and enforcement regimes are not solely about individual investor protection but also serve broader public and market integrity functions. This perspective suggests that ESG-related misstatements, even when their financial impact is unclear, may warrant scrutiny because

current securities fraud regime and ESG-related needs is so severe that we should explore policy alternatives.[48] Among the proposals, one could consider tailored rules to close these gaps by requiring timely disclosure of policy reversals or contradictions, enhancing transparency, and holding corporations accountable when their actions diverge from their commitments.

### 3 *Enhanced Corporate Governance Devices*

This discussion of possible reforms to disclosure regimes naturally leads to questions about how corporate governing decisions are made and by whom. The focus now shifts from transparency to internal governance mechanisms, whereby policymakers must consider whether and how enhanced process, board centrality, disinterested director oversight, and shareholder approval can address the challenges and risks associated with corporate governing in today's environment.[49]

Enhanced Process. Aaron Chatterji and Michael Toffel have suggested CEOs should establish a proactive framework with their executive teams, including chief communications officers, to identify and prioritize issues that align with the company's values and assess their social impact.[50] This process involves carefully

they affect confidence in corporate disclosures as a whole. *See generally* Hillary A. Sale & Robert B. Thompson, *Market Intermediation, Publicness, and Securities Class Actions*, 93 Wash. U. L. Rev. 487 (2015). *See also* Fairfax, *supra* note 32, at 306. Fairfax points out that although the SEC clarified on several occasions that liability is attached to voluntary disclosures, "corporate behavior around voluntary disclosure strongly suggests that corporations do not view the liability risks associated with voluntary disclosure in the same manner that they view the liability risks associated with mandated disclosure." *Id.* (citing a 2020 GAO study and mentioning that this was one of the reasons the Biden SEC sought to impose mandatory climate disclosures).

48 Aneil Kovvali argues that ESG is largely incompatible with the presumption of reliance under *Basic*, which assumes that all publicly available, material information – including misstatements – is reflected in stock prices, thereby eliminating the need for individual proof of reliance in securities fraud cases. *Basic*, 485 U.S. at 247. In his view, this presumption fails in the ESG context because ESG information is not reliably incorporated into share prices. First, the ESG movement itself rests on the premise that share prices do not fully capture socially significant risks and impacts, contradicting *Basic*'s assumption of market efficiency. Second, ESG information is often qualitative, difficult to quantify, and inconsistently acted upon by investors, making it unlikely that misstatements meaningfully distort stock prices. Finally, applying *Basic* to ESG disclosures may chill voluntary corporate ESG reporting, as companies could fear litigation over statements that are inherently uncertain or difficult to measure. *See* Aneil Kovvali, *ESG and Securities Litigation: A Basic Contradiction*, 73 Duke L.J. 1229 (2024) (advocating for limiting *Basic*'s applicability to ESG disclosures and proposing alternative enforcement mechanisms, including SEC action, targeted liability regimes, corporate governance reforms, and market-based incentives).

49 For a critical view of disclosure-only interventions in corporate governance, see Christopher M. Bruner, *Corporate Governance Reform and the Sustainability Imperative*, 131 Yale L.J. 1217, 1228 (2022) (arguing that "disclosure-based strategies … create the impression of regulatory action, but remain unlikely to substantially improve matters on their own.").

50 Aaron K. Chatterji & Michael W. Toffel, *The New CEO Activists*, Harv. Bus. Rev. (Jan.–Feb. 2018), https://hbr.org/2018/01/the-new-ceo-activists, at 11.

weighing the importance of chosen causes against alternatives, considering potential benefits like employee and consumer support, and accounting for the risk of backlash in a politically divided landscape.[51] While this framework should guide most decisions, the authors concede it may not always be feasible in urgent situations.[52]

Lisa Fairfax offers a more detailed articulation of how corporations should approach political speech as a matter of enterprise risk.[53] She proposes a four-part risk management framework: risk identification (which includes mapping speech from all levels of the organization and across informal channels like blogs or marketing), cost–benefit assessment (including short- and long-term brand effects and stakeholder responses), risk mitigation (through internal processes, red flag detection, and crisis response planning), and finally, board oversight (ensuring visibility, interdepartmental communication, and subject-matter expertise).[54] Her approach does not seek to constrain corporate speech, but to embed it within the same internal systems used to govern other high-risk corporate activities.[55]

Operationalizing any of these best-practice processes into actual policy requirements is not easy, but this is where existing open-ended standards like fiduciary duties come in handy, particularly in jurisdictions with specialized corporate judges like Delaware, who could introduce procedural requirements as prerequisites for meeting safe harbors, the business judgment rule, or any other legal defenses.

*Board Centrality*. Many in the literature, some writing on corporate political spending, are critical of leaving the practice in management's hands.[56] Thus, if there is appetite and political preconditions for a bolder intervention, board empowerment, and enhanced accountability are some of the tools to consider when addressing the risks of corporate governing.

[51] *Id.* The authors reckon that CEOs statements are inevitably linked to their companies and because separating personal views from the firm is rarely successful, they suggest forming rapid response teams – including board members, investors, senior management, and employees. In their view, while seeking consensus may delay timely messaging, informing this team in advance can mitigate stakeholder unpreparedness and potential backlash. *Id.* at 16–17.

[52] *Id.* at 11.

[53] Lisa M. Fairfax, *Reframing the Corporate Political Speech Debate*, Working Paper (2025) (unpublished manuscript, on file with author), at 6–9 (arguing for enterprise-wide, risk-based approaches to managing corporate political speech).

[54] *Id.*

[55] *Id.*

[56] *See for example*, Bebchuk & Jackson, *supra* note 16, at 89–90 (arguing that political speech decisions are different from ordinary business decisions and that, like other types of corporate decisions involving diverging interests, different rules are in order); Leo E. Strine, Jr., *Good Corporate Citizenship We Can All Get Behind? Toward a Principled, Non-Ideological Approach to Making Money the Right Way*, 78 Bus. Law. 329, 366 (2023) (arguing that "[i]f the company purports to take positions on external public policy, its positions should result from a deliberative process of the board of directors based on the direct relevance of the policy question to the company, and not just reflect the personal view of the CEO without board backing.").

This can be done in different ways. One is to require that initiatives always be subject to board approval, thus disempowering management.[57] Another is incentivizing board centrality with tools like standard shifting or burden of proof shifting[58] to reward board involvement instead of leaving corporate governing to management. To that end, courts can consider utilizing a system of enhanced scrutiny for corporate governing, which aligns with what already happens in the takeover field.[59]

Disinterested Directors. Corporations may employ additional mechanisms to enhance board effectiveness and ensure accountability. For instance, an extra step would be to put disinterested directors in charge,[60] either as an actual requirement or, again, as a result of incentives such as standard of review shifting or burden of proof shifting.[61] While this may seem like a sensible policy, its implementation is fraught with complications.

In theory, disinterested directors could provide an objective perspective and check potential conflicts of interest.[62] In practice, though, establishing disinterest on this

57 *See* Omari Scott Simmons, *Political Risk Management*, 64 Wm. & Mary L. Rev. 707, 725 (2023) (framing political risk within broader enterprise risk management and noting that while "[s]ome delegation to a standing committee (for example, a risk or audit committee), a chief risk officer (CRO), or outside experts is necessary, … risk management remains the responsibility of the entire board.").

58 Standard-shifting mechanisms (as in *Corwin* and *M&F Worldwide*) and burden-of-proof shifts (as in *Kahn v. Lynch*) are policy tools the Delaware judiciary has used in connection with fiduciary duties litigation (though some of these cases are no longer good law after the passage of Delaware SB 21, which significantly expanded statutory safe harbors for conflicted transactions: see Morgan, Lewis & Bockius LLP, *Just Passed: Senate Bill Significantly Amends Delaware General Corporation Law*, *Morgan Lewis* (Mar. 26, 2025), www.morganlewis.com/pubs/2025/03/just-passed-senate-bill-significantly-amends-delaware-general-corporation-law). *See* Corwin v. KKR Fin. Holdings LLC, 125 A.3d 304, 309 (Del. 2015) (applying the business judgment rule to transactions not requiring entire fairness after a fully informed, uncoerced vote by disinterested shareholders); Kahn v. M&F Worldwide Corp., 88 A.3d 635, 645–54 (Del. 2014) (applying the business judgment rule to transactions meeting conditions such as approval by an independent committee and a majority-of-the-minority vote); Kahn v. Lynch Commc'ns Sys., 638 A.2d 1110, 1117 (Del. 1994) (placing the burden on plaintiffs to prove unfairness in parent-subsidiary mergers approved by independent committees or majority-of-the-minority votes). It is common to use procedural tools like the burden of proof for purposes of shaping substantive policy in corporate law. *See* Matteo Gatti, *It's My Stock and I'll Vote If I Want To: Conflicted Voting by Shareholders in (Hostile) M&A Deals*, 47 U. Mem. L. Rev. 181, 281 n.260 (2016) (providing a series of examples). On burden shifting, see generally Louis Kaplow, *Burden of Proof*, 121 Yale L.J. 738 (2012) and, with respect to corporate law, Charles M. Yablon, *On the Allocation of Burdens of Proof in Corporate Law: An Essay on Fairness and Fuzzy Sets*, 13 Cardozo L. Rev. 497 (1991).

59 For a brief description, see *supra* Section B.1.b.

60 *See* Bebchuk & Jackson, *supra* note 16, at 101–02 (proposing a requirement that independent directors approve decisions about corporate political speech).

61 *See supra* note 58. For a description of independent directors as a "good governance" tool, see Lipton, *supra* note 10, at 7–9 (noting critiques of their effectiveness in protecting shareholders and perspectives that view them as enhancing corporate legitimacy). Lipton points out that when Delaware adopted the *Unocal* standard of enhanced scrutiny (*see supra* Section B.1.b), director independence played a crucial role. *Id.* at 20.

62 Bebchuk & Jackson, *supra* note 16, at 101–02. *See also* Strine, *Good Corporate Citizenship*, *supra* note 56 at 361. Disinterested directors played a role in the *Simeone* case, as the Chancery Court was

front is not as straightforward as in typical conflicted transactions, in which the director has a financial interest opposite the corporation on a given deal or the company has a controlling shareholder to whom some directors may be too close. Here, the interest in question is a political preference, which everybody has. The challenge of putting disinterested directors in charge would be finding someone without prior political preferences – arguably an impossible task. For instance, when deciding on an issue that, on its face, is progressive, the regime would call for decision-makers to not be progressive. But could anyone consider a conservative director truly disinterested on that same issue? If a progressive director is presumed biased in favor of the initiative, wouldn't a conservative director be equally biased in the other direction? How could we disqualify the former but not the latter? Arguably, even moderate directors could not qualify because they, too, may be deciding the underlying issue based on their prior biases and against the best interests of the corporation.

The same challenges obviously arise in the reverse scenario of boards with conservative directors, either when a conservative issue is at stake or, more in general, when the board decides in ways that conform the political priors of the directors. For instance, could a firm's workplace safety policies be deemed politically biased if the CEO is a known conservative, say Elon Musk? If we adhere to a framework that assigns such decisions to disinterested directors based on political neutrality, the answer would be yes. Would this then disqualify Musk and require liberal directors at his companies – heroically assuming there are any – to take charge of such matters due to their perceived political nature (e.g., worker rights and safety, but also LGBTQ+ rights, of which Musk is a staunch opponent[63])?

Following this logic to its extreme, any corporate initiative involving a socioeconomic issue would require the exclusion of all directors or executives with political leanings – left, right, or center. That is neither practical nor desirable.

More importantly, excluding directors based on their general political identity may lead to strategic misalignment. If, for instance, a progressive initiative is in the company's best interest – as one could argue Nike's Kaepernick ad was[64] – a politically conservative but otherwise "independent" director might oppose it, not out of disinterest, but because of ideological bias. Entrusting such decisions to individuals whose views diverge from the firm's strategic priorities risks undermining sound judgment.

This suggests that disinterest shouldn't be defined by a director's general political affiliation, but by whether their position aligns with the corporation's best interests under the given circumstances. Yet, such an approach creates its own

satisfied that "the weighing of these key risks by disinterested [directors did] not evidence a potential lack of due care, let alone bad faith." *See* Simeone v. Walt Disney Co., 302 A.3d 956, 972 (Del. Ch. 2023).

63 Lipton, *supra* note 10, at 12–13. *See supra* Chapter 1, Sections B.7 and C.1.

64 *See supra* Introduction.

problems. Once a proposal is supported – whether through evidence or credible forecasts – as beneficial to the firm, everyone backing it could be deemed disinterested by default. That flips the logic: disinterest no longer rests on neutrality, but on agreement with a projected outcome. And if interestedness can only be meaningfully assessed ex post – after the dust settles and motives are reconstructed – then fiduciary law loses one of its key procedural safeguards. Courts and litigants are left with tools poorly suited to the political dimensions now embedded in corporate decision-making.

Shareholder Approval. Authors who liken corporate political activity to conflicted transactions suggest using the other primary device to cleanse such transactions, which is shareholder approval.[65] Professors Bebchuk and Jackson propose that, as a default rule, corporate political spending be subject to a veto by shareholders.[66] Former Chief Justice Leo Strine addresses advocacy and proposes that shareholder approval be required "[i]f a company wants to stop doing business in or with a particular American state"[67] on the argument that such an action "may involve the company abandoning services and endangering the employment of lots of residents of that state who do not disagree with the state policy that the company opposes."[68] However, concerns about pluralism and stakeholder protection may not be fully resolved by simply empowering stockholders, who may be non-residents of the boycotted state and thus indifferent to the fate of local stakeholders. In other words, if the primary concerns about corporate governing relate to its broader societal impact, putting shareholders in charge would be mistargeted.[69] Therefore, traditional corporate law and governance responses will inevitably fall short.[70]

65 Bebchuk & Jackson, *supra* note 16, at 98; Strine, *Good Corporate Citizenship*, *supra* note 56, at 370.

66 Bebchuk & Jackson, *supra* note 16, at 98.

67 Strine, *supra* note 56, at 368.

68 *Id.* (noting that "[n]ot everyone in Alabama is pro-life and not everyone in Massachusetts is pro-choice.").

69 To be sure, investors – particularly universal owners – have been cast as potential levers for disciplining corporate externalities. *See* Madison Condon, *Externalities and the Common Owner*, 95 WASH. L. REV. 1, 5 (2020); Jeffrey N. Gordon, *Systematic Stewardship*, 47 J. CORP. L. 627 (2022). Yet, a growing literature casts doubt on whether investor governance can meaningfully address societal harms. Scholars have argued that it may be impractical to promote the value of a portfolio by limiting the externalities of specific companies, that shareholder voting and engagement often fail to convey clear instructions to corporate managers, and that investors lack the representativeness and democratic legitimacy to serve as societal proxies. *See, for example*, Roberto Tallarita, *The Limits of Portfolio Primacy*, 76 VAND. L. REV. 511 (2023); Robert P. Bartlett & Ryan Bubb, *Corporate Social Responsibility through Shareholder Governance*, ECGI Law Working Paper No. 682/2023 (2023), https://ssrn.com/abstract=4354220.

70 For this reason, some authors have argued to reform corporate law to make internal corporate governance more democratic. *See* David G. Yosifon, *The Public Choice Problem in Corporate Law: Corporate Social Responsibility after Citizens United*, 89 N.C. L. REV. 1197 (2011); GRANT M. HAYDEN & MATTHEW T. BODIE, RECONSTRUCTING THE CORPORATION: FROM SHAREHOLDER PRIMACY TO SHARED GOVERNANCE (2020).

## C SHOULD CORPORATE GOVERNING BE LEFT TO THE MARKET?

One of the drawbacks of the policies described above is requiring board (or shareholder) involvement for minor, immaterial initiatives. Given the trade-off with preserving a corporation's flexibility in managing day-to-day operations, any policy intervention should be preceded by evidence of a market failure that justifies departing from the current regime. At a minimum, a workable revised system should distinguish between two levels of decision-making: on the one hand, authorizing and overseeing the overall strategy and initiatives the company plans to adopt, a responsibility suited for the board; on the other hand, more straightforward day-to-day actions or implementation measures (such as social media campaigns or one-off posts), which are better handled by management. Of course, these day-to-day activities would remain subject to board supervision under the existing regime but would not require board or shareholder intervention.

The risk of overreach may help explain why even critics of corporate governing – like Professors Jill Fisch and Jeff Schwartz – propose alternative frameworks rather than calling for hard bans or restrictive reforms.[71] For instance, they argue that corporations can and should engage in what they call "voluntary disarmament," reducing through voluntary collective action their involvement in political posturing.[72] They propose that corporations commit to depoliticization through a pledge akin to the Business Roundtable Statement on Corporate Purpose.[73] In their view, such a commitment would strengthen the ability of corporate decision-makers to withstand the significant pressure from stakeholders to take a stance on public debates.[74] While the proposal is worth considering at the individual company level, whether it can work for all corporations across the business spectrum is unclear. For one, some firms might unnecessarily constrain themselves by taking such a step, particularly given the uncertainty of future circumstances and the evolving nature of societal

[71] Jill E. Fisch & Jeff Schwartz, *How Did Corporations Get Stuck in Politics and Can They Escape?*, 3 U. CHI. BUS. L. REV 325, 330 (2024):

> Although we acknowledge the possibility that some political posturing is based on the selfish motivations of corporate executives, we believe that the phenomenon we described is primarily motivated by sincere efforts to promote corporate value. Moreover, we do not view political posturing as sufficiently different from other business decisions to warrant specific governance mandates or the line between political posturing and other forms of engagement in the political process as crisp enough to form a workable legal boundary

[72] *Id.* at 330–31 & 355–56.

[73] *Id.* at 355. For the Business Roundtable Statement of Corporate Purpose, see *supra* Chapter 2, Section A.2.

[74] Fisch and Schwartz believe corporations could publicly state in the pledge that their role is to serve stakeholders by providing quality goods and services in an ethical and sustainable manner and that they believe taking stances on political issues does not further these goals. Fisch & Schwartz, *supra* note 71, at 355.

and political expectations. While the pledge aims to depoliticize corporate actions, there is a risk that it could hinder some companies from addressing unforeseen crises or engaging in discussions where their corporate voices may ultimately be necessary or beneficial.

In any case, regardless of the merits of an express reform mandating some or all of the measures described in Section B, pragmatism suggests that legislative or regulatory changes in this field will be anything but straightforward.[75] For reasons illustrated in Chapter 2, this is true for any high-stakes reform in the US;[76] it might be even more accurate here, where political parties' views on the phenomenon are mainly dictated by the underlying corporate governing initiative.[77]

Given the risks of counterproductive, heavy-handed policy interventions and the potential for reform inertia, it is worth exploring allowing corporate governing to evolve through market forces. Various market mechanisms have, in fact, already begun shaping corporate governing, including the emergence of anti-ESG funds and the growing impact of shareholder proposals reflecting these viewpoints.[78] At the same time, traditional legal and political counterbalances have played a significant role, driven by challenges from conservative plaintiffs, politicians, and business figures like Elon Musk.[79] Market pressures from the left also persist, with demands for more decisive corporate action on climate change, human capital management, and other social concerns.[80] While the resulting dynamics may appear messy, it ultimately falls to executives, boards, and stakeholders to navigate and strike the right balance at the level of the individual company. This reflects the broader nature of markets, which thrive on competing forces across virtually all domains.

75 Some authors are vocal critics of voluntary regimes. *See* Bebchuk & Jackson, *supra* note 16, at 92 (noting that "[t]o the extent that one supports the mechanisms established by corporate law rules for various situations involving a divergence of the interests of directors and executives from those of shareholders, and therefore is not prepared to rely simply on market forces to eradicate these problems, one should also be reluctant to rely on market forces to eliminate any similar divergence of interests with respect to political speech decisions."). While I agree with their remark, I find it useful and realistic to preplan for a world that will not roll out a full-blown reform of corporate governing.

76 *See supra* Section B.2.

77 *See* Strine, *supra* note 56, at 350 (arguing that the left generally likes corporate governing unless it involves religious freedom, while the right decries "woke capitalism" but engages in "anti-woke" corporate governing and eagerly cashes in on what created woke capitalism: corporate political speech).

78 Mahi Roy & Alyssa Stankiewicz, *What's Inside "Anti-ESG" Funds?*, MORNINGSTAR.COM (Aug. 29, 2023), www.morningstar.com/sustainable-investing/whats-inside-anti-esg-funds (analyzing the composition, strategies, and market reception of funds designed to counter ESG-focused investing). On anti-ESG shareholder proposals, see Merel Spierings, *2024 Proxy Season Review: Corporate Resilience in a Polarized Landscape*, HARV. L. SCH. F. ON CORP. GOVERNANCE (Oct. 12, 2024), https://corpgov.law.harvard.edu/2024/10/12/2024-proxy-season-review-corporate-resilience-in-a-polarized-landscape/.

79 *See supra* Chapter 1, Section C.

80 Spierings, *supra* note 78 (noting that progressive shareholder initiatives and ESG-related efforts have continued to shape corporate governance in 2024, despite rising polarization).

Market forces and institutional investor pressure can contribute to improved corporate governing practices in many ways: informal board-shareholder engagement,[81] shareholder proposals,[82] outright activism,[83] and threatened or actual litigation.[84]

In this latter regard, corporations already operate against the backdrop of potential reprimands or incremental shifts in case law from Delaware and other courts. If they engage in corporate governing in ways that are not beneficial to the business, they may attract plaintiffs' attention and be subject to judicial scrutiny. Until now courts have been lenient because defendants have kept their act together, procedurally. For instance, in rejecting a Section 220 demand in the *Simeone* case, the Delaware Chancery Court was satisfied with the Disney board's deliberative process.[85] With other facts, judges may become less forgiving: Even in the absence of ultimate liability, corporate decision-makers still want to avoid attracting attention, especially given how charged the field is.[86] Time will tell whether the Delaware judiciary will explicitly define the guardrails corporations must implement to protect directors and officers from liability – or even judicial reproach. Some guardrails may already be emerging in other forums adjudicating securities and investment law issues, as seen in cases involving Target's risk factors and American Airlines' 401(k) plans, which could result in chilling effects on DEI initiatives and ESG investing, respectively.[87]

It should come as no surprise that companies have begun developing best practices well before any legal or regulatory intervention. For instance, Leo Strine notes

[81] *Cf.* Matteo Gatti, Giovanni Strampelli & Matteo Tonello, *How Does Board-Shareholder Engagement Really Work? Evidence from a Survey of Corporate Officers and from Disclosure Data*, *in* Board-Shareholder Dialogue: Policy Debate, Legal Constraints and Best Practices 325 (Luca Enriques & Giovanni Strampelli eds., 2024).

[82] *Cf.* Roberto Tallarita, *Stockholder Politics*, 73 Hastings L.J. 1697 (2022).

[83] *Cf.* Ronald J. Gilson & Jeffrey N. Gordon, *The Agency Costs of Agency Capitalism: Activist Investors and the Revaluation of Governance Rights*, 113 Colum. L. Rev. 863, 889–901 (2013).

[84] Jill E. Fisch, *Teaching Corporate Governance through Shareholder Litigation*, 34 Ga. L. Rev. 745 (2000).

[85] *Simeone*, 302 A.3d 956, at 970 (finding that the board "held the sort of deliberations that a board should undertake when the corporation's voice is used on matters of social significance.").

[86] *See generally* Roy Shapira, Law and Reputation: How the Legal System Shapes Behavior by Producing Information (2020) (theorizing that decision-makers are constrained by fear of reputational harm deriving from litigation regardless of ultimate monetary liability). *See also generally* Edward Rock, *Saints and Sinners: How Does Delaware Corporate Law Work?*, 44 UCLA L. Rev. 1009 (1997) (on the effects of Delaware corporate law litigation on corporate decision-makers).

[87] For Target, see *supra* note 37 and accompanying text and Chapter 3, Section E.1. In the American Airlines litigation, a federal district court ruled that the company and its Employee Benefits Committee breached their ERISA duty of loyalty by prioritizing corporate ESG objectives over the financial interests of plan participants in managing the company's 401(k) plans. Spence v. American Airlines, Inc., No. 4:23-cv-00552 (N.D. Tex. Jan. 10, 2025) (holding that American delegated significant authority to BlackRock despite its known ESG activism, creating conflicts of interest that led to improper fiduciary decision-making, and ultimately prioritizing corporate and third-party interests over plan beneficiaries).

that "Microsoft's management has decided to ask a 'three-pronged question' as a gating matter: Does the issue affect the interests of its customers, its employees, or the business itself?"[88] Approaches like this are sensible, particularly given the intensity of conservative angst surrounding these issues. To contain such concerns – and mitigate the associated risks of declining revenue and stock prices – corporations may need to demonstrate that they have an orderly process for engaging in corporate governing activities.

This aligns with the views of other scholars. Stavros Gadinis and Chris Havasy frame these issues in terms of corporate legitimacy,[89] arguing that corporate governing may sometimes lack sociological and moral legitimacy, that is, public or stakeholder acceptance of corporate actions and their normative foundations.[90] To address the legitimacy gap, they look to administrative law – where agencies have long faced similar concerns, and legal tools have evolved to manage them.[91] In their view, a corporation's internal governance should be reinforced by strong procedural and substantive rules,[92] including:

> increasing participation with stakeholders, improving corporate managerial transparency and disclosure, embracing the use of external experts during deliberation, and standardizing the metrics and methods of corporate decisionmaking.[93]

Lisa Fairfax proposes similar adjustments as she calls for corporations to adopt an enterprise-wide approach that equips them to detect, assess, and manage political risk proactively.[94] That includes identifying political risks across departments and platforms – not just from executives; weighing costs and benefits, including reputational gains and losses; establishing internal processes for mitigation and response; and strengthening board oversight through expertise, monitoring, and information-sharing.[95]

Indeed, to absorb risks stemming from political backlash, many companies are already implementing internal policies to navigate corporate governing or, at the very least, are becoming more transparent about when and how they intervene, as Section D illustrates.

88 Strine, *supra* note 56, at 366 n.102 (citing Patrick Temple-West, *Microsoft's Brad Smith on the Cloud, ESG Backlash and Taxes*, FIN. TIMES (Sept. 23, 2022), www.ft.com/content/4d6f7c5b-9d20-4c73-ad9a-984c847a4a45)).

89 Stavros Gadinis & Chris Havasy, *The Quest for Legitimacy: A Public Law Blueprint for Corporate Law*, 57 U.C. DAVIS L. REV. 1581 (2024).

90 *Id.* at 1596–97.

91 *Id.* at 1586–87

92 *Cf.* Cary Coglianese, *Legitimacy and Corporate Governance*, 32 DEL. J. CORP. L. 159 (2007) (arguing that procedural and substantive rules are the foundations to legitimacy).

93 Gadinis & Havasy, *supra* note 89, at 1664.

94 Fairfax, *supra* note 55, at 7–10.

95 *Id.*

## D A SURVEY OF CORPORATE POLICIES AND PRACTICES THAT ADDRESS CORPORATE GOVERNING

To evaluate the transparency and procedural rigor of corporate governing activities, I analyze disclosures on corporate governing practices and related issues from two subsets of S&P 500 companies: the S&P 100 and those ranked 401–500. This analysis is based on data extracted on December 13, 2024, with assistance from the data mining firm ESGAUGE. The data comes from company securities filings and other "shadow governance" documents available on corporate websites as of such date.[96] I examine how companies manage advocacy, lobbying, and political activities, including whether they disclose policies on supported issues. I also assess whether they disclose if they pursue certain ESG goals such as diversity (gender, racial, and LGBTQ+), climate impact (gas emissions), and certain broader societal concerns like guns and democracy. Importantly, I analyze whether advocacy policies or disclosures specify the issues they address and whose interests they serve.

A few caveats about the findings. First, the data presented here reflects corporate disclosures as of December 13, 2024, offering a snapshot of advocacy and engagement prior to President Trump's second inauguration and the subsequent wave of anti-DEI executive orders.[97] Given the sharp policy shift since then, the corporate landscape on these issues has undoubtedly evolved. To track these changes, I am conducting a follow-up study comparing corporate disclosures and advocacy efforts before and after the start of Trump's second term. However, full-sample disclosure updates are still in progress and will inform subsequent findings. Despite these anticipated shifts, the data presented here remains highly relevant. By late 2024, anti-DEI sentiment had already become a significant force shaping corporate decision-making, yet some companies remained transparent about their advocacy efforts, offering insight into how businesses navigated growing political scrutiny. Moreover, even if DEI were not a concern, the data captures corporate behavior in a comparatively less volatile period. In other words, it establishes a baseline for what companies were willing to disclose to investors when political risks were mounting but had not yet fully materialized.

Second, the data presented here reflects static disclosures – what companies choose to say about their goals and advocacy, not necessarily what they do. Incongruence between talk and action is a persistent challenge in this space – one that some investors attempt to confront through shareholder engagement, including political alignment proposals.[98] Still, the findings here do not address that potential disconnect.

96 *See supra* note 38 and accompanying text.

97 *See supra* Chapter 1, Section C.3.

98 Political alignment proposals, a growing category of shareholder proposals, aim precisely to expose and address potential inconsistencies between corporate advocacy and political spending. These

Third, it is also plausible, if not probable, that some of the disclosures I track here are the downstream result of past shareholder engagement. Jill Fisch and Adriana Robertson document that political disclosure proposals tend to target companies with weaker disclosure practices – and that those companies often improve their transparency after being targeted.[99]

With these disclaimers, the main findings are summarized below.

### 1 *Policy on Advocacy*

First, corporations tend to be transparent about their advocacy efforts overall (especially the larger ones). As per Table 6.1, seven out of ten companies in the full sample have a policy on advocacy (or a policy that combines lobbying and advocacy). In the S&P 100, the percentage rises to 84% (6% advocacy-only policy and 78% with policies covering advocacy and lobbying). In the smallest 100 companies in the S&P 500, only 57% have policies covering advocacy (and three out of ten companies have no policy on either advocacy or lobbying).

### 2 *Disclosure of Specific Advocacy Issues*

The data show that 76.5% of corporations disclose the specific issues they advocate for (see Figure 6.1). However, disclosure rates vary by size, with 89% of S&P 100 firms detailing their advocacy policies, compared to 64% of the smallest 100 firms in the S&P 500. This suggests that larger corporations, under greater scrutiny, are more likely to formalize and communicate their advocacy policies.[100]

TABLE 6.1 *Policy on advocacy and lobbying, by index (2024)*

| | Full sample | S&P 100 | 401–500 in S&P 500 |
|---|---|---|---|
| | n = 200 | n = 100 | n = 100 |
| *Advocacy only* | 13.5% | 6% | 21% |
| *Both advocacy and lobbying* | 57% | 78% | 36% |
| *Lobbying only* | 13% | 12% | 14% |
| *No policy* | 16.5% | 4% | 29% |

*Source:* ESGAUGE & Matteo Gatti, 2025

proposals – though less frequent than others related to political involvement – highlight investors' efforts to police talk-versus-walk gaps. *See generally* Jill E. Fisch & Adriana Z. Robertson, *Corporate Political Disclosure and Shareholder Voting* (working paper 2025) (on file with author).

99 *Id.*

100 *Cf.* Yaron Nili & Kobi Kastiel, *The Corporate Governance Gap*, 131 YALE L.J. 782 (2022) (finding that larger corporations care more about corporate governance than smaller ones).

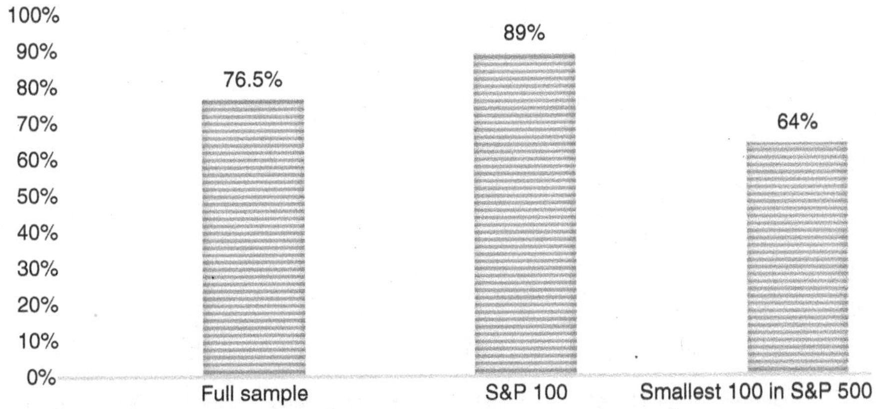


FIGURE 6.1 Policy on advocacy (or other disclosure) refers to specific issues for which advocacy is permitted or practiced, by index (2024)
*Source:* ESGAUGE & Matteo Gatti, 2025

## 3 *What Specific Issues Corporations Advocate On*

The next question is obvious: What are the specific issues corporations advocate for? To better grasp the data, it is essential to preliminarily gauge what ESG goals corporations say they pursue in their disclosures. As we will see, a subset of corporations who pursue ESG goals also advocate for such goals.

### a ESG Goals Corporations (Say They) Pursue

The overwhelming majority of corporations disclosed that their ESG goals included gender and racial diversity and – to a slightly lesser extent – LGBTQ+ diversity. Almost all disclose they pursue climate-related goals (one that did not, Berkshire Hathaway, controls subsidiaries that do). Though about half of all companies disclose having a gun policy, most relate solely to workplace restrictions – such as bans on bringing firearms to work. Only one in ten extends that policy to address gun control measures involving suppliers or customers. Very few corporations are explicit in their efforts to preserve democracy and the rule of law. Figures 6.2–6.4 graphically summarize the data, while Table 6.2 shows the data breakdown relating to gun policies.

### b Breakdown by Advocacy Issues

Returning to our main question: Given these ESG goals – some of which were ubiquitous as of December 13, 2024 – how many corporations explicitly disclose that they also *advocate* for pursuing such goals? The data reveals that corporate disclosures on advocacy vary significantly by topic and company size. As Figure 6.5 shows, across

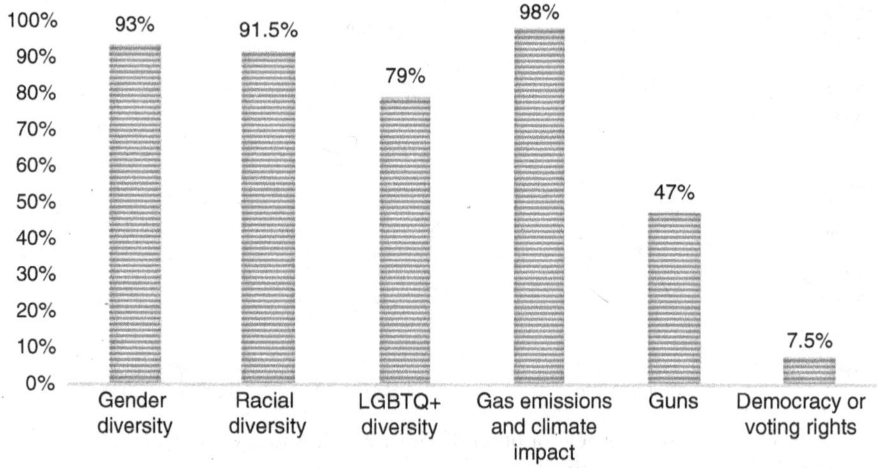


FIGURE 6.2 Disclosure of certain ESG goals, full sample (2024)
*Source:* ESGAUGE & Matteo Gatti, 2025

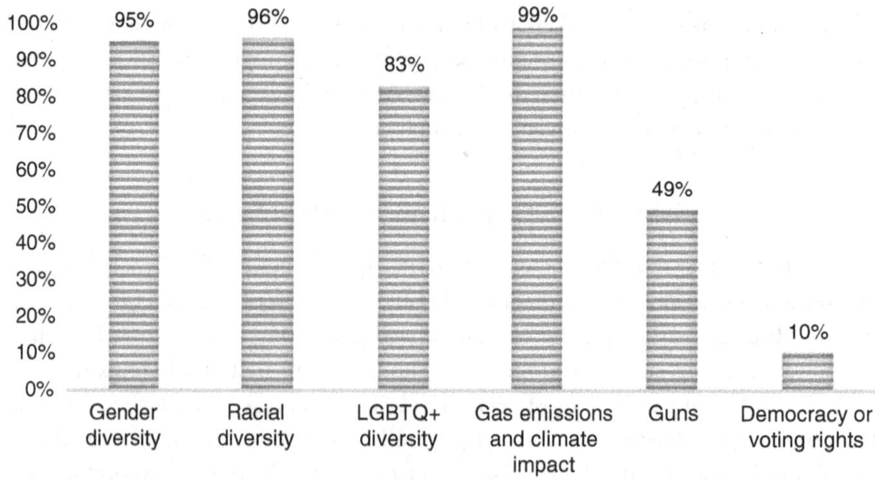


FIGURE 6.3 Disclosure of certain ESG goals, S&P 100 (2024)
*Source:* ESGAUGE & Matteo Gatti, 2025

all surveyed companies, engagement in diversity-related advocacy is the most commonly disclosed, with gender, racial, and sexual orientation diversity each reported by around 30 percent to 33 percent of firms. In contrast, climate advocacy is mentioned by 24% of firms, while democracy or voting rights engagement is disclosed by only 3.5%. No company in the sample reports advocacy on gun-related issues. Notably, S&P 100 firms report higher levels of advocacy than smaller companies – especially on climate issues, where their engagement rate is nearly twice as high.

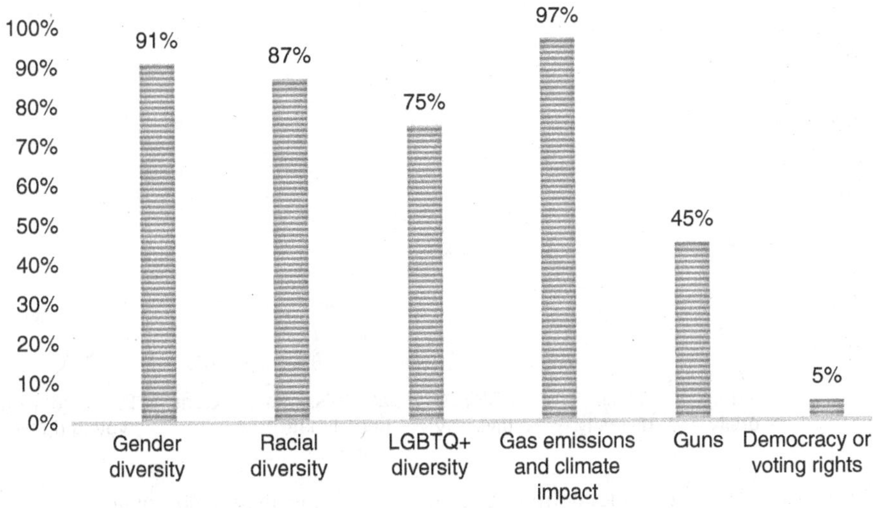


FIGURE 6.4 Disclosure of certain ESG goals, S&P 401–500 (2024)
*Source:* ESGAUGE & Matteo Gatti, 2025

TABLE 6.2 *Type of gun policy, by index (2024)*

| | Full sample | S&P 100 | 401–500 in S&P 500 |
|---|---|---|---|
| | n = 200 | n = 100 | n = 100 |
| *Corporations with gun policy, of which:* | 47.0% | 49.0% | 45.0% |
| *No guns at work/premises* | 90.4% | 85.7% | 95.6% |
| *Gun control policy with customers/ suppliers or other* | 9.6% | 14.3% | 4.4% |

*Source:* ESGAUGE & Matteo Gatti, 2025

Figure 6.6 highlights the gap between ESG engagement and related advocacy disclosure – that is, the difference between companies that report pursuing ESG goals and those that also disclose advocating for them. The data show that significantly fewer corporations disclose advocacy on prosocial issues than claim to pursue related goals. While companies engage in a broad range of ESG initiatives, their willingness to publicly acknowledge these efforts varies significantly depending on the issue. Even among firms actively engaged in diversity-related ESG efforts, a significant majority remain silent about their advocacy, with about two-thirds of gender-diverse firms and nearly the same percentage of race-diverse firms opting not to disclose. Climate advocacy, despite being a major ESG focus, is disclosed far less frequently. Although 98% of firms say they engage in environmental sustainability

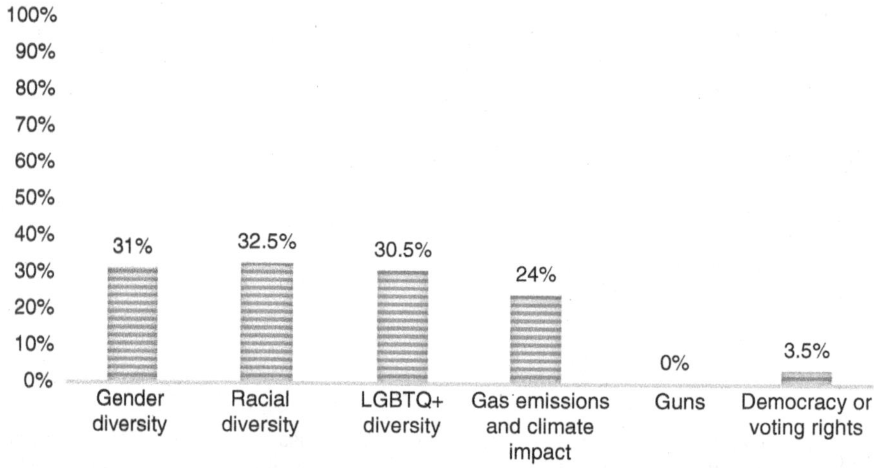


FIGURE 6.5 Advocacy issues permitted or practiced, as specified in corporate disclosures, full sample (2024)
*Source:* ESGAUGE & Matteo Gatti, 2025

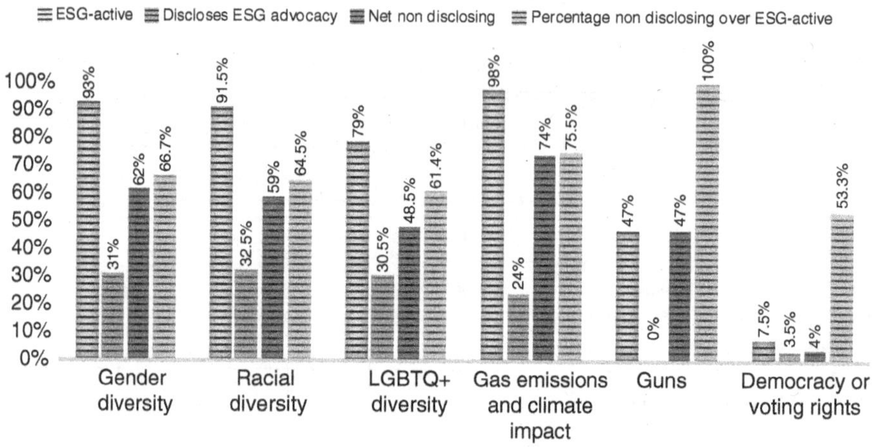


FIGURE 6.6 Gaps between ESG engagement and advocacy disclosure, full sample (2024)
*Source:* ESGAUGE & Matteo Gatti, 2025

efforts, only 24% report lobbying or advocacy on climate-related policies. The avoidance of disclosure is even more striking when it comes to gun-related issues. Despite 47 percent of companies being active in this area, none disclose any advocacy.

### c Breakdown by Industry

The data reveal variation in corporate advocacy disclosures by industry. As a disclaimer, given the relatively small sample sizes for some industries, as shown below, the following findings should be viewed as indicative and interpreted with caution. As subsection D.3.b indicates, gender, racial, and LGBTQ+ diversity receive the most mentions, though the extent of advocacy engagement differs across sectors.

Consumer Staples (52%, n = 21) leads in *gender diversity advocacy*, followed by Communication Services (39%, n = 13). In contrast, Industrials (14%, n = 28) and Utilities (13%, n = 8) report notably lower levels. *Racial diversity* follows a similar pattern, with Information Technology (54%, n = 26) reporting the highest engagement, while Utilities (13%, n = 8) and Industrials (18%, n = 28) report the lowest. *LGBTQ+ diversity* sees the highest engagement in Communication Services (54%, n = 13) and Information Technology (46%, n = 26). *Climate-related advocacy* is most frequently cited by the Energy sector (80%, but a *very* small sample n = 5). The Materials sector follows at 50% (n = 10), while industries such as Financials (8%, n = 26) and Health Care (4%, n = 28) report minimal engagement on climate issues. *Democracy or voting rights advocacy* is rare across all industries, with the highest disclosure in Communication Services (15%, n = 13), followed by Information Technology (12%, n = 26).

### d Breakdown by Advocacy Type

Breaking down advocacy by type, Table 6.3 shows that diversity-related advocacy often occurs through Employee Resource Groups (ERGs), which are instrumental in promoting diversity and inclusion within companies, addressing areas such as gender, race, and LGBTQ+. For instance, among firms disclosing advocacy for gender diversity (31% of those surveyed), 33.9% engage through ERGs. Similarly, in racial diversity efforts, within the 32.5% of firms report advocacy, 35.4% utilize ERGs. Regarding LGBTQ+ diversity, 30.5% of firms indicate advocacy, and 34.4% of them employ ERGs as their engagement method. The data in Table 6.3 suggests that smaller firms are more inclined to utilize ERGs for advocacy in these domains compared to larger corporations like those in the S&P 100.

Beyond ERGs, trade associations are another significant channel for diversity-related engagement, though this time, they are more frequently cited by S&P 100 firms. Among surveyed firms, within the 31% that report engaging in gender diversity initiatives, 24.2% utilize trade associations as a means of advocacy. Similarly, of the 32.5% that disclose being involved in promoting racial diversity, 23.1% collaborate with trade associations. In the realm of LGBTQ+ diversity, of the 30.5% of firms that indicate advocacy efforts, 18% partner with trade associations to advance these initiatives. A smaller subset of firms report engaging through both trade associations and ERGs.

Overall, corporate socioeconomic advocacy disclosures suggest a structured but selective approach, with diversity-related advocacy being the most frequently mentioned, often channeled through ERGs or trade associations. Climate advocacy (24% of the total sample) is more common among large firms (32% among S&P 100 firms versus 16% in the smaller firms). In comparison, engagement on democracy

TABLE 6.3 *Issues and types of advocacy permitted or practiced, as specified in corporate disclosures, by index (2024)*

| | | Full sample | S&P 100 | 401–500 in S&P 500 |
|---|---|---|---|---|
| | | n = 200 | n = 100 | n = 100 |
| *Gender diversity* | | 31% | 30% | 32% |
| *within which:* | *Gender diversity (general)* | 30.6% | 33.3% | 28.1% |
| | *Only via charitable giving* | 3.2% | 3.3% | 3.1% |
| | *Only via ERG* | 33.9% | 23.3% | 43.8% |
| | *Only via ERG and trade assoc.* | 6.5% | 3.3% | 9.4% |
| | *Only via trade associations* | 24.2% | 33.3% | 15.6% |
| | *Only via PAC contributions* | 1.6% | 3.3% | 0% |
| *Racial diversity* | | 32.5% | 34.0% | 31.0% |
| *within which:* | *Racial diversity (general)* | 30.8% | 32.4% | 29.0% |
| | *Only in immigration* | 1.5% | 2.9% | 0% |
| | *Only via charitable giving* | 3.1% | 2.9% | 3.2% |
| | *Only via ERG* | 35.4% | 26.5% | 45.2% |
| | *Only via ERG and trade assoc.* | 4.6% | 0% | 9.7% |
| | *Only via trade associations* | 23.1% | 32.4% | 12.9% |
| | *Only via PAC contributions* | 1.5% | 2.9% | 0% |
| *LGBTQ+ diversity.* | | 30.5% | 31% | 30.0% |
| *within which:* | *Sexual orientation div. (general)* | 36.1% | 41.9% | 30.0% |
| | *Only via sponsoring* | 3.3% | 6.5% | 0% |
| | *Only via charitable giving* | 1.6% | 0% | 3.3% |
| | *Only via ERG* | 34.4% | 22.6% | 46.7% |
| | *Only via ERG and trade association* | 4.9% | 0% | 10% |
| | *Only via trade associations* | 18% | 25.8% | 10% |
| | *Only via PAC contributions* | 1.6% | 3.2% | 0% |
| *Climate* | | 24% | 32% | 16% |

*Source:* ESGAUGE & Matteo Gatti, 2025

and voting rights remains minimal across the board (only seven companies or 3.5 percent of the overall sample). As mentioned earlier, no company in the sample discloses about gun-related advocacy.

## 4 *In Whose Interest Corporations Advocate?*

The data also indicate how corporations frame their advocacy efforts in terms of whose interests they claim to represent. As per Table 6.4, disclosures show that companies most frequently cite they advocate for their own business (45%) and their industry or sector (22%). Larger firms in the S&P 100 are likelier to emphasize these interests, with 52% reporting advocacy for their business compared to 39% of smaller firms and 27% citing industry-related advocacy versus 16% of smaller firms.

TABLE 6.4 *Interests corporations disclose supporting through advocacy, by index (2004)*

| | Full sample | S&P 100 | 401–500 in S&P 500 |
|---|---|---|---|
| | n = 200 | n = 100 | n = 100 |
| *The company or the business* | 45.5% | 52% | 39% |
| *The company's sector or industry* | 21.5% | 27% | 16% |
| *The company's shareholders* | 14.0% | 19% | 9% |
| *The company's stakeholders* | 19.0% | 29% | 9% |
| *The company's employees* | 16.5% | 25% | 8% |
| *The community where the company operates* | 15.0% | 20% | 10% |
| *Society at large* | 3.5% | 4% | 3% |
| *Issues of legal compliance* | 6.5% | 9% | 4% |
| *Issues of security/safety* | 6.5% | 7% | 6% |

*Source:* ESGAUGE & Matteo Gatti, 2025

Some companies also disclose advocacy in the interest of specific stakeholders. Nineteen percent cite stakeholders broadly, with S&P 100 firms (29%) more likely to do so than smaller firms (9%). Despite shareholder primacy, shareholders are mentioned as a focus of advocacy only by 14% of firms, with a similar divide between S&P 100 firms (19%) and smaller firms (9%). Employees appear less frequently, with 17% of firms overall citing them, though larger firms (25%) mention them more than smaller firms (8%). An even smaller portion of companies indicate that they advocate for the communities where they operate (15%) or for society at large (4% in the S&P 100, 3% among smaller firms). Legal compliance and security-related advocacy are cited by about 7% of firms, with little difference between company sizes.

Note that corporations who disclose interests often cite more than one in their disclosures and that many remain silent on advocacy altogether. These disclosures suggest that when companies engage in advocacy, they tend to frame it as aligned with their business, industry, or immediate stakeholders rather than as an effort to promote broader societal concerns.

## 5 *Assessment*

The data analyzed in Section D underscores corporate advocacy's selective and strategic nature. While many corporations disclose engagement in diversity-related initiatives, particularly on gender, racial, and LGBTQ+ diversity, their willingness to advocate explicitly on these issues varies. Larger firms in the S&P 100 tend to be more forthcoming in their disclosures, likely reflecting greater scrutiny from investors, regulators, and the public. Climate-related advocacy is also more frequently disclosed by larger firms. At the same time, issues such as democracy and voting rights receive far less attention, indicating a cautious approach to politically charged topics.

Crucially, corporate disclosures suggest that advocacy is framed primarily as serving the interests of the company, its industry, and its direct stakeholders rather than broader societal concerns. While some firms acknowledge advocating for employees, shareholders, or the communities in which they operate, very few cite society at large as a primary beneficiary of their advocacy. Still, many corporations remain silent on advocacy altogether (see Figure 6.6). This dataset offers a critical baseline for how corporations positioned themselves before the regulatory and political shifts of 2025 – laying the groundwork for future comparisons as the landscape continues to evolve.

## E SUMMARY

This chapter highlights both the challenges and potential avenues for addressing corporate governing through policy interventions or market-based mechanisms. While policy interventions such as enhanced disclosure requirements, board oversight, and shareholder involvement could bring greater transparency and accountability to corporate advocacy, their implementation faces constitutional, legal, and practical obstacles.

In particular, *Citizens United* limits direct restrictions on corporate advocacy, making disclosure one of the few viable regulatory levers. Even here, striking the right balance is complicated – too much mandatory disclosure risks overwhelming investors with excessive information, while too little leaves key stakeholders in the dark.

Beyond disclosure, stronger corporate governance mechanisms such as board oversight or disinterested director involvement might improve decision-making, but they, too, present challenges.

Given these difficulties, one might argue that corporate governing should largely be left to market forces, allowing companies to self-regulate in response to investor expectations, consumer sentiment, and broader economic incentives. Market-based constraints, including institutional investor pressure, litigation risks, and consumer backlash, have already begun shaping corporate approaches to ESG and advocacy. This dynamic has led many companies to develop internal policies to structure their advocacy efforts, signaling a preference for self-imposed guardrails rather than external regulatory mandates. However, self-regulation has limits, mainly because corporate governing decisions affect broader societal interests that fall outside traditional corporate governance protections and are unlikely to get proper considerations by internal decision-makers.

Ultimately, corporate governing remains a contested and evolving practice. While companies may respond to external pressures with increased transparency and structured processes, this does not necessarily mean their actions align with the public interest. The legal and political landscape will continue to shape corporate behavior, influencing whether advocacy remains a prominent feature of corporate governing or is scaled back due to regulatory and market pressures. As policymakers, investors, and corporations navigate this space, the degree to which it is disciplined – whether through legal rules, market forces, or internal governance – will determine its role in shaping economic and political outcomes in the years ahead.

In any event, we should not lose track of the big picture: traditional corporate governance mechanisms can help mitigate risk at the firm level, but are ill-equipped to manage the broader societal consequences of corporate governing. As Chapter 5 indicates, the growing reliance on private firms to fill policy gaps – whether through environmental pledges, DEI programs, or crisis response – raises questions about their democratic legitimacy and the long-term stability of public institutions. These are not just firm-level risks; they are broader risks. And corporate law, given its dynamics, is not equipped to answer them.

If corporate governance policies and market forces – shareholder activism, stakeholder backlash, reputational exposure – can only discipline corporations around the edges, it is far from clear we can count on meaningful oversight at the societal level. In the worst cases, they may reinforce corporate self-interest, deepen polarization, or create cycles of engagement and retreat.

Addressing these risks is no simple task. It requires ambitious, sustained efforts from multiple actors – not just within corporate boardrooms but across the public sphere. Citizens and civil society organizations must reclaim their role in democratic life, demanding accountability not only from corporations but from the political institutions that have ceded ground to them. Politicians, in turn, must move beyond performative outrage and prioritize the long-term welfare of their constituents – governing with responsiveness, not just rhetoric.

Doing so will take more than regulatory tweaks or well-meaning statements. It calls for a shift in norms, a renewal of political will, and, ultimately, reform of the political system itself. These are transformations that corporate governance can support at the margins – but it cannot lead them. The work of democratic repair belongs to the polity, not the private sector.

# Conclusion

This book has examined the evolving role of corporations in addressing socioeconomic policy issues, corporate governing, which is framed as a combination of both talk (corporate socioeconomic advocacy) and action (government substitution). At times, corporations appear to fill the void left by political dysfunction. They respond to consumer, employee, and investor pressures and can be fast at interpreting the need of changing times, much faster than official policymakers. Yet, it remains a precarious and uneven mechanism, constrained by market incentives, political backlash, and the limits of present-day corporate law and governance. While some have looked to corporations as agents of change, *Corporate Power and the Politics of Change* posits that corporate governing is a problematic substitute for policymaking – it's unstable, prone to calculus, at times conflicted – not completely reliable in the end.

We should not be too surprised. Corporations were never meant to shoulder the burden of resolving deep societal and political dysfunctions. For all the discourse about them stepping in where governments fail – on climate, civil rights, or democracy itself – the reality is more complex. When the stakes become too high, most will prioritize self-preservation over advocacy. While some firms have taken bold positions on issues such as climate action or DEI, their engagement is typically pragmatic rather than principled, shaped by reputational, regulatory, or market incentives. Today, however, the greatest pressure on corporations no longer comes from the legal system or market forces – consumers, employees, or investors – but from political actors seeking to dictate what private enterprises can and cannot support.

This is a form of economic *dirigisme*, more reminiscent of post-war Continental Europe, whereby private sector power is shaped by, and expected to align with, ruling political forces of the day. The irony is evident: Those decrying corporate governing as undemocratic and hostile to dissenting voices are now wielding state power to police corporate speech – punishing companies that step out of line and, in doing so, curtailing the rights of consumers, employees, and shareholders alike. This current battle is not just cultural – it is deeply political. Politicians have grown adept at treating corporations as ideological adversaries when they express prosocial values, especially on DEI or climate issues. But the same politicians often avoid passing structural reforms that corporations oppose – on taxes, antitrust, labor rights, or campaign finance – because they remain reliant on corporate money to stay electorally viable. In effect, they wage public battles for attention and ideological signaling, while leaving the underlying corporate power structures intact. The result is not regulation, but pressure – an attempt to discipline private actors through selective intervention rather than through consistent, transparent policymaking.

While this political fight has been taking shape, Musk and DOGE had their stint at redoing the government. Again, private interests, but expressly empowered by the President of the United States of America, in the name of private sector efficiency over public sector waste. The entanglement between private wealth and political influence is how things are supposed to go, mid-2020s politics seems to say. This is something resembling a modern form of economic feudalism, where power does not derive from democratic legitimacy but from unlimited wealth and control over key industries and platforms in the largest world economy. The ability of the ultra-wealthy to shape policy, sway elections, and dominate discourse through informal channels reveals the fragility of governance in an era where financial and political power blur. If this is what fills the vacuum left first by traditional politics and then by corporate retreat, the main worry is not around whether firms should take public stands and prosocial initiatives – it's the deeper erosion of democratic institutions.

Expecting corporate governing to fill the void left by political dysfunction is misguided. Corporations are designed in an idiosyncratic fashion. Mainstream corporate governance prioritizes shareholder interests, leaving little room for broader societal concerns. Basic public choice tells us that, historically, corporate governance hardly counterbalances strong corporate power – whether stemming from managers or, increasingly, controlling shareholders. External regulation, no matter how difficult to put in place, remains the primary tool to tame corporate externalities and other market failures – that is, the framework that corporate governing often seeks to navigate or circumvent. Even if policymakers wanted to step in, corporate governance itself offers no real levers to correct these imbalances.

None of this is to say that corporations have been irrelevant on socioeconomic issues. *Corporate Power and the Politics of Change* recognizes that firms have, at times, played a consequential role in shaping climate policy, DEI, and even democratic norms. But corporate engagement is largely reactive and strategic – not reformist – and often calibrated to mitigate risk, not drive structural change. When the strategy fails, the fallout can be severe, dissuading others from entering the field of corporate governing. Is that necessarily a loss? Probably not. In the long run, democratic resilience isn't built in boardrooms – it's forged in legislatures, town halls, and civic life. Real reform requires structural fixes: campaign finance laws, lobbying constraints, and institutional accountability. These are the tools for safeguarding democracy – not corporate interventions tethered to brand calculus and political mood.

Could corporate governing regain momentum? With societal shifts, it surely is a possibility, one day or another. If public pressure intensifies, if regulatory landscapes evolve, if the costs of inaction outweigh the risks of engagement, some firms will adjust accordingly. But remember: corporations will not be leading this game – at best, they will follow. As noted, corporations are not built to be political vanguards, nor should they be expected to assume that role. Ultimately, it would be hazardous to count on the strategic leanings of corporate leaders for the preservation of democracy; rather, we must focus on the sustained engagement of citizens, civil society, and political institutions.

So, what does this all tell us about corporate governing? That its help is intermittent at best – an occasional ally when interests align, a hedge when risks escalate, and a retreat when the political winds shift. The real work of democratic governance remains where it has always been: politics, no matter how bleak the prospects of change may be. For all the rhetoric around corporate responsibility, there is no substitute for democratic engagement – at times messy, often imperfect, and always indispensable.

# Index

Printed by Integrated Books International,
United States of America